# THE
# FOOTBALL
# HANDBOOK

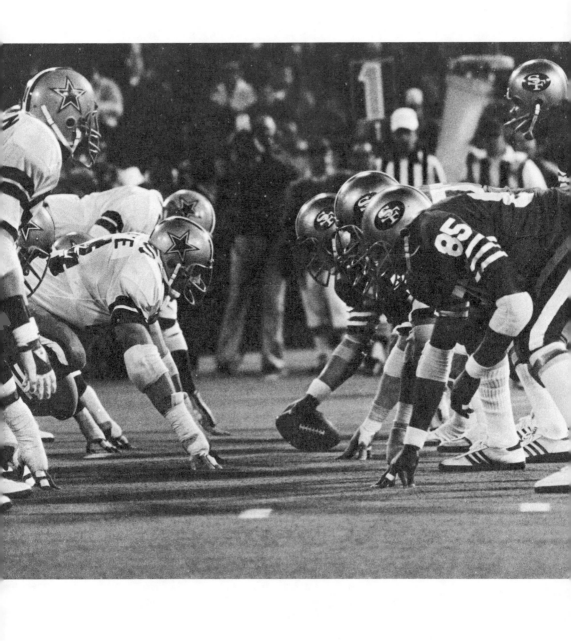

# THE
# FOOTBALL
# HANDBOOK

## by Sam DeLuca

JD | JONATHAN DAVID PUBLISHERS, INC.
MIDDLE VILLAGE, NEW YORK 11379

# THE FOOTBALL HANDBOOK
Copyright © 1978
by
Sam DeLuca

## 1981 Edition

Jonathan David Publishers, Inc.
Middle Village, New York 11379

### PHOTO CREDITS

Baltimore Colts: pp. 31, 130, 134, 193, 223; Buffalo Bills (Robert L. Smith): pp. 69, 165, 230; Chicago Bears: pp. 93, 140; Cincinnati Bengals: pp. 24, 86, 89, 91; Thomas J. Croke: pp. 94, 196; Dallas Cowboys: pp. 143, 228; Denver Broncos: pp. 21, 22, 158, 198; Kansas City Chiefs: p. 141; Ted Kaplan: pp. 126, 309; New Orleans Saints: pp. 28, 195; New York Jets: p. 110; Oakland Raiders: pp. 26, 49, 61, 65, 92, 101, 124, 204, 329; Pittsburgh Steelers: pp. 33, 84, 99, 199, 206, 227; San Francisco 49ers: pp. 64, 138, 169; Seattle Seahawks: p. 226; Tampa Bay Buccaneers: pp. 57, 298.

### Library of Congress Cataloging in Publication Data

DeLuca, Sam.
 The football handbook.
 1. Football. I. Title.
GV951.D358  796.33'22  78-18764
ISBN 0-8246-0274-9 pbk

Manufactured in the United States of America

# TABLE OF CONTENTS

# PREFACE

Football, more so than baseball, basketball or hockey, has always been surrounded by a mystique. Whether this is warranted or not can be debated. It is a fact that baseball, with its slow, deliberate pace, is pretty much predictable as far as strategy goes. Hockey and basketball, with their continuous action, don't lend themselves to detailed, advance planning, relying often on spontaneous variations of a few standard plays. Football, though, is different. For one thing, it permits more players on the field than the other sports and defines rather strictly what these players can and can't do. For another, it allows its players to regroup after each play and consider their next move. These two facts make football a game that can be appreciated by all. It makes it a game of action which appeals to just about anyone. And, it also makes it a complex game which can be studied and debated.

Whether you prefer to be just a casual fan or want to really dig into football, *The Football Handbook* will increase your enjoyment of the game. This isn't a school book and you can use it any way that you like. It was written with you in mind, though, and knowing a few things about how it was put together in advance should increase what you get out of it.

For one thing, you must not allow yourself to be intimidated by the language of the game or its play notations. *X*'s and *O*'s have traditionally been used to symbolize the offensive and defensive players respectively. These symbols for some reason tend to confuse a lot of fans. Perhaps they are put off by a similarity to math. To remove this mental block, we use little footballs and helmets to represent the offense and defense in *The Football Handbook*. We have also kept the number of diagrams to a minimum. Nevertheless, simple diagrams are still the best way to explain football plays and formations and they shouldn't be ignored. Remember that these symbols are not abstract equations; they represent real people. It is not necessary to memorize each diagram, but you should glance at each of them and try to relate them to the purpose of the play and the people and action on the field.

There is no universally accepted dictionary of football terms. Each coach either devises his own terminology or uses the terms which the coaches he played for used. You will therefore often find five or six different words or expressions used to describe the same thing. For example, members of the defensive line often exchange assignments with each other. The defensive tackle moves to the outside to assume the responsibilities of the defensive end, and the end moves to the inside to take up the duties of the tackle. This exchange of assignments may be known as "stunts" or "games" or "tricks" or "deals" or "an exchange." It is easy to see why some fans are overwhelmed by the esoteric jargon used by T.V. colormen, who are also known as "analysts" or "expert commentators" or "the 'ex-jock' in the booth" or simply "the announcer."

Terms are explained as they come up, but occasionally terms are used which may not be sufficiently clear. Thus, there is a rather lengthy section in the back called "The Language of Football" which can be consulted any time you are in doubt. It is particularly good to consult when watching a game. You might want to take a look at this section before getting into the book. In the long run, if you want to understand the game, you have to learn its language.

Since a football team is only as good as its individual players, I have started the book with an analysis of what goes into each position: the physical requirements for the players, the skills they need, the duties they have to carry out, and the things to look for when evaluating a player at a particular position. I started here because this is where the coaches start. The coach (or the fan) must be able to determine if the individual players have accomplished their assignments (or if they are capable of doing the job at all) in order to evaluate a team's potential or performance. Football is a team sport, but the success of a team is determined by the outcome of the many individual confrontations on each play. Choosing the right offensive and defensive plays is important, but, in the final analysis, it is the ability of individuals which will determine which formations and plays a team can use. If your quarterback can't throw deep, long pass patterns will not be of help. If your defensive backfield has no speed, a man to man defense isn't going to work.

Once a coach has evaluated his personnel, he will decide what offensive and defensive formations he can use. In the chapter on formations, you have descriptions of the major offensive and defensive alignments and the basic plays that are run from each. The best way to start this section is to take a look at the explanations on how to read a diagram. Once you see that a diagram isn't so complicated, the rest will be easy.

The section called "Starting the Action" will give you an idea how plays are called in the huddle and how they are changed at the line of scrimmage. You'll see that there is a system to numbering plays. They are grouped so that you don't have to be an elephant to remember them.

O.K. Now you're ready to watch and analyze a game. First, I thought that I would show you the game the way it looks to the players on the field. The obvious choice was to look at the defense through the eyes of the quarterback and the offense through the eyes of the middle linebacker. By getting an idea what these two players look for, you'll have a better feel of what you should be looking for. Another chapter tells what the game looks like from the play-by-play booth.

Now we get to the game plan. Now that the phrase "game plan" is a part of our political vocabulary, I think you'll probably be disappointed to learn that there is nothing much to the game plan itself. It is nothing more than a list of plays which a team decides will work best against its upcoming opponent. What is interesting is how the game plan is formed and the complementary information that is passed along to the team together with it. If you know your team well, and you know its opponent, you ought to be able to figure out what it most likely will be using next Sunday. In this section we will also deal with the game plan of a recent Super Bowl game.

What *The Football Handbook* is really trying to get you to do is to look beneath the surface when evaluating a football game. An excellent example of what can happen when a shallow look is taken at a game was the naming of Harvey Martin, of the Dallas Cowboys, as co-MVP of the 1978 Super Bowl. Martin is a great defensive end who turned most offensive tackles upside down as he set a record for quarterback sacks (23) during the regular season. It was his performance throughout the season, along with the accompanying publicity, that got him the Super Bowl award. Martin was just another good defensive end on Super Bowl Sunday. I would have given the entire award to Randy White instead of the half-share that he received.

SAM DeLuca

# INTRODUCTION

When I was asked to write an introduction to the paperback edition of *The Football Handbook*, I leafed through the book and thought a bit about the turns that have taken place in the game during the last three years. To be sure, faces have changed and team fortunes have risen and fallen, but that came as no great surprise. What particularly struck me were the changes that have taken place in offensive and defensive emphases.

The Rules Committee of the National Football League first began trying to open up the passing game, hoping to thereby create the excitement that only the "bomb" can provide, when it moved the hash marks closer to the center of the field way back in 1972. At that time there was considerable concern that increased use of zone coverage would virtually eliminate the long pass. The Rules Committee's intent was to force the defense to cover the entire field. Instead of opening up the passing game, though, the opposite occurred. Ten running backs broke the thousand-yard mark in 1972—an N.F.L. record.

In 1974, further changes were made to aid the offense. To help protect the quarterback, the penalties for offensive holding, illegal use of hands, and tripping were reduced from 15 yards to 10 yards, and the "bump and run" was eliminated, making it easier for the wide receiver to get free. All of this had less impact than anticipated. The running game and ball control continued to dominate the thinking of the offense—and the defense continued to dominate the offense—during most of the 1970s.

The 1972 and 1974 rule changes did not open up the offense as hoped for because they overlooked what really prevented the wide receivers from catching the ball: what Weeb Ewbank once termed the "alley fighting" in the defensive secondary. Weeb Ewbank—a man for whom my respect has grown steadily over the years—had noted in 1972 that the clotheslining, chopping, elbowing, and attempts to cartwheel the receiver made it all but impossible for them to catch the ball. The Rules Committee finally came to this same conclusion in 1978 when it eliminated all contact beyond five yards of the line of scrimmage. Other 1978 rule changes allowed the offensive lineman to extend his hands and arms while pass protecting. This time the changes achieved their intended result. One need look no further than the stat sheet to recognize that the pendulum has swung back to the offense and, in particular, to the passing game.

The opening up of the passing game in the last few years has helped some teams and hurt others. Don Coryell of the San Diego Chargers has always been a proponent of the forward pass, and his 1980 Chargers were probably the most pass-obsessed *winning* team in the history of the game. In the past, only overmatched losing teams passed as frequently as the Chargers did. San Diego's top three receivers—Kellen Winslow, John Jefferson, and Charlie Joiner—finished 1, 2, 3 in the A.F.C. in receptions and 1, 2, 3 in yardage. Quarterback Dan Fouts has had two consecutive 4,000-yard passing years. The Chargers have exceptional talent, and their passing records would probably be impressive under any circumstance, but the rule changes certainly didn't hurt them.

For the 1980 New York Jets, it was another story. The Jets led the league in rushing in 1979, and everyone expected the 1980 team to improve upon its 8-8 record and perhaps contend for the division crown. Coach Walt Michaels came to the decision that the way to realize this expectation would have to be via the pass, and he drafted Olympic sprinter Johnny "Lam" Jones to pair up with fleet Wesley Walker on the outside. The reasoning was sound. The Jets had an offensive line that could pass protect as well as block for the run. It also had a young quarterback with a strong arm, an outstanding receiver coming out of the backfield, a tight receiver who could go deep, and a wide receiver who most opponents felt a need to double-team. So, the Jets opened up their offense as logic demanded, and they finished the 1980 season with a 4-12 record. What nobody had anticipated was that the Jet switch from a ball control offense would expose a weak and inexperienced defense. For the 1980 New York Jets, the decision to emphasize the passing game proved disastrous.

If the offensive thrust over the last three years has been to develop the passing game, you can be certain that defensive coaches have been trying to find ways to counteract the effects of the rule changes. The efforts of most teams have been subtle and difficult to recognize. Such obvious adjustments as adding one or two extra defensive backs are not the answer unless the offense is in a "must" passing situation. The quarterback would merely check off and take what the defense gives him.

Most teams have begun to change the type of coverage as well as the type of player in the defensive secondary. Despite the fact that the effectiveness of zone and combination coverages stifled the passing game and encouraged the rule changes in the first place, teams have been forced to lessen their dependence on the zone and rely more on man to man coverage. For years quarterbacks have been saying that "given time, they could pick apart the zone." The new rules have given them the time they asked for. The rule that now allows offensive linemen to extend their arms has significantly diminished the number of pass rushes and sacks. Without a solid pass rush, a zone cannot be effective.

As teams are forced to go more to man coverage and limit contact to within five yards of the line of scrimmage, there has been increased demand for the quick cornerback. Before the 1978 rules changes, there was a demand for big, strong corners who could assist in defensing the run and also be able to bump a receiver off his route. The defensive back who could run the 40-yard dash in 4.6 seconds is no longer the ideal. Scouts are now looking for 4.4 people who can run with world-class sprinters disguised as wide receivers. There is once again room on the roster for a 215-pound linebacker like Philadelphia's Jerry Robinson—men who can neutralize the new breed of tight end and also blitz the quarterback.

Defensive units have also started to adjust on the front line in order to put pressure on the passer. There has been more use of situation defenses, blitzing, and stunting than in the past. Defensive linemen now think "pass" first and "run" second. And they no longer have to stand over 6'5" to capture the attention of the scouts. Fred Dean and Gary Johnson of the San Diego Chargers both did an outstanding job of rushing the passer in 1980, and both are under 6'3".

The adjustments of the Pittsburgh Steeler defense have been most noticeable. Back in 1974, when the first priority of the defense was to stop the run, Chuck Noll moved Joe Green into the center-guard gap and had him turn almost at a 45-degree angle toward the center as he lined up as close to the line of scrimmage as possible. Needless to say, the Steelers were effective in defensing the run. During the 1980 season, after succeeding in sacking the quarterback only once over a three-game period, the Steelers abandoned their rush-oriented defense and reverted to the traditional 4-3. Times had changed.

Over the next few years, you will see many more changes as the defense attempts to generate an improved pass rush and defend against the pass without making illegal contact with the receiver. It will take the defense time to adjust to the new pass-oriented offenses. It will take time, but if history is any teacher, it will happen. And when it does, another pro-set or I or wishbone will be worked out on a blackboard somewhere, and the whole cycle will start again. But, regardless of the directions taken by the offense or the defense in the years to come, you can be sure that they will be based on the basic information presented in the pages that follow.

September, 1981 Sam DeLuca

# Part One

# THE POSITIONS OF FOOTBALL

## Introduction

Boxing has always enjoyed a following because it can be enjoyed on several levels. You don't have to be able to analyze advanced skills and techniques to enjoy a boxing match. It is the most basic of battles. Anyone can appreciate at a glance the showmanship and speed of a Muhammad Ali at his peak or the intense desire of a Leon Spinks. An understanding of counterpunching, working the ropes and pacing can come later.

The same principle applies to football. It is a relatively easy to recognize the basic skills of running, catching, and throwing which running backs, receivers and quarterbacks possess. It takes some knowledge and practice to appreciate some of the skills necessary at the other positions on a football field.

Working to obtain this extra knowledge, though, is worth the effort. The fan that learns to appreciate the skills required in the defensive backfield, at linebacker, or on the offensive and defensive lines will certainly have a better understanding of what is happening on the field and why a team is winning or losing. He will also discover that there is no reason to be bored at any football game regardless of the score. The knowledgeable fan learns to enjoy watching any one of the many individual battles involving the same hard blows, intense desire, tremendous endurance, skill and grace that make for an interesting boxing match. You may find that you even prefer to watch those individual battles when the action is not dull or the game has not been decided.

Individual battles notwithstanding, football is a team game and the interdependency between each player will become quite evident as you read the chapters on the various positions. It is this interdependency and the failure to understand what is expected at each position that causes the many conflicting opinions about the worth of a player. When you finish the chapters on the positions you will not only be able to evaluate each player on a team more effectively, but should be ready for the more complex chapters on formations and strategy that follow. It's like chess. There is an offense, there is a defense and there are different pieces with different functions. You can see that easily enough by looking at the board. To really understand the game, though, you have to first understand the role of each piece in the game.

# 1

# THE QUARTERBACK

## The Man Who Makes It All Go

"Most football games are won or lost in the fourth quarter."

"Football games are won and lost up front."

"Football games are won by the team that makes the fewest mistakes."

"The quitter never wins and the winner never quits."

"We're beating ourselves."

I could fill this page and probably a chapter with cliches about football, some of which would be true and others only partially true. Some may have been true at one time, and others never true. There is one that I used to believe until Joe Namath joined the Jets in 1965: "A quarterback is only as good as his team." Now, I am not at all certain that it shouldn't be reversed to say: "A team is only as good as its quarterback."

Quarterback is the most difficult position to evaluate and without a doubt the most important position on a football team. If a team runs 90% of the time, the exceptional running back may be more important, but if the quarterback is capable, the team should not be running 90% of the time. An *individual* playing quarterback may not be the most important person on *his* team, but the position itself *is*, and, in professional football, if an individual quarterback is not the most important person on his team, then that team has an inadequate quarterback.

The cliche, "A quarterback is only as good as his team" probably gained favor because the quarterback is almost completely dependent on his teammates. The quarterback cannot pass effectively if he is not getting adequate pass protection. He can't complete his passes if his receivers are inadequate or if the defense succeeds in tying up all of his receivers. The passer's effectiveness is directly related to the success of the ground game because a quarterback who has to pass on every down loses the element of surprise. The quarterback is also dependent on his defense. He can't put points on the board if the other team has the ball. In short, the quarterback is dependent on his offensive line, his offensive backs and the effectiveness of his entire defensive team. The team as a whole though, is also dependent on the quarterback.

A team may win *occasionally* in spite of the quarterback, but will have difficulty doing so *consistently* in pro football.

It is presently popular to criticize Joe Namath. He couldn't win the starting job with the Rams and, in retrospect, he had only one good year with the Jets. Perhaps. But, what an unforgettable year that was. Namath led a team of very average players to the Super Bowl and then delivered the big one. The Baltimore Colts had better personnel at about 18 of the 22 starting positions. They were 17 point favorites and justifiably so if you go on the assumption that a team makes the quarterback. By that reasoning, Earl Morrall and Johnny Unitas should have been exceptional on January 5, 1969 because of the exceptional team in front of them, and Joe Namath should have been very average.

That particular day the Jets were not an average team. They were a very good team capable of beating any other team in the N.F.L. Average players like Gerry Philbin, Paul Rochester, John Schmitt, Pete Lammons and an entire defensive secondary that disappeared the following year played the best football of their careers. Dave Herman, just a cut above an average offensive guard moved out to tackle and ate up Bubba Smith, an all pro defensive end. Someone forgot to tell Herman that the was too short to play tackle. The average Jet players were all good that day and their good players—especially Matt Snell, George Sauer and Winston Hill—were Super. They might have been able to win that particular day without Joe Namath at quarterback, but certainly not as decisively. It was Namath's arrogance and the constant threat of the bomb that kept the Baltimore defensive backs and linebackers loose enough for Matt Snell and Emerson Boozer to establish a running game and make possible that memorable day for the American Football League. Without his quarterbacking, the Jets would never have been in the Super Bowl, and without his presence, those average players would never have been inspired to the heights they were that warm Sunday afternoon in Miami. There can be no doubt that it was the quarterback that made the team, the year the Jets won the Super Bowl.

There is a tendency to look at final statistics and won and lost records and forget everything else in football. Statistics can be a valuable tool in attempting to evaluate the performance of a player or team. They can also be completely misleading when the individual is forgotten. Namath's career statistics are not impressive. His completion percentage would have been consistently higher had the Jets been a stronger and better balanced team. Namath would not have been forced to play "catch up" as often and would have been able to throw more short Fran Tarkenton type passes to his backs and tight end. Namath's independence— or arrogance if you prefer—and his tremendous competitive spirit did not help his stats. Namath was never concerned with his completion percentage or what others thought of him. His only concern was to win, which often meant throwing 40 times a game when everyone knew he was going to throw because his team was behind by three touchdowns. He was not influenced by the fact that there was little hope of pulling out many of those games during the lean years or that those many long passes were hurting his passing rating. Perhaps he should have thrown more short passes and taken a more conservative approach. This might well have helped his statistics but most certainly would not have helped the Jets' won and lost record over the years. They just didn't have the personnel, and Namath won more games than he lost when he dominated the action with the long pass.

With the exception of Howard Cosell, anyone involved with football realizes that quarterback is a difficult position to analyze. Howard is the only person I know who will venture an opinion on a quarterback after seeing him play once. The rest of us have our difficulties even after several times. Perhaps this is the reason Cosell changes his opinion so often.

There are numerous examples of coaches who have made mistakes in evaluating their quarterbacks. Look at the many great ones that have been cut or traded over the years. The Pittsburgh Steeler coaches are particularly notorious for getting rid of good quarterbacks. They have either cut or traded people like Johnny Unitas, Bobby Lane and Len Dawson.

How could the New York Giants have allowed Fran Tarkenton to return to the Minnesota Vikings? Couldn't they see that Tarkenton was a winner and that his teammates on the Giants were the losers? It's not easy to evaluate a quarterback on a losing team or Minnesota would not have traded Tarkenton to the Giants to begin with. When Tarkenton was with the Giants they used to say that he didn't have a strong arm; that he scrambled too much. It's curious that no one in Minnesota seems to notice that Tarkenton doesn't throw long very often. This is probably because Tarkenton doesn't have to throw long as often with Minnesota's more balanced and effective attack. He scrambled so much in New York because he had to. Otherwise, he would never have had a chance with the weak Giant offensive line.

Several years later the Giants made another error in evaluating a quarterback. They picked up Craig Morton. Every time I hear Craig Morton's name, I think of the 1970 season when Morton played for Dallas. They beat the San Francisco 49ers in a playoff game that year despite the fact that Craig Morton only hit 7 of 22 for a total of 90 yards. Morton proved equally inept in the Super Bowl by completing 12 of 26 for 127 yards as the Cowboys lost to the Colts, 16-13. With any other quarterback in the league, Dallas would have won. It took the Giants a while to realize the mistake they made with Morton and, before the 1977 season, they traded him to Denver for Steve Ramsey. Ramsey didn't make the team, but Morton brought Denver to the Super Bowl. The question now is whether the Giants made a mistake when they picked up Morton or when they traded him to Denver.

I think the point has been made. It is difficult to evaluate a quarterback. When coaches who have an opportunity to study a quarterback's every move on film often make poor decisions, the average fan doesn't have much of a chance. The one advantage the fan has is that he doesn't have to cut a player in mid-season.

## PHYSICAL QUALITIES

Size, strength and speed are naturally an asset to a quarterback, but not as important as they are at other positions. Quick arms and hands are more important to the pro quarterback than foot speed. High school and college quarterbacks are frequently required to do most of their passing while moving and are required to run with the ball more often. To them, foot speed is a prime asset. To a pro, a quick delivery is as important.

Quick arms and hands allow the pro quarterback to fake and hand off more effectively on running plays. They are also important to the passing game. The key to good passing is releasing the ball at the right time. That does not mean that the quarterback counts Mississippi 1, Mississippi 2, Mississippi 3, and releases the football. It implies that, although being rushed, he waits until the last possible moment before releasing the ball. This will give the defense less time to react to the ball, and will enable him to hit any receiver who opens unexpectedly at the last moment. If he has a quick release, he'll avoid being guilty of what defensive players call "telegraphing the throw." The quarterback with the quick release will also be trapped less trying to throw the ball, and avoid the necessity of those hurried throws which so often lead to interceptions.

Another physical quality that is important to a quarterback but rather difficult to measure is peripheral vision. This is something that coaches say is important at all positions, but it's vital at quarterback. Many football games are determined by turnovers, and interceptions are turnovers that often occur because of poor peripheral vision. Out of necessity, the quarterback has to shift his eye focus while scanning his receivers. The quarterback with poor peripheral vision will have trouble keeping track of his defenders in these situations. The quarterback with good peripheral vision will always have an idea where the defenders are and avoid interceptions.

Agility is one of the physical qualities required by a quarterback that *is* easy to measure. Greg Landry of the Detroit Lions has agility to spare. Billy Kilmer has little. Most other quarterbacks fall somewhere in between those two.

## MENTAL AND EMOTIONAL QUALITIES

Self-confidence, poise, determination and mental toughness are required of all football players and the quarterback is certainly no exception. More than any other position, though, a quarterback has to have a head on his shoulders. The defensive tackle and the offensive guard can get by with superior physical ability and good technique. The quarterback must be able to think. The quarterback not only has to remember every offensive play and how it fits into the game plan, but must remember the assignment of each man on the offensive team. That information, along with a knowledge of how his teammates are likely to react, will help him to make decisions as he reads the defense. He must get particularly close to his receivers to anticipate their adjustments to the defense.

No quarterback can get by without poise and confidence; but there is a difference between them. A player may believe in himself and his ability to accomplish the job, but lack the poise and polish to sit in the pocket under pressure. It takes something special not to panic when people begin to fall all around you. Poise helps the quarterback to establish a rapport with his teammates and to inspire them during a game. It's called leadership, and it *is* important. A halfback can be a follower. A quarterback should be a leader. He doesn't inspire with rhetoric or cliches like "this is a big one" or "buckle your belts, we need this first down." He simply conveys the feeling that he knows what he is doing, that the play he calls is right, and that it's going to work.

More than anything else, it is the depth of knowledge required which makes it imperative that the quarterback be able to think. The average player has no idea of what is happening on the field while he is playing. Unless he misses a block on the offensive line and the man he is supposed to block makes the tackle, he doesn't necessarily know why a play broke down. He has a specific assignment and knows only what happened to him. In many instances, he doesn't even know what type of defensive alignment the opposition has taken until the quarterback tells him when calling signals. The quarterback, though, has to know what's happening everywhere if he's going to exploit the opposition's weaknesses and move his team.

Of course the quarterback comes into the game with a lot of information not usually given to the rest of the team. In general, the team is not privy to the suggested sequence of plays and strategy the coaching staff thinks will be effective against the particular opponent coming up. These things are discussed during special meetings between the quarterback and the offensive coaches. The only reason the offensive linemen know that a play will work is because the quarterback tells them that it will. Much depends on what they think of the quarterback. A Fran Tarkenton or a Bob Griese gets the most out of his team because the team believes in his judgment.

Both Tarkenton and Griese are exceptionally bright and articulate. They would be team leaders even if they were not quarterbacks. Both have consistently displayed the ability to outwit defenders and lead their teams to victory. Tarkenton has never possesed anything more than an average arm, but his ability to improvise and build confidence in his teammates has enabled him to win many more games than he's lost. Griese has an exceptional throwing arm, but is bright enough to know that the less he uses it, the more effective his passing game will be. In two Super Bowl victories, he combined for only 18 pass attempts but completed 14. In the three game blitz to the Super Bowl VII victory, he attempted only 31 passes and completed 20 of them.

Don Shula has remarked that there are some quarterbacks who throw bombs but can't throw first downs. Shula says that the thing he admires most about Griese is that he throws first downs and bombs. Griese once threw three consecutive passes for touchdowns against New England and, as a rookie in 1967, he set an A.F.L. record by throwing 122 passes without an interception. In fact, Bob Griese had more poise and confidence as a rookie than some quarterbacks have after being in the league for ten years. Craig Morton is a case in point. It took Craig Morton 13 years to develop the poise and confidence necessary for him to live up to his physical potential. This same Craig Morton that finished 2nd in passing in the A.F.C. in 1977 and brought his team into the Super Bowl was the man that cost Dallas the Super Bowl in 1970 and was booed out of New York in 1976. Could that Craig Morton be the same man who is now regarded as a folk hero in Denver? How can a player be less than adequate for 12 years and suddenly become a dynamic leader and a super star? Certainly the answer lies beyond the physical. Morton is no better a passer today than he ever was. There must be other reasons for the sudden transformation.

Morton had this to say after the 1977 season: "I am the same player I was before, but the situation is different. With the Giants I got myself into a lot of trouble trying to make things happen that maybe weren't the best percentage type plays. Here, I'm not doing that. I'll still take some chances, like running the ball, but here we have people who break games wide open, a lot of

Craig Morton—he outlasted his critics.

offensive threats. Otis Armstrong and rookie Rob Lytle are awfully good runners. Haven Moses and Rick Upchurch are excellent pass receivers, and Riley Odoms is as good a tight end as I've ever thrown to."

The reason for Morton's success in 1977 is not a superior Denver team, but simply a superior Craig Morton: a man with a degree of poise and confidence that he never had before. I won't speculate as to what changed him or why it took so long.

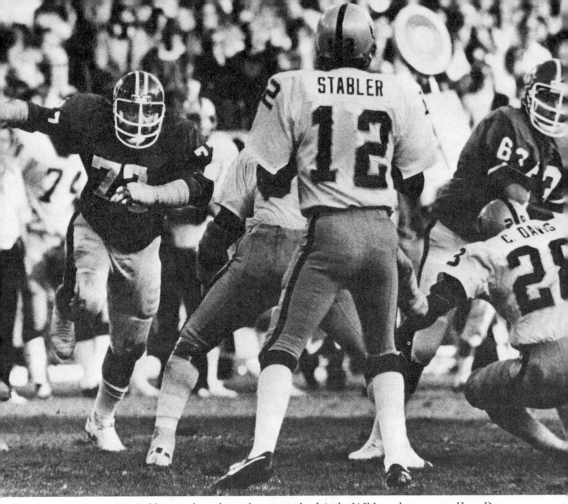

Ken Stabler is perhaps the coolest quarterback in the N.F.L. under pressure. Here, Denver Bronco defensive end Lyle Alzado bears down on him.

Ken Stabler of the Raiders is another quarterback out of Alabama that seemed to have an abundance of poise and confidence right from the beginning. Like Namath, he throws the bomb more often than most quarterbacks and doesn't seem to worry about statistics or criticism. He will do whatever necessary to win. Coach John Madden doesn't worry about Stabler's occasional interceptions: "Being concerned with those interceptions is like being concerned that Rembrandt missed a stroke. I never worry about Kenny. No matter what happens, he just keeps coming at you. That's what makes him so great."

## FUNDAMENTAL SKILLS

The fundamental skills required of a quarterback are harder to measure objectively than at most other positions. You can evaluate an offensive lineman if you watch him closely by determining how often his man gets to the ball carrier. An end can be measured by the number of passes he catches. With a quarterback, it's much more subtle. His fundamental skills can be broken into two areas: those required for the running game and those for the passing game.

## The Running Game

There are four basic skills the quarterback must develop to properly execute the running game. Look for his ability to hand off, to fake, to lateral and to run with the football.

*The Hand Off*—The quarterback has full responsibility for the hand off since the running back is often looking into the line to see where the hole is likely to open. A fumble on the hand off may occasionally be the running back's fault, but if there is nothing unusual that catches your eye, blame the quarterback. The hand off should be smooth and fluid. After taking the snap from center, the quarterback should hold the ball close to his body in order to avoid the possibility of the ball being knocked out of his hands. He should not crowd the runner and yet not reach too far when placing it into his mid-section.

*The Fake*—Coaches teach all sorts of fundamental moves and positions of the body while faking: knees bent slightly, shoulders rounded, elbows in, and body between the defense and the ball whenever possible. The fan in the stands is in a better position to evaluate a fake than a player on the field. Watch the effort which the quarterback expends in carrying through the fake. You should be able to get an idea after a few plays if the defense is going for the fakes or ignoring them.

*The Lateral*—There are two basic lateral passes used by the quarterback: the two-handed pitch-out and the one-handed pitch-out. The two-handed pitch-out or lateral is frequently used on the high school and college levels. It was especially popular during the 1950's and early 1960's when the option play was in vogue. In the option play, the quarterback takes the snap from the center and moves down the line to the position of the defensive end or corner linebacker and either pitches out to a running back moving behind him or runs the ball himself. His choice is determined by the action of the defensive man he is approaching.

The option regained popularity during the early '70's when such major college teams as Texas and Oklahoma had success with the wishbone offense which utilizes a triple option play, one of whose options is a pitch-out. It is doubtful that any type of option will ever become popular in the pros though, because it exposes the quarterback to unusual danger. I doubt that any pro coach would allow his quarterback to be hit play after play by the larger

Bengal quarterback Ken Anderson hands off to Archie Griffin.

defensive ends and linebackers in the pros—something which is inevitable with the option. For openers, it would end the careers of all quarterbacks over 30 years of age. However, the option can be effective on the goal line and will always have some place in the pro football game plan.

One-handed laterals are often seen in professional football on the quick pitch (an end sweep with the on-side tackle, and sometimes the guard, pulling out to lead interference). It develops quickly and involves a fast turn by the quarterback after taking the snap, and an immediate pitch to the running back who has already begun to head for the flank. The one-handed lateral is tossed with a spiral and will travel further. The advantage of the two-handed lateral is that it's easier to catch since it floats and gives the receiver more time to react.

*Running Ability*—The importance of a quarterback's running ability varies according to the level at which he is playing and the offensive philosophy of his coach. Most pro coaches do not want their quarterback to run with the football unless it is absolutely necessary. Although there are several running plays that can be extremely effective when the quarterback carries the football, many coaches would rather not risk injury to their number one quarterback. The quarterback on the high school and college levels, on the other hand, is usually not as important to the team and will frequently be listed among its leading rushers.

The most common play run by pro quarterbacks is the quarterback sneak. Terry Bradshaw, of the Pittsburgh Steelers, will use the sneak as often as anyone. He is big and strong and can frequently bull his way for a yard of two. The ability of the offensive center and the two guards will often determine the success of the quarterback sneak. The offensive line uses wedge blocking, with the center as the apex. The offensive guards and tackles close to the inside and try to move forward as a unit. Each offensive player is responsible for the man to his inside. Ideally, the quarterback will run behind the center, but he may break into another area if a hole opens. The alert quarterback will run the sneak any time an unusually wide gap opens in the defensive line. On these occasions the offensive line may not be aware of his intentions.

The quarterback draw can be highly effective when run by a quarterback with the speed and agility of a Greg Landry or a Terry Bradshaw. The advantage of the quarterback draw is having the use of an additional offensive back to fake or block. He will normally be sent out on a flare to remove the middle linebacker completely, or provide a blocking angle for the center assigned to block the middle linebacker. The quarterback will drop back as he would on a show pass and then key his blockers and take any hole that opens. Some teams will use the set backs as blockers to lead this play.

Archie Manning of the New Orleans Saints sees the pluses and minuses of the quarterback draw: "It gives our team an added dimension and other teams use it with fellows like Roger Staubach and Ken Stabler. Of course, there are good things and bad things about it. The first thing that pops into my head is the injury factor." He readily concedes, though that, when a game is on the line, nobody is worrying about injuries.

Raider quarterback Ken Stabler bootlegging the ball behind guard Gene Upshaw.

The bootleg is another play that can be effective if the quarterback can move. The flow of the backfield goes one way and, after carrying out his fakes, the quarterback goes around the opposite end by himself or in front of one or two pulling linemen. It is most effective when a team has been running the ends consistently and the defense has begun to react quickly to the flow of the backfield. Many teams save the bootleg for a key situation near the goal line when the quarterback doesn't have to run too far and may not be tackled at all if the play is successful. The defense is more likely to overreact to the faking in the backfield when backed up to its own goal line. Speed is of the essence, but you will also see slow quarterbacks run this play since there is usually a receiver downfield to whom he can throw if he sees that he can't outrun the defense.

## The Passing Game

The list of fundamental skills required of the passing quarterback begins with the stance he assumes behind the center when taking the exchange and includes a myriad of little things that most people don't notice. Like most other positions on a football team, you can find people at quarterback that break the fundamental rules, develop their own peculiar skills and techniques, and still enjoy success. Rather than dwell on these minute points which are important only to the quarterback himself, let's get into some of the fundamental skills, visible from the stands, which will help to explain why certain things happen on the field and why one quarterback has more success than another:

*The Quarterback Drop*—After taking the ball from the center, on a show or drop back pass, the quarterback will drop back seven or eight yards directly behind the center. There are several ways to set up which are acceptable and the style a quarterback uses will depend on his physical attributes and his coach's philosophy. The fastest way to get back into the pocket is to turn and run. However, the quarterback that turns his back to the line of scrimmage and does not look downfield until in the pocket will have more difficulty in finding his receivers. Far too many things can happen during the short time it takes him to set up. If he turns his back, he might not see the coverage, the receiver who has fallen or been forced to change his route, or the double coverage on his primary receiver. As a result, there are no pro quarterbacks that turn completely while retreating. Most turn and look over one shoulder, which allows them to see what is happening over a good portion of the field. Some quarterbacks will backpedal into the pocket. This allows them to see the entire field of action while dropping back, at a small sacrifice in time. In the case of quarterbacks with extremely poor mobility, the backpedal may be as quick as turning completely. The disadvantage of the backpedal is that the ball is exposed to the defense at all times. Another problem is a tendency to lose one's balance. Billy Kilmer of the Washington Redskins probably has the most battered and abused body in pro football. He was a fine running quarterback at UCLA but lost most of his agility in a serious auto accident in 1963 that sidelined him for almost three years. As a result, he has taken to backpedaling. In a nationally televised game during the 1976

season, Kilmer was backpedaling when he lost his footing and
ended up on his backside. Those of you familiar with Kilmer's
fiery personality can imagine his reaction to the incident.

Regardless of his style, look for the speed a quarterback
displays in setting up and his ability to release the ball quickly if
necessary.

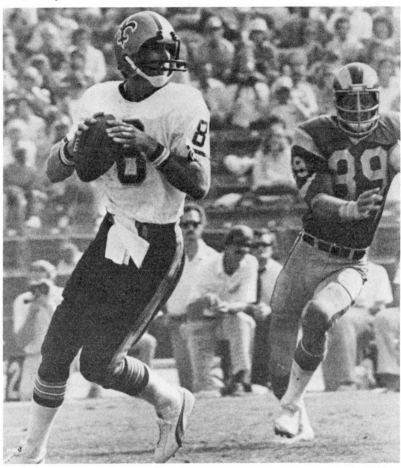

Archie Manning of New Orleans dropping back to pass. How good could he have been
with a winning team?

*The Passing Motion*—Here again there is room for individual
differences. Most experts agree that the overhead release is best
for a young passer. Of course, there have been successful sidearm
passers in pro football, and any release that leads to a completion is
acceptable. Theoretically, anyhow, the over-the-head release
gives the quarterback more control and makes deflections more
difficult.

There are times when a quarterback is almost compelled to release the ball sidearm or close to it. He may have to throw on the run or around the outstretched arms of a pass rusher. This will also influence the follow through. Don't expect to see a quarterback follow through with his arm if he has thrown off balance or around a defender.

*Faking (The Pump)*—The quarterback himself plays a role in breaking a receiver free. The deep backs in the defensive second-ary are taught to look at the receiver at all times. Not all of them listen to the teacher. Many will peek into the backfield peri-odically to see what the quarterback is doing and where he is looking. The linebackers and free safety will look into the back-field more often than the cornerbacks and move in the direction in which the quarterback is looking. The experienced quarterback will try to "look off" the defender by looking in one direction and then suddenly turning and throwing to another man. This is most effective against those defenders that look at the quarterback continually, and should be used when throwing into areas covered by the linebacker.

One of the ways that a quarterback can get the pass defenders to commit themselves is by pumping without releasing the ball. The objective is to get the defenders to move in one direction and then to throw elsewhere. There are many situations where the pump can be used effectively. The quarterback may want to move a linebacker out of a receiver's path or use it to help another receiver with a move. For example, a pump timed with the receiver's turn-in on the "hook and go" can make the receiver's fake more effective. It requires no more than a split second of effective deception for a fake to be successful. Once the defender sees the pump and begins to move in the desired direction, it has been accomplished.

The arm fake is easy to detect by anyone looking at the quarterback. The number of fakes used by the quarterback is not as important as their timing. It takes a degree of poise to look away from the man to whom you intend to throw the ball and still not lose your perspective.

*Timing*—The timing between the receiver and quarterback is the most important element in the passing game. There are certain patterns and routes that require pin point timing. The quarterback that holds on to the ball too long on the sideline route is inviting an interception. He has to work with his receivers and know exactly when they will make their break. Ideally, he will release the ball before the receiver makes that final break. On routes over the middle, he must throw between linebackers and other defenders. On these passes, there is generally little room for doubt as to who caused the interception (the quarterback or the receiver). There is no set time to throw the football when it must sail between the linebackers since it is impossible to know exactly where they will be and what coverage was called. The interception thrown on the slant over the middle can be credited to the quarterback (on any of the sharp breaking routes it could be either the quarterback, or the receiver that broke too soon).

*Scrambling*—Ever since Norm Van Brocklin's statement that his quarterback at Minnesota, Fran Tarkenton, "will win some that he shouldn't win and lose some that he shouldn't lose," the football world has been tuned in to the "scrambling quarterback." It's true that the performance of a compulsive scrambler, who does not have the poise to sit in the pocket and wait for his receiver to break free or to look for his secondary receiver, is unpredictable. He is likely to come up with the great play at times, and thow an interception or be thrown for an unnecessary loss at other times. Fran Tarkenton may have been that type of quarterback at the time of the statement, but he now rarely scrambles and only out of necessity. His scrambling ability was a tremendous asset to a rather weak football team, the New York Giants. It has not been important to the Minnesota Vikings.

Look for the quarterback to move out of the pocket only when he is being pressured to do so. Be critical of those that leave prematurely. The quarterback that is not moving out of design loses sight of everything that is happening downfield. He no longer knows where all the defenders are and can easily throw the ball into an opponent's hands without knowing he was there. Leaving the pocket causes a state of confusion for both the offense and the defense. This increases the chances of an interception.

As an offensive lineman, I always objected to a quarterback who scrambled unnecessarily. A lineman must maintain the proper angle between the pass rusher and the quarterback. When the quarterback begins to scramble, the offensive lineman has little chance of maintaining that angle. There is too much room for the defensive man to maneuver when the quarterback leaves the pocket. The defensive lineman can run around his opponent without being concerned about protecting an area or leaving a rushing lane.

In short, scrambling takes away the biggest advantage that the offense has: knowing where the play is going and therefore what is likely to happen. When the quarterback is scrambling, the offense is no longer in control of the situation and is just as likely to be hurt as to benefit from the conditions created. Van Brocklin's opinion that a quarterback that scrambles unnecessarily will win some he shouldn't win and lose some he shouldn't lose was accurate. His assessment of Fran Tarkenton was incorrect. Tarkenton was not a compulsive scrambler lacking the discipline or courage to sit in the pocket. Minnesota was a weak expansion team when Van Brocklin and Tarkenton were there and, as with the Giants, Tarkenton was *forced* to scramble.

Bert Jones of Baltimore rolling out.

*The Roll Out*—There is a distinct difference between a roll out pass and a pass resulting from a quarterback scramble. The roll out is a pre-determined action in which the quarterback runs to one side of the field before throwing the football. It was designed to put pressure on the linebackers and possibly the defensive secondary since the quarterback has the option of running with the football if someone doesn't contain him on the flank. The more fleet-footed the quarterback, the more pressure exerted on the defense.

The roll out pass most often develops off of play action. The quarterback fakes a hand off to one of his set backs before rolling out on the flank. This puts even more pressure on the linebacker.

The roll out pass has been around almost as long as the forward pass. Nevertheless, the flamboyant Hank Stram was able to convince everyone that his "moving pocket" of the late 1960's was unique. In truth, it was no more than an elaborate roll out pass designed to get the rather short Len Dawson out of the pocket where he had trouble seeing over his tall offensive linemen. It was probably effective for the Kansas City Chiefs because they spent more time perfecting the roll out than the other teams in the N.F.L., all of which have a form of the roll out pass in their playbooks. Even the Jets with Joe Namath had a roll out pass in their repetoire, though it was rarely used.

Fran Tarkenton sums up the changing nature of quarterback play: "I think the quarterback of tomorrow is going to be better than we are today, and he will be able to do a zillion things, including scrambling. He's going to have the ability to throw from the roll, the moving pocket, the drop-back pocket, the bootleg and the busted play. The quarterbacks coming out of colleges nowadays are better athletes than ever before; they can do everything."

Steve Grogen, Richard Todd, and Pat Hayden seem to fit that description. They are all fine young athletes who have an excellent opportunity to become star N.F.L. quarterbacks. The extent that each will be encouraged to run and scramble depends on the philosophy of their respective coaches. I think you will see more and more coaches that will not wince when their quarterbacks leave the pocket, but encourage it when the alternative is throwing the ball away or eating the football. A first down counts as much when it results from a run by the quarterback as from a pin point pass.

## PLAY CALLING

Every quarterback goes into a game with a specific game plan (a list of potential plays for that game). The extent that the quarterback will be allowed to deviate from the game plan will depend on his experience, his coach's philosophy and his faith in his quarterback's intelligence. There are some coaches, like Paul Brown, whose philosophy is to insist on calling every play for the quarterback. Brown not only did this for Ken Anderson on the Bengals, but did it for one of the best, Otto Graham, of the Cleveland Browns, during the late 1940's and early 1950's. Brown has maintained that he will let his quarterback call the signals when he finds a quarterback who knows as much about football as he does.

It is unlikely that a quarterback will know as much about football as his coach, but it isn't necessary for a coach to call every play either. The strategy doesn't change that much from play to

Terry Bradshaw scanning the defense before taking the snap.

play and sideline talks still allow the coach to control the game if he is so inclined. Brown claims that he did not want his quarterback to be exposed to the pressure of calling the plays. He wanted him to be thinking about execution. I personally believe that the quarterback should call the plays based on the game plan since it's advisable to have the quarterback thinking about what is happening on the other side of the line of scrimmage. I played for Paul Brown in the Senior Bowl many years ago and agree with the consensus opinion about him: an outstanding coach . . . but an outstanding ego to match his record.

No matter how well formulated the game plan, it can't hope to cover every situation. The better than average quarterback shows his skill and his ability to adapt to minor changes in the defensive alignment and to adjust to the variables. The score, time remaining, field position, down and distance, wind and weather, and what has happened to that point in the game cannot be predetermined. These are the variables that must be considered, in conjunction with the game plan, by the quarterback, when deciding what play to call.

### The Score

The score naturally plays a major role in determining which plays the quarterback will choose. When a team is ahead by several touchdowns, you can expect the quarterback to make conservative calls. The quarterback should not throw the bomb in the fourth quarter when his team is leading by two touchdowns. He should be trying to run out the clock by staying on the ground. He should not be calling the quick pitch if he's backed up to his own goal line because of the possibility of being thrown for a loss. Both the bomb and quick pitch may be advisable if his team is down by two touchdowns in the fourth quarter. With a two touchdown lead and time running out, though, there's nothing to gain.

### Time Remaining

The time becomes more important as the game progresses. A two-touchdown deficit means more to a losing quarterback in the fourth quarter than with two minutes remaining in the first half. The game does not have to be won or lost at halftime. The quarterback should only start to gamble when his team is behind and the clock says that something drastic is needed.

Every team spends a great deal of practice time in developing what is known as the "two-minute offense." This is designed to enable a losing team to get a maximum number of plays into the time remaining. It is an excellent time to evaluate a quarterback's poise and self control. You have to remember that there is little chance of completing the bomb at this time since the defense will be in a "prevent" defense with instructions to give up the short to medium pass but not the long pass. The quarterback must be able to utilize his time outs properly, hit on the short sideline passes which will enable the receiver to get out of bounds, and throw the incomplete pass when the clock must be stopped and the receiver is not open. Johnny Unitas is the accepted past-master at executing the two-minute offense. Ken Stabler does it as well as anyone in the game today.

## Down and Distance

The general rule is to go for the touchdown on first down and the first down in a third down situation. At mid-field it is probably best to call the bomb on first down. The play pass is also a good call on first down. It's useless on third with 30 yards to go, when the defense will be looking for the long pass and is not likely to be affected by the faking. Look for some variation. If a team has been running all game on first down, a long pass may be effective toward the end of the game.

On second down with ten yards to go, the quarterback should be trying for the first down and not the touchdown. Some quarterbacks will try for the long gainer on second down, but only if there is short yardage required for a first down and he is confident of getting it on the following down if the long gainer fails. On second and ten, the quarterback can be expected to call anything except the bomb. He should be trying for at least seven or eight yards, which can come from almost any play he calls.

Third down situations are usually handled with the pass if more than seven yards are required for a first down. This is a situation when the quarterback is likely to go with those plays that have been successful earlier in the game, provided that he thinks he can get the necessary yardage. There are some who say that certain pass routes are more effective at certain times. I doubt this since, if it were, the defense would fast learn what the offense considers more effective. However, draws and screens are considered good calls on third and long situations. The defensive team's concern over the bomb helps to set up the draw and screen.

## Wind and Weather

The influence that the wind and weather have on the quarterback's calls is obvious. He should not throw deep against the wind, or run the quick pitch often on a very sloppy field. Simple plays that don't require sharp cuts are best. Short passes that are simply designed are advisable.

## SPECIAL PLAYS

There are many *special* or *supplemental* plays in most playbooks. In this section we'll confine ourselves to those plays that are used to supplement the passing game and offer a particular opportunity to evaluate the quarterback. These are the screen pass, the draw play and the safety valve or flare pass. All three plays have a better chance of success if the quarterback has been using the drop back pass frequently.

In most situations defensive linemen will look for the run first and then the pass. However, there are times when *all* linemen play the pass, with little concern for the run. These are the times when the alert quarterback will call the draw or screen plays. Not only do they often break for good yardage, but they have the added advantage of slowing down the pass rush.

### The Screen Pass

The screen pass can be called on any down, but is usually reserved for what the defense may consider a sure passing situation. The play has a better chance of succeeding if the defensive line is charging hard and is intent on getting to the passer. The offensive line sets up as it would on a show pass and invites the defenders to go over them to get to the passer. They make contact as they would on the show or drop back pass and, after two or three seconds of holding the block, they allow the defensive people to get by them and rush the passer. They have to be good actors and not tip the play. The quarterback also has to be a good actor. He sets up at seven or eight yards as he normally does, and, as the rush approaches, he drops back an additional three to five yards before releasing the ball to the set back or receiver standing behind the wall of offensive linemen which has formed.

The screen pass may develop in any area behind the line of scrimmage, and is predicated on timing and deception. It can be tipped by a lineman who leaves too early to get into the wall, or the quarterback who drops back too quickly and looks directly at the receiver as the wall is forming. This is another situation where good peripheral vision is an asset. The quarterback should be looking downfield as he would on a pass play, and still be aware of what is happening directly in front of and to the side of him.

One problem that frequently destroys the screen pass is the difficulty the quarterback has in clearing the outstretched hands of the onrushing linemen with his pass. It is for this reason that he

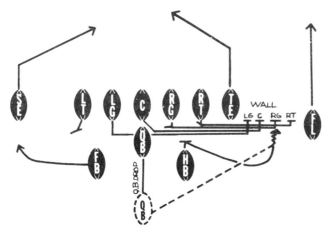

Timing is everything on the screen pass. An offensive lineman that leaves to form the wall too soon will tip the play.

drops back several additional yards as the linemen approach.

The screen pass takes a certain amount of poise if it is to be run well. The quarterback must not panic and throw the ball too soon or take an exceptionally deep set to begin with. Dan Pastorini of the Houston Oilers does it exceptionally well. The screen is sometimes effective on first and second downs. On third down and long yardage the defense may be looking for it. Most teams also run a *quick* screen. Here, the quarterback usually drops back and fakes the draw play to the fullback and then tosses the ball to the halfback setting up out in the flat. There is not as much deception involved here because the play develops much more quickly than the ordinary screen and fewer offensive linemen leave to get into blocking position in the flat area. On this play, the offensive linemen look for specific people to block and do not form a wall in front of the ball carrier. The quick screen seems to be gaining popularity in the N.F.L. This, probably because there is less chance of the receiver being thrown for a loss with it.

## The Draw Play

This is another play that is most effective against a hard charging defensive line. The quarterback plays a minor role in executing the play. The key is the blocking of the offensive line and the ball carrier's ability to pick the proper hole. The play sets up exactly like a show pass. As the quarterback drops back into the pocket, he hands off to one of his set backs who carries into the

Note: For an explanation of how to read a diagram, see the beginning of Part Two: "The Formations of Football."

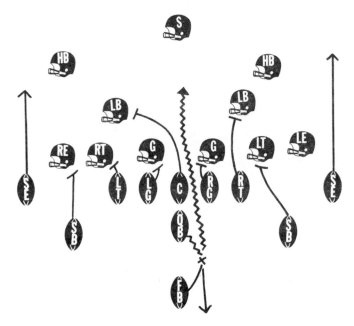

The draw play. It can be used to slow down the pass rush.

line. The linemen set as they would on a show pass and then, after making contact, attempt to take their opponents to one side, opening up a gaping hole for the runner.

The quarterback should set up a little slower than usual on the draw to allow his linemen time to make contact and begin to "turn" their opponents. A clean hand off is important. However, the quarterback's primary job is to make sure that he calls the play at the right time. It is extremely difficult to block effectively when the opposition expects the draw. It should be called in a passing situation or on downs when, in the same situation, the quarterback has called pass plays earlier in the game. Even if it has been successful, the draw should not be called too often. It is predicated on surprise and a defensive line that is rolling off hard in an attempt to get to the passer. If the charge slows down, the play is likely to fail.

There are several types of draw plays. The draw can be directed up the middle or to one side of the line. It can be run with the quarterback dropping straight back or while he's rolling out. If it is run to one side of the line, the quarterback should be certain that the most aggressive defensive linemen are on that side. The slower and more cautious the lineman, the harder he is to deceive with the draw play.

### The Safety Valve or Flare Pass

This can be a predetermined play, can be used to combat a blitzing linebacker, or can be used as a last resort when there are no open receivers downfield. The way the quarterback uses the flare is a good indication of his ability. The quarterback that has an uncovered set back moving out into the flat area should not be thrown for a loss while attempting to pass from the pocket.

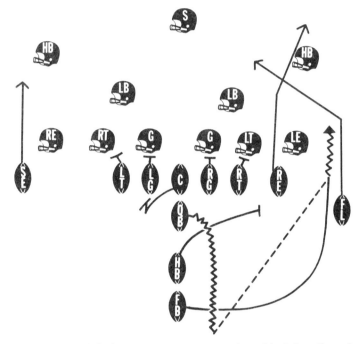

When the quarterback can't find an open primary receiver, he will look for a flaring back.

The flare pass involves no more than the set back moving out into the flat area. To be effective with the flare, the quarterback must be aware of the assignment each man has on every play. The offensive back is assigned to block the blitzing linebacker. (The blitzing corner linebacker presents a problem when the set back on that side is moving out on a flare only if the quarterback does not throw the football to him.)

When the quarterback eats the ball or throws it away, check to see if there was a back open in the flat. It's hard to see him when a couple of 260 pounders are just a few feet away, but the poised and gutsy quarterback will find him.

## STATISTICS, INTERCEPTIONS AND THE QUARTERBACK

Passing the football is a skill that can be developed and

improved in every quarterback. The man with the strongest arm is not necessarily the best passer. Quarterback Fran Tarkenton of the Minnesota Vikings has long been criticized for having a weak arm and not being able to throw the long pass effectively. Yet, few would question his ability to lead a team and his effectiveness in getting points on the scoreboard.

The number of young men with good arms who have not been able to make it in pro football is too numerous to list. Heisman Trophy winner Steve Spurrier is a good example. He had a strong arm and threw a perfect spiral most of the time. Billy Kilmer is an example of the other extreme. His passes sometimes look as if the ball has helium inside, but he gets the job done. The real measure of a quarterback's effectiveness is his ability to get the ball to the receiver at the right time and with the right lead.

The N.F.L. rates its passers each week during the football season in several categories. The factors considered are attempts and completions, completion percentage, yards gained, average yards gained, touchdown passes, touchdown percentage, long passes, interceptions, and interception percentage. Any one category is meaningless if considered by itself. For example, total yards gained is misleading if the completion percentage is very low, because the quarterback is probably throwing more than is advisable.

The completion percentage may be misleading if the average yards gained per completion is not considered. The quarterback may be constantly throwing short passes to his set backs and tight end, and rarely throwing those longer more difficult passes to his wide receivers. A confusing factor here is that since yardage picked up by the receiver after catching the football is credited to the quarterback, it is often hard to tell from the raw statistics whether the credit belongs to the quarterback or to the receiver. Of course, the quarterback that throws to his set backs and tight ends may be doing so out of design. Few will deny that there is less chance of an interception and a greater chance of a completion with the short pass. The coach striving to develop a ball control offense will encourage the short pass. This doesn't necessarily mean that his quarterback cannot throw long.

During the heyday of the Green Bay Packers, few experts regarded Bart Starr as an exceptional passer. His throwing arm was not strong and he threw too many short passes. However, this fit in perfectly with the Packer ball control approach to offensive football, and short passes were encouraged by the coaching staff. Although Starr did not have a great arm, he threw long often enough to keep the defense loose, and completed his share of bombs.

AMERICAN FOOTBALL CONFERENCE STATISTICS

12/19/77
(Final)

LEADING PASSERS
(168 attempts)

| | Att. | Comp. | Pct. Comp. | Yds Gnd | Avg Yds Gained | TD Pass | Pct. TD | LP | Int. | Pct. Int. | Rating |
|---|---|---|---|---|---|---|---|---|---|---|---|
| Griese, Mia. | 307 | 180 | 58.6 | 2252 | 7.34 | 22 | 7.2 | 73 | 13 | 4.2 | 88.0 |
| Morton, Den. | 254 | 131 | 51.6 | 1929 | 7.59 | 14 | 5.5 | 81 | 8 | 3.1 | 82.1 |
| Jones, Balt. | 393 | 224 | 57.0 | 2686 | 6.83 | 17 | 4.3 | 78 | 11 | 2.8 | 80.7 |
| Stabler, Oak. | 294 | 169 | 57.5 | 2176 | 7.40 | 20 | 6.8 | 44 | 20 | 6.8 | 75.2 |
| Bradshaw, Pitt. | 314 | 162 | 51.6 | 2523 | 8.04 | 17 | 5.4 | 65 | 19 | 6.1 | 71.2 |
| K. Anderson, Cin. | 323 | 166 | 51.4 | 2145 | 6.64 | 11 | 3.4 | 94 | 11 | 3.4 | 69.8 |
| Grogan, N.E. | 305 | 160 | 52.5 | 2162 | 7.09 | 17 | 5.6 | 68 | 21 | 6.9 | 65.3 |
| Pastorini, Hou. | 319 | 169 | 53.0 | 1987 | 6.23 | 13 | 4.1 | 85 | 18 | 5.6 | 62.6 |
| Sipe, Clev. | 195 | 112 | 57.4 | 1233 | 6.32 | 9 | 4.6 | 52 | 14 | 7.2 | 61.6 |
| Todd, N.Y. | 265 | 133 | 50.2 | 1863 | 7.03 | 11 | 4.2 | 87 | 17 | 6.4 | 60.6 |
| Livingston, K.C. | 282 | 143 | 50.7 | 1823 | 6.46 | 9 | 3.2 | 49 | 15 | 5.3 | 59.8 |
| Harris, S.D. | 211 | 110 | 52.1 | 1240 | 5.88 | 5 | 2.4 | 78 | 11 | 5.2 | 56.3 |
| Ferguson, Buff. | 457 | 221 | 48.4 | 2803 | 6.13 | 12 | 2.6 | 42 | 24 | 5.3 | 54.6 |
| Zorn, Sea. | 251 | 104 | 41.4 | 1687 | 6.72 | 16 | 6.4 | 82 | 19 | 7.6 | 54.3 |

LONGEST: 94 yds., Ken Anderson (to Billy Brooks), Cin. vs Minn. 11/13 – TD
Rating based on Pct. Comp.; Avg. Yds. Gained; Pct. TD; Pct. Int.

You have to be careful with statistics. They tend to isolate various aspects of the game and conceal basic facts. They do not consider how often the quarterback was forced to rush his throw, the depth of his passes, the caliber of his receivers and the number they have dropped on him, the effectiveness of his running game (which puts additional pressure on the defense), or the type of schedule he is facing.

The game situation that exists when a pass or passes are completed is important and not reflected in the stat sheet. The bomb completed by a losing team with just seconds remaining on the clock is certainly more important than one completed when a team is ahead by several touchdowns and the defensive backs are gambling for an interception. Those many short passes completed by a losing team in the waning moments of a game when the defense is in a "prevent" defense count as much in the season-end statistics as the short pass on third down and two inside the opponents 15 yard line. Eliminating all attempts and completions during the last two minutes of both halves would probably provide a more accurate indication of a quarterback's effectiveness. And, of course, games played in a heavy rain or strong wind also cloud the totals on the stat sheet.

Most coaches would rather see their quarterback throw the ball away than release it when there is a chance of an interception. When the quarterback passes, he must not only try to hit his receiver, but must also throw *away* from the defender in order to minimize the possibility of an interception. The most "public" mistake a quarterback can make is an interception. Everyone in the park knows who is to blame. Every quarterback is going to be intercepted at one time or another, especially when he is playing catch-up. When he is intercepted too often, look to see if he is doing the following:

## Throwing Low

Most passes should be thrown low to the ground. This provides less chance of the ball being batted by the defender or bouncing off the receiver's shoulder pads and into the hands of a defender. The sideline, hook, comeback, and cross patterns (see chapter on receivers) should all be thrown low. These passes may be under-thrown but never overthrown unless there are mitigating circumstances like a blitzing linebacker. The quarterback must then face the dilemma of whether to try to clear him or to throw the ball away. The post and corner routes require the proper lead, but are still considered better passes if thrown fairly low. Only the go or the fly is better overthrown than underthrown. Most teams have "tip drills" for their defensive backs. The ball is tipped into the air and the players are conditioned to react to it while it is in the air. It happens often enough for the drill to be worth the time and effort. The low pass cannot be tipped. Roger Staubach is a master at throwing low.

## Throwing Hard

There's no hard and fast rule here. Just as all passes should not be thrown low, all should not be thrown hard. However, the longer the ball hangs in the air, the more time the defense has to react and the greater the opportunity for an interception. The criterion for the speed with which the ball should be thrown is the distance it must travel. The tight end going over the middle on a quick slant at five yards cannot handle a ball thrown with the same velocity as one thrown to a wide receiver breaking on a sideline route, 17 yards downfield, and off at an angle. As a rule, any sideline pattern should be thrown hard.

The go or fly route is an exception. Certainly the ball must be thrown hard enough to lead the receiver deep downfield, but it must also be thrown high enough to allow the receiver to run under it. A ball thrown hard on a flat trajectory must be timed perfectly, which is difficult on a deep pattern. Again, Roger Staubach seems to have a knack for putting just enough zip on every pass he throws.

## Mix Them Up

There should not only be a balance between the pass and the run, but a proper ratio between short and long passes. The chances are greater for an interception when the ball is thrown long repeatedly. As a rule, the quarterback should be throwing more short passes than long ones. The bomb is an effective weapon and should be utilized. It should be thrown often enough to keep the defensive backs honest; but the quarterback's bread and butter is the short pass. As mentioned before, Bob Griese seems to prefer the short pass for the first down, but also throws the bomb regularly.

### Throwing away from the Defender

The quarterback is taught to throw *to* the receiver and *away* from the defender. For example, he should be throwing to the outside on a sideline so the receiver can utilize his body to keep the defender from reaching the ball. Since the defender tries to take advantage of the sideline (see chapter on defensive backs), he will almost always be to the inside. On the hook or comeback, the quarterback should throw to the side opposite the defender if possible. The quarterback should throw the ball over the inside shoulder of a receiver running a fly route. Not only is the defensive back likely to be on the outside because he may expect help from the inside, but the receiver will be looking over his inside shoulder. It would be difficult for him to turn his head and catch a ball thrown over his outside shoulder.

Certainly passes should be thrown over the middle. However, if the quarterback is throwing many interceptions, check to see if he is not throwing over the middle too often. Some believed that Fran Tarkenton throws an inordinate number of passes over the middle because he had a weak arm and it takes more zip to throw well to the outside. However, Tarkenton has never had the exceptionally high interception percentage which he would have with a weak arm. The reason an interception is more likely over the middle is that there are more defenders there. The linebackers and the free safety, if there is one on a particular play, will be helping the other defenders and are more likely to intercept on passes over the middle.

### Exploiting Weakness in the Defense

It is generally accepted that a quarterback should throw short passes to his set backs and tight end against the zone and deep passes to his wide receivers when the defense is in man coverage. This is only a general rule and like most rules should be violated from time to time. However, it is obvious that the primary strength of the zone is in guarding against the long pass, and a consistent attempt to throw deep against it will lead to interceptions.

### Keeping the Defense Guessing

The quarterback should not allow the defense to *type* him. All too often he will call the same play or pass pattern in a particular situation again and again. His tendencies in previous games will be noted by the opposition and looked for during the game.

Steve Grogan of the New England Patriots had typed himself in goal line situations during the 1976 season. He finished as the top rusher in the N.F.L. among quarterbacks with 397 yards. Grogan's 13 touchdowns also established a new all-time scoring record for quarterbacks. You can be certain that as time went on opposing defenders began to look for Grogan to carry the football in short yardage situations. Coach Chuck Fairbanks recognized the problem and Grogan did not run with the ball as often near the end of the season.

A quarterback should not throw to his wide receiver on first and ten and to his set backs on third and six all the time. Remember that if you or I can predict the play with any kind of success, so can the defensive backs who probably have more information than we do. We can all make intelligent guesses, but if the people in the stands are right too often, then the quarterback has typed himself. The quarterback that can be typed, will be intercepted.

## THINGS TO LOOK FOR

Because of the great number of variables which go into the quarterback's performance, he is more difficult to analyze than players at other positions. The most helpful advice that I can give is to keep in mind the fundamentals of the position as well as the mutual interdependence between the quarterback and the rest of the team. Remember, without a supporting cast, a quarterback is nothing. Without a good quarterback, a team is nothing.

On every incompleted pass there are usually a set of questions that can be asked. Did the quarterback panic and leave the pocket too soon or was there a good pass rush? Were his receivers blanketed? Did the play pass break down because the quarterback or the set back going into the line failed to fake well? Was the interception a great play on the part of the defender, a bad pass, or just the result of a poorly run route by the receiver? Perhaps it was a sudden gust of wind that caused the pass to take off.

The quarterback is sometimes blamed for what appears to be a poorly thrown pass when it is not his fault. The receiver that runs a poor route is the obvious alternative. There may be a number of other reasons for a pass not being on target. The coverage may be such that the play called in the huddle did not have much of a chance of succeeding. The defense may be disguised so well that neither the quarterback nor the receiver picks it up. The defensive secondary may have moved into a different coverage after the ball was snapped.

The quarterback calls his plays based on how he thinks the defense will align itself. If the defense tips a change, the quarterback can audibilize or check off to another play at the line. If the play is not changed before the snap, he must try to make the best of the situation, either by looking for another receiver or by trying to anticipate any changes his primary receiver may make. It can be tricky. For example, say the play called in the huddle has the split end as the primary receiver. After the quarterback begins to call the signals, he sees the defense moving to provide double coverage. He must now make a decision. Will his pass protection hold up and give him time to hit the primary target on the designated route? It will take longer for the receiver to run his route, since one of the people assigned to cover him is trying to hold him on the line. Since the pass rush has been consistently good, it is doubtful that he will be given enough time to throw the fly. However, the split end has been told to hook up into the dead spot on the zone. Will he be double teamed all the way or will the first man stay shallow to cover the flat area? All of this goes through the quarterback's mind in a flash. It's not uncommon for him to come to the conclusion that the best thing to do is to eat the ball or throw it away.

The receiver must also be considered. How long has he been working with the quarterback? Is he noted for running precise patterns or is he a free lancer? When a quarterback has worked with his receiver over a period of time, there is less chance of a completely new situation developing. The receiver and the quarterback get to know each other and can anticipate each other's reactions to a specific situation.

Be aware of how the quarterback mixes up his calls. Not only should there be a delicate balance between the run and pass, but they should complement each other. For example, if a team is running a lot, and the linebackers have tightened up, it is advisable to throw the medium pass just beyond the linebackers. It might be even better if the pass is run out of play action. There should be some kind of recognizable continuity between plays at all times. This is less important at the pro level than elsewhere. But even in the pros you should be able to recognize the same flow in the backfield on successive plays that hit different holes on the same side of the line. The better the faking, the smoother the execution will be and the more difficult for the defense to predetermine the play.

The importance of adequate pass protection has been previously noted. This does not mean that the quarterback will not be touched or hit by a defensive man. Ideally, the offensive guards will keep their men on the line of scrimmage while the tackles ride the defensive ends out beyond the quarterback. However, it is rare that the guard can keep his man on the line for the three, four or five second it takes to complete a pass. Be aware of the penetration that the tackles achieve. It can force the quarterback to alter his throw over the middle. Any forced movement by the quarterback out of the pocket should be noted. His inability to set before throwing can explain a poorly thrown pass. One of the advantages of the drop back pass is that the quarterback can see the entire field and be set when he throws the ball. When the quarterback is forced out of the pocket even a foot or two, it becomes more difficult to complete that pass. This is quite different from the play action and roll out passes where the quarterback is in motion out of design. He knows where he is going and that he has blockers in front of him. When *forced* to leave the pocket, on the other hand, he loses sight of what is happening downfield and may not be in position to throw to a particular man or even see him.

The quarterback is the most important individual on a football team. He has greater opportunity to win or lose a football game than anyone else on the team and yet is more dependent on his teammates than anyone else. In order to evaluate him properly, the play of the entire team has to be considered along with his ability to pass the football, select plays, fake well, run well, scramble when necessary, maintain his poise, and provide a greater degree of leadership than any other individual. It's a big job and it is better filled by an all-around athlete and not just a high-priced kid with a strong arm.

# 2

# THE OFFENSIVE LINE

## The Faceless Heroes

*The halfback, he's a hero*
*And the idol of the mob.*
*No one notes his humble helpers*
*As he weaves his way to fame.*
*And the guard who took the tackler out,*
*A rather nasty job.*
*Well, he's nothing, simply nothing,*
*Just the man who won the game.*

*Quoted by John Kieran*

The above appeared in *The New York Times* almost 50 years ago. Football has changed considerably since it was written, but the status of the offensive lineman has remained pretty much the same. He receives less publicity and less money at the pro level than anyone else on the team, and yet it is generally conceded that he is as important to the success of the team as anyone else except the Quarterback. If this poem were written today, the author probably would have substituted:

*The Quarterback, he's a hero*
*And the idol of the mob.*

For, 50 years ago, the forward pass was not an integral part of football and the quarterback was used primarily as a blocker. In any case, whether the offensive lineman is blocking for the half-back on the run or the quarterback on the pass, he is as important as anyone else on the team. He may not get as much recognition in the press, but he is appreciated by his peers—especially the offensive backs that play directly behind him.

The most frustrating part of being an offensive lineman is not the lack of recognition by the press or the fans; the great athletes are usually self-motivated. It is the fact that the offensive lineman is frequently criticized unjustly. His value to the team is almost completely dependent on the performances of the people around him. A super effort might go completely unnoticed because the lineman next to him broke down and the back was forced to run in the wrong hole. At other times, a quarterback who can't find an open receiver will move out of the pocket and into an area where an offensive lineman has good position on his opponent. This change of position by the quarterback usually changes the blocking angle with the result that the offensive lineman that was making a super effort suddenly finds his opponent lying on top of the quarterback. He looks at fault, but there was nothing he could have done about it.

The defensive lineman can, with a super effort, stop four receivers going downfield on a pass play all by himself by sacking the quarterback. The linebacker that reads a play quickly can burst into the backfield and throw the runner for a loss even if the entire defensive line in front of him is wiped out. The defensive back knocks down passes in the end zone. The quarterback completes touchdown passes to a receiver who ran a super route. And the running back can break one on his own with a super second effort. The offensive lineman can do practically nothing on his own. His effectiveness is completely dependent on the people next to him and behind him. Because of this, coaches choose players who are highly disciplined and can follow directions for their offensive linemen.

Bill Curry, who used to play offensive center for the Baltimore Colts, was once quoted as saying: "An offensive lineman is programmed. I move my right foot and the offensive guard next to me puts his left foot where my right foot was. Everything is done in concert. Great defensive players like Dick Butkus of the Bears and Mike Curtis of our club act instinctively. I think a linebacker has to be a little better athlete than a center." Bill Curry happened to be a pretty good athlete and a fine offensive center. Just the same, his statement is basically true and provides an indication of how most teams choose their offensive linemen as well as an explanation as to why a defensive player is sometimes switched to the offensive line.

A defensive player, whether he be a linebacker, defensive lineman or defensive back, must have good speed, agility and size. There is no way for a defensive player to compensate for the speed necessary to rush the passer, pursue a speedy halfback running an end sweep, or cover a fast wide receiver on a "go" route downfield. The defensive player with an abundance of physical ability can overcome a lack of skill, or manage to hang on until he develops the essential skills and techniques. The opposite is often true of the offensive lineman. He has to have a high degree of skill and technique. This can sometimes make up for physical deficiencies. Only rarely can an offensive lineman get by on superior physical ability alone.

Coaches sometimes tailor their offensive attack to their offensive line personnel. The offensive tackle that lacks the speed or agility to lead interference on such outside running plays as the quick pitch may be good enough in all other areas to warrant eliminating the quick pitch from his side of the line.

Two of the best—left tackle Art Shell (78) and left guard Gene Upshaw (63) of the Oakland Raiders.

The Oakland Raiders run to their left more often than they run to the right side of the line. The two reasons are Art Shell and Gene Upshaw. They list Shell at 280 pounds, but he is over 300 pounds most of the time. He is outstanding when blocking straight ahead and on pass protection. Because of his size, he is not as effective on the quick pitch as on the sweep. The Raiders continue to run to the outside but shy away from the quick pitch where Shell would be a liability.

The individual offensive lineman may find ways to compensate for a weakness without involving anyone else. He can split an extra foot or two from his offensive guard if he lacks speed and is concerned about getting outside on the quick pitch. A slight adjustment in his stance may help him to get off the line quickly and in front of the ball carrier. The amount of weight he places on his hand will also determine how quickly a lineman can pull out. The danger of altering one's stance is that the defensive players may read the adjustment and anticipate the play.

There are other ways that an offensive lineman can compensate for physical deficiencies. The smaller lineman may develop a style of blocking that does not require him to outmuscle an opponent. He may use many different offensive blocks to keep his opponent off balance and rely on position and leverage rather than strength. Defensive players, on the other hand, can do little to compensate for a lack of size or speed, except to try harder. There is no place to hide deficient defensive linemen. The offense will eventually recognize the weakness and attempt to exploit it at every opportunity.

The ideal offensive lineman will posess exceptional size, speed, quickness, intelligence, determination, and a high level of skill. When you find all of those qualities in one man, and he is allowed to play on the offensive line, you have a Forrest Gregg— the most nearly perfect offensive lineman in memory. The average offensive lineman only excels in one or two of the above areas.

I recently came across an evaluation of the Chicago Bear offensive line by their line coach, Ray Callahan. It is still a relatively young line and must prove itself, but they must have been doing something right to get the Bears into the playoffs in 1977 and break Walter Payton free so often. I found Callahan's remarks about his players interesting. Note that one or two of the above qualities was attributed to each player. This was the Bears' lineup:

LT—Ted Albrecht, 6-4, 260, 23, rookie from California
LG—Noah Jackson, 6-2, 273, 26, 3rd year from Tampa
C—Dan Peiffer, 6-3, 254, 26, 3rd year from S.E. Missouri State

RG—Revie Sorey, 6-2, 269, 24, 3rd year from Illinois
RT—Dennis Lick, 6-3, 275, 23, 2nd year from Wisconsin

"Lick is one of the finest offensive blockers in football. He doesn't have great quickness but he gets into his man and is one of the most consistent players I ever had contact with.

"Sorey has both speed and size. We like to get him out on the corner against the cornerback or safety. Pulling is his best asset. He has improved his interior line play a great deal. He just loves to get out there and run.

"Peiffer has had three knee operations, two last year when Dan Neal filled in and did an excellent job. Peiffer is very consistent, very strong and a hard worker. He is one of our captains and a good solid leader.

"Jackson's main asset is quickness and consistency. He does a good job pulling out and getting out on the corner. He has as good quickness as any guard in the league."

Dennis Lick's strength is his blocking skill and determination. A player cannot be a good blocker or consistent unless he is determined. Revie Sorey's greatest asset is speed. Dan Pieffer must rely on his intelligence. Callahan didn't say much about his natural ability. But the fact that he is consistent and the captain indicates he must be bright. Noah Jackson's biggest asset is quickness. Callahan did not comment on Ted Albrecht who was a rookie in 1977 and got the job when Lionel Antoine hurt his knee. Callahan understands that it takes more than a year to draw definitive conclusions about an offensive lineman's strengths and weaknesses. In fact, it often takes that long to determine what his best position on the line should be.

## POSITIONS

Theoretically, there are seven members on the offensive line—the two end men (the split end and the tight end) being considered offensive linemen by the officials. However, their pass eligibility causes the ends to be classified differently by coaches. They are grouped with the flanker back in pro football and called receivers. When you talk about the offensive line in football, you are referring to the five interior men.

The personnel available to a team at a given time often determines where a player will be positioned on the offensive line.

A balanced offensive line

There are, however, certain guidelines to which most coaches adhere. Although size now plays less of a role in determining a player's position than it did in the past, it is still an important consideration. At one time, those players slated for the offensive line that weighed in at over 250 pounds were automatically placed at offensive tackle. Those between 232 and 247 pounds were tried at offensive guard. The player between 247 and 250 was told to lose two pounds and play guard or gain three and play tackle. Those players under 230 pounds, after being rejected as linebackers and fullbacks, were tried at center.

Today, you can no longer tell a player's position on the offensive line from his height and weight. The guards are often as big as the tackles, and just as tall. Guards Terry Hermeling of the Redskins, Elbert Drungo of Houston and Gene Upshaw of Oakland are all 6'5" tall and weigh about 260 pounds. Larry Little of the Miami Dolphins is only 6'1" and has trimmed down to 265 pounds from the 280 pounds at which he made the Dolphins. Offensive centers are now mistaken for tackles. John Fitzgerald of Dallas and Bob Johnson of Cincinnati are both 6'5" tall. On the San Diego Chargers, Billy Shields is 6'7" and weights 270 and Russ Washington is 6'7" and weights 285. Wayne Moore of Miami is also 6'7" tall. Jim Nicholson of Kansas City, Ralph Neely of Dallas, Stan Walters of Philadelphia, Keith Fahnhorst of San Francisco, Warren Bryant of Altanta and George Kunz of Baltimore are all 6'6" tall. Offensive tackles may weigh anywhere from the 245 pounds of Doug Van Horn to the 300 pounds that Art Shell carries around much of the time.

### The Center

The demands made of the offensive center have changed over the last five or six years, which is one reason coaches have placed bigger men at the position. In the past, players that could not fit in elsewhere were often hidden at center. For years, the center had what most of his teammates considered the easiest job on the team. He was the only man on the offensive line who was not engaged in a violent physical confrontation on almost every play. He was assigned to the smaller middle linebacker on most running plays and linebackers are usually more intent on *avoiding* contact than in charging into an offensive blocker. The center was involved in a chase more often than a battle. When assigned to a defensive tackle, a favorable angle almost always existed, and all he had to do was position himself between the tackle and ball carrier.

On pass plays, against the standard 4-3 pro defense, the center was not assigned to a defensive lineman, but asked to pick up the

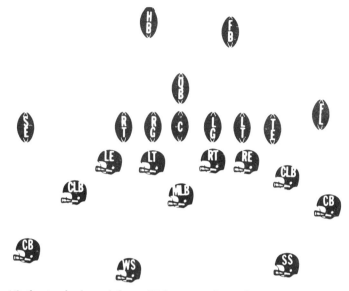

The 4-3, the standard pro defense. With an even front, the center is left uncovered.

blitzing middle linebacker or help where neeed. This meant that he would most often give ground and shuffle from side to side while looking for someone to help. Even when one of his teammates broke down, his job was easier since he did not have to absorb the initial charge of the defensive lineman. It was an easy job and still is the softest on the offensive line . . . but, not quite as easy as it once was.

The difference is the odd man (or odd front) defense which is being used more and more in pro football. An odd front defense simply means that a large and sometimes angry defensive tackle is placed in a three point stance about two inches from the center's nose. The center has primary responsibility for this man on both the run and the pass. To make the center's assignment more difficult, his first responsibility is to get the ball back to the quarterback. This means that his first move does nothing to help him handle the man on his nose. His arms are still moving backward as he moves forward on running plays or straightens up on the pass. This inhibits his impact on the run since the arms play an

An odd front defense. A defensive man is placed directly in front of the center.

important part in a lineman's charge. It provides the defensive man with a better opportunity to grab hold of him on a pass play.

The center is at a disadvantage because of his responsibility for snapping the ball. But, don't feel sorry for him. Most coaches are aware of this and when there is a man opposite him, provide more help for him than anyone else receives. Centers are usually not required to drive a defensive tackle back on running plays, and one of the offensive guards helps him on pass plays. When the defensive team "offsets" the defensive tackle by respacing their line so that he falls into the gap between the center and the guard, the offset defensive man becomes the responsibility of the guard. Teams in the N.F.L. switch back and forth between the odd and even fronts in order to keep the offense guessing. This means the center will rarely have a man on his nose the entire game unless the defense is totally committed to the 3-4 defense.

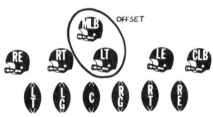

An offset defense. Only the defensive tackles and ends are in three point stances. The corner linebacker stands upright.

Because he does not always have a man opposite him and is frequently assigned to the middle linebacker, the first quality to look for in a center is quickness. There is a difference between speed and quickness. To a football player quickness means the ability to get off the line of scrimmage quickly and move fast for five or six yards. Speed is how long it takes to run the 40-yard dash. Coaches used to time players in the 100-yard dash, until someone finally concluded that football players rarely run more than 40 yards on a given play. A center almost never has to run 40 yards, but he does have to be quick enough to get to the middle linebacker on running plays.

The center should also be more flexible than his teammates on the offensive line. A tight and overly muscular upper body can be a disadvantage to the center when snapping the football to the quarterback or kicker. A quick delivery and the ability to recover the use of the arms is vitally important. The arms provide additional impact and an extended blocking surface for an offensive lineman. The shoulder or option block is not as effective when the use of the arms is restricted. The hands and arms are just as important when pass blocking.

Some coaches teach their offensive center to snap the ball to the quarterback with one hand. This can help the center by giving him one free arm at all times. Whether a center uses one hand or two on the snap will depend on the requirements of his quarterback. A center required to snap the ball with the point up will probably use two hands. It is easier to use one hand when the ball is turned and delivered sideways. On punts and place kicks, the center usually uses two hands.

Flexibility is also important to the center because of his blocking assignments. He has primary responsibility for blocking the middle linebacker on most plays. When the play is designed to run between the offensive guards, his blocking techniques will be the same as those of the other offensive linemen. When the play is designed to go outside of the offensive guard, the center's major problem is reaching the middle linebacker before he moves to the outside. The middle linebacker will rarely remain in his original position and give the center a good blocking angle. Unless the faking is exceptional in the backfield, the middle linebacker will have started to move to the outside as the center approaches. The center has two options. He can attempt to knock the middle linebacker off his feet with a cross body block *or* run after him and make contact when he stops to make the tackle. The center will then strive to drive him beyond the hole in the direction that both are running. The quickness of the middle linebacker will determine the tactic used by the center.

## The Guards

The offensive guard playing pro football today may weigh anywhere from 240 to 275 pounds. Few are shorter than 6'2" and some are as tall as 6'6". The present attitude by coaches is: the bigger the better, as long as they have enough speed and agility to pull out and lead a sweep in front of a fast running back. The guard must be able to leave the line at a 45 degree angle (pull out), in order to clear the feet of the man next to him and avoid his own back who may be blocking or faking into the line. He must then get out to the flank ahead of the running back with the ball. Adjustments can be made for the tackle who cannot pull out effectively, but no such adjustment can be made for the guard.

The guard must be able to perform a larger variety of functions than anyone else on the offensive line. He must block straight ahead on the run against someone who is usually bigger and often as quick as he is. He must pass protect. He must pull out to lead the sweep. At one time or another he must trap block on everyone on the defensive line.

In the past there were more people with less athletic ability playing guard than any other position. If a player was too short or too light to play tackle, he was placed at guard. If he was too slow to be a linebacker, he played guard. The only prerequisites were toughness and the intelligence to develop the essential skills. Now things have changed.

Aside from the quarterback, the offensive guard must have more highly refined skills than anyone else on the football team. In the past he could get by on those skills if he was short on physical ability. This is becoming increasingly more difficult. Coaches have discovered that there is no substitute for size and speed, and are constantly looking for the big man who can perform the necessary skills as well as the smaller man.

Ed White of the Minnesota Vikings is regarded as being among the strongest men in professional football. Twenty years ago he would probably have been placed at defensive tackle because of that strength. Ironically, White has received more publicity because of his strength than because of his All-Pro performances over the last few years. It started when he won the N.F.L. Arm Wrestling Championship several years ago. Arm wrestling has no relationship to playing offensive guard, but it put White in the spotlight and he has been reaping the rewards ever since. He is the only offensive guard in football who does television commercials.

## The Tackles

The offensive tackle is usually bigger than the offensive guard, though the man opposite him is often smaller than the man over the guard. He is almost always taller than the guard, which is important when protecting the passer. The taller the offensive lineman, the more difficult it becomes for the defensive player to use his hands to pull him off balance and get by him.

Height, then, is the primary factor in choosing an offensive tackle. He doesn't require the speed of the guard, nor the quickness of the center. But if he doesn't have some speed and quickness, then he'd better have a lot of size or he won't make very many football teams.

His basic assignments are to block straight ahead on the run and to protect the passer. He does little else except to pull out on the quick pitch. On the quick pitch, the quarterback takes the snap from center, turns, and pitches the ball to the halfback who has already begun to run to the outside. The quick pitch develops more quickly than the sweep which requires both guards to pull and lead interference. The on-side (the side to which the play is directed) tackle is the only lineman to lead interference on the

Tackle Darryl Carlton (70) leading interference for Ricky Bell (42) on the quick pitch.

quick pitch. He does not have to pull out deep to clear people as the guard does, nor does he have to travel as far. It is the only play where the tackle's size works against him.

The tackles are less likely to get help from the center on pass plays than the guards, which means that they may get no assistance at all. The tackle must also hold his blocks in the running game for a longer period of time than the guard when the plays are designed to go outside of him, since the running back has to travel a greater distance to reach the tackle's hole than the guard's hole.

The offensive tackle, like everyone else on a football team, can use all the strength and size that he can carry. Even experienced veterans, who can sometimes compensate for advancing age with

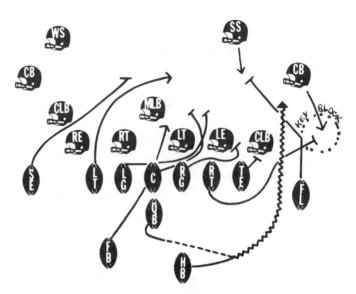

The quick pitch. It develops much faster than the end sweep. The offensive tackle pulls out on this play.

increased know how, find that there are minimum size and strength requirements. Ralph Neely of the Cowboys was in the league for 12 years before he started lifting weights prior to the 1977 season in an attempt to add weight to his 6′6″ frame. Coach Bob Ward helped him develop a technique whereby he could lift heavy weights without them bothering his lower back allowing him to put on 15-20 pounds between seasons, moving up to 254. At 238 pounds, he just wasn't heavy enough to play offensive tackle in pro football.

## FUNDAMENTALS

Fundamentals are probably more important to an offensive lineman than to anyone else on a football team. There are those linemen like Bob Brown, formerly of the Philadelphia Eagles and Oakland Raiders, who break the rules and get away with it; not because what they are doing is right or the best way to get the job done, but because they have enough size, speed and strength. Brown got by with a poor stance and unorthodox techniques because he had enough natural ability to compensate for being fundamentally unsound. The average tackle who drops his rear leg in his stance and is as aggressive as Brown was on the pass would have problems.

None of this implies that all offensive linemen must look and block alike. There is no right or wrong way to block or line up in a stance. Anything that works for the individual with consistency has got to be the right way for him. Each man is different mentally and physically. The length of his legs in relation to his torso, his height and weight, the length of his arms, and the tightness of his build all will have an influence on his style and technique. To require a 240-pound offensive guard to try to imitate 300-pound Art Shell is as ridiculous as to make Shell stay low and use a variety of techniques a smaller man might be forced to develop. There are many ways to skin a cat and many ways to accomplish the tasks of an offensive lineman. There are, however, certain fundamental principles and methods to which most linemen do adhere:

## Stance

The one thing to look for in a lineman's stance is consistency. It doesn't have to look like the stance of the guy next to him, but it must be the same every time he gets down. The offensive guard probably has to be more aware of his stance than anyone else on the line since he has to perform a greater variety of skills. He must be in the same stance whether he is pulling out, blocking straight ahead, or dropping back to pass protect. Everyone on the defensive team, including the tackle playing on his nose, will be looking for tip-offs as to what play the offense may be running. The lineman with most of his weight on his hand will be better able to fire out into the man playing directly in front of him with speed and authority. However, that type of stance is not conducive to pulling out of the line or dropping back to protect the passer. Therefore, most guards try to assume a balanced stance from which they can perform all of their assignments effectively without having to make adjustments which may be picked up by the defense.

The offensive tackle does not have to do as many different things as the guard and can afford to put more weight on his hand—just as long as it doesn't prevent him from moving back to pass block when necessary. He, too, must be consistent and balanced, but if Bob Brown could throw that leg out behind him and still make All Pro, who is to say that it is not a good stance. Then again, his unorthodox techniques and stubborn refusal to change them were perhaps as much the reason for his early retirement as his injured knee.

The offensive center has less in his stance to worry about than anyone else since there is not much room for variation. The quarterback's position behind the center will influence his stance. His feet must be almost parallel to enable the quarterback to move quickly to either side without tripping over his feet. The height of his stance will also be influenced by the quarterback since it must be compatible with the height of the quarterback. The 6'5" quarterback will have difficulty taking the snap from a 6'1" center who assumes a stance low to the ground. Since the center doesn't have much leeway to choose his own stance, it is the way that he distributes his weight that becomes important.

The one thing that everyone on the offensive line must do while in his basic stance is to keep his head up to see where he is going. More important than the stance, though, is what a player does once he leaves it.

## Blocking—The Running Game

There are five basic blocks used on running plays, but at least 25 different names for these blocks. Those utilizing the same basic moves will be grouped together.

*Shoulder, Head, Face, Butt or Option Block*—This is the basic block used by all offensive linemen. It started out as a shoulder block. With the advent of the face mask in the early '50's, it developed into the face, head or butt block, depending on which part of the body the coach favored. The only difference between them is the part of the body that the offensive player aims into the middle of the defensive player. Before the widespread use of the face mask, it would have been pretty dangerous to block with a forehead. The plastic bar and the birdcage on helmets have probably done more to improve the quality of blocking at all levels than any other single factor. It has practically eliminated ducking the head on the part of players and greatly reduced the number of completely missed blocks and tackles. It is much easier and more effective to put the head right down the middle than to hit with the shoulder.

On these blocks, the offensive lineman springs from his stance and hits his opponent as hard as possible without lunging. His feet may leave the ground for a split second, but he begins driving his legs the instant contact is made. It's a question of timing and coordination as well as striking a compromise between firing out so hard that he loses his balance and having such control that there is little impact. Every coach has his own pet theories about how to block straight ahead. The good coach will allow the individual to make adjustments which suit him. I have played for those that suggested, or in some cases demanded, that it might be preferable to step with the near foot to the man being blocked. Others suggested using the far foot on the same play. In most cases it didn't matter.

There is very little coaching on the *head* block in pro football. If the player has not mastered the technique that best suits him, he won't last. Those that try to coach it and make changes, belong at the high school level. Ernie Zwahlen, the offensive line coach for the Jets while I was playing, made this mistake. His contract was not renewed. He tried to change everything that each of his linemen had been doing and to establish a completely uniform method of blocking for the pass and run. The only thing I

Dave Dolby (50) of Oakland with an option block.

remember about it was that his basic drill was to have the lineman walk across the field in a position low to the ground that resembled the walk of a duck. Appropriately, he called it "the duck walk." He taught nothing and succeeded in changing nothing. It was unfortunate since the line would drill his way all week and on Sunday be forced to resume the practices and skills taught the previous year by Chuck Knox, the finest line coach I ever played for. The amusing part of the story is that after leaving the Jets, Zwahlen, who had joined the Jets off the campus at Purdue, realized he was hollering down a rain barrel. He went on to San Francisco and established many of the practices that Chuck Knox had established with the Jets. His stubbornness caught up with him when he was fired by the Houston Oilers. It was one of the few times an assistant coach was fired during the middle of a season.

The *option* block derives it's name from the fact that the offensive lineman does not have a predetermined direction in which he must drive his opponent. His assignment is to stick with him and take him wherever he wants to go. The running back has the responsibility of cutting in the opposite direction. The fundamental moves are the same as the head or face block. The offensive lineman fires out of his stance and aims his forehead at the neck of the defensive lineman while he is still in his stance. This should force the defensive lineman to straighten up since few will take a blow on the face whether they are wearing a face mask or not. After impact with the head, shoulders, and arms, the player must begin driving his legs. The quickness with which he starts to drive his legs with short choppy steps is frequently the key to whether the block will be successful. Many coaches believe leg drive is the most important phase of blocking.

*Crab, Scramble, Cutoff or Leg Block*—This type of block can be an effective change-up for the offensive lineman if used at the right time. Instead of aiming his head at the defensive lineman's neck, the offensive lineman springs from his stance and extends his arm and shoulder beyond and to the side of the defensive lineman. Under ideal circumstances, contact is made with the thigh pad and then the offensive lineman scrambles on all fours after his man. Quite often, he never manages to get his head beyond the man playing over him, but does manage to knock his legs out from under him with his head and shoulders. This block should not be used when the ball carrier is running behind or close to the offensive lineman because the defensive player may reach over him to make the tackle. It is most effective when the runner is going to the other side of the line. It serves to keep the defensive man off balance. The offensive lineman should strive to keep his opponent guessing. Blocking becomes more difficult when the defensive player anticipates the type of block.

*Reverse Body or Reverse Shoulder Block*—This block can be used as an effective change-up when the runner is not directly behind the blocker. Instead of hitting down the middle with his head, the offensive lineman fires out with his head to one side. He does not try to drive his opponent off the line. Instead, he swings his body around in an attempt to collapse him or wall him off by keeping his body between his opponent and the ball carrier. The reverse shoulder block is predicated on the defensive player moving in the direction of his opponent's head. This block is not effective unless used in conjunction with the *cut off* and *hit and turn* blocks. It was more popular when the lineman hit with his shoulder than down the middle with his head. Then, the defensive player would react to the position of the head and seek to work in that direction.

*Hit and Turn Block*—This is another change-up that may be used when on the off-side or when the play is going wide to the same side. It is also effective when the defensive lineman is playing on the outside shoulder of the offensive lineman and a poor blocking angle exists. It is essential that the player step with the proper foot and hit with the correct shoulder. If the right guard wants to block the defensive tackle playing slightly to his outside, he steps with his left foot and hits with his left shoulder. As soon as contact is made, he whips his right arm around the defensive man and moves to a position between the man and his running back. This requires quickness and practice. It cannot be used too often but can be effective as a change-up with larger, slower reacting opponents.

*Cross Body Block*—This is a downfield block that some coaches demand and others abhor. Sid Gillman required his linemen to throw their bodies at a defender downfield whenever possible. Other coaches believe that the lineman has a better chance of making contact if he stays on his feet. Again, the only thing that is important is whether he gets his man. The player throwing a downfield block tries to hit with his hip pads and knock the legs out from under the defender. There is no special technique except to wait until he is as close to the opponent as possible before throwing his body. If the back is right behind him, he should be able to break free whether the defensive man is knocked off his feet or manages to avoid contact. The hope is that the defensive man will be forced to move out of position to avoid the block. This makes a clean hit unnecessary for the block to be successful.

Because of the increased size of the offensive linemen in pro football, the cross body block is seen more often at the high school and college levels. There is a loss of agility that goes along with increased size, so the pro player more often tries to screen the small defensive back or linebacker and force him out of position rather than knocking him off his feet with a body block.

The offensive lineman, as a rule, gets less publicity and recognition than anyone else on the team. His efforts on the line of scrimmage are often obscured by the crowd of players. Viewers tend to overlook the good pass block, remembering instead the

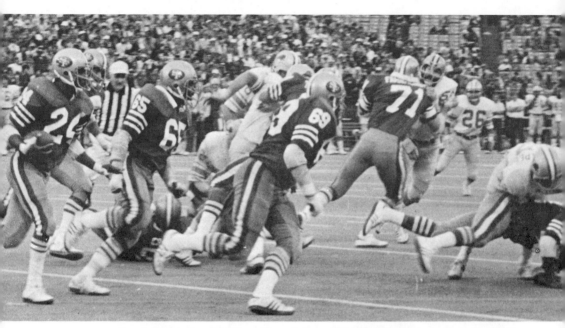

Guards Woody Peoples (69) and Steve Lawson (65) of San Francisco lead interference for Delvin Williams. Notice the key cross body block by Wilbur Jackson (lower right) downfield.

number of the player that sacked the quarterback and the offensive lineman who let him in. One of the few opportunities the offensive lineman has to gain recognition is when blocking downfield where it's wide open and easy to spot the good block.

Except at the high school level, teams rarely practice downfield blocking. The chance of serious injury is too great. The good downfield blocker is thinking cross body block, but should use the shoulder block at times.

I was never much of a downfield blocker because of a lack of speed. I would throw body blocks and knock down people when I could reach them. The problem was reaching them. There are some plays or blocks that a football player never forgets. We used to practice downfield blocking in high school and one block in particular stands out in my mind. The drill required the offensive lineman to pull out of the line with a running back behind him and try to block a defensive back standing 12 yards downfield. I pulled out and the defensive back (a young man who just joined the team) came up to make the tackle. I threw a body block, he did a complete flip and landed in a sitting position. I ran back to the huddle, but he just sat and sat and sat. He claimed to have a broken leg, which he did. The coach didn't believe it and insisted he "run off" the injury. At that point the young man began to wail over and over, "My mother told me I shouldn't play football." She must have been right, since we never saw him again.

You can do it any way you want as long as you get the job done. George Buehler of Oakland doesn't throw a cross body block downfield here but does what he has to anyhow.

## Blocking—The Passing Game

Highly refined skills and self-restraint are the key words when you talk about pass blocking. Walt Sweeney was one of those exceptions to the conception that many have about what an offensive lineman should be like. He was put at offensive guard, not because he didn't have the size or speed to play defense, but because Sid Gillman and Joe Madro thought he was the physically perfect guard: big, strong, tough. However, he wasn't highly skilled and didn't have the quiet, introspective, unemotional personality offensive linemen are supposed to possess. In fact, Sweeney played offensive guard like Bob Brown played offensive tackle. It was on pass protection that his aggressiveness really became apparent. He got by because of his exceptional raw ability.

The thing that amazed me about Sweeney was the fact that he was created almost from scratch by Joe Madro, the Chargers' offensive line coach. When he joined the Chargers, Sweeney had less skill than any other offensive lineman I have ever seen at the pro level. At Syracuse he had played end where his primary job was to block. He had the same problem most rookie linemen have in learning to pass protect. But, he had much further to go than most. He couldn't even block a dummy without looking foolish when I first saw him, and the next time I looked, he was All Pro. What does it mean? Quite simply that there is no substitute for natural ability. Skill and finesse are extremely important when pass protecting, but size, strength and quickness can compensate for many mistakes.

Let's go over some of the basic pass protection maneuvers.

*Drop Back or Show Pass*—This is the most common type of pass protection in professional football. The offensive lineman does not fire out aggressively into his opponent on the show pass. He sets in place and invites him to come across the line and go *over* or *around* him to get to the passer. (He "shows" that it is a pass.) Some teams teach their linemen to "drop back" a step or two when blocking, but the term "drop back" stems from the "drop" of the quarterback to a spot behind the center. The show pass is the hardest type of pass protection that a rookie in pro football has to learn. One of the reasons many have a problem mastering its fundamentals is that it was rarely used at the high school and college levels until recently. Everything that a lineman learned at the lower level was predicated on being aggressive. Show pass protection requires a degree of passivity.

The first thing an offensive lineman must learn is not to pop or strike out at the onrushing defensive player. Most defensive linemen try to finesse the offensive man by grabbing his shirt and pulling him off balance. It takes too long to go over the top of the offensive man and overpower him. The offensive lineman that tries to jar or jolt his opponent is likely to strike nothing but air and find himself on the ground. The experienced defensive lineman will anticipate the blow and use his opponent's forward motion to help throw him to the ground. The offensive player must be mentally prepared to accept the blow and provide just enough resistance to avoid being bowled over. He should be ready to be slapped in the head, elbowed, pushed and finally thrown to the ground. He is fighting for time. The quarterback sometimes needs three or four seconds to release the ball. Not very long, but much can happen during that time.

The offensive lineman has to have the self-control to maintain his composure for those four seconds each time a pass is called. It takes some longer to learn than others, but once a player becomes convinced that passivity is the answer, most can develop the needed self-control. This was not always necessary. Until the early '60's, most defensive linemen tried to get depth when rushing the passer and the emphasis was on overpowering the offensive linemen who could afford to be more aggressive. Ron McDole, defensive end for the Redskins, who was 38 years old during the 1977 season, remembers that back in 1961, when he came into the league: "It was more pushing. The agile linemen weren't there as they are today. Now they are more mobile, a lot lighter and quicker. They're fattening up guys who would have played linebacker then, guys like Jim Marshall, Jack Youngblood and Fred Dryer."

*Fire Protection*—This type of protection is used when a quick pass is called. The quarterback can't set up deep, since he is required to release the ball quickly. The offensive linemen fire out low and hard in an attempt to knock the defensive linemen off their feet or, at the very least, bring their arms down to protect their knees. Hopefully, the quarterback will have a clear line of vision to his receiver.

*Play Pass*—The quarterback fakes a running play and then drops back somewhere behind the line to find his receiver. The offensive lineman fires with a head or shoulder block as if a running play has been called and then drops back and pass protects as he would on show pass protection. The reason for firing out is to draw in the linebackers and deep backs by making them think it's a run. The play pass is more effective when run by a team that is having success on the ground.

*Roll Out Pass*—The roll out is similar to play pass action, except that the quarterback always rolls out (moves back and to his left or right and throws from the flank). The line fires out as on a play pass, and then assumes a position between the defensive man and the quarterback. One or two offensive linemen, usually the guards, may be required to pull out and protect the quarterback on the outside.

We have outlined the fundamental blocks used by most linemen in pro football. Blocking can be defined as keeping an opponent from the ball carrier. It does not necessarily require the offensive player to move his opponent or to follow a predetermined style or form. Remember! Any time an offensive player has kept his opponent from the ball carrier, and the ball carrier has not been forced to alter his course drastically, you can consider it a successful block.

## Use of Hands

Loosely translated, the 1978 rule on illegal use of hands states that the offensive player can place his hands on the defensive man as long as he does not clutch his opponent's shirt. It is legal for an offensive lineman to break his opponent's charge with outstretched arms or to brace himself with a hand on his opponent's chest as the defensive player holds his shirt or shoulder pads in an attempt to yank him to one side. The extent that the offensive lineman extends those arms and hands and the length of time that he keeps his hands on his opponent depends on the style of the defensive player. Extended arms are not as effective or as necessary against the player who tries to overpower the offensive lineman. One of the reasons that an official may not call holding when an offensive player extends his arms and keeps them out in front of him until the defensive player releases his hold is that the defensive player is technically guilty of defensive holding.

You often hear defensive linemen complaining about holding on the offensive line. Offensive players complain just as vociferously about the defensive player that grabs hold and refuses to let go. He doesn't have as much of a chance in convincing the official that his opponent should be penalized, but some have taken steps to prevent it. Offensive linemen have been striving to emulate the "greased pig" for years by loading their shirts with Vaseline. During the 1977 season, one of the league's most respected linemen, whom we won't embarrass here, was observed by a sideline television cameraman, and a national audience learned a new use for Vaseline. During the next timeout, we all saw an official arguing with him as he attempted to wipe off the Vaseline. Both men were smiling, but not the defensive linemen playing opposite him.

Some offensive linemen have taken more drastic measures to prevent defensive players from grabbing them by the shoulder pads. Several players on the Washington Redskins will attest to the fact that ex-offensive guard John Wilbur used to sew thumb tacks inside his jersey so that the points were up. They say that few defensive linemen would grab Wilbur by the shirt more than once. His talent with a needle and thread earned him the nickname, "Betsy Ross."

The view that if the officials could see everything that went on in "the pit" and interpreted the rules literally, holding could be called on every play is probably true. There will be many times, as a fan, when you are concentrating on an offensive lineman and it seems quite apparent that he is holding, but the official does not call the penalty. Quite often, he simply does not see the holding

With the new liberal holding rule, almost anything goes on pass protection. In the past, Joe Devlin of Buffalo, here setting up for a show pass, would have drawn the official's attention for extending his arms.

since the angle and body positions of the players sometimes make it difficult to spot from the ground. It is often much easier to see the holding on television, in the stands or in the game films that the players view on Monday or Tuesday morning than on the field. There are other times when an official sees the holding, but, for one reason or another, choses to ignore it on a particular play. This is strictly conjecture on my part, having never heard any official admit to ignoring an infraction of the rules. However, there are situations when it might be expedient for an official to look the other way. I have seen offensive linemen panic after being beaten quickly on several plays in succession and resort to flagrant holding for the rest of the game. The official might call it several times, but how often can he penalize a team without completely destroying the tempo of the game and the T.V. ratings, or causing the fans to leave the stands and attack him! This is an extreme situation and does not occur very often.

There are other instances when the official doesn't call holding, even though it is flagrant, because he believes the holding did not effect the outcome of the play. There are other times when he simply feels sorry for an offensive lineman who is outclassed, or may feel that the defensive lineman can handle himself despite the holding. In this respect, such great pass rushers as Harvey Martin of Dallas, and Bob Lilly before him, *do* get held more often than a less effective pass rusher.

The outstanding linemen do not normally have to resort to excessive holding. At the same time, all offensive linemen hold on occassion. Holding, therefore, becomes relative. The question you should ask is not whether an offensive lineman broke the rules, but how often he broke the rules and how long he held on any given play.

## SPECIAL PLAYS AND BLOCKING CALLS

There are certain plays run by most football teams that require special blocks or skills on the part of the offensive linemen.

### The Trap Block

A defensive lineman is trapped when blocked by a player approaching from the side, provided that the person blocking him is not the player on either side of the offensive lineman he is directly opposite. The offensive players directly in front of him do not block him at all on the trap. In fact, he is "encouraged" to come across the line of scrimmage where he will be blocked by a player coming from another area.

The offensive guards perform most of the trap blocking on a team, but an interior defensive lineman can be trapped by an offensive tackle or end. This is one of those difficult blocks where anything that allows the ball carrier to pass the man being trapped is acceptable. Trapping guards never know what to expect from the defensive tackle, end, or corner linebacker. He might dive into the ground in front of you, go around the block, dive over you, or try to knock your head off. The trapping lineman attempts to hit with his shoulder and head placed between his opponent and the goal line. It will require him to hit with a right shoulder when pulling to his right and a left shoulder when pulling to his left. The object is to prevent the defensive lineman from closing the hole.

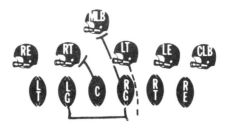

Trap blocking—the block on the middle linebacker is essential.

The defensive player usually tries to narrow the hole to the inside by placing his head on the same side. If he reads trap quickly and closes well, there is going to be a head-on collision when they meet. The problem for the trapping lineman is that he can't be certain that the man being trapped is going to take him on. He must hold back a little in order to avoid missing the man completely if he decides at the last minute to go under, over, or around the block. The further the trapping lineman has to travel, the more difficult it becomes since the defensive player has more time to react.

One of the toughest men in the N.F.L. to trap is Chris Hanburger of the Washington Redskins. He can ring your bell pretty good when he has to, but the problem is not his size or strength. He is quick and fast enough to close the hole even if he doesn't read it quickly, and this same quickness makes him difficult to make contact with when he decides not to take on the blocker.

There are few things as embarrassing for an offensive lineman as missing your man on an outside trap and turning to see him swallow the ball carrier while you are laying helpless on the ground. Everyone in the stadium notices the guard on these occasions.

Two particular trap blocks stick in my mind. One occurred in the A.F.L. championship game in 1963, when I was with San Diego and the Chargers beat the Boston Patriots 51-10. I remember Keith Lincoln of the Chargers picking up 349 yards in total offense including 206 yards from the line of scrimmage. There is one specific play that I particularly remember. I was playing left guard and pulling to my right to trap the Patriots' left corner linebacker Tommy Addison, a former teammate at South Carolina. Tommy went under my block and came up with his head right under Lincoln's number 22. I was on my back listening to the o-o-o-o-h that went through the stands. It was the only time Lincoln was thrown for a loss all game.

The other trap play that sticks in my mind was against the Oakland Raiders that same year. It was a game that the Chargers lost 34-33. I had been given a holding penalty on the play before the trap was called. The penalty hurt us and I was still angry when I reached the line of scrimmage. On the trap play, I caught the defensive end perfectly. He went sprawling over backward and I fell on top of him. When we viewed the films the following Tuesday, Joe Madro, the Charger offensive line coach, stopped the film and ran the trap play back several times. He said: "Watch Sam, I want you to look at this block." We looked at it several times with no further comment from Madro. It was the hardest hit I made all game and probably all season. I was waiting for a compliment which I could have used after the bawling out I had received for the holding penalty on the previous play. Madro finally spoke. Quote, "Have you ever seen lousier technique in your life?" How could I ever forget that block? Madro was a fanatic for technique. The trapping guard had to have inside out position, hit under control, and then move, forcing the man to the outside. To Joe, if the technique was lousy, the results didn't count.

They say that neurotics attract neurotics. Joe and I were attracted. We about drove each other crazy, but there was a genuine friendship because I respected his knowledge of the game. Joe regarded himself as a teacher, which is what a coach should be at all levels. I learned many valuable techniques and skills from him. His one fault was ignoring the basic tenet of a good teacher. He refused to recognize that everyone is different and allow for individual differences. He wanted five linemen like Ron Mix, and of course most of us weren't as good as Ron Mix. Madro would chew out everyone except Mix—only because he rarely had reason to chastise Ron. Some of us didn't need any criticism. I was psyched enough not to need any further pressure.

## Screens

The screen pass probably requires more technique from the offensive line than any other play. Essentially, what the offense tries to do on the screen, is to fake a long pass play and then complete a short pass behind the line of scrimmage. The releasing linemen form a wall of blockers for the receiver. The secret to running the screen well is to have a bunch of hams on the team. I'm surprised that the Los Angeles Rams don't run the screen better because of their exposure to the acting community. The defensive linemen must believe that the play is a pass and that they are legitimately beating the offensive linemen to the passer. The line sets up as it would on a show pass and makes contact for about two seconds. The trick is to then let the defensive man go without tipping the screen. The release of the line is important. If at all possible, the defensive man should pass to the side of the screen. It is also important that each of the offensive linemen release at the same time. Otherwise, the defensive people still on the line are likely to pick it up.

Besides a poorly timed release, the other factor that usually messes up the screen is indecision or duplication of effort once the wall of blockers forms over the middle or to the outside. Quite often, you will see two men run by a defensive player with each assuming the other will pick him up, while at other times you will see two offensive players blocking the same man. The effort must be coordinated. The distance between the running back and the wall after the ball has been caught is also important. In most cases, the smaller the distance the better. The pressure on the defensive players to make a move and take on the offensive blocker is greater when the ball carrier is directly behind the blocker. In this case, the defender has no room to go around the block.

## The Draw Play

The draw play is a running play designed to look like a show pass and draw the defensive linemen across the line as they would when they rush the passer. The quarterback begins to drop back to pass and then hands off to a running back who carries through the line.

The draw is another play that requires a modicum of acting ability or at least the poise and self-control to set up as if it were a show pass and then to move the man to one side or the other after making contact. The draw, and to a lesser extent the screen, are sometimes used to slow down the pass rush. The aggressive pass rusher that has the ball thrown just over his head on the screen, or has the ball carrier run by him on the draw play, may not charge as hard in the next passing situation. In any event, they are more effective against a hard charging defensive line. The key on the draw play is to take the defensive man where he wants to go. The problem that sometimes develops is that the defensive man may not take a side, but instead may try to go over the top of the offensive lineman. If a man is doing that repeatedly, the offensive lineman may try cutting him with a body block.

## Wedge Blocking

The wedge is used in short yardage situations. Each player on the line of scrimmage blocks to his inside, with the center the apex of the wedge. The wedge can be used on the quarterback sneak or when any of the set backs are carrying up the middle. The ball carrier can take any opening that develops or can go over the top if

The quarterback sneak. The quarterback breaks wherever a hole develops.

there is no hole. In wedge blocking, it is imperative that the offensive linemen stay low to the ground. Generally speaking, linemen at the pro level block higher after the initial charge than in high school or college. It doesn't matter how high the blocker is as long as he is lower than the man he is blocking. The idea is to move to the inside and block an area. Adjustments should be made if there is nobody in the area to a player's inside.

## Cross Blocking

When two offensive linemen exchange assignments, they are cross blocking. For example, the defensive tackle lining up on the guard may be slightly to the outside, making it difficult for the guard to block him to the inside. The offensive tackle may be assigned to block down on the defensive tackle. The guard then takes a jab step back to clear the tackle, and proceeds to block out on the defensive end. The ball carrier has to run between the two defensive linemen.

The idea is to create good blocking angles when none exist. The man blocking first on the offensive line has the advantage since the defensive player assigned to the other offensive lineman in the switch has more time to react. Either offensive player may move first when cross blocking. The cross block is used most often when the defensive players are taking unusual splits. Some teams give the offensive line the prerogative of calling crosses at the line if they think it necessary. The age and experience of the people on the line determine the leeway given by the coach.

## THINGS TO LOOK FOR

Nobody can expect to take in all the action on the field at one glance. Trained coaches can't do it, so the armchair quarterback shouldn't expect to either. The best way to enjoy a football game is to keep an eye out for certain things on each play. For example, on some plays try watching the offensive guards to see if they pull. On others watch the defensive linebackers to see if they blitz. You can even watch the referees. The following paragraphs point out some things you might want to look for.

Battles, or *confrontations* if you prefer, are taking place all over the field on each play. However, none is more intense or easier to evaluate and appreciate than the battle being waged by the people up front. It's like a prize fight. There is a winner every round and the final outcome is decided at the gong or whistle. Sometimes it's easy to pick out the winner on a given play and other times it's more difficult because the offensive player is even more dependent on his teammates than the people on defense. But, if you watch carefully you should be able to decide who won and who lost.

Let's take a concrete situation. Number 78 is playing right defensive end over 79 on offense. Number 78 makes the tackle on the running back breaking a slant off the 6 hole in the area of the tight end. You didn't watch the blocking up front and only saw 78 make the tackle. Do you assume that 79, the offensive tackle, broke down. Most people do, but it isn't necessarily the case. The tight end may have been blocking down on 78; the set back on that side may have been assigned to him; the guard and tackle may have been cross blocking; or the offensive guard may have tried to trap him.

There are several other possibilities which may explain why 78 made the tackle. The back could have run into the wrong hole accidentally or could have been forced to run in that area because somebody else broke down on the offensive line. The offensive tackle, 79, may have been trying to block 78 to the outside and succeeded. The offensive guard or center may have missed their blocks and the defensive player may have plugged the area to the inside of the offensive tackle. Rather than running into the free defensive player moving in the hole that the play was designed to hit, he may have chosen to run outside because 79 still had contact with 78.

Things like this happen all the time. This is the reason for the popularity of the option block and run which give the back the option of running wherever the hole develops. What I'm getting at is that a hasty analysis of a play will be wrong far more often than right.

Watch the battles up front and try to determine what the offensive player is trying to accomplish and how his opponent reacts to his moves. Look for change-ups and adjustments. Adaptability is extremely important to an offensive lineman. The good ones don't try to use the same approach all the time. They adapt to the style of the man across the line.

Another thing to keep in mind is that the basic block of the offensive lineman is the head or option block. I learned this from bitter experience.

Warren Geise was appointed as head coach at the University of

South Carolina immediately after my junior year. At the time, there was no unlimited substitution at the college level, which meant you played both ways (offense *and* defense). I averaged about 58 minutes a game during my junior year and was widely acclaimed as the best lineman on the team, which was not saying much since we won only three games. And yet, after the first scrimmage the following spring I was demoted to fourth string.

During the first scrimmage I played over a kid with only fair ability who dug in and submarined (went under) on every play. I was required to get under him and drive him back with an option block. If I turned him to either side, my body would be clogging up the line and not providing an option for the ball carrier. However, I had a problem because my opponent refused to be moved. He never made a tackle all day, but I never drove him back. Almost anyone can dig in and refuse to be moved. I would fall on top of him and knee him, or move to one side and push him sideways, but I wasn't doing what the coach wanted and was demoted the following week. Geise was a good coach and I wound up liking him and naming my son after him. I understood his reasoning, but never did agree with his premise that there is only one way to block a man. The point for the fan to remember is not to look for the picture block, but rather the successful block. Chuck Knox, now head coach of the Buffalo Bills, was the finest offensive line coach I have ever known because he had fewer preconceived notions about how to block than anyone I have ever known. He didn't care what you did as long as it was successful. He never asked me to do the same thing as 330-pound Sherman Plunkett.

The size and speed of a man must be considered in evaluating the things you see him do on the field. Do not expect a 300-pounder to throw as many body blocks on pass protection as the smaller offensive guard. The larger man should utilize his size, while the smaller man must often make adjustments to compensate for his lack of size. Sometimes, the greatest adjustments are those that the small man must make off the field or during the off-season in order to keep his weight up to the minimum most coaches look for at various positions.

Few people would suspect that 256-pound John Kolb of the Pittsburgh Steelers has a weight problem. Kolb is one of the strongest men in pro football and has been known to bench press 550 pounds. He claims that his natural, mature configuration should be somewhere around 210 pounds. As a high school freshman, he was 5'4" and 120 pounds and the only boy in a school with a total male enrollment of 60 not big enough to get a suit. Since everyone goes out for the football team in Oklahoma, Kolb began to eat six times a day and, when not eating, he lifted heavy weights. Needless to say, he made the team the following year. Many football players who must carry more weight than is natural for them are required to lift weights and take dietary supplements. Without lifting weights, many players would be cast away as being too small to play pro football.

When a lineman seems to be getting beaten repeatedly on the pass, look to see if he is fundamentally sound or is "breaking down" for some reason. There are times when a player who is sound will suddenly try something new or begin to fire out on pass protection. You would be surprised how often the man beaten on a pass will be too aggressive by trying to pop the defensive player. He may have lost his cool because of a pressure situation on the field or what happened on the previous day. He may be trying to get back at an opponent who he believes was unnecessarily rough.

Another thing to look for on pass protection is the offensive lineman who, while not being beaten cleanly, is giving too much ground and thus making it difficult for the quarterback to see and throw over him, or over the outstretched arms of the defender. Check to see if one man up front is constantly getting help from the center or one of the set backs.

Everyone breaks down a few times a game. You may never be aware of it since there is often someone waiting to give him help. What sometimes happens is that the man who gets beaten several times early in the game gets all the attention of the extra blocker. He may be beaten repeatedly and yet his opponent may never get to the quarterback. On the other hand, a man may only be beaten twice all game and, yet, both times have his man get to the quarterback. He is the player everyone will notice and criticize for having had a bad game.

Like almost everyone else on the field, the offensive lineman is affected by the relationship between the run and pass. An offensive lineman playing for a team that has not established the running game and must pass 30 to 40 times a game is going to have more difficulty pass blocking. His opponent knows that there is a greater likelihood of a pass, regardless of the down and distance, and plays accordingly. This puts constant pressure on the lineman. At the end of the game, he won't get dressed so quickly.

The type of passes called will also effect the pass protectors' effectiveness up front. The quarterback that throws short is easier to block for than the guy who constantly throws the bomb. It takes longer to throw the bomb and requires the linemen to stay with their opponents longer.

When you see the defensive tackle getting in on the quarterback on a particular play, and you know that he is playing over a particular guard, check to see that there wasn't a blitz or a tackle-end game on the play which caused the people up front to change assignments. The man closest to the one that does the damage is not always the culprit. (This holds true in the defensive backfield as well as on the offensive line.) Suppose there is a tackle-end game with the end coming down into the guard's area first. The offensive tackle doesn't read it and stays with the end, although he is supposed to switch, and at the last minute the guard tries to go across to reach the defensive tackle going around the outside. He gets there a moment too late, just as the defensive tackle lays out the quarterback. Unless you have glanced at the line or watched it the entire time, you will most certainly assume that the guard broke down since he had been blocking that tackle most of the day. What has really happened is that the offensive tackle missed an assignment by not recognizing the tackle-end game.

Proper spacing or splits in the offensive line is important to the success of the running game. Large splits often make it more difficult to pass protect, since the defensive lineman has more room to maneuver the offensive lineman out of position. The line will frequently tip a pass or the area that a running play will be hitting by the type of splits they take. When a team is passing in a critical situation, look for them to narrow their splits. On running plays from tackle to tackle in mid-field, you can expect slightly larger than average splits. The larger the split, the more likelihood of a hole developing between two blockers. The offensive guard prefers a large split when pulling to lead interference on a sweep, but the coach will suggest a narrow split to bring in the defensive people on that side of the line. You can tell how much confidence a guard has in his speed by the size of the split he takes on the sweep. If the center is blocking the on-side defensive tackle (the tackle on the side to which the play is going) on a sweep, it is almost mandatory for the guard to take a narrow split. He must travel a further distance, but the narrow split brings in the tackle and makes the center's block possible.

Teams will split to develop favorable blocking angles on the defense. It is generally easier to block a man who is lined to one side or the other than it is to take on a man head on. Most teams split their line to give the backs more room to operate. If favorable blocking angles develop, all the better. One problem that large splits create is the possibility of a defensive man shooting the gap and coming up with the big play by throwing the ball carrier for a loss. It will happen to the best teams. But, remember that the lineman that shoots the gap is gambling and is as likely to take himself out of the play and put pressure on his teammates by creating an exceptionally large hole as he is to shoot into the right area and make the big play. Try to determine whether the offensive lineman missed his block, or whether the defensive player was indeed gambling and could not have been blocked by anyone on that particular play.

Scott Appleton, who was a much publicized All-American at the University of Texas, and a colossal flop with the Houston Oilers, did a lot of this type of guessing during his short career. What probably annoyed Appleton the most, when coaches objected to his taking a side or shooting the gap, was that he was right more often than he was wrong. He was pretty good at reading the offense and anticipating where the play would be going. He would not try to hit and control the offensive player, but instead would immediately go to the area he thought was going to be attacked. Despite being in the right area more often than not, he was released because he hurt the team too much when he was wrong.

John Mendenhall of the New York Giants is a present day player who is guilty of guessing or taking a side. He does come up with the big play for the Giants on occasion, but he hurts them more often than he helps their cause. The Giants have had a weak team since Mendenhall joined them and he is the best defensive tackle the Giants have had to choose from. As the Giants improve and their defense becomes more disciplined and effective, Mendenhall will either have to change his style of play or suffer the same fate as Scott Appleton.

Lastly, in evaluating the offensive line, don't forget the inherent difficulties at each position. The offensive tackle is playing over a man who has more room to operate; the guard is playing over the biggest man on the defense; and the center has the problem of going after a linebacker who not only has more room to evade the block, but more time as well. Don't look for clean blocks by the center on the middle linebacker unless he happens to catch him with a body block and knocks him off his feet. Many times the center will have to chase the middle linebacker all over the field and will only get a piece of him when he goes to make the tackle (which might be anywhere on the football field). It is controlled and properly channeled emotion that drives a successful offensive lineman. If he were to fire out at the middle linebacker and try to hit him high with everything he had, he would likely wind up on the ground. Instead, he plays it safe and tries to cut him off. If the middle linebacker beats him to the pass, he chases and doesn't stop until the whistle is blown. He'll never create a great running back all by himself, but he sure as hell can help. Just ask any running back about the importance of his offensive line.

# 3

# THE OFFENSIVE BACKFIELD
## The Men Who Earn Their Glory

The transition from college football to pro football seems to be easier for the running back than for anyone else on the football team. Many fine running backs step into the pro ranks and, after a year or two, achieve the same level of stardom they enjoyed in college. As an ex-offensive lineman, I have always been envious of the running back. You cannot appreciate the feeling unless you have lined up at offensive tackle two yards from the goal line, driven your opponent over the goal line with the offensive back right behind you, and then seen the entire team come over and congratulate the back. It's something that every offensive lineman learns to live with. The guy that carries the football over the goal line always gets the ink and the handshakes.

The skills and techniques that a good running back possesses are closer to being natural than those of an offensive lineman. If a runner has exceptional ability and the size essential for pro football, he may find the transition from college easy.

The rookie running back often has his greatest difficulty in learning to protect the passer. Although college backs are required to block on running plays, most colleges do not require their running backs to block the way the pros do on the pass. Blocking is essentially desire and hard work. It takes the desire to stand in there and take your raps as well as put in the hard work that it takes to learn a bunch of new skills which come natural to very few backs. Jimmy Brown was the finest running back the game has ever known, and probably less than a fair blocker. He could have been as good as he wanted to be, because of his size and strength, but had little interest in blocking. The fact that he carried the football about thirty times a game may have also had something to do with the lack of effort he expended when blocking.

On some teams a back can get away with being just a fair

blocker. But, a running back wanting to play in the same backfield as Joe Namath had to be a strong blocker. Weeb Ewbank believed in a quarterback throwing from the pocket. Whether it was Namath or someone else at quarterback, he drafted his backs both for their running *and* blocking ability. Fullback Matt Snell of the New York Jets was as good a blocking back as you will find. He had the size, strength and willingness to put his helmet into the chin of a blitzing linebacker. Emerson Boozer and the rest of Ewbank's running backs were out of the same mold. It is not by accident that they were all fine blockers. Poor blocking in the backfield and two gimpy knees at quarterback didn't go together.

## POSITIONS

Aside from the quarterback, most teams use three offensive backs. You are more likely to find the third back between the offensive tackles in high school and college football, than in the pro game. The traditional backfield alignment in the T formation has two halfbacks and a fullback. In the T, the fullback lines up directly behind the quarterback and, until the recent popularity of the wishbone T, was traditionally placed slightly behind the halfbacks.

These days, you are liable to see any back carrying the ball into any area on the field. Traditionally, however, the halfbacks carried the ball to the outside and the fullback was limited to plays up the middle and off-tackle. The reasons were the physical qualities of the various backs, and their location in the backfield. The outside position of the halfbacks made them the logical choice to carry the football on end runs. The fullback was aligned deeper than the halfbacks in order to prevent his reaching the line of scrimmage too quickly on plays up the middle. The advantages of a quick hitting attack, however, have caused coaches to re-evaluate their thinking and many have recently moved the fullback closer to the line.

Because of the emphasis on the passing game in pro football, one of the offensive backs has been removed from the area behind the offensive line and placed in a split position on the flank. He continues to line up in the backfield to accommodate the rules, but his primary responsibility as a flanker is to run pass routes. Consequently, he is chosen for his pass catching ability rather than his running ability.

You are likely to see almost any combination of the remaining two running backs in the standard pro-set, which is still used more than any other alignment. Since the roles of the halfback and fullback are interchangeable, a team may use a fullback and a

## THE BACKFIELD SETS

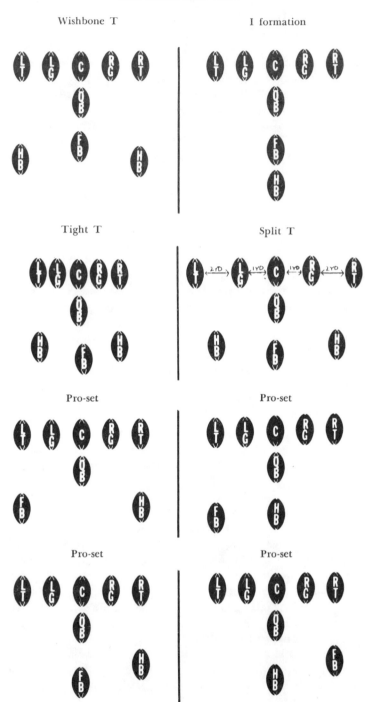

Wishbone T

I formation

Tight T

Split T

Pro-set

Pro-set

Pro-set

Pro-set

halfback, two halfbacks, or two fullbacks. In a short yardage situation, two fullbacks may be advantageous. When five receivers are to be sent out on a pass play, two halfbacks might be used to provide more speed. The alignment of the backfield will vary according to the play and game situation. It changes on almost every play.

Varying the alignment of the backfield not only allows a team to run its plays from the best possible angles, but also prevents the defense from guessing (reading) what is coming up. When in one basic alignment, there is a tendency for a back to vary his positioning slightly ("cheat") in order to be in a more favorable position to execute his particular assignment. This is virtually eliminated when the formation is altered to meet the individual's needs. For example, a fullback lined up in the traditional spot behind the quarterback may feel a need to cheat to the outside when required to be the lead blocker on the off-tackle play. This need is eliminated if he can line up in the halfback's traditional position behind the offensive tackle. The halfback can similarly line up directly behind the center, in the position normally thought of as belonging to the fullback, if it enables the offense to use its best blocker and runner for a particular play to either side of the line.

## PHYSICAL AND MENTAL QUALITIES

The ideal fullback on a professional football team should stand 6'3" tall, weigh between 230 and 240 pounds and run the 40-yard dash in 4.7 seconds. If you cannot find him, you may have to settle for Don Nottingham, of the Miami Dolphins, who goes 5'11", 210 pounds and probably does not run the 40 in less than five seconds. Nottingham was the last Baltimore Colt choice picked in the 1971 draft. He may not look the part, but he made it in pro football.

Like most other positions on a football team, there is room for individual differences in the size and speed of fullbacks. Every coach has a picture in his mind of what his fullback should look and run like, but he will settle for less than the V shape and blazing speed if the man can get the job done. Don Nottingham will never be a super-star, but he is doing the job for the Dolphins. Naturally, a man with his lack of speed will have to compensate with exceptional blocking and constant second and third efforts when he carries the football. Of course in pro football everyone has to make that proverbial second effort or he won't succeed. There are some with exceptional ability who make it without delivering a maximum effort, but that is rarely the case with fullbacks, and such people are never as good as they could be. John Riggins is a case in point. He has truly exceptional ability, but has not played to

Two tough running backs: Franco Harris (32) and Rocky Bleier (20).

his maximum potential since his rookie year when he was still thinking about playing football instead of the dollar figure on his contract. He probably now realizes that he has wasted the tremendous talent with which he was blessed by making a half hearted effort, but it's too late for him to turn around. Football demands 100% dedication—the cliches about eating, drinking and thinking football 24 hours a day are all true. Riggins wouldn't pay the price necessary to be outstanding and has been an average fullback these many years. He has at least as much natural ability as Franco Harris and much more than Larry Csonka and Jim Taylor had in their heydays. However, he has just half the dedication they had. Riggins would probably reply to these charges that he is too intelligent to be used by the owners, and cite the huge contract he received when he joined the Redskins, as proof of his intelligence.

He will discover someday, if he hasn't already, that there is more to playing pro ball than making money. He will learn too late that the man that wastes the ability to be outstanding in any field, regrets it for the rest of his life.

The pro halfback should be 6'2", 220 pounds and also run that 40-yard dash in less than 4.7. But Tony Dorsett at 5'11" and 192 pounds might be a good alternative. And so would Terry Metcalf at 5'10" and 185 pounds or Otis Armstrong at 5'10" and 195. They have all held up quite well to the weekly pounding to which the running back is submitted.

The punishment sustained by the running back is the primary reason coaches prefer large people. Another is the blocking required of all backs. How often can a 5'9", 190-pound running back block a 6'3", 245-pound corner linebacker? Yet, they do. To compensate, most teams with small running backs adjust their offense so that they do not have to block as often as a back ordinarily would.

There seems to be more acceptance of the smaller running back today than there was during the early and mid-'60's. Jim Brown, Jim Taylor and Paul Hornung set the trend towards the big running back, and for a while everyone was looking for 225-pounders. Eventually, coaches realized that they were not going to find another Jimmy Brown—a big fullback who was in a class all by himself—and became satisfied with lighter backs.

My pet theory is that as the defensive players grow larger, the smaller running back has an increased advantage. The defensive player today is bigger and faster than his predecessors. Ordinarily, though, a player loses some agility and perhaps quickness with size. It becomes very much like a circus act with the midgets eluding the much larger clowns by going under and around them. The smaller running backs are usually the game breakers, and a quick look at the rosters in the N.F.L. indicates that there are quite a few running backs near or under 200 pounds. In addition to Metcalf, Armstrong and Dorsett, there is Oakland's Clarence Davis at 5'10"—195 pounds, Greg Pruitt of the Browns at 5'10"—190 pounds, Houston's Ron Coleman at 5'11"—195 pounds, and Walter Payton at 5'10" and 204 pounds. It's hard to believe when you watch him run, but that's all that Payton weighs. Pound for pound he is probably the strongest player in the league, and his style of running is quite different from the other halfbacks mentioned here. He not only relies on his quickness and acceleration, but can break a tackle when necessary. Because of his slashing, reckless style of running and his refusal to go down when being gang-tackled, it remains to be seen how long his body will last.

One of the reasons that it is easier to break in as a running back

It takes more than one tackler to bring down a big back like Boobie Clark of the Bengals.

than at other positions in pro-football is that much of what is required is instinctive. (Nobody taught Walter Payton how to run.) But there is nothing easy about playing the position. Running backs take more abuse than anyone else on the football team. The offensive linemen have complete control when they make contact. They hit with their helmet and shoulder pads. The people on defense can use their hands and arms to ward off the blow in addition to being among the largest players on the team. Linebackers have room to maneuver. Defensive backs and wide receivers make contact only rarely. The offensive back, however, can expect to be hit every time he carries the ball on any part of his anatomy and by any and every member of the defensive unit that can find a piece of him. He has no control of his body when he gets hit and cannot always use his protective gear to absorb the blow. He may have to take the blow on his free arm (if he is lucky), on his ribs, his back, or even his shins. He will be pulled, tugged, clawed at, pounded and, unless he crosses the goal line or goes out of bounds, always thrown or knocked to the ground.

The running back in professional football takes a beating on almost every play. When he is not lugging the football, he may be blocking people 50 to 90 pounds heavier than himself. When not carrying the ball or blocking, he is either a potential receiver or faking into the line—which is likely to put him into position to be clobbered once again by some larger opponent. As a receiver, whether out on a flare route, curling up over the middle, or going through the line to catch a pass, he will be hit harder and by more people than the deep receivers. What's more, the back receiving a flare pass is expected to get yardage on his own, since the pass may only be thrown three or four yards upfield. There's no getting away from it, the running back must be tough.

To make things even more difficult for the running back, he has to carry the football wherever he goes. This not only occupies an arm that could be used to ward off tacklers and protect himself, but also takes away from his speed—his greatest asset. The football may not be a heavy object, but carrying it takes away a couple of vital tenths of a second from the time it takes him to run the 40-yard dash.

The running back gets one break, though. His offensive plays are not hard to learn. If anything, they are easier for the offensive back than for the offensive lineman. Regardless of the defense, the running back has the same assignment whether he is running with the football or carrying out a fake. Even when blocking there will not be that much variation in his assignments. When blocking, he is likely to be assigned to the end man on the line or to a linebacker. Those running backs required to block the larger interior linemen will have their careers shortened by the constant pounding.

## FUNDAMENTALS

Because most of the things that a running back does when carrying the football are instinctive, his basic skills take on a different character than other positions. There is not much time for thinking when running with the ball. The offensive back is more likely to react to a movement he sees out of the corner of his eye. He might use a cross over or a side step, but won't be thinking about it at the time.

There are, nevertheless, certain skills which offensive backs have to develop and we'll devote a little time to them.

## The Stance

The further a player, whether on offense or defense, lines up from the line of scrimmage, the less important his stance becomes. It's a lot like track, where, the longer the race, the less important the start. The offensive and defensive linemen must have a well balanced and functional stance. They make contact immediately and their stance will have an effect on the block of the offensive lineman, and the charge of the defensive lineman. The running back does not make contact as he leaves his stance and can compensate for a poor start with exceptional speed.

There is no prescribed stance for a running back. His stance will vary according to the type of offense and his function within that offense. In the split T offense, the running backs will be going straight ahead most of the time. This allows them to place most of their weight on the hand that is down on the ground. The set back required to run laterally on a quick pitch, as well as perform other varied functions, will probably take some of the weight off his hand. This will make it easier to get to the outside and set up to pass protect. Whatever the stance, it should be the same every time. It is variations in stance which help the defense "read" or anticipate the play.

Just as there is no prescribed stance in the backfield, the offensive back also has some latitude as to where he lines up. Again, the only stipulation is that he does not tip the play. For example, a running back may want to cheat by moving a foot to the outside on the quick pitch enabling him to turn the corner faster. This is okay as long as that back assumes the same alignment on several preceding and following plays so that the defense can't read the quick pitch.

## The Start

On quick hitting running plays, it is important for every member of the offensive team to get off with the snap of the ball. On a show pass, this is not necessary and sometimes a player deliberately delays his movement. The linebacker and defensive secondary key on the offensive line and the set backs. Since the set back has more time to react, the experienced back remaining in to protect the passer may delay before setting up at the snap of the ball. This will sometimes cause those keying to hesitate for a split second which can make the difference between a successful play and one that fails.

On the running play, there is seldom a valid reason for any offensive player to be late in getting in motion after the ball has been snapped. The running back who gets a slow start may have a poor stance, but the problem is more often mental. It can be due to lack of concentration on the starting count or indecision caused by not being certain of his assignment. The problem seems to be more common among rookie backs. Mark Van Eeghen of the Raiders and Chuck Foreman of the Vikings are just two examples of running backs who had trouble with their starts until they learned the systems of their new teams.

A poor stance may cause a poor start at times. The player who has too much weight on his hand may have a problem moving laterally. On the other hand, the back with *not enough* weight on his hand may be slow in moving straight ahead. There are prescribed ways for offensive linemen to pull out of the line of scrimmage. Most coaches do not stress this technique with running backs. Occasionally, a back will develop a flaw in his start. If a back seems to be slow to the outside, look for any false or unnecessary steps he might be making. Each step should bring him closer to his target.

Cincinnati running back Pete Johnson covers the ball with both arms as he is about to be tackled.

### The Hand Off

The responsibility for the hand off is the quarterback's. The running back should be looking straight ahead at the offensive line to determine where the hole is developing. The only thing you might look for is that the running back have the proper arm raised. The elbow closest to the quarterback should be raised with the other arm underneath and ready to close in on the ball. It's so basic and automatic that it is rarely the reason for a fumble. The fumble on the hand off is usually caused by poor timing or interference by the defense.

### The Fake

The faking of a ball carrier when carrying the ball is one of those techniques that is hard to define and will vary from play to play. Much of it is instinctive. Faking by the running back when not carrying the ball is equally important, and something which requires no special ability—only a desire to carry out the fake. The running back should run into the line as if he were taking the hand off from the quarterback. When faking a sweep to the outside, he must run at full speed and continue five yards upfield. This may seem unnecessary when viewed from the stands, but can sometimes fool a defensive lineman or linebacker busy fighting off a block.

The back should of course *always* carry out his fakes. But, this becomes especially important on certain plays. The play action pass, when the quarterback fakes into the line before dropping back, is an exapmle. The effort expended on the fake by a back can, and often does, make the play a success. It can also help make a quarterback's attempt to call a progression of related plays successful. For example, when a back carries the football between the guard and center on one play, his fake into that hole on the next play may bring the defense in tight enough to open up the area off-tackle for another running back.

### Running with the Football

Every running back has his own particular way of running with the football. Moves that are basic and effective for one may be completely ineffective for another. Some use little things like the head or shoulder fake, and others rely on their speed or power almost exclusively. These differences in style notwithstanding, there are certain basic moves and techniques that either come naturally or are taught to all young running backs. The modifications come later.

Tony Dorsett of the Cowboys didn't find the transition from college to pro ball especially difficult.

*Use the Blocker*—The most important single thing a runner can do is to use his blockers whenever possible. He should know every blocker's assignment and which way he is likely to take his opponent. The good back gets to know the people in front of him and can anticipate how they will react when there are alternative choices. He will wait a split second if he knows where his blocker is supposed to be.

The running back who has taken a quick pitch can often beat the offensive tackle who has pulled to block for him, to the outside. It is wiser, though, to fake running to the outside and then to cut back inside the approaching offensive tackle. This is usually safer than trying to outrun everyone including the cornerback, and, if done well, can make the tackle's job easier.

The secret to effective downfield blocking is running backs

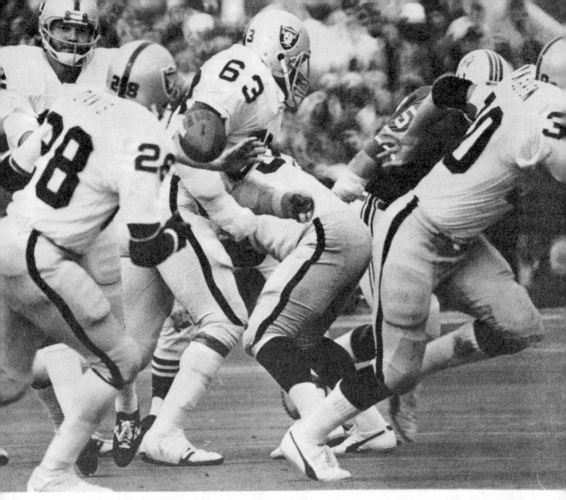

Oakland Raider running back Clarence Davis (28) takes a pitch out from Ken Stabler and sweeps behind guard Gene Upshaw (63) and back Mark van Eeghen (30).

who stay as close as possible to their linemen running interference. The further away the blocker is from the runner, the more chance the smaller defensive back has to elude the block. There are times when the running back is so close to the pulling lineman that he will actually tap or push him in the direction he wants him to move. If he is that close, the offensive lineman might not have to make contact to keep the tackler from the ball carrier. The defensive back may *take himself* out of the play as he attempts to avoid contact.

The running back moving into the line of scrimmage can also help his blockers at times. The defensive lineman tries to hit and control the offensive man opposite him. He will aim at the middle of the offensive lineman which will allow him to move in any direction the back does. If there is time and the back sees the block developing, he can make an early move to one side and then break the other way at the last second, upsetting the defensive man's balance. The offensive lineman will then be able to drive his opponent off the line to give the back room to operate more easily. The lineman must keep contact while the running back sets up the defender.

*Change of Pace*—The last thing a runner wants to do is make contact of any kind with a defensive player. He should have his free arm ready to stiff-arm his opponent if necessary, but a good change of pace can sometimes help him to avoid contact completely. The change-up is best used when a defensive player is

Walter Payton (34) of the Bears has one of the best stiff arms in football.

pursuing from an angle. The defensive man is running to what he thinks is a cut-off point to make the tackle. He determines where that cut-off spot will be by gauging the speed of the runner. If the ball carrier can confuse him, he may misjudge the cut-off spot. One way the running back can achieve this is by slowing down and then putting on a burst of speed when he thinks he can outrun the defender. Another type of change of pace can be accomplished by shortening his stride and then running full out at the proper moment.

*Stop-and-Go*—When a tackler is approaching from the side, the stop-and-go can be used. Instead of outrunning the defender, the ball carrier will attempt to stop running completely, thereby causing the defender to overshoot the tackle. The change of pace and stop-and-go may be used on the same play. The running back starts with the change of pace and, if the defender does not slow down, he switches to the stop-and-go.

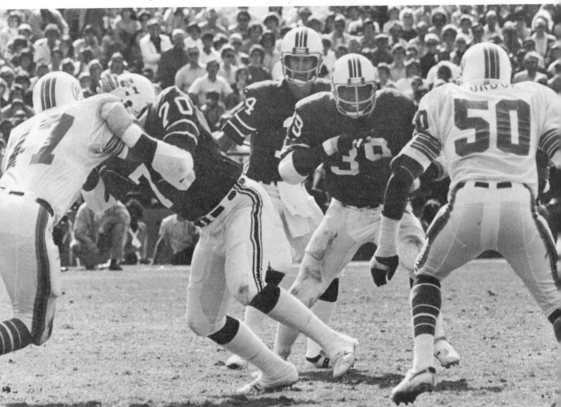

New England running back Sam Cunningham getting ready to break to the outside.

*The Side Step*—The side step is a good move in the open field with only one defender between the runner and the goal line. It's not a good move when there is a crowd around the ball, because the runner must slow down as he approaches the defender. In using the side step, the runner stops and plants a foot to one side of the tackler and then springs to the other side. The ball should be in the far arm to enable him to use the stiff-arm, if necessary.

In the side step, the right leg should be kept limp after springing to the side so that it will give, if the tackler gets a piece of it. This is the famous *limp leg*. It was used more often in the past when tacklers were taught to hit low. The limp leg is ineffective against a tackler aiming his head at the ball carrier's numbers.

*The Cross Step*—The cross step is exactly what it sounds like. The ball carrier crosses one foot in front of the other and takes a long step. If the step is long enough, and he has set it up well, he should then be able to continue his trip to the goal line. He should not slow down when approaching the defender.

*Lower the Head*—There are times when the ball carrier has no room or time to maneuver and elude the tacklers. When there is nothing else for him to do, he has to lower his head and try to bull his way for an extra yard or two. It requires no special skill except a willingness to blast in there and fight for the inches. Every good back will do it when there is no alternative. However, there is also a time for the runner to go down after being tackled. The back that keeps struggling on his feet with three or four people on him is inviting injury.

Not all running backs use *all* of these techniques. Some rely more on their speed, and others more on their power; but every good back will develop *some* elusive moves. There is no point in looking for specifics. Look for a variety of moves. In time, you will come to notice that the smaller the back, the more moves he has.

The better running backs generally have a smooth and fluid style when carrying the football. Some people used to accuse Jim Brown of only making a half hearted effort and running at less than full speed. Nonsense! It was his exceptional agility, speed and coordination that made it look so easy. Regardless of the fakes or moves of a running back, he should appear natural and in complete control of the move and of his body. Question unnecessary motion, particularly a great many steps that do not bring the runner any closer to the goal line.

John Brockington was the number one draft choice of the Green Bay Packers, and then went to Kansas City. Although he didn't play very much last year, he always seemed to excite the crowd when he was in there. It wasn't the yardage which he gained, but his style of running that captured the imagination of the fans. There were arms and legs going in every direction all at one time. It seemed as if he was making a tremendous second and third effort every time he carried the football, and that he was expending a great deal of effort in attempting to avoid would-be tacklers. Much of it was false, unnecessary movement.

The running back lacking body control often has to take two or three steps when one would suffice. His legs may be moving quickly and the fans may be cheering, but the defender is getting time to recover and adjust to the situation. The back should be shortening the distance between the goal line with each step he takes.

## Catching the Football

The running back is given a contract each year that reflects his total yardage and average yards per carry the year before. IN PRO FOOTBALL THE RUNNING BACK GETS PAID FOR RUNNING WITH THE FOOTBALL. The Coaching staff will constantly stress the importance of being able to catch and block, *as well as* run with the football. However, when the season ends and it's time to talk contract, the only thing anyone remembers is the won-lost record and the yardage accumulated by the back.

Blocking and the ability to catch the football may not earn a player a high salary, but it can make the difference when two marginal players are fighting for a position and both have equal running ability. Then, the coach will evaluate a player's ability in other areas, especially pass receiving. As zone coverage in the defensive secondary grows in popularity, pass receiving ability could become an even more important yardstick for backs. During the early '70's more and more teams in the N.F.L. went to the zone, and more and more quarterbacks began to look for their set backs and tight ends when dropping back to throw the football.

Rocky Bleir is a perfect example of a running back that beat out several superior runners because of his all-around ability, even though it took him six years to earn a starting position. Bleier played exclusively on special teams for the first five years of his career. Eventually, Chuck Noll realized that the Steelers were a better football team when Bleier was in at halfback than any number of faster and more talented runners. He won a starting berth in the fifth game of the 1974 season and was instrumental in helping the Steelers win their first league championship that season. He has had much competition since, but is still the Steelers' starting halfback.

Catching a short pass from his regular position in the backfield, or a long pass when set out wide, presents no particular difficulty for the back. On occasion, though, he is required to run a long route from his regular backfield position. This requires excellent protection by the offensive line since the set back must travel a long way to get downfield and there will be no one to pick up a defensive lineman on the side that he has vacated. Most of the pass routes run by a back, however, will be of the short flare variety.

When running a flare pattern (the most common route for backs), the back is usually covered by the corner linebacker on the side that he is flaring. The corner linebacker looks at him and the

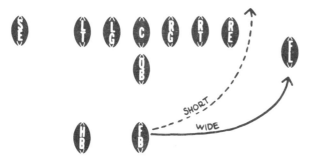

The wide and short flare passes.

back in turn is aware of the movement of the linebacker. If the linebacker moves out into the flat too quickly, the set back may curl back over the middle into the area he vacated. This move forces the linebacker to change direction and may provide the split second necessary for the back to break free and catch the ball. Look for the curl over the middle if the back has been tackled several times immediately after catching the football.

Although the distance covered on a flare pass is short, it is not an easy one for the quarterback to throw or for the back to catch. There are two problems for the running back on the flare pass. The first is the ever-present knowledge that he is likely to be clobbered by that corner linebacker, and maybe several other defensive people, as soon as he catches the ball. Yet, he is expected to pick up most of the yardage needed *after* he catches the ball. As a result, there is more of a tendency than usual for him to take his eyes off the ball to see who is approaching and where he should break after catching the football. He cannot catch the ball and fall down like the wide receiver snaring a long pass 40 yards downfield.

The other problem is the angle at which the ball approaches. If not thrown perfectly, the flare requires him to turn, bend, or reach, and with little time to make the adjustment. The extra movement also leaves him in a poor position to elude the linebacker. Catching the flare pass requires at least as much and maybe more concentration than is necessary for the bomb thrown downfield. Superior concentration makes the difference before the catch, and a good lead by the quarterback will determine how much yardage the back picks up after the reception.

When running other pass routes, the offensive back is confronted with the same problems as any other receiver. When evaluating him, look at the preciseness of his moves, the sharpness of his breaks and the aggressiveness he displays when going after the football.

## Blocking

When a running back is tearing up the league you will probably find an excellent blocking back in the same backfield who deserves much of the credit. There are many possible blocking combinations, but, generally, when a play is run to the strong side (the side where the tight end is situated), there is an offensive blocker for each defensive player on the line or at the linebacker position. Assuming straight blocking is called, the center will block the middle linebacker, the guard will block the defensive tackle, the offensive tackle will block the defensive end, and the tight end will fire out on the corner linebacker. The set back not carrying the ball may be used to fake another play, lead through the hole to "clean up" anyone that breaks free, or block downfield on one of the deep backs. When the play is run *away* from the tight end (to the weak side), which happens about 50% of the time, there is an extra man on that side of the defensive line. He may be assigned to one of several offensive players, such as the pulling off-side guard. In many instances, the non-ballcarrying back is required to block him.

The number of plays in an offensive attack that require a back to block will vary with the type of attack and the proficiency of the backs. Whether the backs are utilized extensively in blocking or not, it is a definite asset to have two good blocking backs. It is as important to the success of the passing game as it is to the running game. The offensive backs not only help the offensive linemen in front of them on the pass when necessary, but are also responsible for blocking the corner linebacker when he is blitzing.

The Oakland Raiders have always handled to blitz well, because of their fine blocking backs. Needless to say, Ken Stabler's ability to read the blitz along with Fred Biletnikoff and the other receivers plays an important role. However, the main reason for the team's success in this area remains the excellent blockers in the backfield. Blocking ability has always been a prime requisite for consideration as a backfield candidate with the Raiders. Stabler's loss of mobility is now an open invitation to blitz against the Raiders. He rarely moves from the pocket anymore even when his knees are feeling good. Solid blocking backs are a necessity.

Chuck Noll also spends a great deal of time in developing the blocking skills of his backs. They employ the same techniques as do his offensive linemen. The defensive player is looked right in the eye and hit under the chin with the back's helmet. Noll does not believe in throwing cross body blocks when pass protecting since it is often a hit or miss situation. Many times, with the cross body block, the defensive player can reach over the back lying on the

Back Rocky Bleier (20) ready to help tackle John Kolb (55) on a show pass.

ground and make the tackle. In ordinary situations, a normal head and shoulder block will be enough to take out the corner line-backer. If the back is greatly overmatched, look for a change-up in the form of a body block.

Bill Mathis, the ex-Jet, was a fine blocking back who believed whole-heartedly in staying up and taking on the defensive player and not resorting to a body block. If he was not completely sold beforehand, I convinced him of it during the 1966 season. I was playing over 6'9", 320-pound Ernie Ladd, who played with me in San Diego and them went on to Houston and Kansas City. I was rather small toward the end of my career. At the beginning, I was considered a fair-sized guard at 240 pounds. Each year, as the rookies came in bigger, I was considered smaller. Since I was not particularly tall either, I had trouble with gigantic Ernie Ladd.

During one game, I decided that I needed some help. I had to slow Ladd down some way and decided to try to cut him and knock his legs out from under him. Weeb had told us to be certain to tell the back behind us if we intended to cut so that he could help if the lineman missed the block (the back would then throw a block). I told Mathis who accepted my decision calmly.

He was anything but calm when I returned to the huddle after missing Ladd completely. It was about the fourteenth time that Mathis had had his nose broken, and the blood to prove it was all over his pants and face. He said, "Thanks for letting me know you were about to cut him, but next time do it when Matt [Matt Snell] is behind you." Bill never thought much of the body block after that.

As on the offensive line, pass protection is harder to master for the back than blocking for the run. The back that is willing to run full speed at a defensive player, and throw his body around, will block well on the run. It takes more skill and self discipline when pass blocking. Like the offensive lineman, he cannot be too aggressive. He must learn to absorb the charge of the defensive lineman or linebacker, and be prepared to get knocked down and bruised, if it will give the quarterback an additional second to release the ball.

When pass blocking, the offensive back first looks for the linebacker. If he is not blitzing, the back will look to help where needed. Since the offensive center is normally restricted to assisting the guards, the set back will often look to help the tackle on his side of the line. There is a tendency in this situation to become overly aggressive and try to unload on the defender a split second before he gets by the tackle. The back sees an opportunity to hit the defender. It seems like the logical approach, but it is frequently a mistake. Instead of trying to jar the defensive player, he should position himself next to the tackle and help when necessary. This approach is likely to enable the tackle to maintain his balance and the two offensive players can continue to double team the defender. Together, they are more likely to succeed than by hitting him one at a time.

## THINGS TO LOOK FOR

Most fans have a pretty good idea of the running ability of a back; primarily because they keep their eye on him whenever he is given the ball. It is easy to determine if the ball carrier is slashing and driving for extra yardage or if he just happens to be getting enormous holes to run through. The offensive line should always be the first consideration in evaluating a running back. If a back

Anyone could run through this hole provided for Pete Banaszak (40) by the Oakland offensive line.

seems to be picking up a lot of easy yardage, try to see if the back is opening his own holes, or if his blockers are making it so easy, a baby could have gone through.

There are other factors which may not show up in the statistics. Try to determine if one particular back is always called on to carry in short yardage situations. This will cut down his average gain per carry even though he's doing a great job. Look for the column that lists the number of times he carries in a given game and how many touchdowns he scored. It may help you to determine if he is getting the call in the tough situations.

Bud Grant of the Vikings was recently comparing Chuck Foreman to Walter Payton in this regard: "No back in football has got it all together like Foreman," said Grant. "He and Payton have entirely different programs. Foreman may not go all the way as often as Payton. Foreman is a slasher and pounder. The linebackers around the league will tell you about the moves he's got. The thing about his totals, he's never going to have a big average per carry because he's the guy who gets the tough yardage for us." The number of carries (without regard to total yardage) will indicate the value of the running back to his team. When you see a back carry the football over 15 times a game you know that he is earning his salary.

Hugh McElhenny, one of the great running backs, and recently inducted into the Hall of Fame, once said that he questioned O. J. Simpson's greatness because he did not break the long one often enough during his first two years in the N.F.L. McElhenny said that all of the great runners break one on their own regularly, despite the quality of the offensive line in front of them. The factor that he may have overlooked is the number of times O. J. carried the ball. Most great runners have carried the ball at least twice as often as O.J. did his first few years. That offered them at least twice the number of opportunities to break the long run. O.J. certainly isn't a great blocker so why didn't he carry the ball more? One answer is that Buffalo was the weakest team in football when O. J. was drafted. This meant that for the comparatively short period that the opponent's defense was in the game, they were particularly fresh. It's pretty tough to gain yardage against a defense which is always fresh. As the Bills' offensive line improved, O. J.'s performance and ability to break the long one improved. He certainly proved McElhenny wrong, and did it with just an average offensive line, Joe DeLamielleure being the only outstanding lineman in front of him.

In evaluating the performance of a star, try not to forget the team he plays for. Look to see if it has a balanced attack. Just as it becomes more difficult for the quarterback to complete his passes when he is forced to throw repeatedly, so it becomes harder for the running back to pick up yardage when his team stays on the ground a good part of the time.

Look for the back's ability to get the first down. Does he dive under or over the top when inches are important. Most defensive teams will give two or three yards at mid-field on first down. It is a completely different situation near the goal line or on third and two yards to go. Be aware of these variables.

The fumble is the unpardonable sin for the running back. Most backs will not make it to the pros unless they have learned to hold on to the football. All backs will fumble occasionally. There is not much that can be done to prevent it after the ball carrier has learned to hold the ball properly. You will sometimes see defensive backs or wide receivers hold the ball in one hand and move it about unnecessarily. They do not get paid to run with the football. Most running backs tuck it into the elbow crease and hold tight. Many coaches try to get their backs to place the free arm over the ball when about to be tackled. Yet many of the finest runners do not do it, with resulting fumbles.

The running back is often said to be only as good as his offensive line, but it works both ways. The good back must hit the line fast, pick the right hole, set up his downfield blockers, and, finally, bull his way for those extra inches when cornered. The good back often has an opportunity to make his linemen look good, when running with the ball. When he is not carrying the ball he should block with the abandon, if not the skill, of an offensive lineman, or go after the pass with the determination and concentration of a highly skilled wide receiver. In evaluating a back, see what he can do in addition to running with the ball.

Don't be overly impressed by speed alone. There are some coaches that have preconceived notions about how fast a running back should run the 40-yard sprint, and will not play anyone who cannot meet minimum standards. If the Baltimore Colts required their halfbacks to run the 40 in 44 or 45 seconds, Lydell Mitchell might be doing something else for a living. That would be a shame since Mitchell has had over 1000 yards in each of the last three years. Mitchell doesn't have outstanding speed, but he does have the necessary quickness and does everything well. Mitchell believes that his lack of blinding speed may be a blessing in disguise: "Some of the players in the league are good because they can run fast, but when they begin to lose a half step, they can't get a job anywhere. I won't have that problem because my greatest asset is quickness, not straight ahead speed." Ex-Colt great Lenny Moore had this to say about Lydell Mitchell recently: "I always knew he was going to be a good one. Lydell isn't a flashy runner with lots of moves like Walter Payton or O.J. Simpson but he gets things accomplished in his own way. He keeps running the ball for six or seven yards and all of a sudden he has his 100 for the day." Moore made those remarks after Mitchell surpassed Moore as the Colt's number one career rusher in his sixth season in the league. (Moore was around for 12 years though he did spend some time as a wide receiver.)

Mitchell holds another record which is equally impressive. He had 72 receptions in 1974, the most ever by an N.F.L. running back. He caught 60 more passes in each of the two years followng the record. There is no way for me to document his blocking ability. You will have to watch him in action for that. When you put it all together, Lydell Mitchell is one of the most effective all-around backs in the league, and is as valuable to his team as any running back in the league. All this, despite being "slow."

# 4

# THE RECEIVERS

## The Men Who Fly

Football is unique among team sports because of the contact that pervades every moment of the action. Yet, one of the most interesting and exciting aspects of football involves a minimum of contact. It is the individual battles between the receivers and defenders which get more attention than any other confrontation on the field. There is the ever-present threat of the bomb for the easy score with the equal possibility of an interception and long runback. It's all done in the wide open spaces, and you don't have to be a coach to appreciate the skills involved. Perhaps it is the simplicity of the passing game that makes it the focal point of attention in professional football. The quarterback throws the football and the receiver runs, jumps, and catches it—skills that anyone can relate to and everyone can understand.

The rule book states that the two end people on every offensive line are eligible to go downfield and receive a forward pass. It also states that there must be seven men on the offensive line, which makes the five interior linemen ineligible receivers. All members of the offensive backfield are eligible to receive a pass, but technically they are not called receivers unless they wear a number in the 80's and line up on the flank. Of course, there are exceptions, Fred Biletnikoff of the Raiders insists on wearing number 25 on his football jersey; and Ken Burrough of the Oilers wears 00.

Until the pro-set and its many variations came into widespread use, there were few problems in recognizing the eligible receivers and finding names for them. The two ends on the offensive line were the receivers and everyone behind the line was a back. The pros confused things by choosing to operate from a basic formation that utilized three receivers and only two set backs. In the pro-set, the receiver lined up in the traditional position of end is called

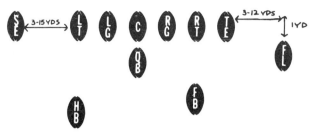

The pro-set. There are five potential receivers.

the tight end. The end man on the other side may be split anywhere from 3 to 15 yards from the offensive tackle. He is called the split end. The receiver lined up from 3 to 12 yards outside the tight end is called the flanker back. If the flanker lined up on the line of scrimmage, the tight end would be an ineligible receiver; so he lines up a yard or so behind the line of scrimmage. Because of the many variations in the traditional alignment of the receivers in pro football, the official team programs no longer attempt to distinguish between the split end and the flanker back. They are now known as wide receivers. The players and coaches, though, continue to use the original terms.

## FLANKER BACK

Regardless of what letter of the alphabet you assign to him, the flanker must have speed and must be able to catch the football. The extent of the flanker's split varies with the game situation and the team's field postion. If the ball is on the right hash mark and the flanker is sent to the right side of the line, a narrow split is almost mandatory. When a wide receiver lines up too close to the sideline, the outside move is taken away.

The predetermined route called by the quarterback in the huddle also influences the split of both the flanker and split end. Any of the wide receivers is likely to cheat out a few yards on the post pattern or tighten up when running a corner route (see diagrams ahead). This gives them more room to operate and elude the defender. If a running play is called and the wide receiver is required to throw a crackback block (when a wide receiver blocks someone to his inside) on the corner linebacker, he may take a narrow split which will help him get the job done on that play.

Most flankers are chosen for their speed, ability to elude the defender and ability to catch the football. Blocking is usually of secondary importance, though there are exceptions. Much depends on the type of offense being used and where a team prefers to run with the football. The team that sweeps the ends with consistency (which is becoming rare) and requires the wide receiver to crack back, will choose its personnel with an eye toward a player's ability to block. Sid Gillman, former coach of the San Diego Chargers, insisted that his wide receivers learn to block. When the Chargers were viewing the game films of the New York Titans during the early days of the American Football League, you could count on his stopping the projector to tell the team to look at Don Maynard's blocking. He would then run the play over and over while getting a good laugh and pointing out how not to block. However, he would never laugh when Maynard was running a pass route. Gillman said repeatedly that Maynard was the most dangerous receiver in the league.

The main reason for the use of the flanker is to open up the offense and make it more explosive. This allows the offense to get another receiver downfield quickly in an open area of the field. The defense sometimes attempts to hit a receiver as he leaves the line of scrimmage and make it difficult for him to run his pre-designated route. Corner linebackers often try to do this to the tight end. The split of the flanker enables him to avoid being detained at the line. In sure passing situations, the corner line-backers will sometimes move out and line up *directly in front of* the wide receivers, trying to detain them or force them to change their predetermined route.

The flanker's position outside the tight end allows the defense to employ the use of specific combination (two man) pass patterns. These combination patterns can be run by any two eligible pass receivers including the offensive backs, but the proximity to each other of the tight end and the flanker make them highly effective. Other combinations are frequently run between the set back and tight end, the two set backs and even the two wide receivers.

## SPLIT END

There are few differences between the flanker and split end. The bigger receiver will probably be placed at split end since he may have to block more than the flanker. There is no tight end on his side and he may be forced to block down on the corner linebacker or defensive end on outside plays. Like most pro football players, split ends are getting bigger all the time. Nevertheless, there is still a wide range of shapes and sizes. Harold Jackson of the Los Angeles Rams stands 5'10" and weighs no more than 175 pounds, while Harold Carmichael of the Philadelphia Eagles stands 6'8" tall and weighs 235 pounds.

Coaches prefer split ends to be in the 6'2" to 6'5" range, but will give the shorter player a good look if he has exceptional speed.

He must be tough and display the ability to catch the ball in a crowd. The big man may be given the benefit of the doubt if he drops the ball once or twice when the defender is breathing down his neck, but the little guy rarely gets a second chance.

Many wide receivers in pro football today were running backs in college. Charley Taylor comes to mind immediately. The player that is too light or not durable enough to play in the offensive backfield will be tried as an outside receiver. Some fine running backs have extended their careers several years by switching to wide receiver after an injury. Rick Upchurch of the Denver Broncos and Ron Jessie of the Rams were fine running backs in college but weren't big enough to make it to the pros as runners and turned out to be outstanding wide receivers. Frank Gifford started out as a pro running back and then drifted to wide receiver after sustaining a serious head injury which forced him out of the game for an entire season.

The reasons for splitting the end are the same as those for splitting the flanker. The split also forces the defense to adjust (rotate) to him, in an attempt to take away some of his operating room and assist the defender assigned to cover him.

## TIGHT END

The tight end is stationed right next to one of the offensive tackles. Whether in the pros, on a high school team, or in college, he is always cut out of the same mold. He should be tough enough to block down on the defensive end and fast enough to get downfield to snare a pass. They seem to be getting bigger and faster all the time, but it is doubtful that anyone will come up with tight end bigger than Morris Stroud of the Kansas City Chiefs. He was 6'10" tall and weighed 265 pounds, but lacked the speed and agility to last long in the N.F.L. Other abilities being equal, size not only aids the tight end's blocking effectiveness in the running game, but helps him in going over the middle to catch a pass. Most receivers dislike catching anything over the middle where they are likely to be hit by two or more people after catching the ball. The bigger the tight end, the better the chance of his outfighting the defender for the ball.

Teams throw to their tight ends more often when the defense is in a zone or when they expect to see double coverage on the wide receiver. Almost all the tight ends in the N.F.L. now have the speed to go long, but most of the time the tight end will be used to run short routes. There may be enough time for him to run deep routes but the chance of his being detained on the line of scrimmage by the corner linebacker makes the shorter pass more attractive to the normally conservative N.F.L. coach. The reason the tight end is used more against the zone is the difficulty of throwing deep to anyone when the defense is in zone coverage. Most teams use the wide receivers to spread the zone (since they can get off the line faster), and then try to hit their tight ends and set backs on short and medium patterns between the defenders in the dead spots (see diagram on page175). Because of the increased use of the zone in pro football, the prerequisite for a tight end is speed. Coaches now seem to be willing to sacrifice some blocking ability for a 4.4 second time in the 40-yard dash.

Much depends on the coach and his philosophy. Rich Caster was originally placed at the outside receiver position for the Jets. They moved him to tight end in order to capitalize on his size and (more importantly) his speed. The change brought Pro Bowl status for Caster. He was a constant threat as a receiver, but his blocking left something to be desired. When Walt Michaels took over as Jet head coach in 1977, he moved Caster back outside and the smaller Jerome Barkum was placed inside. Blocking was never mentioned as one of the reasons for the switch, but it had to be the underlying reason.

## VARIATIONS IN ALIGNMENT

When aligned in a standard pro-set, many teams will flip flop the flanker and split end. (The flanker will always be on the side of the tight end.) However, the physical requirements of the two wide receivers are similar and, in most instances, flip flopping is not essential. Those coaches that require it contend that the tight end and flanker get to know each other better and operate more efficiently. It also forces the cornerbacks on both sides to learn the moves of both wide receivers. Those coaches that always keep their wide receivers on the same side, regardless of the position of the tight end, claim that it is a definite asset for a wide receiver to play opposite the same cornerback on every play. He has a better opportunity to learn the cornerback's weaknesses and set up his routes. It is an individual matter in most cases. Some receivers feel better on one side of the field. Others are better blockers and if a team prefers to run to either the strong or weak side it allows them to use their best blocker more often.

Professional teams will sometimes use three wide receivers in a game at one time. The third wide receiver may replace either a set back or the tight end, and line up on the wing or in the slot to either side. This set up is most often used in an obvious passing situation or when a team has fallen behind by several touchdowns and every play is a passing situation.

The reasons for using three wide receivers are the same as those for placing both the split end and flanker on the same side of the field. It enhances the prospects of completing a pass by getting both downfield more quickly and increases the prospects of isolating one defender on a receiver. The third wide receiver requires no special skills and will generally be a reserve split end or flanker.

## FUNDAMENTALS

The receiving corps uses many of the skills required by players at other positions. The tight end is like another offensive tackle on running plays to his side of the line. In such cases, he might be assigned to block the linebacker or defensive end to his inside. He uses the same technique as the offensive linemen in this situation. When the wide receiver cracks back or throws a block on someone else downfield, he uses the same technique as any other player throwing a downfield block. After catching the ball, the receiver becomes a ball carrier using his techniques. Let's look at the fundamental skills that are *peculiar* to the receiver.

### The Stance

Generally, of the three receivers found in the standard pro-set, the only one that is likely to be down in a three point stance is the tight end. You will sometimes see a wide receiver down in a three point stance, but rarely at the pro level. The two wide receivers stand erect (usually with their hands on their hips), and look at the quarterback in order to better hear the signals. Standing also allows them to scan the defensive secondary which may help when running patterns.

The tight end gets into a three point stance since he is likely to have someone nearby that he must block. Placing one hand on the turf puts him at the right height to make a block and allows him to leave the line with the impetus required for effective blocking. It is virtually impossible to block effectively from a standing position.

Another reason the tight end should be in a stance on every play is because he is the one receiver the defense is likely to try to hit and slow up on the line regularly. He does not have the room to elude the defender as the wide receivers do.

### Faking

Faking a defender while running a pass route is an art. Fakes vary with each receiver's style, speed and experience. The particular pattern called and the type of defense used also have to be considered. Here are the more basic fakes used by receivers:

*Head and Shoulder Fake*—The receiver throws his head, shoulder and arms in one direction, and breaks the opposite way. For this reason, all young defensive backs are advised not to look at the receiver's upper torso. They are told to look at the belt buckle (which many claim doesn't work either). At the pro level, you may find the defender looking at almost anything to get a tip as to where the receiver will make his final break. Some will look at a receiver's eyes to see where he is looking. Others claim that the feet are the answer. The only thing that is for certain is that there is

Jerome Barkum has planted his foot after the reception and is in good position to cut around his defender.

no consensus of opinion. The receiver should make his fakes without breaking his stride.

*Foot Plant*—If time permits, the receiver can plant a foot in one direction before breaking the opposite way. This maneuver will often be combined with the head and shoulder fake. The foot plant is really a means of making a cut, rather than a faking tactic. But, it often has the effect of a fake.

*Look Back*—The receiver may stop his forward motion completely or merely turn to look at the quarterback as if he were expecting the ball. Again, the arms and hands play an important role, since the receiver should look as if he is about to catch the ball. Remember that the defender does not look into the backfield all the time. He generally looks for the ball only when the receiver does. The "look back" is done to distract the defender and cause him to begin looking for the ball. The receiver then continues to run his route.

*Change of Pace*—This type of faking does not require any extraordinary movement on the part of the receiver. He merely runs directly at the defender at ¾ or ⅞ speed and then suddenly begins to run at full speed in an attempt to outdistance the defender. The change of pace may also be effective if the receiver moves his legs at full speed but uses short strides, and then breaks into a full stride.

*Blocking Fake*—This is used most often by the tight end, but wide receivers sometimes fake a block on a player before running a pass route. Excellent pass protection is required when used by the wide receiver since the play will be slow in developing. The tight end can fake the block on either the corner linebacker or the defensive end. If the strong safety is assigned to cover him, he may look to help elsewhere when he sees the end block on the line.

*Lull the Opposition to Sleep*—The receiver attempts to cause the defender to relax by running several sloppy patterns at half speed when he is not the primary receiver. On the third or fourth play, when he *is* the primary receiver, he comes off the line "hell bent for election."

## PASS PATTERNS

The terms "route" and "pattern" are used interchangeably in most quarters. However, professionals regard the "route" as the path of the individual receiver and the "pattern" as the combination of routes by all receivers. The precision with which one route is run is likely to affect the position of the other receivers in relation to the defenders. Look for sharp cuts and exact timing on those passes that are thrown at a predetermined time or spot on the field.

It may often be difficult to determine whether it was the quarter-back or receiver that did not time the break perfectly. The pass rush put on the quarterback, the type of coverage used by the defenders, or the pattern the receiver ran might provide a tip-off as to who fouled up. If the quarterback was about to be hit and the ball was thrown before the receiver made his break, it probably was the quarterback who threw too soon. If the quarterback was not rushed, but the receiver was harrassed by an interfering linebacker, it probably was the receiver's fault.

After running a proper and well-timed route, the next thing the receiver should be thinking about is looking at and catching the ball. Many receivers claim that concentration is the key to catching the football. Remember that there are many distractions while the receiver is simultaneously running his route and keeping an eye on the ball in mid-air. He must be aware of the sideline, the goal posts, the defender covering him and other people in the secondary who may have a shot at him after he catches the ball. He must be aware of all these factors, but should not be distracted by them. If he takes his eye off of the football to look at the sideline or an approaching defender, his chances of dropping the ball are much greater. It's like finding a mosquito flying around a room. If you lose track of it, you may not find it again until it lands on a wall. When the ball approaches, the receiver should catch it with his hands extended from his body. He must remain relaxed and try to keep his hands soft as the ball touches them. They should give slightly on impact.

Here is what John Madden has to say about hands and the receiver: "You can't hear good hands. There is no loud slap of leather on skin. That's because with a good receiver the fingertips are stopping the ball, not the palms." Madden claims that his outstanding receiver with the Oakland Raiders, Fred Biletnikoff, has those good hands. There isn't a pass defender in the league who would disagree, although some have complained about the amount of "stickum" used by Biletnikoff. (It is commonplace for some receivers to place a sticky substance on their hands before a game and at halftime.) I have asked several receivers the official name of that substance, but none seem to know. There are defenders who would swear that Biletnikoff sprays not only his hands, but his arms, legs and football jersey as well. If you look at his sweat socks you will see globs of the paste-like form of stickum in case the spray has worn off while he is on the playing field. The substance can help a receiver, but there is no rule against using it and Fred Biletnikoff is a great receiver with or without "stickum."

After the receiver catches the ball, there is only one thing for him to do. Run in the right direction. This is something that can't be taught or developed very much. Running with the football is probably the most instinctive skill of all those developed by any player. Some players have exceptional ability to pick up yardage after the catch has been made; others can only pick up a few yards.

## Individual Pass Routes

A successful pass offense is highly dependent on individual successes. On each completed pass play, the quarterback must throw the ball well and the defender must be outmaneuvered by the receiver. The accompanying diagrams give the basic individual routes used by most teams. The individual routes become patterns when two people run them in the same area of the field.

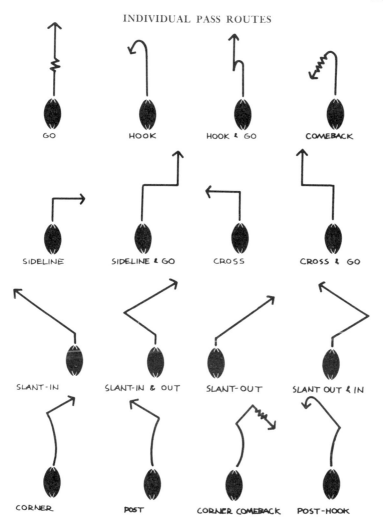

INDIVIDUAL PASS ROUTES

GO    HOOK    HOOK & GO    COMEBACK

SIDELINE    SIDELINE & GO    CROSS    CROSS & GO

SLANT-IN    SLANT-IN & OUT    SLANT-OUT    SLANT OUT & IN

CORNER    POST    CORNER COMEBACK    POST-HOOK

Multiple patterns are plays that have three or more receivers running routes that influence each other. Every team has its own terminology and favorite patterns. Here are brief descriptions of the basic routes and what the receiver and quarterback are trying to accomplish:

*Go, Fly, Streak*—The receiver runs straight up the field as quickly as possible without altering his course. He may use a head or leg fake to the outside along with a change of pace, but speed is of the essence. This is one of the few routes where the receiver tries to outrun the defender.

*Sideline, Out, Square Out*—On this route the receiver usually runs 8 to 12 yards straight downfield and makes a 90-degree cut toward the sideline. Receivers vary in the way they run this route but there is seldom much faking. Sharp cuts and timing between the quarterback and the receiver are more important. The quarterback must work with the receiver and anticipate his cut. The ball should be thrown before the receiver makes his final break for the sideline. The receiver should try to assume a sideline position with his body that will force the defender to go over him to reach the ball in the event that he has anticipated the break. Timing must be perfect since an interception on the sideline is likely to be returned for a long gain or a touchdown.

*Sideline and Go, Out and Up, Square Out and Go*—The receiver runs a sideline route, but after making his break and feinting an attempt to catch the ball, he breaks straight up the field on a "go" route. This is an excellent route if the sideline has been run several times and the receiver expects the defender to anticipate and try for an interception. The fake by the receiver, in this instance, may not be as important as a pump (fake throw) by the quarterback, since the defender will probably be looking for the ball after the sideline break.

*Cross, Square In, Cross In*—This route is run exactly like the *sideline* except that the break is made to the inside. Timing is equally important although the quarterback does not try to anticipate the receiver's final cut. On the cross, or any pass over the middle, the quarterback must throw *between the linebackers* and not on the break of the receiver. The chance of an interception is greater on the *cross* than on the *sideline*, since the football tends to attract a crowd and there are more people to attract over the middle.

*Slant, Look-In, Diagonal*—Some teams distinguish between a slant and a diagonal route. The difference, if any, is minor. The receiver runs two or three steps and then breaks over the middle at a 45 degree angle. Once again, the quarterback must wait until the receiver comes free and throws the ball between the linebackers.

This is a tough route on the receiver since he is likely to be hit by any number of people after catching the ball. The ball, on this route, is thrown at waist level and the receiver only has a split second to decide whether to catch it with his hands up or down

*Slant-In and Slant-Out, Look-In and Look-Out*—The receiver starts to run a slant route and hopefully the defender will close in on him as the quarterback fakes a pass. The receiver will then complete the pattern by running at an angle toward the sideline.

*Corner, Flag*—The *corner* can be run from anywhere on the field, but is usually run to the wide side of the field. The term *flag* comes from the fact that the receiver breaks toward the red flag at the corner of the field. Once again, it should be pointed out that each receiver will run these routes differently. The position of the ball in relation to the sideline will determine whether or not the receiver moves toward the middle of the field before breaking toward the corner. This pattern requires an exceptionally strong throw by the quarterback.

*Post*—The post route is run similarly to the corner, except that the final break is made toward the goal post. The receiver tries to run straight at the defender, as he does on most routes, to prevent the defender from giving him only one side on which to make his break. The distance the receiver travels before breaking for the goal post will vary according to the depth of the defenders and the distance required for the first down.

*Hook, Comeback*—Most teams distinguish between these two routes. Basically, they are similar. The receiver may or may not run full speed as he leaves the line. Some prefer to hold back a little and then put on a burst of speed as they approach the defender, hoping that the defender will think that he is going deep on a *fly* or *go* route. The receiver then stops abruptly and turns to face the quarterback. As on the *sideline* route, the quarterback attempts to anticipate the receiver's move and release the ball before the receiver stops and turns. This is the *hook* route.

The *comeback* is run exactly the same way with the receiver coming back two or three yards toward the quarterback to catch the football. Unlike the hook, the ball is not thrown before the receiver turns. The ball is thrown low to the ground and the position of the receiver's body is expected to keep the defender away. The defender must always go over the top of him to stop the play.

*Hook and Go*—After running the hook, the quarterback pumps once and the receiver then breaks on a *go* route upfield. The success of the *hook and go* depends on how closely the defender is playing the receiver. If he is laying off and looking for the long pass, there is not much chance that it will work. This route requires good pass protection since it often takes longer to run than other patterns.

## Combination Patterns

It should be easy enough to distinguish between the various routes when looking at individual receivers. However, it takes more concentration, study and a high seat in the stadium to see the total pattern developing. You can see some of the most common combination or two man patterns in the accompanying diagrams. The combination pattern is used against the zone to force the defender to make a choice and cover one of the two receivers in

COMBINATION PATTERNS

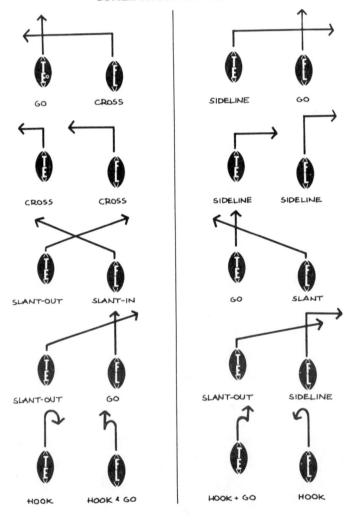

| GO | CROSS | SIDELINE | GO |
| CROSS | CROSS | SIDELINE | SIDELINE |
| SLANT-OUT | SLANT-IN | GO | SLANT |
| SLANT-OUT | GO | SLANT-OUT | SIDELINE |
| HOOK | HOOK & GO | HOOK + GO | HOOK |

his area. The quarterback reads the defender and not the receivers. He knows where his receivers are going, but does not know which receiver will be covered by the defender. In many cases, the quarterback will key or read two defenders to help determine which of his receivers running a combination pattern will be free.

The defender that the quarterback reads against the zone will vary with each pattern and with the type of coverage. This is why the quarterback looks for tips as to what the coverage will be doing before the play starts. A tip-off will give him more time to read the important defenders after the snap of the ball. Exactly who the defenders will be, will depend upon whether the zone defence is rotating to the strong side or to the weak side.

MULTIPLE PASS PATTERNS

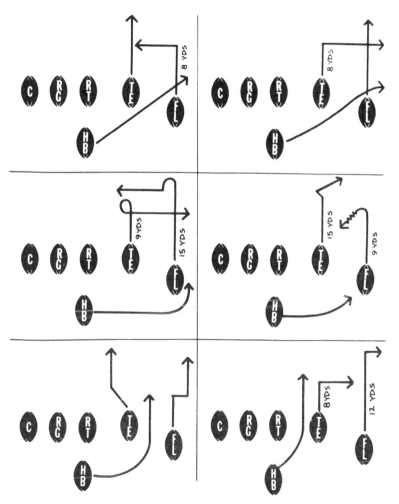

Against man for man coverage, the combination pattern helps to assure that all defenders in the area will be occupied. This allows the quarterback to isolate the primary receiver on the play. In this case, the quarterback may not be looking at either of the defenders he expects to be covering the two men involved in the combination pattern. He may look at a third defender, close to the area, who may provide assistance to one of the primary defenders. He will throw to the receiver furthest from him. The thing that makes it difficult for the quarterback is that he never knows where the defenders will move after the play begins.

## Multiple Patterns

The multiple patterns shown here are based on similar principles. They are used to flood (send more receivers into an area than there are defenders) or dissect (spread apart) the zone. Multiple patterns are also effective in isolating a defender on a wide receiver or running back. It stands to reason that the more receivers involved in the pattern, the greater the chances of breaking one free. The disadvantage of multiple patterns is that they take longer to develop and usually require that a back come out of the backfield. This removes an extra pass protector at a time when he is most needed. Most multiple patterns are run from drop-back (show pass) protection.

I have not included the split end in any of the multiple patterns diagrammed. He can be worked into patterns with the set backs or into slower developing patterns with the two other receivers coming from the opposite side of the line. When the split end moves into the slot on the side of the flanker, many possible combinations develop with what should be the two best and most dangerous receivers on the team.

## Special Situations

In addition to the patterns discussed above, there are certain basic situations which all fans should understand.

*Timing Patterns*—When devising patterns, there are different approaches a team may employ to help the quarterback find the free receiver. Some teams run "timing patterns" which help the quarterback find his second and third receiver if the primary one is covered. Each receiver runs downfield a different distance before breaking and looking at the quarterback. For example, the flanker may break to the sideline at seven yards. If he is not free, the quarterback knows that the tight end will be running a *comeback* at 14 yards, and if he is not free, he knows that the split end will be making a deep cut for the post or corner. Because of

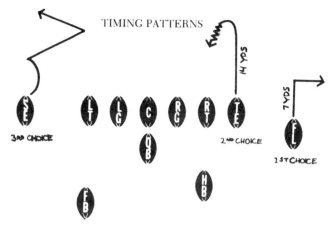

the varying distances each receiver will run, each will be making his final break at a different time. Knowing this helps the quarterback adjust and find the free man.

*Choice Patterns*—Experienced quarterbacks and receivers sometimes practice running choice routes. The receiver will be given the option of breaking in one of two or three directions as he runs his route. He keys the defender covering him and others close by as he moves downfield. The final break is made in the direction where he will receive least resistance. Both the receiver and quarterback should be on the same wave length since the quarterback must read the defense the same way as the receiver. All this takes practice and experience and should only be attempted by veteran players who have been playing together for an extended period of time.

*Scrambling*—Granted that it's hard to take your eyes off of Terry Bradshaw or Fran Tarkenton when he begins to scramble after being forced from the pocket. However, it's interesting to take a peak downfield from time to time to see what the receivers are doing. The first thing you are likely to see are many people waving their arms in an attempt to attract the quarterback's attention. The longer the quarterback scrambles, the more frantic the arm waving becomes. When the quarterback scrambles, it is not hard to break free of a defender, even if the defense is in man coverage. All this points out the importance of giving the receiver enough time to elude the defender. Almost any receiver can get free if he is given enough time. The problem the scrambling quarterback has is that he often loses sight of his receivers and has trouble finding them again.

When the quarterback begins to scramble, most receivers will drift back toward the line of scrimmage in the direction the quarterback is running. The receiver that stays by himself on the opposite side of the field might be free, but it is doubtful that he will be spotted by the quarterback unless he changes his direction.

*The Pick*—A "pick" occurs when an offensive receiver moves between another receiver and the defender assigned to cover his teammate. Because of his size and closeness to the middle of the field, the tight end is often called on to pick or screen for a teammate. The tight end may "pick" the corner linebacker, safety or middle linebacker. When you see both backs flaring to the same side, check to see where the tight end is moving. If he is running an extremely shallow slant and manages to force the middle linebacker to go over or around him, he is running a pick.

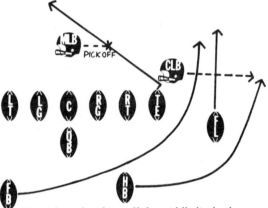

The tight end picking off the middle linebacker.

Remember that blocking beyond the line of scrimmage is prohibited on a pass play. However, there are no restrictions on where a receiver may run to catch a pass. Any receiver may run a path that "accidentally" causes him to obstruct the path of a defender attempting to cover another receiver.

*Man in Motion*—The man in motion should be watched from time to time. Most often he is a decoy. Offensive teams use a man in motion to distract the secondary and force a last minute adjustment. The man in motion running in front of a defender draws his attention, and at times confuses the defense enough to allow a completion. The way the defense reacts to the man in motion will indicate whether the defense is in zone or man coverage. If the defense makes an adjustment, they are probably in man to man coverage; if it doesn't, they are in a zone.

## THINGS TO LOOK FOR

There is more room for individuality among receivers than at any other position on the team. Routes and patterns are important, but what is more interesting is how the individual reacts and moves to get to his assigned area. An experienced receiver, like Haven Moses of Denver, may run three corner routes in a row, each time making a different series of moves and occasionally changing the route itself. This is why it is so important for the receiver and the quarterback to get to know each other. The receiver may very often be forced to alter his course because of the position of the defender assigned to him or the position of someone else in the secondary. For the quarterback to adjust to these unplanned changes, he and the receiver have to be thinking almost as one. Moses is reading the defender while running a route and will make adjustments. He looks primarily at his eyes and feet. If the defender is looking or has his feet going in one direction and Moses believes his quarterback can adjust, he is likely to break in the other direction. Craig Morton has to be ready to anticipate and adjust to his movements.

The increased use of zone coverage has complicated the lives of receivers. Fred Biletnikoff gives us some idea of the problems facing the receiver: "With these damn zones it's harder than ever to get open, but that only makes it more fun when you do. You've got to read them as they develop, and then show them different looks from the line of scrimmage to keep the defenders guessing. If you give a guy the same look every time, he'll play you the same way. But, if in the first 10 or 12 yards you are doing something different but ending up in the same spot, then you've got him guessing. That's how you find out how good a defensive back is, by putting a little challenge to him. He starts asking himself: 'What are you going to do to me now?' For me, that's the fun part of the game, when it gets to be a guessing game."

The best receivers not only have a knack for getting free, but also for hanging on to the ball. Coaches are usually unimpressed by the player that comes up with the outstanding one-handed catch repeatedly. The great players at all positions frequently have a facility for making the difficult look easy. If at all possible, receivers are encouraged to get two hands on the football.

Even the finest receivers in the N.F.L. will drop passes that they should hold on to. There are certain things to look for when a receiver doesn't hold on to a ball that hits his hands. One of the most frequent causes is what is commonly called "hearing foot-steps." All this means is that the receiver is paying more attention to the defender than to the ball. Look for this over the middle where there is likely to be a defender in front of the receiver coming up hard and fast to make the tackle. The good ones will ignore the potential tackler and concentrate on the ball. Rich Caster, of the Jets, had a problem holding on to the ball during his first years in the league. He was not dropping them in a crowd though. It was merely a problem of concentration which caused him to take his eyes off the ball. Weeb Ewbank stayed with him and by the end of his second season, he had overcome his problem. Wesley Walker had a similar problem in his rookie year. Walt Michaels vowed to stick with him, but it's too early to tell if he will have the same success as Caster. He certainly has the speed and ability to lose a defender.

There are certain passes that are harder to catch than others. The receiver on a "go" or "fly" pattern is looking for the ball over his inside shoulder. A ball that is thrown to the outside requires him to turn at the last minute and makes the reception much more difficult since he must take his eyes off of the ball for a split second. The ball that is thrown directly overhead when running this route is even more difficult to catch. It is hard to follow while in the air and most receivers have a problem extending their arms directly in front of them, because of the backward position of their head.

Another pass that frequently makes both the quarterback and the receiver look bad is the quick pass to the tight end over the middle. He too is looking over his inside shoulder. Because the pass does not travel very far in the air, he has trouble turning to catch the ball if it is thrown behind him. Many tight ends have a problem holding on to this type of pass. They know the linebacker assigned to cover them and other defenders are not far away and this hurts their concentration. They are also thinking about what they will do once they catch the football instead of about holding onto it.

Catching the ball is only one aspect of the receiver's job. Getting into a position to be able to catch the football is just as important. We mentioned the importance of speed; but there are and have been many outstanding receivers without exceptional speed. Few receivers brag about how they outran a defender, but they all seem to receive great satisfaction from putting on a few moves which enable them to move (turn) the defender out of position. The good, experienced receivers attempt to get the defensive player to turn one way and then break in the opposite direction. Watch the receiver's moves as he proceeds downfield. The good ones will cut and fake without slowing down. Their moves will be sharp and precise rather than rolling or looping cuts. Those with exceptional speed are often guilty of that type of sloppy move. The question is if those with great speed avoid making sharp moves because they rely on their speed and don't concentrate on their moves, or if the speed at which they are running makes such moves more difficult.

The fan should try to determine whether the defense is in man or zone coverage. Specifically, he should see if the defense is doing anything that might cause the quarterback to favor one receiver and ignore another. The Baltimore Colts double teamed Don Maynard much of the time during their Super Bowl Game. Maynard didn't get to touch the football very much that day, but his role was important. Namath ignored him and threw to the other receivers, well aware of the fact that there are not enough defenders to double cover every receiver. Just because a receiver is double covered or only a decoy on a play is no reason for him to stop running precise patterns at full speed. Many receivers take it easy when they know they are not going to get the ball. What they should be doing is attempting to set up the defender for the next play or experimenting to try to determine where he is vulnerable. Fred Biletnikoff is one receiver who excels because of his diligence and the preciseness of his routes.

The fan that has a basic understanding of combination and multiple patterns should have a better chance of determining who is at fault when the quarterback throws the ball and there seems to be no receiver in sight. If you see two receivers close enough to shake hands in one area, and the ball falls near no one in particular, you can safely assume that the receiver broke his pattern. When the receiver is well covered by one or two men and the ball lands far from everyone, you can assume the quarterback threw it away intentionally in order to avoid an interception or getting thrown for a loss.

Everyone is aware of the necessity for the quarterback to be able to read defenses. The *receiver* must also be aware of what the defense is doing. It does not help for the quarterback to read the weak safety blitz unless the split end also reads it and has the presence of mind to cut over the middle into the area vacated by the safety. This is standard procedure whenever the offense reads the blitz, since the cornerback will have difficulty in covering the area without tipping the coverage. Since the offensive team does not know whether the defense will be in zone or man coverage, constant adjustments are necessary. The quarterback may have called a *go* route in the huddle, anticipating man coverage. The defense may be in zone coverage, however, making the *go* route difficult to run. Instead of continuing with the route, the wide receiver should hook up into one of the dead spots of the zone. Many hook passes which develop against the zone are pre-planned adjustments of this type.

Another important factor to be considered in evaluating the receiver is the aggressivenss he displays when attempting to catch the football. The good ones don't wait for the football when it is underthrown or comes down in a crowd. They go up prepared to fight for the ball and try to catch it at the highest point possible. If the receiver can jump as high as the defender and he catches the ball at its highest point, there is not much chance of an interception. The good receiver that sees that the ball is underthrown, will try to slow down momentarily and then catch the ball on the dead run rather than sit and wait for the ball to come down. Remember that the defender is unaware of when the ball is thrown until he

Fred Biletnikoff catches the ball at its highest point while ignoring the "footsteps" behind him.

sees the receiver going for it. The defender is constantly looking at the receiver as they both run downfield. This gives the receiver an opportunity to dictate terms to the defender.

Before each play, the viewer should be aware not only of the type of coverage, but whether the cornerbacks are playing tight or loose. Their depth depends on the receivers' speed and the situation on the field. As a general rule, the defender in man coverage will play a "move" man, tightly and a receiver with exceptional speed, loosely. By knowing where the first down marker is, the receivers' strengths, how the defenders are playing them, what patterns have been working, the condition of the field and the wind factor, you can often come close to predicting who is likely to be the receiver and when he will make his final break.

The weather and field conditions will influence the extent to which a team uses the forward pass and the type of passing game it goes with. I have never been able to get a consensus of opinion as to who has the advantage on a sloppy field. Some claim that the advantage is with the offensive player since he knows where he is running and is therefore better able to cut. The defensive player, on the other hand, has to react to the movement of the receiver and can't plant his feet securely. Others claim that the key to a receiver's success is his ability to run precise and sharp patterns. Since this cannot be done on a sloppy field, the advantage lies with the defender. I tend to believe that the advantage is with the receiver if it has stopped raining and the ball is dry. If it is still raining, his advantage will be negated by the wet ball which is more difficult to throw and catch.

One aspect that should be considered in evaluating a receiver, and rarely is, is the way that he positions his body. One of the primary responsibilities of a pass catcher is to maintain a position that prevents the defender from having a good shot at the ball. Most of the time it means keeping his body between the defender and the ball or moving into that position as the ball approaches. On short and medium distance passes, this is particularly important. When an end goes up over the middle, he knows that he will be hit. There will be less chance of the ball being jarred loose if his body is in front of it.

Passes that are on target, but are intercepted, are almost always the result of a gamble by the defensive back. In effect, this means that he was playing unusually tight and not guarding against the bomb. As a result, he was in good position to cut in front of the receiver or dive for the ball. He may also have anticipated a particular pattern and been in the right spot at the right time. If he is constantly playing tight, you can bet that he will be burned for a long pass before long. Interceptions may even occur when the ball

Rich Caster protects the ball by getting between the ball and the defender.

is thrown well. But a receiver who has too many passes intercepted on him may not be using his body well, or may be neglecting to fight for the football.

Look for consistency and the ability to deliver under pressure from the receivers. The flashy or speedy receiver isn't always the answer. There have been too many Olympic sprinters who tried to make it and failed miserable for anyone to believe that speed alone is the answer. Ray Norton and John Carlos are two examples. Raymond Berry, of the Baltimore Colts, is probably the best example of a player with just average ability who achieved stardom. He had less than average speed, but an abundance of the mental and emotional qualities required for success. He was tough and dedicated to being the best at his business of catching the football, and the stories about the many hours he devoted to perfecting his pass routes have become legendary. The proof of the pudding is that he held the record for the most career receptions with 631 for many years until Don Maynard surpassed it with 633. Charley Taylor of the Redskins now holds the record with 647.

Statistics alone don't tell the story. A wide receiver working with Ken Stabler is likely to have more bombs thrown his way and more total yardage than a receiver playing with the Washington Redskins with Billy Kilmer at quarterback. Kilmer is regarded as a good quarterback, but is not widely heralded for possessing a strong arm. His completion percentage is always high, but most of the yardage comes after the ball is caught.

To show how a quarterback can influence a receiver's statistics, Don Maynard was not a serious threat to Berry's record until Joe Namath joined the Jets in 1965. If he had played with Namath from the beginning of his career, he would have surpassed Berry's yardage total sooner. Berry was on the end of passes thrown by one of the all-time greats in John Unitas. A winning team with a balanced attack makes it easier for a receiver to catch the football and Berry played most of his career on good teams. Charley Taylor had the opportunity to be on the other end of Sonny Jurgenson's passes for a good part of his long and illustrious career. Jurgenson was one of the better passers the N.F.L. has seen.

Lance Alworth was the most exciting and dangerous receiver I ever saw. He could make the "impossible catch" seem ordinary. Alworth has played on some good teams and some weak ones. But, he has had the advantage of playing on a team with an explosive offense. For most of his career, the San Diego Chargers, with John Hadl at quarterback, were fond of the passing game. Playing with other good receivers also helped. Alworth was not quite as effective after moving on to the more run-conscious Dallas Cowboys.

The effect of the quarterback on the success of the receivers is obvious. However, the importance of the effectiveness of the running game is often neglected. The running back must be good enough to keep the defense honest, but not so good that the running game becomes the dominant factor. A dominant running game might make for a successful team, but not for high priced receivers. The wide receivers on the Green Bay Packers under Vince Lombardi probably received less acclaim than the offensive guards. A coaching philosophy that places equal emphasis on the pass and run represents the ideal situation for the receiver.

In conclusion, there are many factors that go into making an outstanding receiver. He should have good speed. He should be able to hold onto the football (good hands). He should be bright enough to read defenses and work together with the quarterback. He should be a good blocker. He should be able to run after catching the football. He should have the perseverance to continue to run good routes even when his team is running the football or he is not the intended receiver. Obviously, the receiver should be a good all-around athlete.

Be aware of the difficulty in evaluating the performance of the receiver. As with the quarterback, it frequently cannot be done after watching him perform in one game.

# 5

# THE DEFENSIVE LINE
## The Men with Baser Instincts

Before Fred Dryer left the New York Giants to join the Los Angeles Rams, he saw fit to blast the New York sportswriters. His words have special meaning to anyone who has ever played in the middle of the offensive or defensive lines. The headline stated: "Defensive end says those who cite statistics on pass rush fail in objectivity." Dryer then went on to complain about those reporters whom he claimed did not really understand the game, but insisted on drawing conclusions based on facts which are readily apparent but which may or may not tell the entire story. He was talking about things like: Is the Giant pass rush inadequate and worthy of criticism, or is their defense against the running game the actual weakness? Dryer went on to say: "It irritates me to have somebody criticize my profession unless he knows what he is talking about." Amen!

Dryer's complaint is probably universal among football players, and especially among those up front on both the offensive and defensive lines. It is the total effort of a lineman or unit that must be evaluated, and not isolated aspects of their play. The fan or reporter should not conclude that Fred Dryer or any lineman is not getting a good rush on the passer simply because he has not thrown him for a loss. This is not to imply that statistics are meaningless or that what is most obvious is invariably misleading. However, other aspects of play must be considered. Has Fred Dryer been double teamed throughout the game? Did the offensive team use maximum protection by keeping the tight end and running backs in to block most of the time? Has the offensive team run with the football most of the time and provided few opportunities to throw the passer for a loss?

I found Dryer's statements particularly interesting because the viewer who does have a basic understanding of the play of the defensive end, and has watched Fred Dryer closely, will certainly avoid criticizing his pass rush. He is more likely to find fault with other aspects of his play. His weakness is the running game, not the passing game.

## POSITIONS

There are usually anywhere from three to eight men on the defensive line, depending on the level of football you are watching and the situation on the field. For a while, it was fashionable for football broadcasters to identify the defense with such terminology as the 6-1-4, the 6-2-3, or the 6-3-2. The first number in the group identified the number of defensive people who lined up on the line of scrimmage; the number in the middle represented the number of linebackers; and the last digit represented the number of people in the deep secondary. Eventually, they simply eliminated the final digit and said 6-1, 6-2, or 6-3 assuming that the listener could add to 11 and that those not accounted for would be found in the secondary. The pros almost always utilize four defensive linemen—two tackles and two ends.

Let's take a look at the people who make up the defensive line.

### The Defensive Tackles

The two interior defensive linemen, whether they both line up over the guards or one is on the center's nose, are called defensive tackles. Back in the late '50's and early '60's players were chosen to play defensive tackle solely on the basis of size. Big Daddy Lipscomb, of the Baltimore Colts, and Rosie Grier, of the Giants and Rams, had to be defensive tackles since they were the biggest men on their teams and the biggest men were always played at defensive tackle. They were placed in the middle because it was thought that less running and speed were required there.

Attitudes toward size have changed, but weight is still considered important for the defensive tackle. He no longer has to be of the Rosie Grier variety, but if he doesn't scale at least 250 pounds, he probably will not be able to handle the position. A defensive tackle's weight affects his ability to stand his ground. It becomes especially important when a player is hit from the side and doesn't have an opportunity to brace himself and unload on the offensive lineman with a forearm and shoulder. This is likely to happen to the defensive tackle when being blocked by one of the two men flanking the one he is playing opposite.

The need for size in the middle of the defensive line was even more important during the era of the single wing, and immediately thereafter, when there was more double team blocking. There is no substitute for size when a player is fighting off two men at one time.

There is less double team blocking in professional football today. Most offensive teams now rely on speed and versatility rather than power. Today's blocking strategy emphasizes quickness and technique. A defensive lineman does not have to be moved clear out of the runner's path for his coach to pat him on the back. The offensive lineman that manages to keep contact just long enough for a fast running back to squirm by the defensive tackle has done his job well. Consequently, many teams have gone

The Baltimore Colt front four—one of the best. From left to right: John Dutton, Joe Ehrmann, Mike Barnes and Fred Cook.

to the smaller and faster defensive linemen, and no longer necessarily place the biggest men on the inside. The Green Bay Packers and the late Henry Jordan probably did more to convince people that it wasn't necessary to weight 300 pounds to be a defensive tackle, than anyone else. Jordan probably never played at more than 245 pounds, but once he had his fundamentals down, he was as good as they come. Paul Brown didn't make too many mistakes, but giving up on Henry Jordan, when coaching the Cleveland Browns, was one of them.

## The Defensive Ends

Defensive ends are required to have quickness and good lateral movement. They also need size. Their primary responsibility is to stop the off-tackle play, but they are also expected to contain the passer and help stop the outside running game. Quickness and good lateral movement are important for the latter two responsibilites, but size is an asset in stopping the off-tackle play. The offensive tackles are almost always the largest people on the offensive team. In many cases, they are now the biggest men on the entire team. The defensive end will not be double teamed or blocked from the side as often as the defensive tackles, but he must contend with the large offensive tackles. He should weigh a minimum of 245 pounds.

In the past, the defensive ends were almost always smaller than the defensive tackles. A defensive end with the dimensions of Fred Dryer would have been more effective when the offensive tackles were not as large as they are today. For many years, one of the finest defensive ends in the N.F.L. was a 230-pounder named Andy Robustelli. He would never even be considered for an end slot today. In fact, the way players have been increasing in size, he might be considered too small for middle linebacker and be forced to try to make it as a corner linebacker. The difference between Robustelli and Dryer is that Andy was only 6'1" and couldn't handle much more weight, while Dryer is concerned with keeping his 32" waist and V shape. Anyone that lifts weights as Dryer does should be able to put on additional weight if he chooses. At the time Robustelli played, weightlifting was frowned upon by coaches for fear that their players would become "muscle bound." The theory has proven to be an old wives tale and today's player is encouraged to train with weights. This is one important reason that he is bigger and stronger than those of the Robustelli era.

## PHILOSOPHY OF THE DEFENSIVE LINE

The trend today seems to be toward selecting defensive linemen on the basis of speed and quickness. A larger man lacking somewhat in agility will be used at offensive tackle if he has the other required skills. Today's defensive lineman, like Harvey Martin of the Cowboys and John Dutton of the Colts, can run with the offensive guards and sometimes with the fullbacks. If he weighs 275 pounds and still has that speed and quickness, all the better. This is extremely rare. The 275-pounder may have good straight ahead speed, but must sacrifice some quickness and agility. Therefore, the coach must still decide on a defensive line philosophy: bigger and stronger, but perhaps a little slow getting started; or smaller and quicker.

Whether a player should be used at defensive end or tackle is not always a rational decision. Some players simply seem to function better at one of the two positions for no apparent reason. The great Bob Lilly was a defensive end until being moved to tackle during his third year with the Cowboys. He was better at tackle. Randy White was an interior lineman at the University of Maryland. Because of his comparative lack of size—he weighs 245 pounds—and exceptional quickness, he was placed at linebacker with the Cowboys. He earned a starting position, but probably never would have been a great linebacker. Tom Landry decided to put him on the defensive line and, fortunately for White, decided that it would be at the tackle position and not at end. White was named to the All-Star team his first year at tackle. Tom Landry, when asked if he had reservations when he moved Randy White to the line, said: "Yes, but I also had reservations when I was with the New York Giants and moved Sam Huff to middle linebacker. He was an offensive lineman in college, but turned out to be a great one." Hunches are great when they pay off, but experienced coaches know that they don't always work out.

Height is more of an advantage to a defensive end than to a defensive tackle. That the offensive tackles (who play opposite the defensive ends) are taller than the offensive guards is the obvious reason. The defensive lineman intent on rushing the passer should have a degree of leverage on the offensive blocker. Height provides this leverage. The other reason that height is more of an asset at end than at tackle is the necessity to look into the backfield. The tackle reacts to blocks by those opposite him. The end must look over the blocker.

## MENTAL QUALITIES

In contrast to the offensive lineman, the defensive lineman must be aggressive and can afford to be reckless on occasion. Defensive linemen take the play to the offense. Though they sometimes may be burned on a draw or screen play, they are generally rewarded by aggressive play. There is little to think about before or after the play, except perhaps a new move which will help them reach the passer. Defensive line play is primarily a game of emotion and reaction. That does not mean that defensive linemen are necessarily stupid or highly emotional off the field.

Actually, everyone is emotional on the football field. The only difference is that the offensive people have to exert greater control over their emotions.

Alan Page of the Minnesota Vikings is a good example of how a bright and imaginative player can compensate for certain deficiencies—in Page's case, a lack of size. Page weighs only 240 pounds. To counterbalance, this law school student prepares for each game and looks for variations during the game in much the same way as does a quarterback. He is constantly aware of the opposition's strengths and tendencies, the score, field position and time remaining. Since Page's lack of weight makes it difficult for him to always be fundamentally sound, he often tries to anticipate the opposition's next move and make adjustments in his style of play. This can help a player come up with the big play, but if overdone and a player starts to gamble on the accuracy of his anticipatory instincts, he can cost his team a touchdown. Page seems to keep it in balance.

## FUNDAMENTAL SKILLS

Football is a game of fundamentals. If I have heard that statement once, I have heard it a thousand times from every coach I have ever played for. Of course it's true. However, football is also a game for the spirited, imaginative and innovative. There is room for the thinking man on both offense and defense. Nevertheless, there are still fundamental skills and maneuvers that players at every position adhere to most of the time, though fundamentals are not as important to the defensive lineman as they are to his offensive counterpart.

### The Stance

The lineman must have a stance suited to the position he is playing. All defensive linemen use a three or four point stance which means that they put one or two hands on the ground. At the lower levels, this is determined by the coach. The professional player is given the prerogative of placing one or both hands on the ground. There is a tendency to stay lower when charging if both hands are on the ground. This is why it is popular at the high school level. In most instances, it is merely a question of what a player has become accustomed to.

You will notice a greater variety of stances being used by defensive linemen than those on offense. One reason is that the stance is less important to the defensive player. He does not have to worry about tipping the offensive play and assuming the same stance on every play. He can crouch lower when expecting the run

The stance of a defensive lineman is less important than on the offensive line.

or put all his weight forward when it's a sure passing situation. The defensive lineman is likely to have different assignments and people to block him when in different alignments. This will require adjustments in his stance.

In the standard 4-3 defense, the two defensive ends find themselves in completely different situations. The end opposite the weak side tackle (the tackle on the other side of the line from the tight end) does not have to worry about being hit by the tight end. He can place more weight on his hands and concentrate on the tackle. The set back on that side of the line may be assigned to block him, but he will have time to react before he reaches him. The defensive end on the side of the tight end (strong side) will often place less weight on his hands in order to be able to react laterally to the block of the tight end.

The defensive tackle should have a wider base and a more balanced stance than the defensive ends. This will help him to react to the blocks of any one of the five or six people who may be assigned to block him. A well balanced stance with the feet spread and head up will also assist him to survey the offensive line before the snap. The charge required of the defensive lineman will determine the type of stance he uses on a particular play.

## The Charge

More important than the defensive lineman's stance is his charge. The defensive lineman does not know when the ball will be snapped by the offensive center. He reacts to the first movement of any kind by the offensive team. Years ago, the defensive lineman was taught to sit and read the offensive line for a split second before moving across the line of scrimmage. He would then aim his blow directly at the offensive player assigned to block him. If he moved without reading, he would charge into the man opposite him and would not be able to deliver a blow on a man coming from the side. The defensive lineman had to be much bigger and stronger than the offensive lineman in order to play it this way, since he did not have the forward momentum of the offensive lineman. Coaches thought it essential to have their defensive linemen sit back and read because of the prevalence of the double team block.

With the advent of the more explosive present-day offenses that rely less on double team blocking, coaches began to encourage their players to move across the line more quickly. The increased size of the offensive linemen makes this mandatory today. The defensive lineman is advised to react to the blocker assigned to him while charging across the line. The assignment is more difficult, but there is less likelihood of being blown off the line or reacting slowly to the pass. The term used to describe this movement across the line is "rolling-off." The more a player is intent on rolling-off quickly, the more weight he will have on his hands when in his stance.

The other part of a player's charge is the blow delivered when contact is made. Players are advised not to absorb the block, but to deliver a blow which is at least equal to the force of the block delivered by the offensive player. The blow should be made low and hard with the forearm and shoulder. The objective of the charge is to control a predetermined territory while being able to move laterally, in pursuit, to help close a hole or make a tackle. After delivering the blow, the defensive lineman should attempt to lift and straighten up the offensive blocker. A blocker has little forward thrust when standing straight. When the defensive lineman has his opponent in this position, he is in control, and is able to move to his left or right to make the tackle. The defensive lineman must avoid taking a side on his opponent which will allow the back to break in the opposite direction.

### The Tackle

After making a defensive charge and controlling the offensive blocker, the defensive lineman strives to break contact with the offensive player and make the tackle. The defensive player can use his hands to throw his opponent to the ground or push him away. He must do one of the two to break contact and make a clean tackle. Quite often, he will not be able to break contact completely and will not be able to get his body in front of the ball carrier. An arm will not stop a good runner. This is the reason that good team pursuit and gang tackling is important.

Most coaches suggest aiming the head for the ball when tackling, but the only real consideration is bringing the ball carrier down. While with the San Diego Chargers, Big Ernie Ladd was asked how he attempted to make a tackle. He answered that he didn't care how he tackled, as long as got his man. He said he would hit him with shoulder, grab his head or leg, or pull him down by the jock strap if he had to.

In evaluating the efficiency of a tackle, the size of both players should be considered along with the opportunity available to unload on the ball carrier. A 190-pound cornerback should not be expected to aim his head high for a Franco Harris in the open field. However, if Harris has already broken two tackles and is off balance, the smaller man has an opportunity to unload that he should exploit.

### THE PASS RUSH

The defensive lineman's responsibility on passes is to maintain a rush within prescribed lanes, thus containing the quarterback. He must also guard against the draw play. The width of the lane that he must maneuver in is slightly wider than his area of responsibility against the run. If an undersized defensive end like Jim Marshall of the Vikings ignores his responsibility to rush the passer from the outside to keep the quarterback in the pocket, which he does more than most ends, and the quarterback picks up good yardage scrambling, blame Marshall even though it might look like he had a good rush and almost got the passer. (However, don't be too hard on Marshall. He should be applauded for just taking the field at age 40.) Most teams assign linebackers to the draw and screen play, but once again everyone on the defensive unit has an assignment. The middle linebacker cannot be expected to stop the draw up the middle if both defensive tackles take a wide outside rush. The hole will be too large for one man to fill.

The good pass rushers will not try to use their size and strength to get to the passer by going over the offensive lineman. Instead, they will use their hands and quickness to get *around* him. If you see a defensive lineman pounding his opponent into the ground, you can be certain that he isn't getting a good pass rush. Most defensive tackles can maul and drive the offensive guard to the ground, and most guards want him to try it on every play.

Because it takes too much time to overpower the offensive player, most defensive linemen have become handfighters, which was a dirty word to me in high school and college. I had no respect then for a guy who wouldn't take you on by delivering a shoulder and forearm blow. Back in those days, defensive football meant hitting with impact.

Then, one day, some tall and skinny defensive guy probably said to himself: "Why should I try to *knock* him off balance when I can use my hands to grab his shirt or shoulder pads and *pull* him off balance?" Not only doesn't he get bruised if he does it this way, but, he has greater success since his opponent cannot use his hands (theoretic-a-l-l-y). The next thing we knew, people like Bob Lilly were destroying quarterbacks.

The good pass rusher will vary his charge. He will grab, pull and tug most of the time, but will change up, and occasionally try to go over his opponent. Some will merely try to knock him back and get penetration while others will use the forearm to try to get under the face mask and detach the head from the neck. The defensive ends have more room to operate than do the defensive tackles and some try to utilize their speed by outrunning the offensive tackle to the outside. It doesn't work very often, unless the end has great speed and sets it up well. But, it often helps to set up another move: The end takes off to the outside as if he is trying to outrun the tackle, and then stops short, as the tackle attempts to make contact. He lets one arm hang loose at his side which he slips under the tackle and uses his momentum to throw him and establish a lane to the quarterback. I first saw that move used by Ron Nery who was a member of the San Diego Chargers' "Fearsome Foursome," from 1960 to 1962. Nery said that he learned it from Andy Robustelli who picked it up from Gino Marchetti. Nery had a particular advantage on this sort of play because of his physical dimensions. He weighed about 230, stood 6'5", and ran with a jerky motion of his head which resembled the movements of a goose. He had a complete set of false teeth which he would remove before practice and replace with a large wet ball of cotton. He claimed that this not only kept his mouth moist, but prevented his gums from banging together. We would tease him by saying that the only reason the move on the tackle would work was because of the goose-like movements of his head.

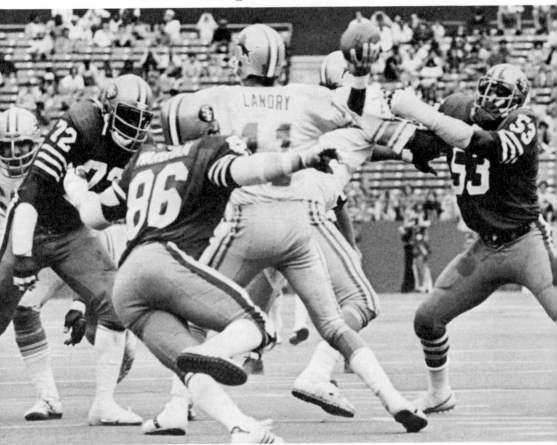

San Francisco defensive end Tommy Hart (53) must have been angry after his opponent grabbed his face mask.

A favorite expression of many high school and college coaches is: "Your body goes where your head is pointed." It is used to impress on young people the importance of keeping their heads up. The blocker that ducks his head before contact is likely to either miss his man completely or fall to the ground after making contact. The "head slam" or "head slap" has been used with success as a change-up by many defensive ends and tackles. The defensive lineman comes across the line and, just before making contact, he reaches out and slaps the opponent on the side of the head with an open hand. I speak from experience when I say that the body goes where the head goes, and in this case it is right to the ground the first time an offensive lineman experiences it. Gordy Holz, who played for the Denver Broncos and later the New York Jets, was one of the first to experiment with it and later used it all the time. He lacked the variety of charges and the foot speed to be a good rusher, though, and you can't expect one move to carry you through on every play. He made it go a long way, though.

Others then picked it up and expanded it into a double and triple slap. Recently, it was barred by the N.F.L. Rules Committee which pleased more offensive linemen than it displeased defensive linemen. Some players never used it at all and the good ones only used it as a change-up. There are other factors to be considered according to Ed "Too Tall" Jones of the Dallas Cowboys: "When we had the head slap, it was harder for offensive linemen to hold us. Now they're all grabbers." If timed perfectly the head slam was an excellent way to keep the offensive player from "getting into" his opponents body. Obviously, if the only contact between the two was a hand on a head, the offensive player didn't have much of an opportunity to hold. Personally, I believe the defensive man has enough of an advantage without it and the elimination of the head slam has created more balance.

Henry Schmidt was one defensive tackle who had just one good move, but perfected it to such a degree that it carried him for four full seasons. I played with Henry in San Diego with the Chargers and in New York with the Jets. If he wasn't the toughest guy I ever met, he had to be the one who enjoyed the physical side of football most. He would ask Ron Mix and me to stay after practice and fire into him while he simply absorbed the blow and tried not to flinch as we made contact. To top it off, he only wore a bar-type face mask, instead of the usual lineman's cage, and absorbed our blows on his face and chest. It could get messy.

He begged us to do it for two reasons. It was his way of psyching himself into believing he was tough, and it helped him develop his pass rush. He had perfected one move. He would charge across the line and dip his head to one side while letting his arm hang loose at his side. He was prepared and would take the blow on the helmet and face mask without using the arm and shoulder to ward off its impact. The harder the better! When the offensive player made contact, he would then "club off" with the loose arm. The key to his success with the move was his ability to get the offensive guard to commit himself and try to unload on Schmidt's unprotected head and chest. The hanging arm would give the opposition a false sense of security and encourage him to deliver a hard blow. The moment he did, Schmidt would use his own momentum to get past him. He was home free.

Defensive tackle Wally Chambers of the Bears being triple teamed on a pass rush. This is what happens when you are too good.

A defensive lineman may put on a good pass rush without getting to the quarterback a single time during a game. The man that is double teamed with consistency should not be expected to get to the quarterback. The defensive lineman may come close enough to upset the quarterback, making him throw the ball away or alter his intentions drastically. This must be considered along with the number of sacks (throwing the quarterback for a loss) a player chalks up. Unless there is a complete breakdown and the defensive player approaches practically untouched, there is little excuse for the experienced quarterback to get trapped with the

Houston middle guard Curly Culp (78) using his hands to get to the Kansas City pass protector who has braced himself for the blow.

ball. The good ones will usually find some way to get rid of the football.

The Houston Oilers have been using a three man front since Curley Culp joined them several years ago. Culp is quick, strong and short at 6'1". He is idealy suited for the nose guard position. His lack of height is not an advantage, but rather less of a disadvantage when playing opposite the center than at the traditional defensive tackle or end positions. Culp has had more than his share of quarterback sacks since joining the Oilers. He is widely appreciated by the fans, but his biggest fans are the Oiler defensive ends. You can give Culp credit for about half of their sacks. Culp has created such a problem for opposing offensive centers that he usually draws the attention of both offensive guards leaving the offensive tackles in a one-on-one situation with the defensive ends. When three men are blocking him, don't expect Culp to get very close to the quarterback, but his value to the team is obvious.

Harvey Martin of Dallas had his best year ever in 1977 with 23 sacks, (more than some teams). One of the reasons was Randy White, who was moved from linebacker to the defensive tackle spot next to Martin. Even before the season began, Martin realized that this would help him: "They cannot double-team me forever with Randy there," said Martin. "They just can't; he'll kill them if they do. Line me up one-on-one and we're goona have a party."

Ideally, the offensive guards will pin the defensive tackles on the line of scrimmage, enabling the quarterback to step forward into the pocket if the defensive ends are applying pressure from the outside. The defensive ends almost always rush from the outside because of their responsibility for containing the quarterback. The defensive tackle who gets penetration and raises his arms to obstruct the quarterback's vision may have done a good job even if no one sacks the quarterback. The defensive end may have not performed his function of forcing the quarterback to step up. However, the raised arms of the tackle may have forced the quarterback to alter his throw.

It often takes a team effort to sack the quarterback. The mobile passer should not have much difficulty in avoiding one pass rusher approaching with his arms raised. When you consider that the defensive lineman rarely manages to get rid of his opponent completely, the difficulty of getting to the quarterback alone becomes more apparent. The defensive end may be repeatedly beating his opponent to the outside only to have the quarterback step into the pocket, giving the offensive tackle a chance to

Defensive tackle Harvey Martin of the Cowboys had 23 sacks in 1977—as many as the entire San Diego team had in 1976.

recover, and drive the end beyond the quarterback. The end may have forced the quarterback to step into the arms of the defensive tackle with all he credit going to the tackle.

Most of the time, you will see the defensive linemen rushing the passer with their arms extended overhead to obstruct the quarterback's vision. They are taught this, and I'm certain that it is effective in blocking the quarterback's vision *on occasion.* I personally think it's a mistake, though. If linemen were taught to simply tackle the quarterback and to forget about obstructing his view, quarterbacks like Terry Bradshaw would not be as effective in eluding people while scrambling. How many times have you seen a quarterback duck under the arms of the defense and pick up yardage? How often have you seen a quarterback pump the football and watch a lineman stop his rush and jump up into the air only to give the quarterback that extra tenth of a second to spot his receiver? The quarterback who knows that he is going to get a hard helmet stuck into his ribs or face is more likely to hurry his throw than the one confronted with a pair of waving arms. Like most areas of football, it is wrong to formulate hard and fast rules to cover any situation. Against a Terry Bradshaw, I would suggest that the defensive people forget waving their arms and try to make a hard clean tackle. Against a Craig Morton, who rarely moves from the pocket, the defense might be advised to raise their arms, but never to stop their forward motion.

## SCREENS AND DRAWS

The middle linebacker, specifically, is assigned by most teams to stop the draw play between the defensive tackles. He cannot do it without the help of the defensive tackles. If the tackles leave their lanes to rush the passer, the best of the middle linebackers will have difficulty in stopping the draw play. The offensive back has the option of breaking anywhere a hole develops, which makes it even more difficult for one man to stop the draw play. The coach may say that he is assigning the linebacker to the draw, but the tackles had better provide assistance.

The same situation exists on the screen pass. The corner linebacker has direct responsibility for the screen, but it is rare that he can stop it unassisted. There will be three or four blockers out in the flat in front of the ball carrier and a lot of ground to cover. At times, it may be advantageous for the linebacker trying to bring down the ball carrier by himself to be in the open field with a lot of room to maneuver; and at times you will see one quick corner linebacker slice between the blockers to make the tackle. However, most often, he will need help from the defensive linemen coming over in pursuit. Neither the tackle nor the defensive end should be pinned on the line of scrimmage. It is especially unforgivable for the end, who has outside responsibility and lines up on the outside shoulder of the offensive tackle.

## THE TRAP

Essentially, the offensive line on the trap is trying to buy the quarterback as much time as possible to execute the pass play. The defense tries to cut this time to a minimum. If they try too hard, they make themselves vulnerable to the screen, draw and trap plays. The well executed trap play (see chapter on the offensive line) is often the most effective means of holding a good pass rusher on the line of scrimmage an extra second. The defensive lineman that is trapped several times is likely to hold back just a little. If he is blindsided (does not see the blocker coming) there is a better chance he will slow down on the next pass play.

The trap play is also an effective running play that helps to set up other running plays with the same initial movement of the linemen and backs. On the trap play, the defensive back keying the pulling guard cannot tell whether the guard is trapping or just pulling out to lead interference on an end sweep. Some teams run the trap play as one of their basic plays, while others use it only if they believe that a defensive player is vulnerable to it. Either way, it is effective if done right.

There are several things the fan should look for in attempting to evaluate how well a defensive lineman plays the trap block. Most teams concentrate their trapping efforts on the defensive ends. The trap on the tackle develops quickly, since there are only a few feet separating the trapping guard from him. All defensive tackles will be trapped successfully at times. There is less reason for finding an excuse for the defensive end. The distance separating him from the trapping guard should give him enough time to play it well.

The style of the defensive player will determine the frequency offensive teams attempt to trap him. The hard charging tackle, who sometimes anticipates the count in his effort to reach the passer, is the type most teams will attempt to trap. If he is quick and does get to the passer more often than the other tackle on his team, he is more likely to be the target of the trap play. The more he penetrates, the easier the trap block should be for the guard. John Mendenhall, Randy White and Alan Page are among those that are vulnerable to being trapped.

When a player is trapped, his style and success in putting pressure on the passer must be considered. If he has been getting to the quarterback (or close) with regularity, you can excuse his being trapped. Would you ask Harvey Martin to slow down his pass rush to guard against the trap? Not unless it happens repeatedly. The situation on the field and the time remaining on the clock must also be considered. The lineman who is trapped for the first time during the fourth quarter after pressuring the quarterback all game should not be given any demerits. However, you can find fault with the lineman trapped three times during the first quarter, regardless of his style of play. A player's style or quickness off the line is important, but an awareness of the trap and what the offensive people in front of him are doing frequently accounts for a player's ability to handle the trap block. A good defensive lineman should not be trapped time after time.

The defensive alignment or the lineman's assignment on a particular play will also influence the effectiveness of the trap block. Some teams require the defensive tackles to get a piece of the offensive guard if he releases inside and seems to be trying to get at the middle linebacker. This accounts for much of the success of many of the middle linebackers in pro football. If a tackle is hitting a guard attempting to release inside, he will be more difficult to trap. If a tackle is moving to the outside because of the defensive alignment or a tackle-end game, he should be easy to trap. In this instance another player should be compensating and covering his area. If the defensive tackle is closing down and keeping the guard off the middle linebacker, you might expect him to be logged in (see chapter on the offensive line). However, if he does keep the guard off of the middle linebacker, he should make the tackle.

The defensive lineman being trapped should try to close the hole and put his head to the inside. In this case, there is usually insufficient time to get rid of the blocker and make a clean tackle. Most defensive linemen try to push the trapping lineman into the ball carrier. The defensive lineman may never touch the ball carrier, but should be given credit if the ball carrier bounces off of the trapping guard and is eventually brought down by someone else.

## SPLITS IN THE LINE

Each player must assume a particular position in relation to the offensive team, and his teammates. By not aligning himself in the exact position specified by the coach, he may make his task more difficult and create problems for his teammates. For example, the defensive tackle should line up opposite the offensive guard on the 4-3 defense. If for some reason he lines up to the inside, without an appropriate adjustment by his teammates, the offensive guard will be given a blocking angle which will help him on any play run to his outside. If the offensive guard can take advantage of the angle, he is likely to drive the tackle down the line of scrimmage. The tackle will look bad on the play, and he will make the jobs of the middle linebacker and defensive end more difficult. They will have to compensate for his loss of position and help close a much wider hole in the defensive line.

When you see unusually wide splits in the offensive line, try to determine how the defense adjusts. Defensive linemen are given specific instructions as to where to line up on the offensive man. It is usually on the inside shoulder, on the outside shoulder, head-up, or directly in the gap between two offensive players. They will retain these positions unless the splits in the offensive line become exceptionally wide. Predetermined adjustments will then be made.

At one time, defensive players were merely advised to maintain a relative distance to each other regardless of the splits in the offensive line. The theory behind maintaining relative distances is that, although blocking angles may develop in some areas, the only area that is vulnerable is to the outside. It was thought that the additional time it would take to get around the split offensive line would give the defense time to compensate for their poor outside position.

The relative distance approach does not always serve to neutralize the team taking wide splits, unless other actions are taken to capitalize on the gaping holes. If the splits are wide enough, a defensive lineman might shoot the gap trying to disrupt things in the offensive backfield by throwing the ball carrier for a loss. By taking it to the offense in this manner, the offensive team may be dissuaded from continuing to split.

Another means of discouraging wide splits is for the defensive linemen to move off the line of scrimmage and play like linebackers. Moving back will give them more time to react to the charging offensive blocker. The combination of additional time and an expanded area in which to work should help to compensate for the improved blocking angles.

## GOAL LINE AND SHORT YARDAGE SITUATIONS

Goal line and short yardage situations are where you want to be particularly aware of what is happening up front. Some teams send their larger people to replace the linebacker or safety in a short yardage situation, while others merely tighten up the defensive alignment and use the linebackers as defensive linemen. In pro football, when the corner linebackers assume a three point stance and move into the line, the defense is called a 6-1 instead of a 4-3.

There is rarely an excuse for a defensive lineman to be driven back off the line of scrimmage. There is never an excuse for anyone to be pushed back on the goal line. I have never met a coach that would accept an alibi in this situation. The defensive lineman should have only one thing on his mind, and that is not to give ground under any circumstance. He must dig in, but he can't bury his head in the ground, for this would limit his mobility considerably and allow the running back easy passage "over the top." The good lineman will stay close to the ground with his head up, and will always know where the ball carrier is running.

In a short yardage situation, the interior defensive linemen will frequently have two men blocking them. Look for it and don't expect them to do much pursuing if the play does break to the outside. The defensive lineman who has been double teamed will have done his job if he simply manages to hold his ground, and is not pushed backward or laterally. He will have done a super job if he can straighten up and prevent the back from going over the top.

Short yardage situations vary according to the position of the ball. The situation in mid-field is altogether different than the one on the goal line. The size of the defensive lineman and the size of his opponent must be considered in evaluating the charge of the defender. In mid-field, he should try to deliver a nearly normal charge and only after making certain that the ball is not being run at him, does he help elsewhere. In a goal line situation, you might expect a smaller defensive lineman to "submarine" his opponent (charge lower than his opponent). The offensive player always attempts to charge lower than the defender, and will fire out as low as he can. If the defensive player is extremely low, he will lose his mobility whether his head is up or down. Therefore, it is suggested that the defensive lineman refrain from burying himself in a mass of humanity, unless absolutely necessary. That means you can expect smaller tackles like Rubin Carter of the Denver Broncos and Sugar Bear Hamilton of the New England Patriots to submarine when playing in front of George Buehler and Gene Upshaw, the 270-pounders of the Raiders. The defensive lineman is first responsible for the run in his immediate area, but he is also expected to pursue the ball carrier and help elsewhere. When a player must submarine repeatedly to avoid being driven back off the line, he is making someone else's job more difficult.

## PURSUIT

You hear the word "pursuit" bandied around in football almost as if it's an end in itself. Pursuit is an asset to a football team ... *if* it follows a fundamentally sound defensive charge. Some players, like John Mendenhall of the Giants, do an excellent job of pursuing the ball carrier at the expense of their primary responsibility of stopping the run directed into their area. Mendenhall pursues well because of his exceptional speed for a lineman and the quickness with which he sheds the offensive blocker. He accomplishes this by going around the block or doing what coaches call "taking the easy way out." He rarely delivers a solid charge, which would enable him to control the blocker and move to his left or right. He hits and immediately takes the side where the least resistance is offered. If the play is directed at him, he has a 50% chance of having moved in the right direction. Because he avoids confrontations with the blocker on most plays, he manages to make tackles in areas where you would not expect to find him. He will look great in those situations where he has moved in the right direction. But, when he gambles and moves the wrong way, he not only looks bad, he also makes it more difficult for his teammates to make the tackle, because of the increased size of the hole he allows to open.

The experienced offensive lineman will fire out under control and look for the defender to take a side. He will then drive him in that direction with the knowledge that the runner will break into the open area. The blocker that tries to hit with all his force is the one that will miss his man completely and fall to his knees, when the defender takes a side. Faster defensive linemen justify their actions by claiming they have the quickness to go around the block and still make the tackle if they have taken the wrong side. It just doesn't work out that way. Football is a game of fundamentals and the player that disregards them hurts his team more often than he helps.

Look for pursuit after a player has fulfilled his primary responsibility. Watch the angle he takes to cut off the ball carrier, and try to determine if he is running at full speed. He should not chase the runner unless he is responsible for stopping the reverse. Instead, he should choose a path of pursuit which will enable him to cut off the runner at a spot downfield. He has to gauge his speed in relation to the ball carrier and to his position on the field.

When a play is going wide to the defensive lineman's side of the field, some linemen will gamble by charging across the line in an attempt to come up with the big play by throwing the runner for a loss with a bone crushing tackle. This may or may not be the thing to do depending on the situation. The lineman should risk wasting himself in this manner only if the prospects of reaching the runner are good. This usually requires the defender to dive for the runner and if he misses, he will certainly take himself out of the play and not be able to pursue the runner. A better indication of a player's value than his ability to come up with that type of big play is the regularity with which he gets an assist on tackles made when the runner tries to cut back.

Look for the loafer. At all levels of football there are players who feel that a play run to the other side of the field is a signal for them to take a breather. This is never true. There are numerous situations where the defender has no chance to overtake the runner if he continues unmolested in his present path. Suddenly, for some reason, the runner may be forced to change his direction and what seemed like an impossible task becomes an excellent opportunity to make a tackle. You can tell much about a player's attitude by the amount of effort he expends when pursuing the ball carrier. There is nothing that will excite a coach more on a given play than watching a player that has been knocked down once or twice get up to make the tackle.

Good pursuit not only prevents the long run, but also serves to slow up the runner by punishing him physically. The runner who is hit by three or four tacklers each time he carries the ball is less likely to come up with the second and third effort to pick up extra yardage. Coaches claim that they can determine a team's mental readiness by the number of people in on the first few tackles. You cannot have gang tackling without adequate pursuit, and good pursuit generally indicates that the adrenalin is flowing.

A danger of good pursuit, and the gang tackling that goes with it, is the possibility of an unnecessary roughness penalty. It is most often the result of being overanxious and should be expected if a team is playing aggressive football. Another possibility, though not very common, is an intentional effort to injure the ball carrier. It is possible to determine whether the player accused of piling on could not stop his momentum, or was intent upon punishing the ball carrier. The impact and type of blow delivered will often tell the story. If a player hits late, but uses his hands to break the impact, or merely falls on the runner, it was probably unintentional. If he places a well-aimed shoulder into the ribs of the ball carrier, you can be fairly certain the penalty was justified.

Earlier in his career, Ben Davidson of the Oakland Raiders was notorious for doing a swan dive into the ball carrier after his forward motion was stopped. Once he was accused of breaking Joe Namath's jaw after he released the ball. Game films revealed that it was another Raider lineman that did the damage. When a player, like Davidson, gets the national publicity that rarely goes to a lineman, he may rationalize that the publicity is worth the 15-yard penalty. Davidson had that handle bar mustache going for him before hair was popular, which may have helped him achieve national recognition after the Namath incident. Like the professional wrestler who travels from one part of the country to another, Ben's role later changed to that of the good guy. He raised his hands overhead whenever there was a question that he might accidentally have run into someone after the play had ended.

I think it was Ben Davidson's show boating and occasional cheap shot that gave the Oakland Raiders the reputation of being a dirty football team. Once they had that reputation, a very small percentage of the Raiders may have felt a need to live up to their press clippings. It all culminated when Steeler coach Chuck Noll charged Raider defensive back George Atkinson with being part of a criminal element in the N.F.L., after almost removing wide-receiver Lynn Swan's number from his football shirt. I think Noll may have overreacted. The Raiders have received their share of unsportsmanlike conduct penalties over the years, but they also have been one of the legitimately hardest-hitting teams in the league since Al Davis took over as head coach back in 1963. Davis has been accused of many things over the years, probably because of his success, but no one that knows him would accuse him of condoning the cheap shot. Curiously, both Davis and Noll were rookie pro football assistant coaches under Sid Gillman back with the then-Los Angeles Chargers in 1960. I clearly remember Davis admonishing me for taking what he thought was a cheap shot on an Oakland Raider defensive back. We debated the issue and although he never convinced me it was a cheap shot, I did admit the forearm blow I threw might be called extra-curricular. (At that time, I used to teach during the off-season and was fond of terms like "extra-curricular.")

## STUNTING

Stunting occurs when, after the snap of the ball, members of the defensive team exchange assignments with each other. Its purpose is to confuse the offensive line and cause a defensive player to break free in the backfield. It also makes blocking assignments more difficult. The term "stunting defense" is usually reserved for teams that employ stunts that involve the linebackers and all the defensive linemen on almost every play. A stunting defense might have the defensive linemen charge into the first man to their right, and the linebackers move to their left to compensate for the movement of the line. The stunt can involve half the defensive line and one or two linebackers; one lineman and one linebacker; two linemen; or just about any combination. The only must is that the stunting players be close enough to exchange assignments with a minimum of risk so that one player will not be cut off. To prevent this, stunting teams will use looping as well as slanting stunts. When looping, the defensive player *first steps* laterally and *then* toward the line of scrimmage and the offensive player.

Professional teams have never used team stunting defenses to the extent that they are used at the lower levels. The pros have preferred to use small group stunts called "games," "tricks," or "an exchange." The three games seen most often are those involving the defensive tackle and end, the two tackles, and the middle

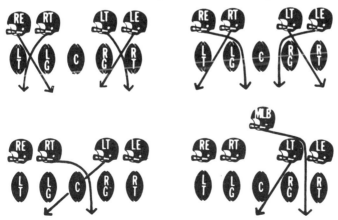

Small group stunts.

linebacker (who exchanges assignments with either tackle). The diagrams are self-explanatory. Either player involved in a game can move first. It is incumbent upon the man that moves first to try to occupy both offensive linemen in the area in order to allow his teammate to break free. For example, if the tackle is moving first on a tackle-end game, he will usually hold onto the offensive guard as he moves toward the tackle. Most offensive teams area block the tackle-end game, which requires the guard to pick up the defensive end coming into his area. If the defensive tackle succeeds in occupying both offensive linemen, the defensive end should break free into the backfield.

When using games, the defensive linemen will frequently alter their alignment to make the exchange of assignments easier. For example, the tackle may move closer to the line with the defensive end dropping off a little before executing the tackle-end game. This can be read by the offensive team or the alert fan in the stands. If the defensive end moves into the offensive guard first, the terminology changes to "end-tackle game."

Games are usually called in passing situations. They are weak against the running game since the linemen are moving laterally and not charging straight into the offensive linemen. If the defense resorts to games, they are creating blocking angles for the offensive linemen and making their job easier.

## THINGS TO LOOK FOR

The ultimate compliment for a football player is to be referred to as the "complete football player." It implies that the player does everything well. The complete football player does not have a mental or physical weakness. When used to describe a defensive lineman it implies a degree of speed, size and quickness that enables him to perform all of his assignments well. He plays the run, rushes the passer, tackles and pursues the ball carrier with equal effectiveness. He does not make mental errors and gives a maximum effort at all times. He is Bob Lilly, the best defensive tackle I ever saw play.

There are few complete football players. Most players have a weakness or a function that they do not perform well. Some do not have the speed to pursue well. Others lack the quickness to get to the passer and come up with the big play. Players that lack size or strength may be vulnerable against the run. Look for the complete football player, but don't expect to find him very often. Look for consistency, and don't be fooled by the player looking for headlines. The big play is not as important to the success of a team as steady performance. The consistent, fundamentally sound defensive lineman without a glaring weakness is more valuable than the player that can deliver the big play, but has deficiencies that will be exploited by the opposition.

Coaches will sometimes tolerate the player with deficiencies, but only until they find a good fundamentally sound player with which to replace him. When they can't get the complete player, coaches try to complement strengths and weaknesses. It is possible to cover for the player that can get to the passer but is weak against the running game, if he is placed on the line next to a steady player who is strong against the run. A tough linebacker behind him will also help cover for his weakness. When you notice one man rushing the passer extremely hard, look for the possibility that someone else is covering for him against the run. You will rarely read about the fundamentally sound player that gives that maximum effort and consistent performance, but he is at least as important as a player that is getting the headlines. He is Joe Ehrmann and Mike Barnes, of the Baltimore Colts and Jerry Sherk, of the Cleveland Browns.

The only unspectacular yet good defensive lineman that received his fair share of publicity was Dick Modzelewski, of the Giants and Browns. His recognition stemmed largely from playing on winning teams. Modzelewski rarely got to the passer himself, but his toughness against the run allowed the people next to him to be more aggressive and daring in rushing the passer. After leaving the Giants, he finished his career with the Cleveland Browns and helped them to the N.F.L. title his first year with the club. His value to the Browns was primarily the inspirational leadership he brought with him from the many championship teams he played on while with the Giants. The Brown players said at the time that he taught them to think and act like champions. He was also a fine defensive tackle.

It is not surprising that the finest defensive lineman on the Cleveland Browns today has a style similar to Modzelewski's, because Dick has been coaching with the Browns since he retired after the 1966 campaign. He has an ideal pupil in Jerry Sherk. Sherk has more to work with than Modzelewski did and is capable of putting a consistent rush on the passer. Modzelewski provided the example and taught him to be an all-around defensive tackle and not just a pass rusher, which is where most defensive linemen build their reputations. This type of lineman may not gain wide recognition from the fans, but is fully appreciated by the coaches. There is a Dick Modzelewski or Jerry Sherk on every team. Look for him.

Each player on the defensive team, like his offensive counterpart, has an assignment on every play. He has a specific area to protect, and if he is not expected to make the tackle on that play, he is expected to close the hole and not give the running back much room to maneuver. For example, the defensive end may not be expected to make the tackle if the ball carrier breaks between the offensive guard and tackle. The end lines up on the outside shoulder of the offensive tackle, at times, and has outside responsibility. If the offensive tackle takes an exceptionally wide split and the defensive end moves with him and does not close the hole with his charge after the snap of the ball, he has created an impossible situation for the middle linebacker and defensive tackle. They may theoretically be responsible for the play between the offensive guard and tackle, but the end is expected to help close the hole and confine the running back. This is the key to good defensive line play.

You should not assume that a particular defensive lineman is at fault because an offensive team seems to be running directly at him, unless you are watching him and are aware of what is happening to the people next to him. Each man can only cover a limited area. Unless he is supported by the men next to and behind him, he may experience difficulty against the run and in rushing the passer. Against the pass he is likely to be double teamed consistently if he is putting on a good rush and his teammates are being held on the line.

As with the linebackers, the defensive lineman can be evaluated by his proximity to the ball carrier after he has been tackled. The good lineman is never "wiped out" or blocked completely. He will be close to or in on the tackle if the ball carrier runs to his side of the field. If the play is to the other side, he will be in hot pursuit. It may be necessary to target in and focus on him exclusively for several plays if the offense seems to be attacking him, but there is also an excellent opportunity to study the defensive linemen when targeting in on other positions. You will notice him when studying the offensive lineman, when checking pass protection, and when keying the running back.

The thing to keep in mind, when evaluating the defensive line, then, is not to confuse anonymity with insignificance. You might not have heard of many of the people on the opponent's defensive line because most of their work is basic, subtle, and unspectacular. If you want a simple test of how much you understand football, it will come when you begin to appreciate the unrewarding work of the men in the pit.

# 6

# THE DEFENSIVE BACKFIELD
## The Men Who Take The Blame

The long pass is to football what the home run is to baseball. Just as a slip by the pitcher can cost his team the ball game, a slip by the defensive back can negate the efforts of a 40-man football team. Both the baseball pitcher and the defensive back are assisted by their teammates, but basically they're out there alone: the pitcher against the batter; the defender against the receiver.

The defensive backfield's first responsibility is to stop the forward pass. Only after the ball has passed the line of scrimmage does it assume its secondary role of assisting in defensing the run. Coaches break down the role of the defensive secondary (another name for the defensive backfield) into three areas: stop the bomb or long pass, stop the short pass, help stop the run. Although all defensive coaches stress the necessity of defending against the bomb, those that use a zone (when men in the defensive secondary cover areas instead of individuals) are probably more acutely aware of the danger of the bomb. It is the increased use of the zone in pro football (college teams have been using it for years) that has made it more difficult to evaluate the play of the defensive secondary.

For the average fan, the play of the defensive secondary is hard to understand. It is not as easy as just looking at a receiver catching the football and pointing an accusing finger at the nearest defensive back. Several years ago, when most teams in pro football were using man coverage (when each man in the defensive secondary is assigned to cover a specific receiver on the offensive team) this was a fair thing to do most of the time. No more!

In the defensive secondary, things are not always as they appear. The good cornerback will earn recognition regardless of the type of coverage or the personnel playing next to him. He will look even better if the safety playing next to him and the linebackers in front of him are working with him. His effectiveness is also dependent on the type of defensive line he is playing behind.

Free safety Paul Krause of the Minnesota Vikings broke Emlen Tunnell's record 79 career interceptions at the end of the 1977 season. Krause is quick to credit the fine defensive line he has played behind most of his career. Defensive backs generally agree that, given time, most N.F.L. quarterbacks can pick even the best defensive backfields to pieces. There is no substitute for the good pass rush or the effective drop by the linebacker in front of the defensive back. Credit at least half of Krause's 79 interceptions to Carl Eller, Alan Page and Jim Marshall.

Let's see what goes into the building of a defensive secondary.

## POSITIONS

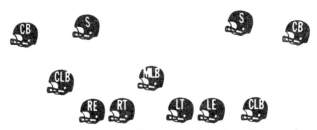

The two cornerbacks and the two safeties form the secondary.

You will find anywhere from three to five defensive backs in a game at any given time. In recent years, professional teams have tended to use four deep backs in their basic coverages. When in a prevent defense (see diagram), a fifth defensive back sometimes replaces a defensive lineman or a linebacker. This is usually in a long yardage situation, when the offense can be expected to throw the long pass. Occasionally, teams go with three deep backs, though you are more likely to see this in college ball than in the pros.

In the standard four deep defense, you will find a left and right cornerback, as well as strong side and weak side safeties. The weak safety is often referred to as the free safety, since he is sometimes not assigned to cover a specific man and is free to help wherever he thinks necessary. He varies the depth at which he positions himself according to the defense called. When free, he will line up deep in order to be able to help the cornerback guard against the bomb. The strong side safety lines up in the area in front of the tight end and usually much closer to the line of

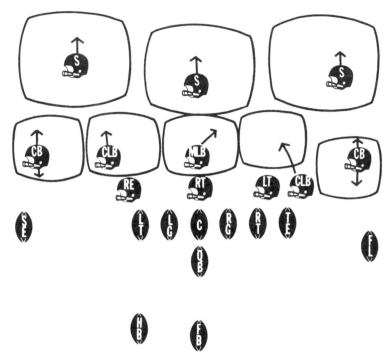

A prevent defense—used in long yardage situations.

scrimmage than the weak safety. The cornerbacks are positioned in front of the wide receivers and 3 to 12 yards off the line.

### Weak Safety

In the past, the weak safety position was often filled by the bright and dedicated player who had neither the size, nor the speed to play any other position on the defensive tam. Like the small, slow offensive guard, he has become hard to find. Nowadays, most teams will sacrifice a couple of points in a player's I.Q. for a few tenths of a second in the time it takes him to run the 40-yard dash. To combat the increased speed of all receivers, many teams are converting cornerbacks to weak safeties and simplifying their coverages.

A quick glance at the rosters of the teams in the N.F.L. will verify this change. That is, if you don't look at the name of the player listed as the weak safety for the Washington Redskins. Pat Fischer was too small at 5'9" and 170 pounds to make it in pro football 17 years ago and he was still too small during the 1977 season. Everyone kept telling him that when he was drafted in the 17th round by St. Louis in 1961, but he refused to believe that size was that important. His greatest concern as a rookie was finding a uniform that fit properly. For the first three days of practice, he simply ran around the edges of the field because the Cardinals didn't have a uniform to fit him. During his first exhibition game, his football pants were so large that they actually fell to his knees and had to be held up with tape. Fischer had two things going for him originally. He was a hitter and a student of the game. He was proficient at reading patterns and analyzing offensive strategy, which enabled him to help where needed. I'm not certain that he would be able to make it as a pro football rookie today, with his height being more of a disadvantage than his weight. He has survived the last few years because of his experience.

Billy Thompson of the Denver Broncos—one of the best safeties in football.

The weak safety, though, can still get away with less physical equipment than those playing most other positions. Since there is no tight end on his side of the line, the corner linebacker playing in front of him is expected to help stop the off-tackle play and turn in the end run. When using man coverage, the weak safety is normally assigned to a set back and rarely has to cover a larger tight end by himself.

The weak safety's greatest asset is a "feel for the ball." The ability to anticipate the release of the ball and react to it quickly may be partially instinctive, but it can be developed with experience. The weak safety having this ability should be able to react to and approach almost any ball thrown more than 10 or 12 yards downfield, in those cases where he is free to roam the secondary.

## Strong Safety

The strong safety should be bigger than the weak safety. If the weak safety happens to be big, the strong safety will probably be more rugged and a better tackler, though slower. Since he is often assigned to cover the slower tight end, he is not required to have the speed of the others in the secondary. However, he must be aggressive and tough enough to help stop the off-tackle play and turn the end run to the inside. He will not get as much help from the corner linebacker as the weak safety does, since the tight end is assigned to block the linebacker. He must be strong enough to take on a pulling guard as well as to bring down a fullback by himself in the open field.

These are the "book" requirements. What makes some strong safeties better than others is the ability to think on their feet. When the tight end does not release on a pass play, the strong safety is free to help where needed. In this situation, the strong safety becomes just like the weak safety and his ability to read patterns becomes important. The secret to good play in the secondary is to get strong individual efforts backed up by good teamwork.

## Cornerback

Next to offensive lineman, the most unrewarding position on a football team has to be cornerback. Very few cornerbacks have received the salaries or recognition of those they are assigned to cover. In return, they usually find themselves isolated on a wide receiver with comparable speed in the middle of the field in full view of everyone in the stadium. The fan will soon forget the big pass play he broke up, but rarely will overlook the touchdown pass caught on him.

Willie Brown of the Oakland Raiders, who at age 37 was the oldest starter in the American Football Conference during the 1977 season, is quite explicit about what it takes to last at cornerback: "The cornerback has to concentrate more than anyone else on defense. A receiver can run anything he wants, but I don't hear the crowd or anything else. I key on him all the way. Another thing about cornerback is that you have to forget things in a hurry. You have to forget a T.D. pass thrown over you in a hurry, and an interception in a hurry. The reason some cornerbacks break is that they can't forget. Either you forget or you're out of the league."

One of the reasons that Brown has lasted 15 seasons at a position where there is little room to compensate for a lack of the mandatory speed and quickness is hard work. "Extra effort" and "unusual dedication" are usually terms used to describe players with average or less than average physical ability. It is frequently their extra effort and willingness to work hard that enables them to make it in the N.F.L. However, even those with exceptional talent must put forth the proverbial "maximum effort" if they are to live up to their potential and perform on an All Star level over a prolonged period of time. John Madden has a rather sophisticated explanation for Brown's prolonged success: "I've always believed a player has a chronological age and a performance age," explains Madden. "Willie has a young performance age; he's always been that way. He's a guy who has kept up his efficiency by working. He has something that's very unusual for a veteran. The older, more experienced and more successful he's become, the harder he works. Usually it's just the opposite. When the season ends, Willie takes one or two days off and then comes around to the clubhouse to start working for next year."

Tom Landry said pretty much the same thing about Bob Lilly during his last years as a player and Chuck Knox will tell you a similar tale about Merlin Olson. What do these aged vets work on, you might ask. Two things: staying in top shape year 'round and fundamentals.

## FUNDAMENTAL SKILLS

The fundamental skills required of a defensive back are somewhat different and harder to recognize than those necessary for success at the other defensive positions. The defensive back rarely makes contact with an opponent of his own volition. On running plays, his objective is to avoid contact completely until he is in position to make the tackle. His skill against the run can be measured by his ability to elude offensive blockers and bring down the ball carrier. His tackling ability is regarded as a skill, but tackling in the open field is more often the result of a desire to make the tackle than any fundamental skills the back may possess. Any method that succeeds in bringing down the ball carrier in the open field is acceptable. Tackling is an important skill required of all defensive players, but a cornerback or weak safety is rarely cut because of his tackling ability. Tackling ability is more important in evaluating the strong safety.

## The Stance

A proper stance is important to success at every defensive position except in the defensive secondary. The receivers are so far from the deep backs that almost any stance will give them enough time to adjust before the receiver approaches. A false step or poor balance will mean little unless the defender is on the line of scrimmage preparing to bump the receiver as he comes off the line. Because instant contact is made in this case, the defensive back must be in a well balanced stance.

Most defensive backs do line up in a ready position with their feet spread shoulder width apart, ready to react to the movement of the offensive team. The coach would not have it any other way. Every football player is expected to be mentally as well as physically prepared to handle every situation. To some coaches, a poor stance will indicate a poor attitude. A seat on the bench will be dusted and polished immediately.

## At the Snap

The defensive back's first movement after the snap of the ball also allows for individual differences. As the receiver leaves the line of scrimmage, the defensive back is expected to move backwards. He should now be well balanced and prepared to move in any direction. Most will bounce back briskly on the balls of their feet and do not take a side until the defender approaches. However, the speed of retreat will vary according to the individual and the man he is covering. All defensive backs strive not to cross their feet or turn their bodies completely. However, some slide sideways while others backpedal as the receiver leaves the line of scrimmage. It depends on the individual.

## Reading Keys

The most important fundamental skill for a defensive back is his ability to "read" specific people (keys) on the offensive team before and after the snap in order to determine whether the play will be a pass or run. If it is a pass, the keys may indicate where the man to whom he is assigned will run and to whom the quarterback will throw the football. Next to speed, ability to "read" is the most important factor in evaluating a defensive back. And yet, the ability to read keys is one of the most difficult things to evaluate in football.

There is no sure key for a back to study. Most offensive teams go to great lengths to confuse the defense. The play pass and roll out pass are designed to look like running plays initially. The screen and draw plays both start out looking like pass plays, but are both designed to pick up yardage on the ground. Teams will pull offensive linemen in the direction opposite to that in which the play is going in order to destroy the keys of the defense. The screen play is often set up by the offensive line to both sides of the field simultaneously. All fakes in the offensive backfield are designed to mislead someone and make it more difficult to read the offense.

Many college and high school teams require their defensive backs to first key on the uncovered offensive lineman, then into the backfield and *then* on the receiver. (The uncovered lineman would be anyone who does not have a defensive lineman directly opposite him.) If he crosses the line of scrimmage and comes downfield, a run can be expected. If he does not cross the line, the defensive back must play for a pass. In the pros, they have to be more careful.

The position the pro defensive back is playing and the offensive formation will influence his keys. The cornerback playing against a pro-set is forced to read different keys than one playing against the tight T. The cornerback covering a wide receiver split 10 yards from his tight end will be vulnerable to the quick pass if he looks in at the uncovered lineman. He must cover the receiver until he is absolutely certain a run has been called. Let's take a closer look at some of the keys used by most pro defensive backs.

### Cornerback

Some cornerbacks look only at the wide receiver they are covering. These are generally the young and inexperienced ones. They are afraid of giving the receiver an edge by taking their eyes off of the receiver for an instant. With experience, most cornerbacks will take a quick peek into the backfield and try to keep the receiver within their field of vision at the same time. The direction of the flaring back on a pass play may give the cornerback an indication of the direction the wide receiver will take. The wide receiver can be expected to break to the inside if the offensive back is flaring wide and seems to be headed deep downfield. More than one quick look may be necessary to determine the depth of the set back's route. Of course, taking your eye off of the receiver can be dangerous. The defensive back does not want to take his eyes off the receiver as he makes his final break.

The cornerback looking into the backfield may try to look through the tight end if he is lined up on the strong side of the offense. The term "looking through" a player is of course technically inaccurate, although used by most coaches. It means that the keying player should be aware of the movement of more than one player at a time. The cornerback looking through the tight end tries to determine his direction as well as the direction of the set back on his side of the field. The tight end's movement may also provide a clue as to where the wide receiver will make his final break. Against man coverage, offensive teams rarely send more than one receiver into a confined area. If the tight end is moving toward the sideline, the wide receiver may be expected to break over the middle or head out on a deep route.

## Strong Safety

The strong safety often has an extra second to study the offense after the snap. The strong side corner linebacker tries to get a piece of the tight end as he releases from the line of scrimmage. Even if he does not make a serious attempt to hold up the tight end, the closeness of the two will force the receiver to alter his course somewhat. The corner linebacker must react to the movement of the tight end. If he comes directly at him, he must anticipate a run and deliver a blow.

Because of the assistance provided by the linebacker, the strong safety has more time to spend reading keys. He will look through the offensive guard or tackle into the backfield. Some players prefer to key the offensive guard since they are frequently pulling out of the line if the play is not directed to their side. Others prefer to key the tackle since he is closer to the tight end which the strong safety is most often assigned to cover on man coverage. The offensive lineman will tip whether the play is a pass or a run and, if it is a run, where the play is directed.

The direction that the set back runs may indicate where the tight end will break. If the back is coming through the offensive line on a pass route, the tight end may be expected to break outside. The depth of the quarterback's drop may provide a further clue as to the depth of the pass. He will set deeper on a long pass. All of the defensive backs that look into the backfield will keep their eye on the quarterback. Along with the depth at which he sets, the direction in which he is looking may indicate the primary receiver. It can also be misleading.

When the strong safety begins to drop back while covering the tight end, the progress of the flanker may help him to anticipate the direction of the tight end's final break. It may not be possible to gather all this information on every play, but when possible it provides valuable assistance to the experienced defensive back.

## Weak Side Safety

There is no telling what a weak safety may be looking for or on whom he may be keying. His assignments vary, from play to play, more than the others in the secondary. He is likely to look through the line and into the backfield for the same reasons as the strong safety. After doing this, his keys will be determined by the type of coverage the defense is using. In man coverage, he may be assigned to the weak side set back, tight end, wide receiver to his side, or be free to assist where he thinks he can be most helpful.

When covering the set back on his side; he may try to determine the path of the wide receiver to get a clue as to where the back will break. On those coverages that require him to cover the tight end, he is likely to look at the set back on the strong side of the offense. When double covering the wide receiver with the cornerback, his keys will depend on whether he is primarily responsible for deep or for shallow coverage on the wide receiver.

## The Interception

If the bomb or long pass is the most exciting play an offensive team can make, then the interception is the biggest play for the defense. It is the kind of play that can turn a game around in a hurry.

The art of intercepting a football may not be considered a fundamental skill by everyone, but there is a degree of skill involved in making most interceptions. Some, of course, are the result of being in the right spot at the right time because of sound fundamental play, while others are made because the defensive back was willing to anticipate and gamble on picking one off. It's the gamble which leads to most interceptions.

The defensive back considers the quarterback's call frequencies, the receiver's ability, previously successful routes, the game situation and the personal preferences of the receiver and quarterback. He then looks for a particular pass and, if the time is right for taking a risk, he may have an interception. The smart back only tries for an interception when the risk is minimal. He knows that his coach is not always impressed with the interception. Interceptions are measured against blown coverages and long passes allowed.

There are many defensive backs who believe that most interceptions are the result of luck rather than outstanding play. When Dave Elmendorf of the Rams was asked why he had no interceptions at one point during the 1977 season, he said: "I believe you have to be lucky to grab an interception. You either have to be in the right place at the right time, or the quarterback has to misread

Did cornerback Dwight Harrison (28) gamble on this interception?

the defenses."

Free safety Paul Krause of the Minnesota Vikings who has intercepted more passes than anyone else in N.F.L. history believes that there is more than luck involved; but, he also thinks luck is important: "You have to be around the offensive man when they're throwing the ball to him. You try to read the quarterback's eyes and watch the films. Most of all, you've got to be lucky. There is so much that is beyond your control."

Krause also believes that the type of defense a team uses has an effect on interceptions. The weak side safety allowed to roam "free" in man coverage will come up with more interceptions than a safety playing in the middle of a disciplined zone defense. The Vikings play the zone most of the time, so Krause doesn't have a whole lot of freedom. His area is usually the deep middle, and most quarterbacks don't throw much deep down the middle, going more for the short pass to the back over the middle or to the sidelines.

Whatever the primary reasons for interceptions, few would deny their importance. Defensive backfield coach Rich Petitbon, of the Oilers, as an ex-defensive back, may have a tendency to over-emphasize the importance of the interception. He said before the 1977 season that he would like his defensive backs to average two interceptions a game. He maintains that 28 interceptions means playoff football in most cases.

## The Safety Blitz

The defensive back must not only be a "cool cat" when the pressure is greatest, but should also possess more gambling instincts than those at other positions. A team is almost always gambling when the safety blitzes, but sometimes it just doesn't have a choice. It simply has to come up with the interception. Some coaches think that it's worth the risk because the safety blitz is one of the few "home run" type plays available to the defense. The defense is gambling that the quarterback will be pressured into throwing an interception or at least be thrown for a sizeable loss.

The safety blitz became prominent back in the early '60's when the late coach, Chuck Drulis of the St. Louis Cardinals decided to take advantage of Larry Wilson's quickness and toughness and put some pressure on the offense. Larry Wilson recalls the first time that it was used: "It was the first game of 1961 against the Giants. The idea was to outman their blockers. Up until that time we had been blitzing our middle linebacker and sometimes the outside linebacker." Wilson seemed to enjoy reminiscing as much as he enjoyed blitzing. He went on: "This time I crept up into position and when the ball was snapped I just shot in there and got him. I don't even remember whether it was Charlie Conerly or Y.A. Tittle, but I do remember what Drulis told me before the game. He told me that as soon as I tackled the quarterback, to get up and get back to the defensive huddle so he wouldn't know who hit him."

There is another reason for blitzing the safety aside from surprising the offense and possibly forcing a turnover with an interception or quarterback fumble. Even if the offensive backs read the blitz and block the safety, the defense has probably forced them to do something they wouldn't normally do. However, it also forces the defense into a vulnerable position and if the safety does not get to the quarterback it could mean six points for the offense. Larry Wilson admitted: "I got burned now and then, like when the cornerback didn't force the play outside and the receiver got into the area I would normally be covering."

Most teams in the N.F.L. have a weak safety blitz somewhere in their defensive playbook. However, no team presently uses it with the frequency that the Cardinals did in the '60's. Blocking techniques have become more sophisticated and quarterbacks taught to look for it and how to react when they see it coming. Some teams will occasionally blitz the strong safety, but most often it will be the weak safety since the strong safety normally has responsibility for the tight end in man coverage. When the safety blitzes, the defense is compelled to use man coverage since the quarterback will be forced to release the ball quickly, if at all, and the defenders must blanket the receivers immediately.

## BASIC PRINCIPLES

There are certain basic principles to which the defensive back should adhere. They are the things that make for individual and team success:

### React to the Ball

It is understood that the defender will attempt to intercept or deflect the ball when thrown to the receiver to whom he is assigned. He should be concentrating *on the receiver* and is often unaware of the precise instant that the ball is released by the quarterback. Once he sees the receiver look for the ball, he must react to the ball. The other defenders should also move toward the football once it leaves the quarterback's hand.

The distance that the ball travels and the defender's proximity to the intended receiver will determine his chance of deflecting the football. The interception of the long pass by the weak safety is frequently the result of reading well and reacting to the ball. The defender anticipates the release of the ball after several seconds. The free safety will look at the quarterback and, by moving in the direction to which the quarterback is looking and then reacting to the ball, he can often intercept. The defender may cover as much as 10 to 15 yards, from the time that the ball is released to the time that it is caught. Reacting to the ball is important even if the defender does not reach it in time to intercept or deflect it. If it is completed, he can help to make the tackle.

### Fight for the Football

The airborne football belongs to no one. The defender has as much right to go after it as the receiver. Both men can be as aggressive as they like as long as they are legitimately going for the football. Contact can be made as long as it is part of an attempt to reach the football and is not an attempt to ward off the opposition. Coaches tell their people to "fight for the football."

### Use the Sideline

The defender should attempt to use the sideline whenever possible. There is time to react to the football once it is in the air. The amount of time will vary according to the distance the ball must travel. When the receiver is running a route close to the sideline, the defender can safely remain to his inside with the knowledge that the receiver cannot break very far to the outside because of the position of the sideline. The distance downfield will determine how much room the defender can safely give the receiver to the outside.

### Take away the Outside

This principle applies more to the cornerbacks than to the others in the secondary. There are several reasons that cornerbacks play to the outside of the wide receivers. The basic premise on which most defenses are built is to force everythig to happen in front and to the inside of the secondary. There are several reasons for this. Running plays to the outside have a greater chance of breaking for long yardage than plays directed toward the middle of the line. The same holds for passes. In addition, the cornerback can get help more readily on plays directed to the inside. This help can come from the safety or one of the linebackers. There will be no assistance coming from the outside in making the tackle or deflecting the pass. Finally, the number of people in the middle of the field also make it more difficult for the quarterback to find a throwing lane.

### Watch the First Down Marker

Like the receiver and the ball carrier, the defensive back must be aware of the location of the first down marker. It should influence his play no matter where he is on the field on third down, and quite often may help him anticipate a play on second down. On third and 15, a 10-yard pass will not do much damage if the

Defensive back Lem Barney of the Lions taking away the outside from wide receiver Gene Washington of the 49ers.

receiver is not allowed to run for a first down. The cornerback should play it loose. On third and six from the offense's own 20-yard line, he should play tight and be more willing to risk the touchdown pass.

## Assist Others

There are times in every coverage when the defender will not have to cover a receiver. When the receiver to which he is assigned in man coverage stays in to block, he should look to help elsewhere. When his zone is clear, he should abandon it and help in the area that is overcrowded.

## Play It Safe

The defensive back should be thinking about the possibility of intercepting the ball every time it is thrown in his direction. However, he must never lose sight of the fact that preventing the bomb is his primary responsibility. The defensive player must sometimes gamble when attempting to intercept the ball. He can afford to take the risk when there is another defensive player in the area to make the tackle if he fails to come up with the interception. There is rarely an excuse for gambling when it may lead to a score. In such cases, he should not only *not* try for the interception, but should strive to deflect the ball with one hand while placing the other arm around the defender to make certain that he does not break away if the pass is completed. This is playing it safe.

## Use Teammates

The offensive player has the advantage of knowing where he is going to go when running a pass route. The defensive player has the advantage of knowing the type of coverage and where he is likely to get help. The experienced defensive back will utilize that knowledge. If a receiver moves into an area that the defender knows will be covered by a teammate, he can maintain a position that will enable him to defend against a more dangerous pass. Much of the success experienced defensive secondaries have is due to their ability to work well together. This requires that everyone know the location of the people around him. The Miami secondary played as well as any unit in memory when they won Super Bowls in 1972 and 1973. Jake Scott, Dick Anderson, Tim Foley and Curtis Johnson were outstanding individually and even better as a group.

## Do Not Tip the Coverage

Defensive backs, like almost everyone else on a football team, have ways of cheating to make their jobs easier. The safety assigned to double cover the wide receiver can cheat out a yard or two to make it easier to get in proper position once the ball is snapped. If he moves over too far or looks in the direction to which he will be moving, he can tip the coverage to the quarterback and wide receiver. This is one of the things that the quarterback will be looking for while scanning the defense. Unless the defensive philosophy dictates that no attempt be made to disguise the coverage, the deep scondary should try to align itself the same way each time. This is something that Don Shula, Bud Grant, Chuck Knox and all successful coaches demand of their players.

## COVERAGES

There are professional football teams that claim to have several hundred different defensive alignments to meet each one of the several hundred different offensive plays claimed by other teams. In most cases, what is called a "change" in defensive alignment is merely an adjustment to the set of the running backs or the splits of the receivers. Almost every change in position by an offensive player requires an adjustment by the defense. Only those that strive to develop the mystique surrounding pro football call each minor adjustment a different defense.

For example, when the offense lines up in a slot formation with both wide receivers split wide to one side of the field, the defense must make an appropriate adjustment. If the defense is using man coverage, someone must move into position to cover the wide receiver in the slot. The weak safety must move further to the outside and cover him or the cornerback may come over from the other side of the field and line up between the cornerback and the safety. Offensive teams will place a wide receiver in the slot to isolate him on a slower safety or to assure single coverage on at least one of the two wide receivers on the same side of the field. The defensive adjustment will depend on the speed of the safety and the coach's philosophy.

There are three broad categories of coverage in the defensive secondary with many variations on each. These are classified as zone, man to man (abbreviated as "man") and various combinations of the two. If each minor change in alignment and variation is counted for each of the coverages, a team can say it has several hundred defenses. This is especially true if the changes in the alignment of the front four and linebackers is considered. The diagrams provided show the basic coverages. The principles remain the same regardless of the variations in alignment. People cover *areas* of the field in *zone* coverage and *individuals* in *man* coverage.

## The Zone

The zone defense has long been the basic coverage used at the high school and college levels. In the pros, until 10 years ago, it was used primarily as a change of pace and in long yardage situations to prevent the long pass. In the zone, each man is assigned to a specific area to cover, but tries to help his teammates when possible. The defensive secondary normally covers the deep areas, while the linebackers are assigned to the shallow areas (see diagram). When the defense uses four deep backs, one normally covers a shallow area with the linebackers. The players in the deep secondary drop back quickly with the snap of the ball. This makes the zone sound against the long pass. The defensive backs do not have to concern themselves with stopping the quick passes over the middle and in the flat, and can concentrate on stopping the bomb.

The weakness of the zone is that there are not enough people to cover all of the flat, short and hook zones. In the past, it was generally accepted as gospel that any good quarterback, given time, could pick apart the "pure" zone by hitting his receivers with these flat, short and hook passes. For that reason some pro teams, such as the Oakland Raiders, stayed exclusively with man coverage longer then they should have. Field position and the other variables will determine when a team uses the zone and how tight the defenders will play. As a team backs up to its goal line, for instance, it must tighten its play if it chooses to remain in the zone. Inside the 20-yard line, there is no zone defense.

The zone has traditionally been popular at the high school and college levels because there are few good passers to be found there. They are not relying on the basic soundness of zone coverage, but on the unrefined passing of most young quarterbacks. The original word on the zone in the pros was that it was to be used only when a team did not have defensive backs capable of staying with good receivers in a one-on-one situation. The weak links could then be hidden in the zone. Gradually, as the passing art became more sophisticated, and the long pass more devastating, the pros drifted toward the zone. They recognized its versatility when combined with man coverage. The zone is now the staple for most pro teams.

There are several ways to attack the zone defense. The first is to flood an area with several receivers with the hope that the defensive people will not leave their pre-assigned areas to help the defender assigned to the flooded area. There comes a time in every zone defense when the defenders must abandon the zone and cover individuals. The trick is to make sure that the offense does not fill up the abandoned areas.

Some teams attempt to *dissect* the zone. Receivers are sent through various zones and into others in an attempt to draw the defenders to the extremes or edges of their zones. Hopefully, a gap will open between the two defenders who have been drawn to

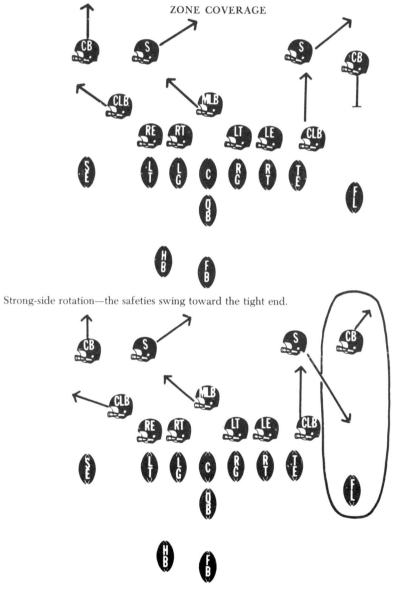

ZONE COVERAGE

Strong-side rotation—the safeties swing toward the tight end.

Safety-cornerback cross—the left safety and left cornerback exchange areas.

the opposite edges of their respective zones and the quarterback will hit another receiver in the expanded area in between. The key to picking apart or dissecting a zone is giving the recivers enough time to confuse the defenders, thus causing one defender to break too early or another not at all. Good pass protection is the key.

The basic premise of the zone is simple, but not necessarily easy to teach. It takes some experience to play it like the pros do, since each player must learn not only his assignment, but where everyone else is and how they are likely to react.

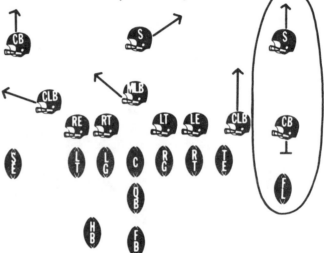

Pre-rotated strong-side zone—the left cornerback moves closer to the line of scrimmage prior to the snap.

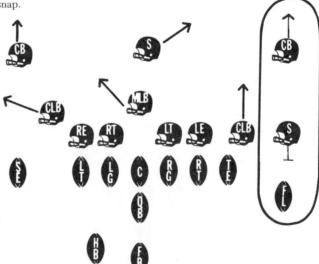

Pre-rotated safety-cornerback cross—safety and cornerback exchange assignments prior to snap.

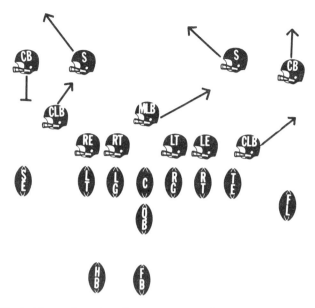

Weak-side rotation—the safeties swing away from the tight end.

Another way of attacking the zone is by sending receivers into what offensive people call the natural dead spots (difficult areas to cover) in any zone. As you can see from the diagram, they are located in the fringe areas between the zones. When two receivers

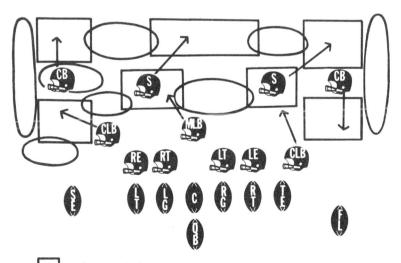

Squares designate area assigned to each defensive player.

Ovals indicate dead spots in the zone (vulnerable areas).

are sent into the dead spots on either side of a defender, a quick decision must be made as to which receiver he will cover. His decision, if not predetermined, will be based on who is playing next to him and where the other receivers are at the moment. This is a situation where the quarterback keys the defender and throws away from him and to another receiver who is open.

The viewer who has learned to recognize zone coverage, and knows how most quarterbacks will attack it, should be able to narrow the choice of defensive culprits after a completion to one or two players in the secondary.

## Man to Man

In man to man coverage, each deep defender is assigned to an eligible receiver on the offensive team. The cornerbacks are usually assigned to wide receivers, and the strong safety covers the tight end wherever he runs on the field. The weak side safety has the greatest variation in assignments among those in the secondary. He may be assigned to one of the set backs coming out of the backfield to run a pass route. When the linebackers are assigned to the set backs, the weak safety is often free to roam and help where needed (hence the designation "free safety"). The broken arrows and the variations given with the diagram indicate the other assignments often given the weak side safety.

An obvious advantage of man coverage is that the defender never allows the receiver to break completely away from him. His assignment is to follow the receiver wherever he goes. Unlike the zone, in man coverage, there should never be a complete break down allowing the receiver to wind up all by himself in the middle of the playing field. The completion should not be made unless the ball is thrown well.

Man coverage has several weaknesses. The football field has many open spaces. When a receiver is isolated on one defender and the offensive player has enough room to operate, the defender's assignment becomes extremely difficult. Given enough time, a top flight receiver can almost always beat a deep back one-on-one. This is the reason that defensive teams double cover the opposition's outstanding receiver. Man coverage breaks down against the great receivers, regardless of the indirect assistance many coaches attempt to provide by the deployment of linebackers. There are few cornerbacks that can cover a Lynn Swann play after play without direct assistance from the safety.

The other disadvantage of man coverage is that the linebackers are almost compelled to play the pass before the running game. When a linebacker is assigned to cover a faster running

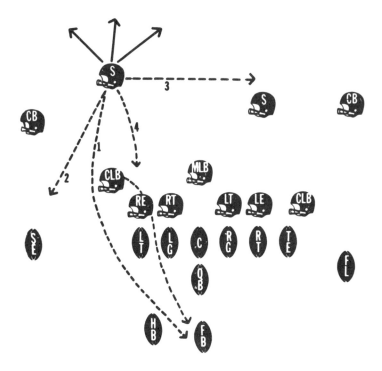

Man coverage with the weak safety free. The assignments are as follows: the split end is covered by the right cornerback; the halfback by the right corner linebacker; the fullback by the middle linebacker if he moves out into a pass route to his left and by the left corner linebacker if he moves out to his right; the tight end by the strong safety; the flanker by the left cornerback. The weak safety assumes various assignments: (1) blitzs; (2) helps double cover the split end; (3) covers the tight end while the strong safety helps double cover the flanker; (4) covers the halfback while the corner linebacker blitzs.

back, he cannot afford to allow him to get the jump on him. If the back breaks quickly to the outside on a flare route, the linebacker must respect the move. The outside fake of the running back may cause the linebacker to delay for that split second which will make the running play up the middle a success. Many believe that it is unfair to ask a linebacker to cover a running back in a one-on-one situation at all. The difference in speed is just too great.

The Oakland Raiders always had good defensive teams using man coverage. Despite good personnel in the secondary, they eventually had problems defensing against the pass. Richie Mc-Cabe, a defensive coach, actually quit the coaching staff because he believed the Raiders should be using more zone coverage. He stated his beliefs publicly when he announced his decision to take another job. Dave Grayson, one of the Raider's outstanding defensive backs, supported McCabe and spoke out after he retired.

Grayson: "Ninety percent of the defensive backs on the Raiders were in agreement with McCabe's contention that more zone coverage was needed." He went on to talk about the problems man coverage creates for the cornerbacks and the linebackers. "The corners are left hanging out there. There is no doubt that they put themselves in a frantic position. The Raiders have good personnel, and our backs and linebackers cover well. You can't ask a linebacker to cover a faster back on every play. Sooner or later he's going to panic."

The Raiders have gradually added more zone coverages over the years and for the last few seasons have been using as much zone as most other teams in the league. The stubborn Raider refusal to convert to the zone when Dave Grayson was playing was probably based on a belief that their personnel was best suited to man coverage. This becomes evident by the following statement made during the 1977 season by John Madden as he talked about his great cornerback Willie Brown. "It didn't take us long to realize how good Willie was. On man to man coverage he was just super. . . . he'd let a receiver get a step or two on him in practice just to encourage the quarterback to throw his way. At the time, we had two fine cornerbacks in Dave Grayson and Kent Mc-Cloughan. We saw how good Willie was and moved Grayson, who played corner in the All-Star Game the previous year, to weak safety." Another reason the Raiders held on to man coverage longer than anyone else was because of the bump and run (or bump and go) which was used more often by Oakland than any other team during the early '70's. A defensive back played bump and run when he lined up close to the line of scrimmage and repeatedly made contact with the receiver as they moved downfield. On certain teams, like the Raiders, the bump and go was a fundamental skill for the cornerbacks. It could be used in zone coverage, but was best suited to man coverage. The object was to "take it to the offense" by not allowing the receiver to run a predetermined route unmolested. He was forced to make adjustments each time he was hit. It became less effective as offensive receivers learned how to handle it. Eventually, in an attempt to increase offensive scoring, contact with the receiver was limited to one blow by each defender after he moved three yards beyond the line of scrimmage. The rule passed in March, 1978 states that receivers can no longer be bumped or "chucked" once they get five yards beyond the line of scrimmage. The defender can ride the receiver—keep pushing him as long as he doesn't break contact—as long as they stay within the five-yard area.

The key to good coverage in the secondary is teamwork. It is as important to zone as to man coverage. Although each defender has an individual assignment in man coverage, he still has the opportunity to help the people around him. There are five potential receivers on every pass play and seven defensive people that are usually assigned to guard against the pass. Depending on how many men the offensive team sends into the secondary, the defense may have anywhere from two to four extra people. Those linebackers and safeties that do not have to cover a receiver on a given play should find a way to help and not twiddle their thumbs. When the tight end does not come out on a pass play, the strong safety should be able to help the cornerback on his side. The linebacker assigned to a set back that stays in to block can move in and force the quarterback to throw over or around him on any pass over the middle. All this is a big help.

### Combination Coverage

Few professional coaches reject completely either zone or man coverage. Each has its advantages and both are used by most pro teams. The decisions as to how much of each will be used is determined by the offensive and defensive personnel and the coach's personal preference. The accompanying diagrams give examples of the many combination coverages that can be used.

Combination coverage allows a team to use man coverage if it has exceptional people in the secondary and at linebacker, and still put two people on an Lynn Swann. Combination coverage allows a team to cover up a weak link in its defense most effectively. Another advantage of combination coverage is the increased difficulty the quarterback has in reading the defense. Teams attempt to disguise the defense if possible. The quarterback and receiver that know whether they will be going against zone or man coverage have an advantage since certain routes and pass patterns are stronger against one than the other. By using combination coverage, the defense can keep the offense forever guessing.

### THINGS TO LOOK FOR

There are certain passes that are almost impossible to stop. Every defensive back must guard against the bomb or easy touchdown pass. Regardless of the coverage, he must remain between the goal line and the receiver. The defensive back goes into a game with the thought that the opposition may complete one or two short passes, but they will not get the easy touchdown pass from him. The cornerback will line up anywhere from 3 to 12 yards from the line of scrimmage. The distances will vary according to the speed of the receiver and the situation on the field. The defensive back and the viewer should be aware of the condition of

## COMBINATION COVERAGES

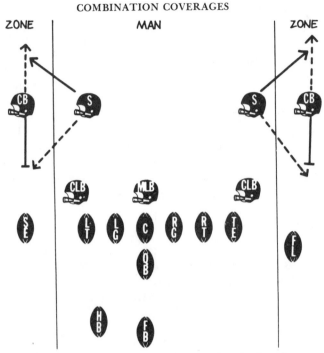

The linebackers are responsible for the halfback, fullback and tight end in man coverage.

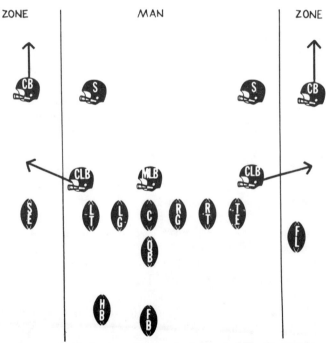

The safeties and middle linebacker will cover the halfback, fullback and tight end in man coverage.

the field, the down and distance, the time, the strength of the quarterback's arm, what passes have been working, the proximity of the goal line and any unusual weather and personnel considerations.

If you agree that a cornerback who usually plays six yards off the line should be 12 yards back in a particular long yardage situation, don't knock him if an eight yard pass is completed. He may not deserve to be criticized even if he is playing only six yards off the line and an eight yard pass is completed. Again, you have to bear in mind that the defensive back's primary responsibility is to prevent the long completion for a touchdown. As the receiver leaves the line of scrimmage, the defensive back must move backward to prevent being outrun. His distance from the receiver will vary, but the likelihood of his breaking up a short perfectly timed sideline pattern is under fifty percent. It is this type of route that Johnny Unitas and Raymond Berry made famous and about which we have read so much. If the quarterback and the receiver have worked together and the quarterback releases the ball before the receiver makes his break, there isn't much the defender can do to deflect the ball. The defensive back does not look at the quarterback, and does not know when the ball is thrown. He is looking at and concentrating on the receiver and will only look for the ball when the receiver turns to look. His only hope, if the ball is on target, is to make a jarring tackle just as the ball touches the receiver's fingers and try to shake it loose.

The linebacker can play an important role in helping the deep backs to prevent these quick out or short sideline patterns. If the team is in zone coverage, the linebacker may be assigned to the short flat area. Stopping the quick out pass is his direct responsibility. In man coverage, although not directly responsible for the flat area, he can assist by the way he drops back to cover the tight end or running back (see chapter on the linebackers).

The short sideline pattern is difficult to defend against even with certain zone coverages. It can readily be seen from looking at the diagram on page 180 that the cornerback who has rotated to the strong side, and is responsible for the short zone, has an excellent chance to stop the short pass. However, the corner linebacker on the other side has a difficult assignment in trying to get out to the flat to cover the split end on a short pattern. He can, and probably will, cheat out a few yards to get into the flat faster. By doing so, he risks tipping the coverage, or inviting the quarterback to check off to an off-tackle play if he moves too far to the outside.

With some study of the diagrams of the various coverages, you can recognize them and evaluate the performances of the players involved. The defense will attempt not to tip the coverage until the ball has been snapped. They must then move quickly. But, with some practice, most coverages can be recognized just as quickly. The keys outlined in the section: "Seeing the Defense Through the Eyes of the Quarterback," will provide a lot of useful information. Don't get discouraged. It takes time.

The fan interested in the passing game should be aware of whether the primary coverage is zone or man. This will help to explain some of the quarterback's calls. For example, knowing that the defense is in a zone will explain the reason for two or three receivers going into or through an area. It will also explain why the quarterback is not throwing long more often, and seems to be favoring the short pass to his tight end and set backs.

The many other factors that must be considered make it impractical for a fan to spend too much time determining the specific assignment of each man in the secondary. Recognizing the coverage may indicate who should have been where, but other things may have to be evaluated in determining why he was not in the right spot at the right time. The effectiveness of the offensive team's running game will affect the pass defense regardless of whether they are using a zone or man coverage. The defensive backs play pass until the ball carrier crosses the line of scrimmage. However, the linebackers have a dual responsibility and are directly influenced by the running game. The team that has established a potent running attack will cause the linebackers to tighten up and think of the run as the primary danger. Since the deep secondary is dependent on the linebackers, they will be indirectly affected. Good running and good faking will also influence the strong safety who has more responsibility for stopping the run than the weak safety.

Any effective ground game will make things more difficult for those in the defensive secondary. Even the cornerbacks will have a tendency to tighten their alignment if the defense is getting burned by the sweep. The play pass and roll out pass become more dangerous when used in conjunction with a good ground game. Don't criticize the deep back that has made several tackles against the run and then gets burned on the play pass. Remember that the good defensive back will take a peek into the backfield, and can be influenced by the fake of an offensive back into the line. This is the reason that many coaches discourage their defensive backs from ever looking into the backfield.

The rule of thumb is that one mistake may be forgiven if there are extenuating circumstances, but it should not happen twice in the same game. For example, you can find excuses for the deep back who goes for the play action fake against a team like the

Pittsburgh Steelers in a game where their running attack is effective. Franco Harris is an exceptional runner and Rocky Bleier is a fine all-around back. They not only run well with the football, but carry out their fakes into the line as well as anyone. When a team is running repeatedly, the secondary must be wary of the run. When Bleier hits that line with the same force on a fake as he would display on a run, almost any defensive back might be inclined to take the fake. The situation and personnel must be considered. The defensive back that takes the fake on third and two may be forgiven, but not the player that plays run on third and 10.

Look for the quickness the back displays in coming up to tackle the ball carrier once the run has become evident. The safety may be expected to make tackles behind the line of scrimmage, but not necessarily the cornerback. If the cornerback does come up fast enough to make tackles behind the line of scrimmage, you will probably find that he was covered deep by the safety and had the shallow area against the pass. Look for a player's toughness in making head-on tackles and not the ferocity displayed when tackling the receiver from behind. It doesn't take much guts to hit someone when he is up in the air reaching for the football and has his back exposed.

Fred Williamson was quite an actor long before he signed a contract to star in movies. He made a reputation for himself by hitting hard in a situation when the receiver's back was his target. I never saw him hit with the same abandon when a running back was approaching head on. He nicknamed himself "The Hammer," which is what he called his forearm. The newspapers gave "The Hammer" a lot of attention, but it was a joke to everyone in the league, including his teammates.

Evaluating the defensive back is sometimes as difficult as evaluating the offensive quarterback. Individual skills and qualities cannot be isolated and evaluated without considering almost every other aspect of team play. The pass rush, the ability to stop the run, the individuals next to the player being judged, the linebackers in front of him, the coverages, and the skill of the opposing receiver and quarterback all have to be considered. Statistics tell us little about the defensive secondary. As with the quarterback, it's the ability to perform at a high level over a long period of time which tells the story.

# 7

# THE LINEBACKERS

## Jacks of All Trades

The linebackers are the most misunderstood people on the football team. For many years they were overlooked by most fans—as an extension of the defensive line by some, and as a part of the defensive secondary by others. Whatever they were labeled, most fans paid little attention to their activities on or off the field. Most reporters and broadcasters are anxious to please the fan and will write and talk about the people on a football team that the fans find interesting. Traditionally, that has always been the quarterback, the receivers, and the running backs. Then, one day in the mid-1950's, a reporter covering the Cleveland Browns decided that he wanted to be a little different and wrote an article about the middle linebacker and his responsibility for stopping those big running backs up the middle. In this way, the defensive player was introduced to the fan.

Sam Huff of the New York Giants was not the best middle linebacker of his day, but he was good. He probably became the most famous defensive player of his time because he had the opportunity to play against Jim Brown during those years when the Giant-Brown rivalry was at its peak. Huff was a tough, hard nosed football player who gave his best. He was also bright and gave the press some good copy. What made him stand out from other defensive players was that he got the ink.

In the 1950's, a series of national articles was written about him and he was the subject of a network television special, "The Violent World of Sam Huff." It showed Huff playing against Brown and the viewer had an opportunity to hear some of the dialogue on the field. From that point on, everyone knew of the middle linebacker and the important role he played in stopping the run.

Of course, Huff's sudden attention caused problems with his

fellow players. His fame occurred before the Joe Namath era, when the show biz approach to pro football was still frowned upon. Football players were not expected to have an outspoken show business type of personality. Any attempt to draw attention to oneself was regarded as "bush" unless the individual happened to be an exceptional football player. Huff was not an exceptional football player in his day. The inside joke, that even made its way over to the fledgling American Football League, was that Joe Schmidt, the middle linebacker of the Detroit Lions, would be given the role of Sam Huff if they ever made a motion picture called "The Life of Sam Huff."

The middle linebacker has always received more attention by the fans and the members of the press than the men that play on either side of him. After Huff and Joe Schmidt, it was Ray Nitschke, Dick Butkus and Mike Curtis. Today, middle line-backers like Jack Lambert of the Pittsburgh Steelers, Bill Bergey of the Philadelphia Eagles, Jeff Siemon of the Minnesota Vikings, and Randy Gradishar of the Denver Broncos get most of the publicity. Certainly, outside linebackers like Chris Hanburger of the Redskins and Jack Ham of the Steelers get their fair share of recognition. However, the middle linebacker is right in the middle of the action and has a greater opportunity to be seen by the fan (taking away some of the attention due the average outside linebacker). Jack Ham is certainly visible enough when the op-position runs to his side of the field. However, he can't do much when they run to the *other* side. The middle linebacker, on the other hand, is instrumental in stopping *any* play run by the offense.

Another reason that the middle linebacker has captured the imagination of the fan is that the position allows him to be more aggressive than the linebackers that play on either side of him. The experienced outside linebacker almost always tries to outrun opposing blockers. Running plays are often directed right at the middle linebacker, though, and there is no place to run. He must take on the blocker, defeat him and then make the tackle without giving any ground at all.

Although the middle linebacker can be more aggressive than the two outside or corner linebackers, there is much more to playing linebacker than hitting people. Isiah Robertson, the fine corner linebacker froom the L.A. Rams gets to the heart of the matter: "You can't single out just one asset which is more impor-tant than others to the play of the linebacker." Robertson goes on to talk about aggressiveness. "Agressiveness? Yes, you need ag-gressiveness at the position, but I would not call it more important than the ability to read plays or how hard you hit a ball carrier or how well you defend against the pass. They all have to fit in together, and you can't name any one of them and say it is more important than the others."

## THE POSITION OF LINEBACKER

Until the mid-'70's, all pro teams used the 4-3 as their basic defense. The normal pro alignment utilizes four defensive linemen, three linebackers and four defensive backs. Some teams will use four linebackers on occasion, pulling a man from either the secondary or the defensive line. A team expecting the short pass might replace a defensive lineman with a fourth linebacker. In a long passing situation, the lineman may be replaced with a fifth defensive back. Conversely, in a short yardage situation, either the linebacker or defensive backs may be replaced with an extra lineman or two.

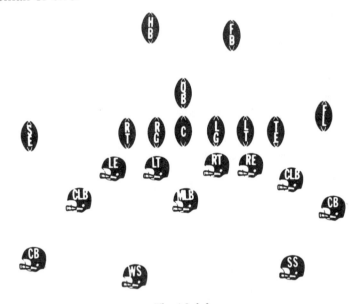

The 4-3 defense

The normal alignment in the 4-3 pro defense will have the middle linebacker directly in front of the offensive center and the strong side corner linebacker head-up or slightly to the outside of the tight end. The weak side corner linebacker will normally line up outside and behind the defensive end. The alignment of all three linebackers will vary with the front, the number and the positon of the defensive linemen.

The role of the linebackers has changed since such teams as New England, Denver, Houston and Oakland have changed their basic defense to a three-man line with four linebackers. It is called

The 3-4 defense. The middle guard, or noseguard, plays right opposite the center. There are two inside linebackers and two outside linebackers.

the 3-4 defense. Since there is no universally accepted dictionary of football terms, and coaches can call a play or formation anything they want, some have chosen to call it the "thirty defense" for the three down linemen on the line of scrimmage. These teams no longer have to put in a fourth linebacker in special situations, although they might replace one of the linebackers with a fifth defensive back in a long passing situation.

The use of the 3-4 defense in pro football reaches back into the 1960's. The Oakland Raiders, then coached by Al Davis, had a defensive player named Dan Birdwell who was a little too small to play defensive tackle and a little too slow to play linebacker. It seems that Davis just couldn't decide what to do with him. Birdwell was a hard-nosed player and Davis has always been partial to the gutsy type player. Since Davis wanted to keep him in the lineup and knew that he could leave him at at neither defensive tackle nor at linebacker all game, he put in a new defense. Oakland used the defense almost half the time while Birdwell was there. He would never leave the game. One play, he would be lined up in the traditional tackle spot, and on the next play he would be the fourth linebacker. Of course, the other defensive players would adjust their alignments when Birdwell moved to the two point stance used by a linebacker. The other defensive tackle would move head up on the center. This was the 3-4 defense, although the term was not yet in use.

Later, Davis began to move Birdwell to other positions on the defensive line as well. After first leading the opposition to believe that he was going to play the position of linebacker as they broke the huddle and approached the line of scrimmage, he might then line up in a three point stance opposite anyone on the offensive line. Birdwell would leave his linebacking spot and jump into the line at the very last minute. It was quite a difficult assignment since most players have enough trouble mastering the finer points of just one position.

Davis' original intention was to confuse the opposition by

moving Birdwell from the defensive line to linebacker as well as to take some pressure off of Birdwell since the offense couldn't attack him if they didn't know where he would be playing. When that proved to be successful, he decided to take it one step further and put him into different positions on the line. If it would not confuse the offense, it would at least force them to spend more time preparing for Birdwell at the expense of something else. That is the way most coaches think.

New England and Houston switched to the present day pure 3-4 defense in 1974 and other teams later followed suit. A team's personnel is usually the determining factor. If a team has more and better linebackers than defensive linemen, they are more likely to use the three man front, since there is nothing that makes the 3-4 intrinsically better than the 4-3 defense. The size of a team's linebackers also figures heavily in a coach's mind when deciding whether to switch to the 3-4. It almost necessitates large linebackers to compensate for the loss of beef on the defensive line. The 3-4 will be covered more extensively in the chapter on defensive formations since it has become increasingly important. However, the basic defense used by the vast majority of pro teams is still the 4-3.

It seems that, over the years, as offenses have become more explosive, the defense has always adjusted by substituting linebackers and defensive backs for defensive linemen. The use of the 3-4 is just another step in this direction.

In an odd front defense, the defensive tackle lines up in front of the center. The middle linebacker will move to his left or right. The two corner linebackers will also make the appropriate adjustments based on the position of the defensive lineman in front of him as well as the alignment of the offensive backs.

There is a relationship between the alignment of the linebacker and the positioning of the backs. The position of the offensive backs varies on almost every play in the pro-set. Since there are only two set backs, there is a vacant spot where the third back would be stationed in a full house backfield. The offensive backs will be lined up in the most advantageous position to run the play called in the huddle. The linebacker must adjust to the postions they assume. For example, the weak side corner linebacker can safely move one yard directly behind his defensive end when the two set backs are lined up on the strong side of the line. He will then be in good position to handle the run or the pass. Because the set back will have to move a greater distance to get to his outside, he will have more time to react to either the run or the flare pass.

All linebackers make appropriate adjustments according to

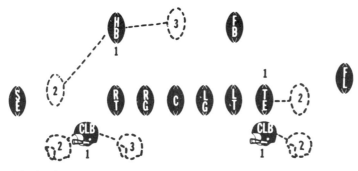

Normal linebacker alignment. The left corner linebacker adjusts to the position of the halfback. The right corner linebacker adjusts to the tight end.

each offensive formation. They cannot assume the same alignment against the I formation as they would against the double wing. The linebackers are responsible for stopping the short pass over the middle. It does not matter much whether the coverage is man or zone. In order to assume the responsibility of covering the set backs and tight end on the pass, they must move as the offensive alignment changes. If the set back moves out into the slot, somebody must go with him. The position of the other running back may determine whether the safety or linebacker covers him. If the remaining back is lined up to that side, the corner linebacker must concern himself with the run. Look for these adjustments.

## PHYSICAL QUALITIES

The linebacker has a greater variety of assignments than anyone else on the defensive unit. He must be able to take on a 270-pound offensive tackle who has had a couple of yards to build up momentum before making contact, handle a trapping guard approaching at full running speed, and stay with a speedy running back going out on a flare pass. He is required to be a bone crushing tackler, blitz the quarterback, run backward, straighten up an offensive center, catch the football, and read the offensive plays.

The defense lineman may get by on size and strength. The defensive back can get by with outstanding speed and a light frame. The linebacker must be an all-around athlete. He will not last in pro football unless he has an abundance of size, speed, strength, agility, and intelligence.

Despite the numerous skills required of the linebacker, there are rather wide variations in their physical characteristics. There are corner linebackers as light as D. D. Lewis, of Dallas, at 210 pounds, and as heavy as Sam Hunt, of the New England Patriots, who weighs in at over 250 pounds. They go as tall as 6'7" Ted

Hendricks of the Oakland Raiders and as short as Denver's Tom Jackson at 5'11". Middle linebackers are usually the biggest of the linebackers since they are in the middle of the action and have more responsibility for taking on the offensive lineman, with less room to maneuver.

They come in all shapes, but the middle linebacker should have sufficient size. In pro football today, the acceptable minimum is the 230 to 235 range. One of the smallest middle linebackers in recent years was Nick Buoniconti at 5'11" and 220 pounds. Buoniconti played pro football for 15 years and relied on his experience more than on his size. When he started playing, the average offensive guard and center was in the 230 to 240 range. When Buoniconti joined the Boston Patriots in 1962, I was considered a big guard at 242 pounds. Today we would both be small. Buoniconti was never bothered much by his lack of size. He used to say: "When Butkus hits you, you fall the way Butkus wants you to fall. When I hit you, you fall the way you want."

The middle linebacker is in a vulnerable position. He can be hit quickly by the center or either guard as well as by just about anyone else on the offensive team. He has more time to react than the defensive tackles, but does not have much room to operate on plays up the middle. He cannot give ground. Therefore, he must have the size and strength to neutralize an offensive guard, and maintain his balance when hit from the blind side.

The best of middle linebackers will occasionally be hit from the blind side. An exceptional fake in the offensive backfield may cause him to step in the wrong direction and be blocked by a lineman trying to take him in that direction, before he can recover and turn to neutralize his charge. More often, the middle linebacker will realize he has been drawn out of position and see the lineman approaching, but will not have enough time to react properly. He may not be able to plant his feet and get lower than the opposing player. In these cases, there is no substitue for size.

The corner linebacker has more room to evade a blocker, or give ground after making contact, than the middle linebacker. He frequently has enough time to go around the block or take a step or two backwards which makes it easier to get rid of the blocker. As a result, he does not have to be as big as the middle linebacker; but he should be at least as fast. He often has responsibility for covering the set back coming out of the backfield on a pass route. In man coverage, he may sometimes be required to stay with the back wherever he goes. If the quarterback has enough time, this could mean a 40-yard sprint downfield. There are not many linebackers that can stay with a halfback in a 40-yard sprint, so many teams try to help their corner linebackers in this situation.

## MENTAL QUALITIES

I don't believe that different positions require different temperaments for a player to be successful. The image created in the minds of many fans about linebackers is the one Ray Nitschke, Dick Butkus and Mike Curtis helped to create. All three were fiery, emotional and instinctive, but there are just as many with the outwardly quiet and introspective demeanor characteristic of the offensive lineman. Willie Lanier and Jeff Siemon come to mind.

There are no specific things to look for when watching a linebacker being interviewed on television, but there are things to look for on the field. He must move instinctively. There is little time for any player to think on the football field, but probably less for the linebacker than anyone else. He has no time to ask himself: Now what did the coach say to do in this situation? He must react!

This is not to say that reactions on the football field are not developed. The finest of natural athletes would not make the right move unless he had thought about it consciously at one time and practiced until the move had become instinctive. The linebacker that seems to be doing things naturally is the product of a lot of repetitious training. He has not been programmed as completely as the offensive lineman, since there would be too many wires to connect. However, he is carrying out well-planned assignments geared to get him to the right spot at the right time. Once he gets to that spot, he has more freedom for individual expression than the offensive lineman who is always somewhat restricted. The linebacker has the option of going around, over, under or taking on the offensive lineman. He probably will not decide what he will do until the last possible instant.

The many things required of the linebacker make intelligence important. For years, I marveled over Lee Roy Jordan of the Dallas Cowboys who retired in 1977. He was very quick. That was the only exceptional physical quality he possessed. He was not tall, he was not heavy, he was not strong and he did not have exceptional speed for a 215-pound middle linebacker. He was quick. But he was also tough and bright. Jordan was one of the most knowledgeable players I have ever met. Tom Landy was quoted as saying that having him in here was like having another coach on the field. I never saw Jordan attempt to overpower anyone on the football field. He knew he wasn't equipped for it. Instead, he used his quickness and experience to handle most situations, and he rarely made the wrong move on the football field. As far as I'm concerned, this was all made possible by his intelligence.

Jordan also called defensive signals for the Cowboys. The defensive calls are not as complex as those called by the offensive quarterback, but calling them requires the ability to think under pressure. One of the reasons that most teams assign a linebacker to call the defensive signals is that most of the deception by the offense is directed at the linebacker. The defensive linemen are looking at the people blocking them, and the deep backs at the receivers assigned to them. The linebacker becomes the logical choice to try to move out of position with a fake. This in turn demands an intelligent player at linebacker—the type of player best equipped to call defensive signals.

## FUNDAMENTAL SKILLS

The linebacker must be fundamentally sound. There is no way for the middle linebacker to plug a hole between his defensive tackles unless he is in good position and capable of taking on the offensive lineman attempting to move him out. However, the ability to read and react quickly (considered a fundamental skill for a linebacker) is more important. In many instances, he may not ever make contact with the offensive lineman if the play is removed from his immediate area. If he reads the play quickly enough, he may be able to beat the blocker to the hole.

### The Stance

The linebacker has more time to react and get set for the lineman blocking down on him than the defensive lineman. Therefore, his stance before the snap of the ball is not particularly important, as long as he is ready when and if contact is necessary.

All linebackers assume a two point stance, meaning, they must be in a semi-upright position in order to see the offensive backfield. There are coaches at all levels that insist that their linebackers place a particular foot to the rear depending on which side of the line he is stationed. This is really unnecessary. The important considerations are that he be well balanced, with his knees flexed, feet spread about shoulder width, body bent slightly at the waist, and his arms hanging loosely in front of him. Some coaches demand clenched fists and special ways of positioning the arms. The only important factor is that he use them when delivering the blow.

### Reading the Offense

"He who hesitates is lost." I don't know who said it first, but it must have been a middle linebacker just after having his bell rung by an offensive tackle blocking down on him. The hesitation may have resulted because he was not reading properly or reacting

How *not* to tackle Lydell Mitchell, using the proverbial stiff arm here. The defensive player should use a shoulder if at all possible.

quickly enough. Quick reaction is the primary factor in evaluating a linebacker. The biggest, toughest and most vicious tackler in the league is worthless unless he can get into position to make the tackle.

Each of the linebackers in the standard 4-3 or 3-4 defense has different keys (people to watch) at different times. Most will first read or key on the lineman playing directly in front of or closest to him. The offensive lineman will do one of six things. He will block straight ahead, to his right or left, pull out to his right or left, or set up to pass protect. The linebacker's assignment will vary from team to team and from one defensive alignment to another on that team. Some coaches will require him to shoot the gap vacated when the offensive lineman blocks left or right, while others will teach him to move in the opposite direction from the blocking lineman. When the guard pulls, the linebacker almost always moves in the same direction. If the offensive lineman fires out straight ahead, the linebacker must deliver a blow and plug the hole. (For this reason some teams call their linebackers "pluggers.") When the offensive lineman sets up on a show pass, the linebacker will drop back into the secondary to protect against the pass if he has not already started to blitz. The linebacker's reaction to the movement of the lineman near him should be automatic. The correct reactions come with practice, experience . . . and intelligence.

It takes a split second for the experienced corner linebacker to read the offensive linemen. He then looks at the tight end if he is on the strong side or into the offensive backfield if on the weak side of the line. When teaching a corner linebacker to read, rather than tell him to look at one man and then another, the coach will instruct him to look through the linemen into the backfield or to keep his eye on the tight end while looking to see what the offensive linemen are doing. Once again the football player with good peripheral vision has an advantage. The middle linebacker looks through the offensive center and tries to key the quarterback and set backs at the same time.

Every linebacker will be faked out of position once in a while, but it shouldn't happen too often. Don't look for the linebacker to be faked out completely. Look for a split second delay or moment of hesitation. This is usually enough to make the play a success.

## DEFENDING AGAINST THE RUN

The linebacker's assignment against the run is to make the tackle or, at the very least, plug the hole in the middle of the line and force the ball carrier into another defensive player.

There are two types of defensive charge normally used by linebackers. They are the shoulder and forearm charge and the hand shiver. When the play is coming at the linebacker, he must deliver a sufficiently crisp blow to stop and straighten up the offensive lineman. In this instance, the shoulder blow delivered under the charge of the offensive lineman is preferable. The problem for the linebacker is that he cannot always tell exactly where the play is going. When the runner is going into another area, the hand shiver may be more effective. When delivering the shiver, the defensive player hits the offensive blocker with the

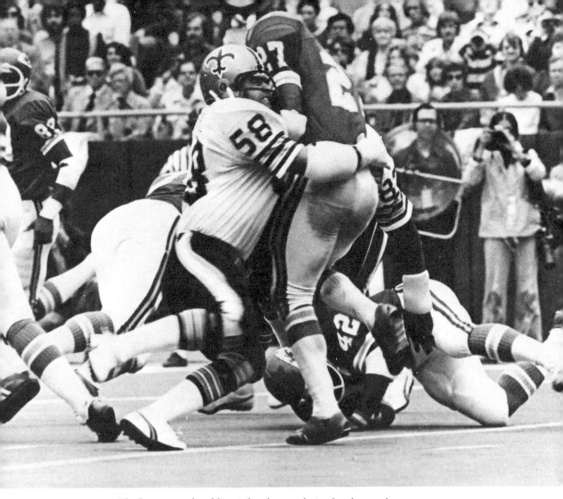

The key to good tackling is head up and aim for the numbers.

heels of his hands on the blocker's head and shoulders, with his elbows locked. He then pushes off and continues toward the ball carrier. It is effective in keeping the offensive lineman from reaching his body, and allows the linebacker to begin his pursuit more quickly. It is similar to the defensive lineman attempting to rush the passer. He will have a better opportunity to reach him if he can avoid the offensive blocker by going around him.

Again, being able to read the offense becomes important. The linebacker must quickly decide where the play is going and what kind of approach he should take to the charging offensive blocker. Some coaches teach their linebackers to use the shiver regardless of where the play is directed. This is a mistake. The linebacker should only use the shiver when the play is going into another area and he has time to avoid contact and sufficient room to maneuver. I have never seen a linebacker with the arm strength to *stop* an offensive lineman with a hand shiver.

If possible, expect the linebacker to avoid contact completely and try to outrun the offensive blocker. His assignment is to make the tackle and not knock down the charging lineman. It is less likely that the middle linebacker will be in position to make a tackle on an end sweep if he makes contact with the offensive center, than if he begins to move outside immediately. He should be able to read his keys and start his pursuit before the center can reach him. This is a perfect example of why the linebackers must key on more than one person at a time. If he restricted his reading,

This is gang tackling. The New York Jet ball carrier doesn't have a chance.

and reacted only to the movement of the offensive center (or guard in a 3-4 defense), he would make contact with him on the line of scrimmage, and often be out of position. However, if he sees the back running to the outside and the quarterback moving in the same direction on the sweep, he knows that there is no other place the play can go but to the outside, unless it develops into a reverse.

A defensive lineman may have played a fair game without making an unassisted tackle. The offensive team may not have run much in his direction and he may have held his ground despite being double teamed when they did run at him. Many fans will not accept this from a linebacker. A linebacker is *expected* to make his fair share of unassisted tackles and to be in the right spot at the right time.

There are plays, though, on which the linebackers have other primary responsibilities and are not expected to make the tackle. For example, the corner linebacker is usually responsible for turning in the end sweep. The linebacker that is out there in good position and forces the ball carrier to cut back to the inside and into the arms of the pursuing lineman has done his job well. The middle linebacker who has plugged the hole between the center and guard against the quarterback sneak, and forces the quarterback to run to the outside, has also done his job. Against wedge blocking (see glossary)—normally used on the quarterback sneak—the thrust of the offensive line is directed into the middle. There should be defensive players free to make the tackle on the outside. These are things for which linebackers are sometimes criticized unjustly.

## DEFENDING AGAINST THE PASS

Most linebackers prefer to use a type of zone coverage rather than straight man to man. There are few if any linebackers who can stay with a running back for more than 15 yards downfield. The corner linebackers usually take the set back to their side on man coverage, while the middle linebacker takes the second back to the same side. Both assignments are difficult. This is one of the reasons the zone, or variations of the zone, has become popular in pro football in recent years. The zone takes the pressure off the linebacker and prevents the bomb. At the snap of the ball, when it is obvious that the play is a pass, the linebackers drop back and cover a relatively small area of the playing field. When the potential receiver leaves his zone, a defensive back picks him up. The alternative man to man coverage would create situations where a linebacker would be involved in a 40-yard sprint with a running back. Strictly no contest!

There are three ways to defend against the pass: rush the passer, cover the potential receivers, hold up the receiver and prevent him from running his route. The linebacker is involved in all three. The linebacker will rush the passer when blitzing. His assignment is then the same as any other pass rusher . . . scratch, claw, run, dive or crawl to the quarterback. When covering a

Linebacker Randy Gradishar of the Broncos looking for the back on the flare pass.

potential receiver, he must remain between the receiver and the goal line to prevent the bomb or touchdown pass. In zone coverage, he guards his area, but tries to help elsewhere, if possible. The third method of defending against the pass by the linebacker deserves special attention.

The success of some linebackers in detaining the tight end is what first spurred people in the deep secondary to use the "bump

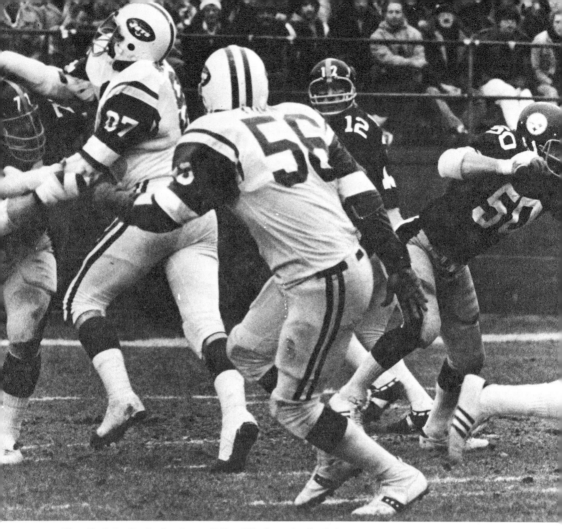

New York Jet linebacker Larry Keller (56) dropping back into pass coverage.

and run" (or "bump and go"). The intention of the cornerback playing bump and go was not to hold the receiver on the line of scrimmage for the duration of the play. The purpose was to force the receiver to alter his route and destroy the timing between the quarterback and the receiver. The linebacker often devotes much effort to holding up and causing the tight end to alter his release from the line. He can afford this luxury since the corner linebacker playing in front of the tight end knows that the strong safety is assigned to cover the tight end after he escapes from his attack. What will influence the intensity of the corner linebacker's attempt to hold up the end is the play of the set back he is assigned to in man coverage. If the back does not release, the linebacker will attempt to stay with the end as long as he can.

Since many of the tight ends in pro football are as large or larger than the corner linebackers, many coaches have stopped trying to detain them on the line. New York Jets' coach Walt Michaels thinks that it is improbable that a linebacker will be able to hold up a tight end consistently. If he succeeds, Michaels believes, he is often taken out of position and unable to cover the flaring back properly. The strong side corner linebacker on the Jets will therefore line up over the tight end and try to push or shove him as he releases. He does not deliver a shoulder which would risk his getting tangled up with a tight end and losing a step to the back coming out on a flare route.

As with the defensive backs, it is much more difficult to evaluate the play of the linebackers when they are in zone coverage. It requires more than being aware of the side to which a back has aligned himself and blaming the corner linebacker on that side if he catches a six-yard pass downfield. Be aware that the weakness of the zone is covering flat, hook, and short passes. These passes are generally the responsibility of the linebacker, since the deep backs are retreating rapidly to guard against the bomb. The key to successful zone coverage then lies with the linebacker. Look for the speed he displays in dropping back to cover his assigned area, after reading the pass. Remember that when assigned to a set back in man coverage, there may be no valid reason for the linebacker to move back quickly. This is because the back must travel further to get past the line of scrimmage. In the zone, the linebackers have responsibility for any receiver passing through their zone including those releasing from the line. This means that the middle linebacker must defend against the quick pass to the tight end over the middle and the corner linebacker must help defend against the quick slant-in pass to the wide receiver. If possible, his initial movement should be backward and to the outside to prevent the slant-in to the wide receiver.

When using the zone, the defensive secondary and linebackers have more opportunity to look into the backfield and anticipate the throw of the quarterback. They can evaluate the rush of the front four in relation to where the quarterback is looking and the location of receivers in their area. The good linebacker should be moving in the direction of the ball as the quarterback releases. He does not have as much time to react as the deep backs since the ball does not travel as far. However, the linebacker that can anticipate the throw may come up with an interception when the ball is poorly thrown.

The offensive team will attempt to flood an area of the zone or spread the defenders and hit a receiver in the seam or dead spot. The difficulty in playing the zone for the linebackers is trying to determine just how far they should go with each receiver coming through their area and when to break the zone and cover an individual moving into another area. The linebacker tries to read the pattern and be certain that nobody else is coming into his area. He should try to determine if his teammate has been drawn out of position. That information and the pattern may tell him who to cover.

There are times when there are two potential pass catchers in his area and the linebacker can really only guess. The quarterback may be keying him on the play, and throwing to the man he does not cover. In this situation, the linebacker must choose to cover the receiver furthest from another defender. It is essential that he know where his teammates are and try to watch the entire pattern as it unfolds. He may not be able to watch the wide receiver out of the corner of his eye for more than a few steps, but by knowing whether he took an inside or outside release, he may be able to make the right choice when the tight end and set back come into his area.

The roll out and the play action passes are used primarily to put pressure on the linebacker. The way he reacts to them shows how he reads the offense.

On the play action pass, the offensive linemen will fire out as they would on a running play in order to draw the linebackers in or cause them to delay a split second before dropping back into pass coverage. Since most linebackers key the offensive linemen as well as the backfield, they are likely to be held momentarily by the back's fake into the line and the aggressive action of the offensive line. The linebacker should never be faked out so completely that he actually tackles the faking back or provides no help at all to the pass coverage. It should take only a split second for him to diagnose the play if he is reading his set of keys well.

The roll out pass which takes the quarterback out into the flat area presents a different problem for the linebacker on that side of the field. He must not only be aware of the position of the quarterback and the receivers in the flat, but also of the position of his own defensive end. Since the quarterback may run with the ball if a path is clear, the linebacker must be certain that his defensive end has not been knocked off his feet and is in position to contain the quarterback. This is another example of the interdependence of the defensive unit. When the defensive end does not pursue, the linebacker may be blamed for the completion on the roll out pass even though he was forced to contain the play.

## SPECIAL PLAYS

There are three plays on which the linebackers have a heavier responsibility: the screen pass, the draw play, and the trap play. Let's go into them in detail.

## The Screen Pass

The primary responsibility for stopping the screen is usually assigned to the linebacker on the side to which the screen is being run. On the screen, you will frequently see the linebacker break into the backfield, get behind the blockers forming the wall, and hit the receiver as he catches the ball. If the linebacker reads the screen quickly, his play is not as difficult as it may appear. Since the offensive lineman cannot go across the line of scrimmage and attack him, he is often stationary as the linebacker approaches. The linebacker has another advantage since the offensive lineman does not know where the receiver is standing and when the ball arrives. Occasionally, you will see a linebacker get past the offensive linemen untouched, even though three were assigned to him. This happens because each of the three men looking at him thought the next fellow was going to pick him up. The problem for the corner linebacker becomes greater when he has not read the screen pass quickly and he has three 250-pound linemen moving full speed directly at him. In this case, he may have primary responsibility for stopping the screen, but he will not do it alone. He must have help from the middle linebacker and the rest of the defensive line coming over in pursuit.

The small and quick corner linebacker usually has a better shot at stopping the screen than his bigger counterpart. Many coaches have attempted to attack 215-pound Paul Naumoff of the Detroit Lions. It has rarely worked. Although Naumoff is relatively small, he is extremely quick and reads the screen as well as anyone who ever played the position. He has a knack of slicing between the blockers or going under one and coming up in the quarterback's lap. He has embarrassed more than a few offensive linemen intent on "creaming" the little guy.

## The Draw Play

The middle linebacker is responsible for the draw play on most teams. Of course, the defensive lineman must take care to rush within his prescribed lanes and not open an area in the middle that will be impossible for any middle linebacker to cover. The corner linebacker should also help on the draw play. Remember that the offensive back has the option of running into any hole that opens on the offensive line. The middle linebacker cannot be expected to plug every hole from end to end. He should plug the hole between the defensive tackles with the corner linebacker covering the area outside the defensive end. The corner line-backer must also help close the hole between the guard and tackle if the defensive end takes a wide outside rush. Bill Bergey of the Eagles is probably the toughest middle linebacker to run the draw against. His 250 pounds do not help in pass coverage. But, it is hard to fool him or move him out on the draw play.

## The Trap Play

The trap play is usually not considered a special play, but it does present special problems for the linebacker. If the linebacker is blitzing and happens to choose a spot between the trapping offensive lineman and the man being trapped, the offensive player is instructed to trap him. Don't expect much from the linebacker in this situation. There is little time to read or react and he will probably be blocked clean and totally embarrassed.

The offensive guard trying to put a predetermined trap on the corner linebacker should not be as successful. The corner line-backer has time to react and should be able to close the hole if he cannot make the tackle himself. When the ball carrier is forced to break to the outside, the play should be slow enough in developing to allow the deep backs to come up and make the tackle with help from those in pursuit.

Another problem for the linebacker on trap plays is the size of the hole that sometimes develops in front of him. Linebackers are required to plug the holes between the defensive linemen in front of them. Have you ever tried to plug a four-inch hole with a three-inch plug? The larger the space between the linemen, the more difficult it is for the linebacker to make the tackle. Because of extreme blocking angles on the trap play, large holes sometimes develop. Do not point a finger at the linebacker if the defensive man being trapped or the one on the other side of the hole is wiped out, leaving an enormous hole for the linebacker to plug.

## THE BLITZ

Just as the bomb is the most exciting play the offense can run, the blitz is the most exciting maneuver on defense. One reason for the popularity of the blitz is that it is readily discernible from the stands. The forward motion of the blitzing linebacker is often as easy to see as the wide receiver running a post route. The blitz may not result in a touchdown, but it often results in a fumble or a 10- to 20-yard loss.

The blitz requires a member of the defense, other than the defensive lineman, to leave his normal position and charge across the line of scrimmage at the snap of the ball to throw the ball carrier for a loss. Like the bomb, it represents somewhat of a gamble. When the quarterback throws the bomb, there is a possibility that the offense may be burned. Similarly, blitzing linebackers make the defense more vulnerable to the long gain. The defense is gambling that the blitzing linebacker will be in position to tackle the set back on a run or throw the quarterback for a loss on the pass. When he does not get the quarterback, it is hoped that he will force him to throw early or throw the ball away.

The Oakland Raiders blitzing two linebackers from the 3-4 defense: Monte Johnson (58, left) and Willie Hall (39).

If the defensive man does not get to the ball carrier in time, there are a lot of empty holes left in the defense.

The blitz is usually called in a passing situation, with the rest of the defensive team trying to compensate for the loss of a part of its pass coverage.

There are two ways a linebacker may blitz. The first is for him to wait for the snap of the ball and come out of his normal alignment so as not to tip the blitz. There is a greater chance that he will not be blocked if he waits until the snap. However, he will also get a slower start and have to travel a greater distance to reach the quarterback or set back. The alternative is to line up closer to the line of scrimmage and make no attempt to hide the blitz. Many even try to anticipate the count so that they are moving forward when the center snaps the ball. There is less of a chance that he will surprise the offense and remain untouched with this maneuver, but the linebacker will be closer to the backfield and may be able to beat the offensive blocker through the hole. And there is also the possibility that his alignment will intimidate the quarterback into changing his call.

Most blitzing linebackers don't expect to confuse the offensive people completely. They are satisfied to cause a moment of hesitation in the offense which may be enough to break themselves or a teammate free. For example, an active middle linebacker standing in the gap between the offensive guard and the center can cause a great deal of concern to that entire side of the line and to the set back behind them. Because the center is burdened with snapping the ball, he may not be able to block the middle linebacker standing in the gap. Some teams require the offensive guard to pick up the linebacker. This requires adjustments by the offensive tackle and the back. The linebacker that fakes the blitz and does not follow through may cause one of the three offensive players to hesitate a second before attempting to block his usual man. The delay may give the defensive player enough of an edge to get to the passer.

Most teams attempt to have their big offensive linemen block the opposition's linemen, and avoid having a set back block a defensive end or tackle on pass plays. The defensive team would like to have it the other way around. Some defenses attempt to isolate a set back on a defensive lineman by having the corner linebacker move into the line between the defensive linemen. He will do his best to get one of the offensive linemen to block him.

Jack Ham of the Steelers is one of the finest blitzing linebackers I ever saw. Despite Ham's ability to blitz, he is rarely allowed to do so under the conservative coaching of Chuck Noll. The blitz is a gamble and not normally used by teams with good personnel. It is often a hit or miss situation. If the offensive call is a trap play and the corner linebacker blitzes on the wrong side or the back makes a good cut, there is no one else to stop the ball carrier until he reaches the deep secondary.

The amount of blitzing a team does will depend on the coach's philosophy and the situation on the field. When the offensive team is behind, it is more likely to use the bomb. When the defense needs the big play, they may go to the blitz, hoping for a missed assignment, a fumble, or the opportunity to throw the quarterback for a loss.

Another factor weighed by many coaches when evaluating the advisability of the blitz is the caliber of the running backs and the quarterback. Most will rush the good passer and defend against the weak passer. The assumption is that the weak passer will not hurt the defense even if he does have time to find his receivers. The blocking ability of the set backs is equally important in deciding whether or not to blitz. The defense cannot expect to confuse or surprise the offense very often. The linebackers must believe they can get by the set backs.

The *experience* of the quarterback is often a factor in deciding the frequency of the blitz. Many teams will blitz against the young quarterback simply out of principle. It takes exceptional poise to sit in the pocket and continue to search for an open man when all hell is breaking loose several feet away. The opposing coaches are hoping that the quarterback will try to move back from the center too quickly and cause a fumble, throw too soon, or perhaps eat the ball. Any quarterback has to think twice when he sees Bill Bergey of the Eagles standing between his center and guard with the edges of his mustache twitching in anticipation of wrapping his big arms around a quarterback who cannot even use his hands to ward off the blow because he is holding the football.

A final factor influencing the frequency of the blitz is the quality of the people in the defensive secondary. There are two ways a defensive coach can compensate for a weak link in his secondary. One is to overload the weak area with additional personnel. The other is to try to force the quarterback's throw with the blitz. The former may be wiser if the linebackers have good speed and are capable of assisting the deep backs. Otherwise, the blitz may be the best way to relieve the pressure. Of course, the game and field conditions always have to be considered. There is no point in blitzing the quarterback if he is throwing against a 30-mile-per-hour wind.

## THINGS TO LOOK FOR

The linebacker should not be evaluated without considering the defensive line in front of him. The linebacker playing behind a defensive line that is consistently being blown back will be blocked by his own people more often than the opposition. The middle linebacker often has more of a problem with this than the outside linebackers. If his own linemen are reacting properly, he should never have to move around one of his own people to get into

Pittsburgh linebacker Jack Ham (59) straightening up a blocker.

position to make a tackle. There is not enough time.

The size of the holes up front must also be considered each time the linebacker seems to be in position to make the tackle and the back breaks free. This has become increasingly important with the advent of the option block, which gives the running back the opportunity to take the hole where he finds it. For example, the middle linebacker is expected to stop running plays up the middle. However, don't blame him if the play starts to go off-tackle and the running back cuts back into the area over the center because the middle linebacker has beaten the center and is plugging the offensive tackle's hole. The off-side tackle who was cut off and knocked to the ground may be guilty.

The role of the corner linebackers is often misunderstood on the sweep. A corner linebacker may not come near the ball carrier on this play, yet succeed in stripping the interference of the pulling guards. That would be sufficient to satisfy any coach.

The off-tackle play, with a guard leading interference, may also be misleading to fans. Many teams run an off-tackle power play with the on-side guard pulling out and leading interference through the hole. The pulling guard is told to turn upfield and look for the middle linebacker or anyone else who may stop the play. If the set back does not make a clean block on the corner linebacker, the offensive guard may be forced to trap block him. The corner linebacker may have made a fine play in destroying the attempted block by the set back only to be surprised and annihilated by the guard. After being "set-up" by the back, he should not be expected to do much more than occupy the guard.

The depth and speed of the linebacker's drop back when the defense is in zone coverage is important. This is relatively easy to evaluate since the space between the linebacker and the deep backs should not be exceedingly large, so as to prevent the receiver from hooking into the dead spot or seam. If too many passes are completed in the dead spot area, it is possible that the deep backs may be lining up too deep or dropping back too far. It is just as likely, however, that the linebacker is slow in dropping back. When a pass is completed in a linebacker's zone, make certain that the people in the adjacent areas gave him support.

The drop that the linebacker takes in man coverage is just as important. Check the linebacker when the wide receiver to his side catches several "quick out" or "quick in" routes. The drop of the linebacker may be the reason, since on this play the cornerback must lay off and guard against the bomb. The linebacker should try to drop back at an angle to the outside which will force the quarterback to throw over or around him when throwing to the wide receiver—a little maneuver that can be extremely effective.

(Of course, the linebacker should not be expected to move out of position to fully cover the set backs going through the line to run a pass route.)

Most linebackers prefer to stay in the zone defense. However, every defense has its strengths and weaknesses, and there is a place for all of them. Defenses are dictated by the men you have playing. Until recently many teams would place their fastest and best athletes on offense. This meant that the wide receivers were usually faster than the people covering them. This is not true today. The fastest men on the team are often found playing cornerback. They are perfectly capable of covering anyone on a man to man basis. It is the disparity between the speed of the running backs and linebackers that has caused the increased use of zone coverage. Jack Ham and Isiah Robertson are premier all-around corner linebackers. However, neither would relish the thought of covering an O.J., Walter Payton, Tony Dorsett or even a slower Lydell Mitchell coming out of the backfield time after time. Switching from man to zone takes the pressure off of both the linebackers and the deep backs.

As at other positions, look for balance at linebacker. The linebacker must not only be able to stop the run, he must defend against the pass equally well. A tendency to favor one responsibility may cause the offense to make adjustments. The linebackers may be playing for the run exclusively at the expense of defending against the pass. In this instance, the offense would be foolish to insist on running with the football when the defense is inviting them to pass. It may appear that the defensive secondary is failing when it is the linebackers that are inviting excessive passing. Make certain that the linebackers are neither too tight nor too loose.

Football players often have a tendency to try to overcompensate for their weaknesses. The middle linebacker with little speed may be prone to playing further off the line when a zone is called in the secondary. Look for any extremes in alignment which may be putting pressure on other players. The middle linebacker that is too far from the center may be leaving a hole that is extremely difficult for the defensive tackles to close. (It should be kept in mind that the linebackers will adjust their alignment to the game variables and may not be trying to compensate for a weakness.) In a passing situation, most linebackers will cheat back off the line. Their depth and position will also vary with the defense called and the alignment of the offense.

The position of linebacker is not easy to evaluate. Casual fans frequently place excessive emphasis on a player's ability to make jarring tackles and overpower the offensive lineman attempting to block him. Certainly these are importat considerations when seeking to determine the effectiveness of any linebacker. But, they don't tell the entire story. The linebacker's ability to read is equally important and may often make it unnecessary for him to overpower the offensive lineman. It is easier and more effective if he can outrun him when the play is not directed into the linebacker's immediate area. The speed and agility displayed when defending against the pass is as important as the ability to ward off a block and make the tackle.

There are many people who believe that Jack Lambert of the Steelers is presently the best middle linebacker in the N.F.L. Lambert is certainly near the very top of the list. However, my personal selection is Bill Bergey of the Philadelphia Eagles. He may not have quite as much range as Lambert, since he outweighs him by about 30 pounds, but he is much tougher from tackle to tackle and has remarkable range for a big man. It's hard to draw a definitive conclusion about who is better by observing their movements and the number of tackles they make, unless you consider the caliber of the defensive lines in front of each man. There is a big difference between playing in the middle of the steel curtain and playing behind the Eagles' front four. To appreciate Bergey, watch the way he straightens up the offensive lineman attempting to block him and refuses to give an inch, in many cases even penetrating into the backfield. He is strong enough to shed the blocker and fill the hole in front of him before it can open very wide.

Like Bergey, some observers contend that Dick Butkus was slightly overrated, claiming he was also weak against the pass. He may not have been the best middle linebacker in pass coverage, but he certainly made up for it against the run. Butkus made more story book tackles in one game than the average linebacker makes in a season. Any linebacker as big, strong and tough as Butkus is bound to be tougher against the run than the pass. He was the best. Undoubtedly, he would have been more proficient against the pass if he had played 20 pounds lighter. Would he then have lost his effectiveness against the run? It becomes a question of priorities.

# 8

# THE KICKING TEAMS
## A Study in Contrasts

The kicking game consists of kick-offs, punts, extra points, field goals, and any runbacks. One out of every four plays is a kicking play. The importance of the kicking game is often overlooked by the fan, but rarely by the coach. Even players have an occasional tendency to regard it as less important than play from the line of scrimmage. In part, that is because players are rarely chosen as members of the kicking, or "special" teams, as many coaches call them, because of exceptional ability. They are often called "suicide squads" by pro players indicating the enthusiasm with which the average player regards an assignment on one of the special teams. In pro football, they are generally manned by substitute players who are usually young and fighting to keep a spot on the roster.

The term "suicide squad" is appropriate because of the inordinate number of injuries that occur on the special teams. Once the ball has been kicked, most of the blocking takes place in the open field with players on both teams running full speed when contact is made. More body blocks than usual are used in these situations and the chance of knee and ankle injuries increases proportionately. There is also a greater chance of being "blind-sided"—hit head-on by a player whose approach cannot be seen. The unpredictable and wide open style of play and the frequent change in direction of the ball carrier increases the chances of being hit when not expecting it.

Although many players are not enthusiastic about assignments on the kicking teams, they are extremely important to the success of any team. It is a rare team which can survive three missed field goal attempts in the first half, as happened to Dallas kicker Efren Herrera in their 1978 Super Bowl win over Denver. More often, games are determined by the three points provided by the field goal, the blocked punt, and the kick-off or punt return that breaks for a long gain or easy touchdown. The kicking game often determines the outcome of a contest in a less spectacular way that may not be recalled at the conclusion of a game: the extraordinary punt that travels 75 yards and stops rolling on the two yard line. The importance of field position is not to be underestimated.

Virgil Carter, the ex-Chicago Bear and Cincinnati Bengal quarterback who fared better in the classroom than he did on the football field, wrote his M.A. thesis in statistics on the importance of field position in determining the outcome of football games. It didn't surprise anyone that he found that the location of the football when a team receives it influences the type of offensive plays called as well as the tactics of the defensive unit. The pressures and limitations placed on a team backed up to its own goal line make success in moving the football much less likely than when taking over near mid-field. The quarterback must call "safe plays" which are not likely to result in a loss for the offensive team. Passing from behind the goal line or running a sweep when backed up to the goal line can be dangerous and lead to a safety. The defense adjusts accordingly and every play becomes more difficult to run successfully.

During the early years, the "foot" in football was more important than it is today. There are several reasons for this. At one time the field goal was worth five (and later four) points instead of the three it puts on the scoreboard today. The goal posts in high school and college were on the goal line as they were in pro football up until recently. The ball was easier to kick because of its shape. (The football used today is narrower and more suitable for passing.) But, the introduction of the forward pass and the changes it caused in offensive philosophy was the most important factor in the shift of emphasis away from the kicking game. It practically eliminated the use of the quick kick and regular punt as an offensive weapon. Teams in long yardage, third down situations would frequently punt with the hope of catching the defense unaware, thereby improving their field position. The chances of breaking a running play for long yardage in a third down situation were slim. With today's high powered passing attacks, however, even a high school team is no longer considered to be in an insurmountable hole inside its 20-yard line on third down and ten. The quick kick just isn't worth giving up a down for. Today's offensive teams use the punt only when absolutely necessary.

## THE KICK-OFF

After the 1970 season, the New York Jets traded Jim Turner to the Denver Broncos for Bobby Howfield, an English soccer-style kicker. Turner had led the American Football League in scoring for several years while Howfield had been with several teams and was not regarded as a particularly accurate field goal kicker. Weeb Ewbank, who rarely made errors in evaluating players, stated that he was dissatisfied with Jim Turner's kick-offs. Far too many were returned for good yardage. The ideal kick-off is one that travels out of the end zone and cannot be returned. The kicking team will gladly give the opposition the ball at the 20 yard line rather than risk a touchdown or a long runback on the kick-off return. The Turner-Howfield trade points up the importance of the kick-off to the coach if not the players. It also points up the fact that even the shrewdest of traders and judges of personnel can make a mistake. At this time, Jim Turner is still going strong in his fourteenth year, while Bobby Howfield has long since returned to his native England. Turner never was very good at kicking off, but few have been more accurate kicking field goals from inside the 35 yard line.

There are three types of kick-offs. The one most commonly seen is the one where the kicker tries to kick out of the end zone or deep into opposing territory. The deeper the better, since the covering team has more time to get downfield. Height is important only if the ball does not go out of the end zone (which happens less often now that the pros kick off from the 35 yard line).

The second type is the "squib kick," which is kicked in such a way that the opposition will have difficulty in handling the ball. The ball can be placed on its side or merely kicked low to the ground from the kicking tee. Teams use this type of kick-off to compensate for a kicker who cannot get the proper distance.

The third kick-off, the onside kick, is used when a team is behind and needs possession of the football. The rule book says that the kick-off is free and can be recovered by either team as long as it travels 10 yards. Since the defense must line up 20 yards from the offense, the object is to kick short and to the side with the hope that the kicking team will recover the football after it has traveled the required 10 yards. The onside kick will occasionally be used by a team on the opening kick-off if they have seen a weakness when viewing films of the opposition or feel they are out-manned and need some breaks or big plays to win. The danger of the onside kick is obvious; if it fails, the opposition has the ball at mid-field.

There is little variation in the alignment used for a kick-off. As the accompanying diagrams show, the kicking team can either proceed directly downfield or execute a "cross." The cross is an attempt to confuse the receiving team and give the covering people more room to operate in avoiding the blockers. The faster

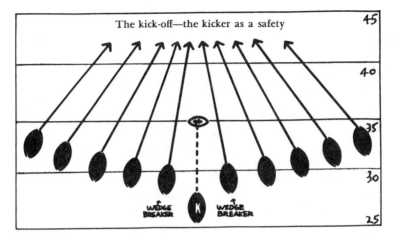

The kick-off—the kicker as a safety

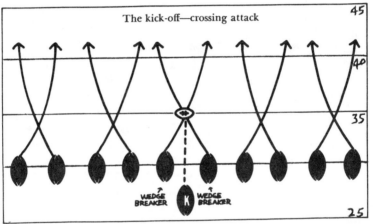

The kick-off—crossing attack

men are generally assigned to outside positions on the kick-off team, while the bigger people are given positions closer to the kicker. Those lined up on the inside will have to take on at least one and perhaps two blockers. The two men on either side of the kicker are called "wedge breakers." Their primary responsibility is to reach the wedge forming up the middle by the returning team and to take out several blockers.

The "wedge buster" has to be a special individual. He not only has to enjoy his work on the suicide squads, but also must have some of that "hari-kari" spirit. Almost every team has one or two especially hungry or dedicated (if you prefer) rookies or free agents who are particularly willing to hurl their bodies through the air with complete abandon on kick-offs in an effort to knock down several players in the wedge. There is no special way to break the wedge. I have seen players go around it, through it, under it and even over the top to get the ball carrier.

Many players have made local reputations as special team players over the years. However, Vince Papale of the Philadelphia Eagles has made a national reputation for his spirited play on special teams. Papale isn't very big and doesn't break the wedge for the Eagles, but his speed and quickness make him especially effective as one of the two outside men covering punts. Regardless of where he is lined up, he will be in on the tackle or near it on kick-off coverage.

The story of how Papale came to be an Eagle probably has accounted for much of the national attention he has received. It isn't very often that a 30-year-old sandlot player who didn't play college ball makes it in the N.F.L. In fact, Papale played high school football only as a senior when he grew to 5'5", 145 pounds. Prior to that, his coach thought he was too small to play football. After high school, Papale didn't play football at any level for eight years. He then enlisted in the Delaware County Rough Touch League and signed to play for a Chester, Pennsylvania bar called The Gross Place. From the Touch League he went to the Aston Kights (a local semi-pro team) in the Seaboard Football League and later was one of 800 players who showed up at a one day tryout for the Philadelphia Bell of the World Football League. At age 28, Papale earned his first dollar as a professional athlete. When the W.F.L. folded, Papale talked himself into a tryout with the Eagles and made it as a 30-year-old rookie in 1976. That's determination!

Most kick-off teams do not line up straight across the field. There is no starting count on the kick-off and the players on the kicking team must be certain not to go offside by passing the ball before it is kicked. By lining up at various distances from the ball, they can watch the approach of the kicker and get a running start.

In theory, the man that kicks off should be making more than his share of tackles, if he is doing his job. He has a running start and does not have to concern himself with being offside. However, in pro football, where the kicker is often a specialist (without the size and speed to cover the kick), this is not true. In order to slow down the kicker in those cases where he does cover, the receiving team may assign a player to charge toward the kicker and block him. In turn, one of the wedge busters may be assigned to protect the kicker before going down to cover the kick. Some of the older and more fragile kickers may be intimidated by the blocker since the follow-through on the kick-off makes him vulnerable before he can take steps to protect himself.

Ben Agajanian, the toeless wonder who gained fame with the New York Giants, finished his career when past 40 with the San

Diego Chargers. During a championship game against Houston in 1961, I remember standing next to him before the halftime kick-off. I asked him to try to put the kick out of the end zone. He said: "O.K. I'll kick it out even if it means getting laid out." Until that time I never realized that a kicker was vulnerable and might hold back a little on his follow through if the opposition was making a determined effort to "lay him out."

The kicker, or some other player, is usually designated as the safety man on the kick-off. He is instructed to proceed slowly downfield to back up the first wave of players. His duty is to prevent the touchdown and he should have good speed and be a sure tackler. The rest of the players on the kicking team should keep relative distances and converge on the opposing player returning the kick. Players should avoid being knocked off their feet or leaving their lanes. If a player is knocked down, the people on either side of him should compensate and close the hole he has created. If they fail to do this, it's all up to the safety.

In pro football, you will find players of varied sizes and positions on the kick-off team. Except for the wedge busters, most coaches choose their people on the basis of speed rather than size. When pursuing on kick-offs, it is just as effective to go around a player as through or over him. In high school and college, where you will see the regular players on the special teams, the interior linemen will line up close to the kicker, with the ends and backs to the outside. Some coaches prefer to place defensive players, especially defensive backs and linebackers, on the kick-off team. Elijah Pitts, the special teams coach for the Rams in 1977, feels that for coverage, you need people who are used to tackling, people who want to *attack* the ball carrier rather than people who are mentally conditioned to protecting him.

On the other hand, Pitts looks for the sort of player who is used to blocking—offensive linemen, tight ends, players who instinctively will *protect* the ball carrier—to play on the kick-off return team.

## THE KICK-OFF RETURN

Staffing the kick return team requires more than determining the fastest and toughest people available. People on the return teams are required to block. In pro football, you will sometimes see the regular offensive linemen on the kick-off return team. They are usually placed between their own 45 and 50 yard line, where the receiving team is required to place five men. Linemen can also be found deeper in their own territory where they may be assigned to form part of the wedge. The blockers up front should

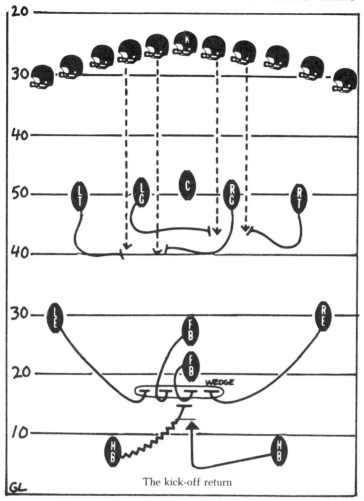

The kick-off return

be throwing cross body blocks while those forming the wedge should line up shoulder to shoulder and simply run over anyone in their way.

There are two places to run the football when returning a kick-off: up the middle or to one side. The type of return is predetermined, but adjustments may be necessary if the kick does not travel up the middle of the field. There is not much chance of running a planned "right" return if the ball is kicked to the left. It would take too long for the ball carrier to get around the wall of blockers. The ball that is kicked to one side will cause the receiving team to form a wedge on that side. The adjustments are all programmed and will be called by the receiver or a member of the wedge if there is some question as to whether they should be made.

Teams at the high school and college level sometimes form a wedge with the five players lined up between the 40 and 45 yard line. This is impractical at the pro level where the kick goes deeper and where a wedge formed so far upfield would be too far from the ball carrier. The pros form a wedge with the four deep people (see diagram); the safety not receiving the ball helps out. The players up front may block straight ahead or use cross blocking.

I have written much about the blocking necessary for a good kick-off return. But, more often than not, a good return on kick-offs or punts is the result of an outstanding effort by the return man. There is probably more room for improvisation when returning kicks than in any other aspect of the game. The return man will frequently abandon the wedge, run away from his blockers or outrun them, or reverse his field.

There is presently a semi-popular song being aired in New York with the title: "Short People." The first lines states: "Short people have no reason . . . short people have no reason . . . short people have no reason to live." The song is only semi-popular because, as expected, it is not popular with short people! If I had to rewrite the song about pro football, the first line would be: "Short people have no reason to play in the N.F.L. . . . unless they return kicks." It is the only area where being short is an advantage. I can't prove it, but I'm convinced that short people are quicker if not necessarily faster. Quickness in acceleration, changing direction and stopping and starting are the keys to returning kicks. Of course, men ranging in height between 5'8" and 5'10" may not be considered short when walking down Main Street, but they are comparatively short when viewed on a pro football field.

As proof that short people are quicker and therefore better suited to returning kicks, I cite the fact that nine regular punt returners in the 14-team National Football Conference were 5'10" or less during the 1977 season. Three more were 5'11" and there was one at 6'. Butch Johnson of Dallas was the tallest at 6'1" and Eddie Payton of the Lions the shortest at 5'8". In addition to quickness, there is also less of a short man for the opposition to get a piece of when trying to tackle him. Since an extra yard or two is meaningless on kick returns, there is little advantage to having a bigger man who can overpower the opposition. The chances of his breaking a tackle which would allow him to go all the way for a touchdown are slim. We may therefore conclude that short people not only have a right to live, but also to play in the N.F.L.

## THE PUNT

Since the early days of football, the use of the punt has changed more dramatically than any other phase of the kicking game. It is now seldom used as an offensive weapon at any level and practically never in pro football. The conditions under which a team may attempt to punt depends on several variables including the skill of its field goal kicker. The rule change of several years ago which moved the goal posts back to the end line, and required that missed field goal attempts which passed the goal line be returned to the point of the kick, put a further premium on good punting.

There are a number of ways to get off a punt. The basic formations in use today are the tight punt, and the spread punt. The spread punt is now the more popular of the two. It spreads the defense and allows the men on the punting team to get downfield faster and cover the entire width of the field.

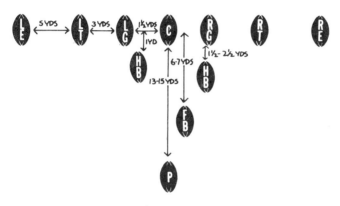

The spread punt

The defensive team occasionally attempts to hold the offensive linemen on the line so that the punt cannot be covered quickly. The chances of detaining the offensive linemen are greater if the offense is in a tight punt formation. It is used in situations where protection for the punter is more important than good coverage.

Since the chance of a defensive player breaking through in the spread punt is greater, the punter is required to line up deeper so he will have more time to get off the punt. The kicker will line up 10-12 yards behind the center on the tight punt. He will line up 13-14 yards deep on the spread punt. A center capable of making a good snap is essential.

There are several ways to align the backs on the spread punt. Some coaches prefer to place the backs close to the line to plug the most dangerous holes in the offensive formation. The coaches have several considerations: the shortest distance between two points is a straight line; the opposing player coming straight up the

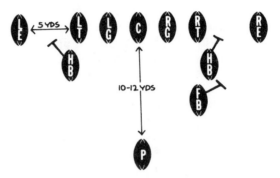

The tight punt

middle has less ground to cover and will reach the punter faster if he is not blocked; it is easier to block a defender as he comes through a hole in the offensive line; the further the backs line up from the line of scrimmage, the more room the rushing player has to maneuver and the more difficult it is to block him. On the other hand, the back that lines up six or seven yards from the line of scrimmage will be able to help in any area necessary and will not be confined to blocking in one small area.

Each member of the punting team has two duties. He must block; he must cover the punt. Blocking for the punt is not difficult since it requires little more than making contact with the rushing player. Blocking sometimes breaks down because the defensive linemen are overly anxious to get downfield and make tackles. Ideally, the offensive lineman should fire out into his opponent and drive through him in an attempt to get downfield. The momentum created by moving into the defensive player will allow him to break away if his opponent is attempting to hold him at the line.

All men on the covering team must maintain a relative distance to each other and converge on the punt returner. If the timing is perfect, the receiver will be hit just as he catches the football. This does not occur too often, though, and the covering linemen are forced to come under "control" by slowing down before making the tackle. They may not hit as hard as the player that keeps running at full speed, but the runner will find them more difficult to avoid.

## THE PUNT RETURN

The receiving team has two alternatives here. It can attempt to block the punt or attempt to return it all the way back for a touchdown. A punt can be blocked by any man on the defensive side of the line. However, most often, the man that does the damage comes either up the middle or from the outside. Success can be the result of a hard rush for the punter after several half-hearted efforts to hold up the opposition on previous punts. It can also be the result of a concerted effort on the part of several defensive players. Offensive linemen may be pulled out of position by one man to allow another to come free, or one area may be overloaded forcing the blocker to make a decision. This maneuver is used most often on the end man of the line. Here, an opposing player approaches to his inside and another to his outside. Hopefully, one of the two will come free. In all instances, the individual that blocks the punt must have speed and quickness.

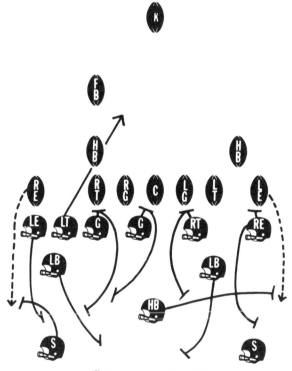

Punt return up the middle

The punt may be returned up the middle or to one side. However, the return up the middle is used more often as a change of pace, since it is much more difficult to execute successfully. It is extremely difficult to hold up the offensive linemen and then beat them downfield to block them again. The return up the middle also requires the return team to block those covering wide on both sides of the field, since almost everyone has an opportunity to get into position to make the tackle on a middle return. On the other

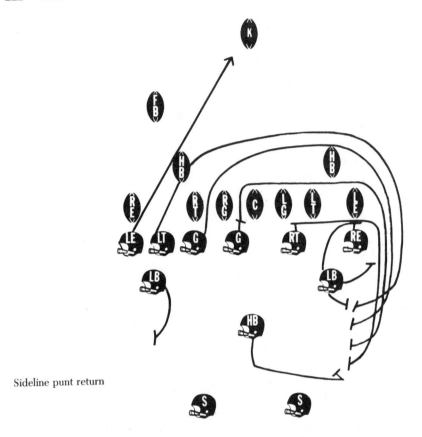

Sideline punt return

hand, when the return is to one side, the defensive men on the other side of the field will have to travel too far to be in on the tackle. The key to a successful sideline punt return is the duration of time the defensive linemen can hold those covering the kick on the line. The first block by the non-receiving safety is also extremely important. After holding the linemen on the punting team, the players on the return team spring downfield and form a wall along the sideline. The spacing and ability to pick out an individual without doubling up on one man is important. Like the block of the safety or halfback downfield, the first block by the end is often vital. Success on the special teams is sometimes due to luck, but more often it goes to the team that emphasizes them during the practice week.

## FIELD GOALS AND EXTRA POINTS

The formation used for both the field goal and the extra point is identical. The offensive linemen are toe to toe with only the

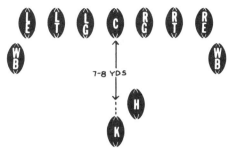

Field goal and extra point formation

slightest splits permitted. Most teams require their players to block an area by taking any rusher that comes to a player's inside. Protecting the inside will also assist the center who is at a disadvantage because his head is down to make the snap. The team that blocks individuals instead of areas has specific rules to follow and

Wedge blocking on the place kick.

the linemen are told to talk freely if there is any chance of confusion. There is no reason for deceptive practices, nor a need to keep blocking assignments a secret on the special teams. Everyone knows what is coming. Since protection is extremely important in this situation, size and strength are the deciding factors in assigning men to the place kicking team.

## BLOCKING THE PLACE KICK

The place kick is blocked as often from the outside as it is up the middle. The same procedures that are used to block the punt are used here. An area is overloaded or rushers try to pull away offensive linemen and have a teammate move through the hole created. When a kick is blocked up the middle, the height of the kick becomes a factor. This is one of the complaints coaches have against soccer-style kickers. Most soccer-style kicks are supposedly blocked up the middle. The increased height of the defensive linemen and linebackers has made the arc of the kick even more important. When players like 6'7" linebacker Ted Hendricks of the Oakland Raiders leap, the kicker has a problem.

When a field goal or extra point can decide a game, the defense is likely to try anything that might work. Players used to climb on teammates to get higher and have a better chance to block the ball. It rarely worked. The N.F.L. Rules Committee recently ruled it illegal.

## INDIVIDUALS IN THE KICKING GAME

The two key individuals in the kicking game are the punter and the place kicker. At one time, it was common for a player to assume kicking duties in addition to playing a regular position. Lou Groza, of the Cleveland Browns, was probably the best known of the place kickers while playing offensive tackle for many years. Ben Agajanian also played another position during his early years. At the pro level today, however, the place kicker, like the punter, is almost always a specialist. Eventually, as players at the lower levels begin to develop their kicking skills earlier, teams will probably find one player to perform both skills. We mentioned Bobby Howfield earlier. He had several good years with Denver but was disappointing after being traded to the Jets and did not last very long. Another New York kicker, Pete Gogolak, also had his ups and downs. Pete was the first sidewinder or soccer-style kicker in pro football. He was a celebrity in Buffalo and New York after being the first player to jump from the American Football League to the New York Giants in the N.F.L. Gogolak seemed to lose his ability overnight. Jan Stenerud cost Kansas City the American Football Conference Championship when he missed three field goals against Miami in a playoff game in the early '70's. It seemed at the time that he had suddenly lost his skill but that was just an off day and Stenerud is still active and near the top of the N.F.L. kicking list.

The question, then, is why a kicker can be on top one day and a bum the next. The quick answer is that it must be the blocking, the snap, or the hold. The truth is that all of these factors can be corrected quickly when they break down. When a kicker goes sour, *he's* the one to blame.

There is only one reason for a kicker in his physical prime to suddenly lose his skill. Like the quarterback, the kicker must be a cool cat. He has no place to work out his frustrations. He does not block and tackle. He does not catch the football or run with it. He sits on the bench and he thinks about his next kick. If he thinks too much and begins to worry, he may lose that coolness and the magic of his leg. You can't make an effort when kicking the football. It is a smooth and methodical skill that starts the same way every time. The only thing that can vary is the follow through. I don't pretend to know why each of the kickers mentioned above had off years or lost their skills prematurely, but, I think that if you look into it, you'll find that it was a question of outlook rather than a breakdown of skills. I know this was the situation in Bobby Howfield's case. He had marital and emotional problems—or perhaps more accurately, emotional problems which led to marital problems—about the time his kicking deteriorated.

This is what Tony Fritsch of the Houston Oilers had to say about kicking. "To be a good kicker you've got to have ice water in your kidneys. I played eight years of professional soccer in Austria. I have played before 100,000 people. When I kick the ball I cannot worry about the crowd, the wind or the grass. What am I to do if the grass is too high? Call time out and cut it before I kick? I concentrate on the ball under any conditions. If I miss, I concentrate on the next kick."

Although most of a kicker's success is due to his emotional outlook and ability to handle the pressure, certain mechanical skills are essential. Let's take a look at them.

### Place Kicking

The place kicker is more dependent on his teammates than the punter. The ball must be snapped accurately and quickly from the center to the holder, and then placed in a predetermined spot by the holder. It has to be done the same way each time. Any variation, even the slightest, will throw off the timing. The mechanics of the snap and the placing of the ball are as simple as they appear. The key to mastery is repetition and concentration. Charlie Waters, who is the holder for the Dallas Cowboys, takes perhaps 100 center snaps on an average practice day. Allowing for days off, that comes to about 2,000 a month or 12,000 during an average season. Waters says it's all concentration. A receiver at Clemson, Waters obviously takes pride in holding. It's the first thing he does every day before practice and it's the first thing he does on game day. That is why, although Charlie Waters has had a lot of close calls, but has never missed a snap.

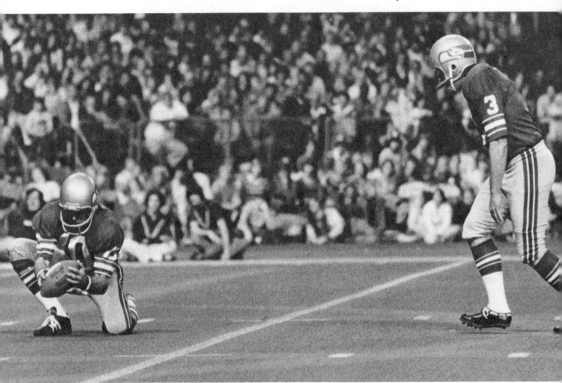

The holder is essential on the place kick.

Look for a snap from center that strikes close to the position of the holder's hands and a quick, smooth placement. The holder's hands will usually be held out in front of the body to provide a target for the center. If the kicker has to take a stagger step, you may assume that the snap or hold was at fault. It may have been due to an early start by the kicker, but you can give him the benefit of the doubt the first time it happens.

Charlie Waters had this to say about the importance of the snap and Dave Manders, the center from whom he took the snap for several years: "Manders spoiled me when I first started to hold. He could hit you in the hands every time with a perfect spiral. The incredible thing was that the strings were almost in perfect position every time. Ideally, the strings should be away from the place

Not all kickers keep their heads down. Roy Gerela of the Pittsburgh Steelers.

But, Efren Herrera of the Cowboys does. His is the traditional, straight-ahead approach to the ball.

kicker's shoe. Oh, maybe a few times I would have to give the ball a half-twist, but mostly it was perfect."

There is little to say about how to kick the football. The best way is the one that causes the ball to travel through the uprights. The American style kicker looks down at the spot where the ball will be placed before the snap and stands about one long step from the ball. There is no time to stand back any further. Most kickers take a short step with the foot that will strike the ball and then a step with the other foot before making contact. Almost all place kickers make a determined effort not to look up too soon after making contact. This prevents them from taking their eyes off the ball before following through. Jim Turner thought it was funny when I asked him why he looked up immediately and did not follow the ritual of most kickers. His reason: "I want to see where the ball is going just like you." Jim believed he was experienced enough to follow through whether he kept his head down or not.

The soccer-style kickers have done much to convince coaches that the number of steps and style is unimportant as long as the kicker gets through the uprights. However, the ball should also have enough arc to clear the on-rushing defensive lineman. If too many are blocked up the middle, the coach should start to ask himself some questions.

The only difference between the place kick and the kick-off is that on the kick-off the kicker has a running start and does not have to get an immediate arc on the ball. Nothing has to be cleared on the kick-off, but height is an asset if the ball does not travel out of the end zone. This gives the covering team time to get downfield. Most kickers take seven to nine strides on kick-offs. Once again, it's a question of individual preference. The speed of the leg is more important than the speed of the individual. Englishman John Smith of the New England Patriots might explain that it is the "pendulum velocity" that determines the distance a ball will travel. In translation, that means that the speed of the lower leg as it strikes the ball determines the distance it will travel.

## Punting

The punter requires protection and a good snap from the center. The rest is up to him. Ideally, the ball should hit the numbers on the punter's chest if he doesn't catch it. Any snap that does not require the punter to bend or reach excessively is acceptable. Since the snap for the punt is more difficult than on the place kick, there will be more variations. If a punter had a choice between a low snap and a high one, he would prefer a low one.

The coaching manuals have a lot to say to the punter. He should lock his ankle joint and keep his foot turned or pointed down. The foot should also be straight and not turned in or out. The punter should try to *place* the ball on his foot and not drop it any more than is necessary. The punter should look at the ball until it meets the foot. Punters generally adhere to these guidelines. However, in analyzing the effectiveness of a punter, look for height, distance, and forget about technique.

It is probably coincidental, but both pro teams that I saw service with in the American Football League had punters that were out of the same mold. Neither Paul McGuire of the San Diego Chargers, nor Curly Johnson of the Jets had especially strong legs or any other physical attributes that would make them good punters. Both were loose as a goose most of the time, and

Marv Bateman of Buffalo punting. Notice the extended toe.

nothing seemed to bother their temperaments. That may have been the reason that both enjoyed more than a medicum of success. Steve O'Neal, who replaced Johnson as the Jet's punter, was the complete opposite. He is quiet and deeply introspective. Maybe that's why he didn't last.

# Part Two

# THE FORMATIONS OF FOOTBALL

## Introduction

In 1869, Rutgers beat Princeton 6-4 in the first intercollegiate football game ever played. The rules decided upon by the captains before the game were quite different from those used today. There were 25 players on each team, and the goal posts were set 25 feet apart on a lot 100 yards long. The ball could be kicked or butted with the head, but a player could not run while carrying the football. A team was awarded one point for kicking the ball between the uprights. The first team to score six points was the winner.

It's hard to imagine the use of any particular formation during that first game. Most of each player's time must have been spent trying to disentangle himself from the 49 other players on the field. The rule that allowed a player to run with the football did much to change the nature of the game. Formations became more important to a team's success, as the number of players was reduced. In the early years, a formation similar to the present day rugby scrum was used. This evolved into the V formation and then the flying wedge.

In the V formation, the players grouped together and lined up in a "V"-shaped alignment. The flying wedge took many different forms during the relatively short time it was used in the 1890's. It was first used by Harvard against Yale in 1892. The line of scrimmage was a little different than today's, though. The ball carrier was positioned in the middle of the field with the remaining ten players divided into two groups stacked 20 yards on either side of him. They began to converge on him in a single file, while running at full speed with the larger men placed at the front of each row. As they converged on their teammate with the ball, he either handed off or kept it himself as he tried to lose himself in the middle of the wedge. The obvious advantage of the wedge was the forward momentum each player on the offensive team was able to gather before approaching the defenders.

The flying wedge was barred after the 1893 season, but the offense was still allowed to move toward the line of scrimmage before the snap of the ball. Until major rule changes in 1906, players were allowed to support the ball carrier and even lift and throw him over the opposition. The wedge and forward motion toward the line of scrimmage dominated the game until that time.

The rules involving the forward pass were modified significantly in 1910 and again in 1912. In the beginning, an incomplete forward pass could be recovered by either team, and there were restrictions as to where and when a forward pass could be thrown. As the restrictions were lifted, the pass became more of a weapon.

Despite the rule changes, the power running game dominated play until 1934. The object of most teams was to get as many blockers as possible in front of the ball carrier. In 1934, the National Collegiate Athletic Association recognized the importance of the passing game developed by some college teams, and instituted three important changes. The circumference of the ball was reduced, a five-yard penalty for more than one incomplete pass in the same series of downs was thrown out, and the offensive team was no longer required to give up the ball if an incomplete pass was grounded in the end zone prior to fourth down. The new streamlined ball made for better passers, and the new rules made the forward pass less of a gamble.

The next significant change was the introduction of the T formation in the 1940's. Emphasis was changed from power, to speed and versatility. Its universal usage at all levels is testimony to the revolutionary importance of the T and its variations. It is unlikely that we will see a major innovation of this kind in the future. There are only so many ways to align eleven men. The only thing that could precipitate another major change in offensive outlook would be a major rule change. The present popularity of the game makes this unlikely.

The story behind the evolution of the defense is similar to that of the offense. During the early years of American football, when the offensive team relied on masses of bodies rather than formations, the defense pitted its own bulk against the opposition's. The only similarity between defensive football then and now is that the big men were always placed in the front. As rules were changed and formations along the line of scrimmage were established for the offense, the defense also began to spread itself and assume well-defined alignments.

The basic premise upon which all defenses are built is that offensive strength must be countered with defensive strength. When offensive football meant running with the ball, the defense could bunch up opposite the offense. With the advent of the passing game and more diversified offensive formations, the defense was forced to spread itself and remove men from the line of scrimmage to defend against the pass. Today, it is common for a team to balance its defense so that it is equally effective against the run and pass.

Many coaches insist that there has been nothing new in football since the advent of the T formation. They claim that the wishbone and I formations are merely variations of the T formation since the quarterback still takes the snap from under the center. The question is unimportant. Teams may not be using *new* formations, but they are employing *more* formations. In the past, it was common for a team to remain in one basic offensive formation for an entire game or season. Today, it would be unusual for a team not to change its backfield set or the alignment of its receivers several times a game.

Nevertheless, there are still many coaches that do not believe in deception or the use of many different formations on either offense or defense. Chuck Knox is one such coach. The answer to such coaches is simplicity and mastery of the fundamentals. They work on the simple premise that the time needed to install an additional offensive or defense formation would be better utilized by working on fundamental execution. Yet, even these coaches will use minor variations in their offensive and defensive alignments. These simple changes are easy to implement and generally enhance the offensive attack while creating problems for the opposition.

The many different offensive and defensive formations and their variations sometimes make it difficult to understand team strategy and what is happening on the field. The purpose of this chapter is to familiarize you with the basic offensive and defensive alignments and the strengths and weaknesses of each. Offensive formations are usually easier to recognize. It is not difficult to distinguish a pro-set from a tight T. Defensive formations are sometimes harder to recognize and name. With a little practice, though, anyone can understand them.

## READING DIAGRAMS

There is nothing mysterious about understanding diagrams of offensive and defensive maneuvers. It's more or less like studying math in school: once you understand the symbols, you're in business.

Traditionally, *O*'s have been used to designate the offensive players and *X*'s to designate the defense. But, this designation is really only arbitrary, and to make things more graphic, we will use a football to designate the offense and a helmet to designate the defense. To see how to read diagrams, let's take an example.

If the offense lines up in a pro-set and the defense in a standard 4-3 it looks like this:

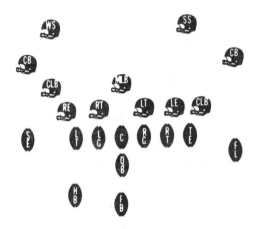

Now, say that we want to show the offense running a screen pass. On a screen, the quarterback goes back as in a regular passing situation and the line forms the usual pocket. At the same time, the receivers are proceeding on their normal pass routes. It looks like this:

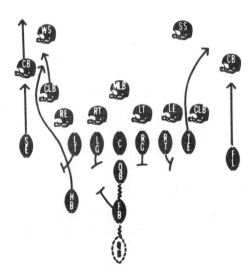

The solid lines indicate where each man is going and the symbol looking like an inverted Y indicates where a man will hold his block.

On the screen play, after holding their blocks for two to three seconds, the linemen pull out to one side to form a wall and the fullback moves behind that wall to catch a short pass from the quarterback.

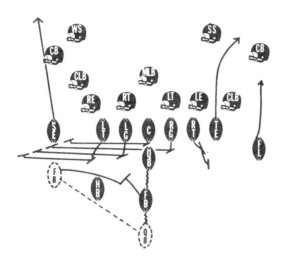

You see a broken line here from the quarterback to the fullback. This just indicates the path of the ball.

Now let's see how the defense reacts to the screen.

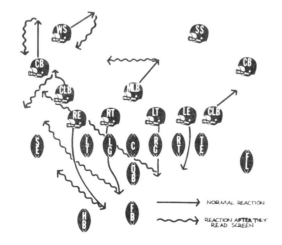

Finally, let's put it all together in one diagram.

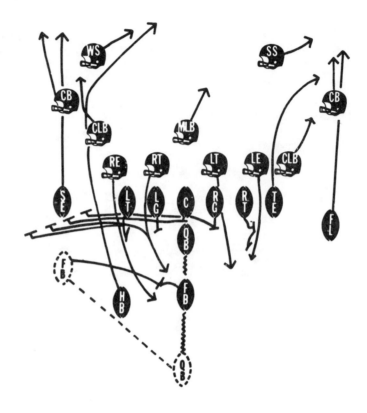

# 1

# THE OFFENSIVE FORMATIONS

On the back of every envelope that the leaves the offices located at 7811 Oakport Street, Oakland, California, there are four words: "Professional Football's Dynamic Organization." I am not certain who had the idea of placing this motto on the back of each envelope that carries Oakland Raider press releases to all parts of the country. I would strongly suspect that it was the brain storm of the Managing General Partner of the Raiders, Al Davis. The reason I'm certain that it was Davis are the words themselves. If it had been at the suggestion of one of the coaches, the phrase probably would have read: "Professional Football's Dynamic Team" and not "Organization." Since Davis is not a coach, although many still believe that he pulls the strings, the word had to be "organization."

John Madden has done a good job on the field, but it was Al Davis who created the dynamic organization that has come up with the players who have kept the Raiders at or near the top since the mid-'60's. The Raiders have had excellent drafts, but they have also been able to reclaim many players with good natural ability, but lacking the discipline or emotional qualities necessary for success. It started with Art Powell back in the '60's and today the tradition has been picked up by such problem children as Carl Garrett and John Matuzak.

On the field, however, the Raiders have become less dynamic, although certainly not less successful. During the late '60's and early '70's they had a wide open attack which was not very different from the offensive formations used by other teams in the league. There are only so many ways to align 11 players, and no team uses more formations than the Dallas Cowboys. It was the Raiders' *philosophy* of offensive football that was different. They were a team capable of striking with the bomb from any place on the football field. The running game was used to complement the passing attack, by keeping the linebackers and defensive backs honest. Most teams have a completely different philosophy. They use the passing game to keep the defense honest and set up the run.

The Raiders have gradually changed their offensive philosophy over the years. They now prefer to operate a more conservative ball control offense. Ken Stabler, one of the top passers in the league, will still throw that bomb from any place on the field, but today the Raiders are more likely to start with a running game and see where it takes them before throwing the ball with any consistency. Like most successful teams, the Raiders now use the passing game to keep the defense honest and prefer to push and probe the defense with the running game. It may be more than coincidence that with a weak pass rush and players no better than they have had for the last five or six years, the Raiders won the Super Bowl in 1976.

It was probably a combination of factors which caused the Raiders to become more conservative. After they gave up on Daryle Lamonica, it would not have been wise to ask an inexperienced quarterback like Ken Stabler to continue the big play philosophy. Their new emphasis on the run probably helped to improve their running game, and Al Davis was reawakened to the fact that it is not formations or philosophies that win football games, but rather physical abilities and mental and emotional readiness. In that respect, the pro game and football on the high school and college levels have been moving closer together. I don't mean to imply that the Raiders don't pass the ball. They throw as often as most teams in pro football, but they don't throw the bomb or try to break the long one quite as often. They have become more conservative like most teams in pro ball.

Most coaches agree that the way to win football games is to have the horses who are sound fundamentally and do not make mistakes. All things being equal, or close to equal, the team that makes the fewest mistakes or "costly errors" will win. These mistakes to a coach are: missed assignments, fumbles, interceptions and penalties. Coaches expect people to miss a block or drop a pass occasionally, but strive to completely avoid costly errors.

The team that makes the fewest mistakes quite often wins, but if the offense is such that it enables a team to put enough points on the scoreboard, they may be able to overcome costly errors. All coaches strive to keep the number of errors to a minimum, but many are concluding that to err is indeed human and that the total yardage a team accumulates is meaningless unless they come out on top on the scoreboard. They realize that the "three yards and a cloud of dust" offense does eat up the clock and, through possession, prevents the opposition from scoring. But, they also realize that the more plays a team runs, the greater the chance that one of those plays will result in a mistake. It takes four plays from scrimmage to get back the 15 yards lost on a holding penalty if you are only getting four yards a crack. Of course, the high school or college coach that does not have a capable quarterback may have to stay on the ground most of the time, but there are runs that are more daring than others and passing plays that don't require exceptional skill from the quarterback. This is the road many college teams have chosen to take. They still do not pass as often or throw as deep as the pros, since their quarterbacks are relatively inexperienced. However, they have devised more imaginative offensive formations that break more long running plays and strive to keep the defense honest with the passing game.

The reason for the tremendous success pro football has enjoyed since the 1960's can be attributed to the emphasis on the passing game and a more explosive running attack. Many claim that the similar change in play on the high school and college levels was an attempt to get the fan back. Not true. The average coach wants to win and does not think twice about the number of people in the stands or the number of dollars his university is getting for television rights. He is opening up on his offense and using the pass more because he is more likely to win that way. The change has really been taking place *gradually* over the last six or seven years. People just haven't noticed. Slowly but surely, more coaches are *first* looking for a quarterback and then worrying about the rest of their team. Such West Coast teams as U.C.L.A., U.S.C., and Stanford, and others like Notre Dame, have been using the pass with greater frequency, for the last five years.

This is not to say that the running game has disappeared from winning football. There continue to be pro teams that are noted as running clubs, and enjoy a measure of success that way. The Minnesota Vikings have been winning for years with solid defense and a sound running attack. However, they too put the ball in the air with a much greater frequency than the "three yards and a cloud of dust" college team. The Vikings have succeeded because of exceptional personnel. Joe Kapp was an exception. He was an asset because of his experience and ability to sell himself, and not because of his throwing arm. The reacquisition of Fran Tarkenton put them back up there in the classic quarterback mold.

Bart Starr was one of the reasons the Green Bay Packers were consistently winners. He was never a great passer, but he did get the most out of the Packers by concentrating on their strengths and not trying to be the star of the team. The Packers were basically a running team, but Bart Starr threw the ball more often than most people thought he did.

Green Bay was successful, not because Lombardi was an innovative coach who was years ahead of his time, but because he had the ability to get the most out of his people, including Bart

Starr. As an ex-high school teacher, I know that fear is the most effective, if not the most desirable, way to motivate people and keep them alert. The Green Bay Packers were alert and made few mistakes because of their fear of Lombardi. They were afraid of being cut from the team or bringing the coach's wrath upon them. No football player, or anyone else, can remain unaffected by the type of treatment which often made 260-pound men feel like little boys. What made Lombardi so special was that somehow he got away with it. I wonder what would have happened if the Packers had lost those two close championship games with the Dallas Cowboys in 1966 and 1967.

The other thing that Vince Lombardi did well was utilize his personnel properly. He not only got the most out of them and played them at the right position, but also tailored his offense to his personnel. The end sweep would not have been as successful for the Packers if Paul Hornung and Jim Taylor could not block as well as run with the football, and if the offensive guards could not pull out to lead interference.

What Lombardi did with his offense was the exception. The pro coach does not often have the problem of adapting his offense to his personnel. More often he will draft people that fit into his scheme of things rather than change his offense to capitalize on the strengths of his people. The high school and college coach has to make more adjustments in his offense than his professional counterpart. To the high school and college coach, the type of offensive formation is not as important as execution and proper utilization of personnel.

The answer then is: Look hard enough and you will find a successful team using every conceivable offense. The question is: Which offense is best? There are high school teams that still use the single wing and are successful. Several years ago, the wishbone T was the favorite and it received the attention due any new successful formation. Before that, it was the I formation that was getting most of the attention. In pro football in the late '60's, it was the Kansas City Chiefs' "Multiple Offense of the '70's."

An innovative offense frequently has initial success, but the defense usually catches up and neutralizes its effectiveness. A case can be made for using every offensive formation including the single wing. There are a few older coaches who still use the single wing because they know it well. They argue that opposing coaches do not see it often and do not know how to defense it; that defensive players are usually unaccustomed to the double and triple team blocking used when running from the single wing. This makes it worth using.

The type of offense used at the high school and college levels is relatively unimportant as long as the coach is running it properly and getting maximum utilization of his personnel. If he has big backs that can block well, they should be used on what is called an "isolation type" block in which a defensive lineman is ignored by the offensive line and then blocked by the set back. This maneuver is not seen very often in pro football, since the defensive linemen are generally too large for most offensive backs to block. A high school team that has backs that are bigger than the opposing linemen can use it well from any formation.

A team with good speed should run to the outside. It's not essential to have exceptionally fast backs to sweep well, but it helps. The Taylor-Hornung Green Bay Packers did not have exceptional team speed, but swept the ends as well as any team. They executed well. A high school or college team with one great runner should utilize him. He should not line up on the same side of every play, but should change positions so that he can carry a maximum number of times to both sides of the line.

A team with big backs is probably better off if it lines up in a tight formation and pounds away at the inside with power plays. An unbalanced line might also be advantageous under these conditions. If the offensive linemen are small, it may be wise to use double team blocking and trap more often. A 170-pound offensive lineman cannot be expected to block a 240-pound high school player consistently. He needs help. Flip flopping people from one side of the line to the other can be done with linemen as well as offensive backs. Teams with one good guard and tackle sometimes have them move from one side of the center to the other (flip flop) depending on the plays. This makes it more difficult for the linemen since their blocking angles are different, but can be effective if there is a big gap in ability.

Professional teams do not flip flop linemen, but they do occasionally shift into an unbalanced line by moving one guard to the opposite side of the center. This is not done very often since the defense will almost always adjust at the pro level, and there are as many disadvantages as advantages. Such a move might serve to deter a defensive team from placing a man head up on the offensive center, but at the risk of placing a highly skilled pro lineman at an unaccustomed position. For example, offensive tackles are not expected to pull out or trap as well as guards. A shift into an unbalanced line might require him to do so. The change in position and assignment may hurt the offense more than the defense.

It is fun to try and determine if the local team is using an appropriate offensive formation, but, in analyzing, don't mix up razzle dazzle with good coaching. Most of the commonly used offensive formations provide the opportunity to incorporate enough razzle dazzle to satisfy anyone. Remember, football is a game of execution and not deception. The team that blocks and tackles hardest is the team that usually wins if mistakes are kept to a minimum. Be skeptical of the coach that talks of deception rather than execution.

There is a place in offensive football for the Statue of Liberty and the naked reverse, but they should not be attempted more than once or twice a game unless the defense is doing something very unusual. The offensive plays that rely too heavily on the element of surprise or deception should only play a small role in the offensive game plan.

There are several basic considerations which go into the choice of offensive running plays. First, there are running plays which are designed to be used at any time with no relationship to any other play in the system. It matters little what precedes or follows the play. Other plays are included in the game plan to capitalize on a specific weakness of the defense as seen in the game films or by the scout in the stands. They sometimes work extremely well, and just as often fail completely. This often depends on whether the play is trying to exploit a particular player's individual weakness or a flaw in the way a defense or individual is aligned. Unfortunately for the observant coaching staff, poor alignment is likely to be spotted by the guilty team when they watch their own movies and corrected before the next game. It is therefore individual weaknesses which are most often exploited.

Finally, there are offensive plays which are designed to be part of a series, and should be set up by running one or two related plays in succession. All of the plays in a series generally begin with the same basic movements on the part of the offensive line and backfield. The play may look identical to a play previously run, but will break into a different area. For example, the trap and sweep may start with the offensive guard pulling out of the line and the backs flaring in the same direction, but the point of attack will be different. The attempt here is to keep the defense honest by preventing it from anticipating where the ball carrier will wind up based on his initial movement.

Pass patterns are designed with the same considerations in mind. Some pass patterns are favored because they are sound and the team executes them well. Others are incorporated to take advantage of a cornerback or weak side safety's weakness. Play progression is also considered important when devising pass patterns. The receivers speak of setting up a defender by running a route that looks like the one run on the previous play, but requires a last minute change. The receiver hopes that the defender expects the same route he previously ran. Of course, the defender may anticipate the movement of the receiver and stop the play cold. For example, say the wide receiver has run two sideline routes in a row. The next time he comes downfield in the same manner, the cornerback might expect the same route that was successful twice in the past, or anticipate the "sideline and go" which could lead to a touchdown. Does he gamble or play it safe?

The average fan doesn't have to overly concern himself with the intricacies of the various offensive and defensive formations. He should, however, have a fundamental understanding of the basic nature of each, the objectives of each, the differences between the various formations and the variations which can develop out of each formation. In time, you will learn that all those X's and O's aren't so complicated after all.

## SINGLE WING

The single wing formation got its name because one halfback is positioned on the "wing" or "flank" just outside the offensive end. The single wing is rarely used today, but it dominated football for decades. Like most of the offensive formations diagrammed and discussed in this section, there are variations to the

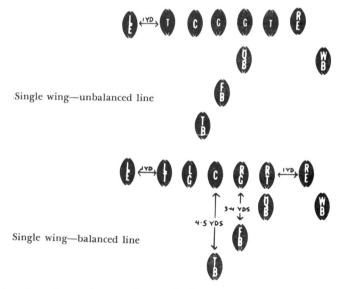

Single wing—unbalanced line

Single wing—balanced line

single wing. It can be run from a balanced or unbalanced line. The unbalanced line has four linemen on one side of the offensive center. There is also a box single wing, "Y" formation single wing,

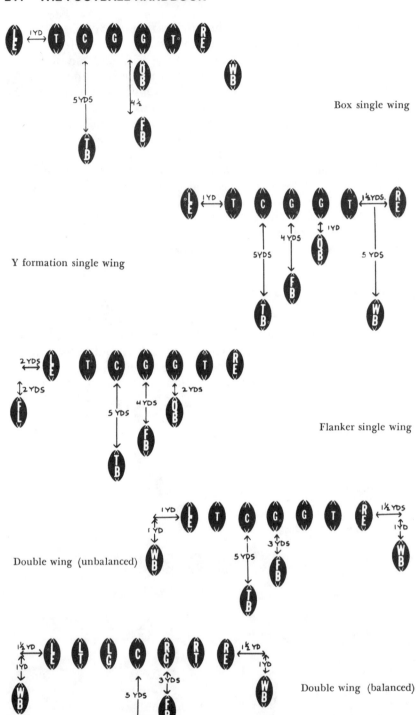

Box single wing

Y formation single wing

Flanker single wing

Double wing (unbalanced)

Double wing (balanced)

"A" formation single wing, flanker single wing, and a double wing. Each represents a minor variation in alignment. It would be pointless to discuss each of these formation since most have been long forgotten. The obvious difference between the single wing and the T formation is the fact that the quarterback does not line up directly behind the center and take the snap on every play. The ball is snapped under the center's legs directly to the tailback or fullback.

The single wing is still used by at least one team: New Dorp High School. Some teams switch to the short punt or shot gun formation when in a passing situation or when trying to confuse the defense. Both the shot gun and short punt are derivations of the single wing.

## Strengths

The single wing is a power formation which relies on good blocking backs and double team blocking by the offensive line. There are many people on the strong side which is where most of the running attack is directed. The single wing can be an effective ball control type of offense. Its advantage on running plays is that the quarterback can be used as a blocker and does not have to hand off the football. Its primary strength is its ability to outnum-

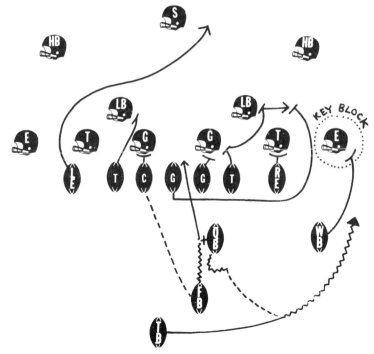

Buck lateral from unbalanced single wing

ber the defense at the point of attack. It is also an especially deceptive offense because of the great number of people bunched together and able to move in different directions.

### Weaknesses

The original single wing formation was not effective to the weak side. This was the primary motivation for developing most of the other single and double wing formations. It is slow in developing on both running and passing plays, and was the original "three yards and a cloud of dust" offense. It is difficult to break the long run from the single wing because of the great number of people concentrating their efforts at the point of attack and the slowness with which the plays develop. This also makes the long pass hard to complete.

The only advantage of the single wing today is that few have seen it in action, much less played against it. In its original form, it does not compare favorably to the swift and quick hitting present-day offensive systems.

### SHORT PUNT

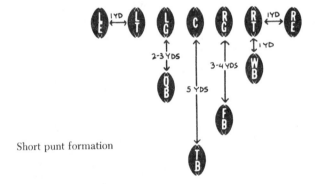

Short punt formation

### Strengths

Like the single wing, the strength of the short punt formation is inside the ends. The quarterback is used as a blocker and the offense can outnumber the defense at the point of attack. The possibilities for deceptive faking are excellent, and when the ball is actually punted, it can put the opposition in a hole.

### Weaknesses

It is slow to the outside and difficult to throw long from the short punt. It requires exceptional blocking backs and should only be used when the backs are bigger than the linemen. Even then, there are better choices. The center is also at a disadvantage since he usually has his head down to see where he snaps the ball and cannot see the defensive player opposite him.

## SHOT GUN

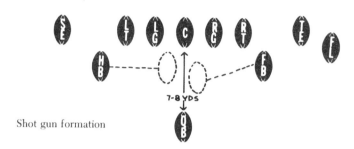

Shot gun formation

The shot gun formation may have been derived from the single wing. The similarity exists because the center snaps the ball under his legs to the quarterback seven or eight yards behind him. However, the shot gun formation used extensively by the Dallas Cowboys and the San Francisco 49ers for a time bears little resemblance to the single wing. It is a passing formation and good for little else. The advantage is that the quarterback does not have to run back to the pocket. He is already back there when he receives the ball and is ready to throw. He has more time to survey the defense downfield and there is less chance that he will be thrown for a loss while attempting to pass the football. The Cowboys use it primarily because it adds a wrinkle to their attack and Roger Staubach seems to work more effectively from it than most other quarterbacks.

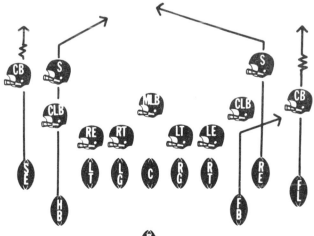

Shot gun—five man pass pattern

As with every offensive alignment, there is room for variation. The set backs may be in the backfield between the guard or center, on the wing, or in the slot. When they are in the slot formation, the shot gun offers an excellent opportunity to get five people downfield very quickly, with a minimum risk of getting the quarterback trapped and thrown for a loss. The shot gun is normally limited to use in sure passing situations or at the end of the game when a team is behind.

There are two major problems with the shot gun, aside from the absence of a balanced running attack. The first is the difficulty in running the screen pass and and the impossibility of running a draw play since the quarterback cannot hand off to another back. The absence of the quick hitting running attack, the draw and the screen allows the defensive linemen the edge in this situation. A three-man rush will probably be able to pressure and contain the passer and the extra pass defender will help to neutralize the passing advantage of the shot gun formation.

## TIGHT T

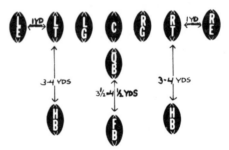

Tight T formation

In the early 1940's there was a rule change which no longer required the quarterback to stand five yards behind the line of scrimmage when passing the football. Many claim that this change in the rules precipitated the placing of the quarterback directly behind the center. In this position, he could take the ball directly from the center's hands and throw it to any one of his receivers. The T formation would have revolutionized football whether or not the rules were changed. The quick pass had little to do with the initial success of the tight T. (*Tight* refers to the fact that the offensive linemen are spaced close together. *T* and *Tight T* are interchangeable here.) Its major asset was versatility, and the fact that it allowed a coach to fully utilize all the talents of each of his players.

It was probably the adaption of the T formation as much as

anything which heralded the age of specialization in football. The offensive halfback had to have speed and quickness while carrying the football. The quarterback had to be able to pass the football. The end could no longer be a small tackle. The offensive lineman could no longer hide behind the double team block. It was now a one-on-one situation for everyone on the offensive team. The tight T is rarely used in its pure form today.

## Strengths

Speed was and is the key to the success of the T formation. The back hitting the hole no longer had to wait for the ball to reach him before moving toward the line of scrimmage. It is true that the offensive center did try to lead his running back with the ball when snapping from the single wing, but it was quite different from the all-out sprinter's start a set back could use from the T formation. He now could be running close to full speed when he took the hand off from the quarterback.

The T also allowed as much deception as the single wing without all the spinning and turning which took so long to execute. Because of the speed in getting the back into the line, the double team block was no longer necessary on almost every play. There was little choice for the running back out of the single wing. He had to run in a prescribed hole because of the double team blocking that frequently took place on either side of the opening in the line. Initially, in the T formation, the running back often chose to run in the "wrong" hole. If the prescribed hole was not there, coaches found their backs running to daylight. It was only in the mid-1950's that the option block and option running were built into the T formation. The T provided more choice for the back and the blocker and more flexibility for the offense.

The life of the center became much more pleasant with the advent of the T. He no longer had to bury his head between his legs; instead, could look his opponent in the eye. Previously, the center had almost always been covered since the defense attempted to capitalize on his vulnerable position. Men in motion and flanker backs were used more extensively from the tight T. Since double team blocking was not absolutely essential on every play, a team could afford to place a man in a flanker's position to spread the defense and enhance the passing game. Coaches discovered the running game was not weakened when the flanker was used, since the defense had to make adjustments for him.

## Weaknesses

Compared to the single wing, the T formation had few weak-

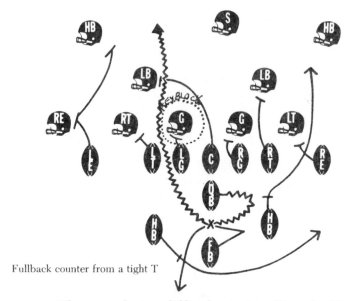

Fullback counter from a tight T

nesses. The one glaring difficulty in installing the T was that it required specialized skills. If the T was to be effective, the quarterback had to be a good ball handler and, more importantly, a good passer. If he could not keep the deep secondary honest (loose), the effectiveness of the quick hitting running attack would be diminished. A tight defensive secondary could create many problems for any T formation. The T does not employ the pulling lineman with backs pouring through a designated hole like the single wing. With the single wing, the offensive line could often handle a defensive back that was not concerned with the pass and came up to close the hole quickly. When running from the tight T formation, there is nobody to pick up an extra man on the line of scrimmage. The defensive backs are blocked downfield by the off-side linemen or outrun by the offensive backs. For this reason, the T also required fast running backs. There was no place to hide the tough kid who could block but lacked running ability. In addition, with the T, the offensive linemen had to be faster off the line and be able to handle a man in a one-on-one situation.

Of course, these factors are not really weaknesses of the T. They merely point out the differences between the single wing and the T. I do not know of any team that uses a straight T today. Most teams use one of the following variations.

## WINGED T

The winged T formation was probably an attempt to retain single wing type blocking and capitalize on the explosiveness of

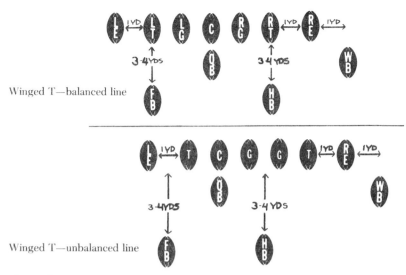

Winged T—balanced line

Winged T—unbalanced line

the T formation. The wing back is used in the same way as he is in the single wing formation. Today, you will see the winged T used with a balanced line at all levels of football, including professional football. Most teams use it with variations like a split line, split end, and double wing. Some shift into it from the I formation. With the increased popularity of the multiple offense, the winged T and variations of it will be seen more often.

One maneuver very popular from the beginning of the winged

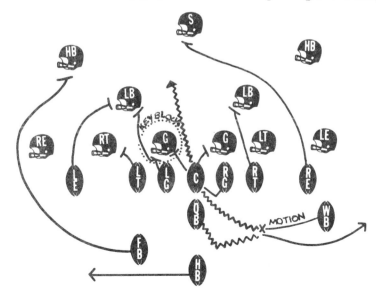

Winged T—trap left

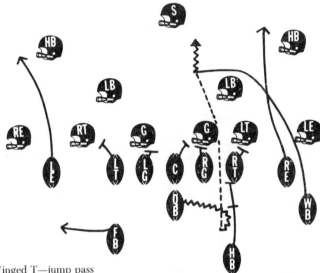

Winged T—jump pass

T is the man in motion coming over the middle. In fact, the idea for using the winged T may initially have stemmed from the use of the man in motion in the tight T. Why put a halfback or fullback in motion if he is to be used as a blocker off-tackle, when he can be aligned on the wing to begin with? The position of the wing back is the only difference between the tight T and the winged T. When he goes in motion over the middle, the strength of the formation is once again the same as the tight T (see diagram).

### Strengths

The winged T enables a team to use double team blocking more effectively on the strong side than the tight T. It also provides an opportunity for the offensive team to utilize a good blocking back more effectively by placing him on the wing. This helps the passing game by getting another receiver into the secondary quickly, and allows the use of combination pass routes in a confined area. The wing back is not lost completely as a running back, however, since he may be sent in motion and used as the ball carrier in the middle of the line. This forces the defense to adjust quickly.

### Weaknesses

When the play goes to the side away from the wing back, he is virtually useless. He cannot be used as a decoy or lead blocker unless the play is going to his side. The wing back position is also difficult to fill properly. He should be big enough and strong enough to be an effective blocker, and, yet, fast enough to get downfield quickly. He also has to be able to carry the ball into the middle or around the opposite end on a reverse. This combination of offensive tackle and halfback is hard to find.

## SLOT T

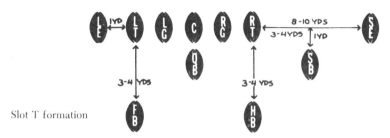

Slot T formation

The slot T is an adaption of the winged T in the same way that the winged T is an off-shoot of the tight T. The only difference between the slot T and winged T is the alignment of the ends and wing back. In the slot T, one or both ends split eight to ten yards from their offensive tackles and the wing back moves out a yard or two into either slot between the tackle and split end. The difference in alignment will necessitate the use of players with different abilities at each of the two positions. The player used at split end is chosen for his pass catching ability with little regard for his blocking. The slot back does not have to be as big or as good a blocker as the wing back.

Like the winged T, the slot T is used at every level of football. It will almost always be included as one of the formations in a multiple offense, and it is used as a change-up by most teams using the winged T. In pro football, it will be seen in passing situations when the offensive team wishes to isolate a wide receiver on one defender. It is difficult to use a pure zone against a slot or double slot formation. Many pro teams use a third wide receiver or move the wide receiver from the other side into the slot. Hopefully, he will be covered by a safety, who is usually slower than the cornerback.

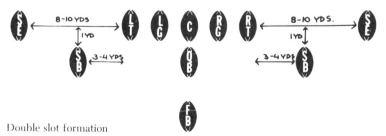

Double slot formation

Another variation of the slot T can be made by placing two men into the same slot. Like the double slot, this will leave only one man in the backfield. It is used only as a change-up in an attempt to create a problem in pass coverage for the defense.

### Strengths

The slot T causes the defense to spread out to cover the man in the slot, and allows the offense to get three receivers downfield quickly. It is more difficult to hold a receiver on the line of scrimmage when he is lined up in the slot and the receiver has more room to maneuver and elude the defender. Since the defense must spread out to cover the man in the slot, the running game up the middle may not be adversely affected. The double slot (see diagram) allows the offensive team to get four men out on a pass pattern quickly. This is a formidable passing formation, but not good to run from.

### Weaknesses

The slot T is primarily a passing formation that can be defensed when used as the basic formation. The defense spreads, which may help plays up the middle, but the outside attack to the slotted man is weakened. The slot man is usually a wide receiver or a set back and probably not capable of taking advantage of the blocking angle to the inside.

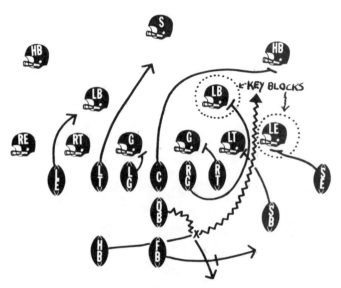

An off-tackle play run from a slot T formation. The split end has a tough blocking assignment on plays run to the outside such as this.

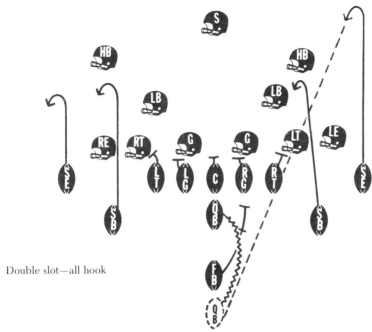

Double slot—all hook

## SPLIT T

Don Faurot, of the University of Missouri, is generally credited with having devised the split T in the 1940's. Nevertheless, it took almost ten years for the split T to gain national acceptance. Initially, the split T was successful because the defense did not

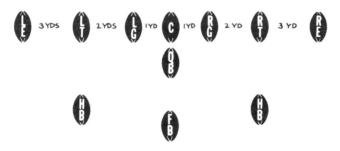

Split T formation

know how to adjust to the wide splits. As with most revolutionary offensive formations, the defenses caught up with the split T. Today, there are few teams that use it in its original form. However, most T formations continue to use the splits in the offensive line introduced by the split T and many of its other features.

### Strengths

The split T formation gets its name from the wide splits between the offensive linemen (compared to the tight T). In addition, there are other basic differences between the split T and other T formations. In the split T, the quarterback moves *up and down* the line of scrimmage. He rarely moves more than a yard into the backfield when handing off or running the option play. The advantage is the ability to hand off even faster than in the tight T where his first move is *away* from the line. The increased speed contributed to the formation's success, but the splits in the offensive line contributed to it even more so. It created blocking angles for the line and provided more running room for the offensive backs. There were times when the slightest brush block proved to be enough to break a back free into the secondary.

The rule of thumb at the outset was a split of a yard between the guard and center, one or two yards between the tackle and guard, and two to three yards between the tackle and end. However, the splits that the tackle and end took were often larger. Coaches simply did not know how to defend against the splits and speed of the split T in its early years. If the defensive linemen split with the offensive line, huge holes would develop. If they kept a relative distance, blocking angles would develop.

### Weaknesses

For quite some time, few found any weaknesses at all in the

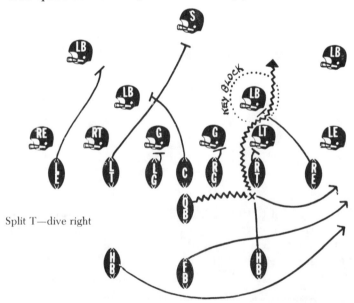

Split T—dive right

split T. Those that used it properly in the early years had considerable success. Don Faurot, Bud Wilkinson of Oklahoma University, and Jim Tatum of the University of Maryland were three coaches that had great success with the split T. Eventually, the defense caught up to it as coaches had their defensive linemen shoot the gaps in the large splits which developed. Stunting linemen and linebackers were introduced following the success defensive teams had shooting the gaps. Linemen found they could counteract the quickness of the split T and get more time to react by playing further back off the line of scrimmage. Linebackers placed inside the offensive tackles also limited the effectiveness of the split T. They had more time to react to the quick opener which had been doing so much damage.

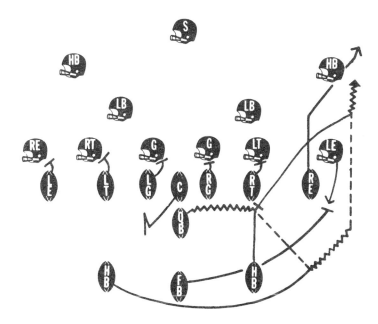

Split T—option pass

The split T was also extremely fundamental. There were only four or five plays (which could be run to either side) in the original split T. The quarterback was the ball carrier half the time. He had to be a good runner as well as a good passer. The linemen had to be quick and mobile, which is necessary for most formations. However, the wide splits made quickness the overriding qualification. The splits made drop back pass protection more difficult and forced the use of play action passes. Often, an offensive team simply couldn't find the manpower to run the split T effectively.

## DOUBLE WINGED T

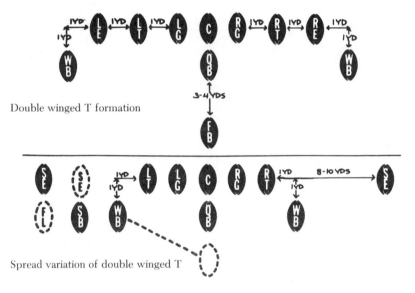

Double winged T formation

Spread variation of double winged T

The double winged T, or a variation of it, is another formation that many multiple formation teams use as a change-up to keep the defense guessing. In its basic form, each side of the double wing is the same as the winged T. The double wing is nothing new. There was double wing formation that developed as an off-shoot of the single wing. It was then used to strengthen the attack to the weak side of the single wing. The present-day double wing can take several forms. The ends can be split or tight, there can be one back or no backs, and any one of the potential receivers can be up on the line. The wing back may be lined up one yard outside the tight end or one yard behind and outside the offensive tackle (see diagram).

### Strengths

The double winged T is primarily or exclusively a passing formation depending on what form it takes. If a set back remains in the backfield, the run is not out of the question. As with the winged T, one of the wing backs may be sent in motion to carry the ball or to fake into the middle of the line. Its primary strength, however, is the pass. It almost *forces* the defense into man coverage, and enables the offense to flood the secondary with four or five receivers very quickly.

### Weaknesses

The weakness of the double winged T is the run. There is only

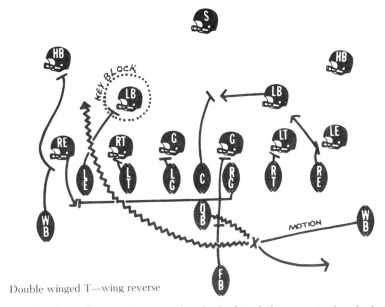

Double winged T—wing reverse

one back and sometimes no backs behind the quarterback that the defense must be concerned with. When everyone is out on the flat, and the quarterback is the only one in the backfield, he will have to either carry himself or hand off to someone in motion or coming around on a reverse. There can be no faking if there are no backs and that means nothing to distract the people in the pass defense from their coverage.

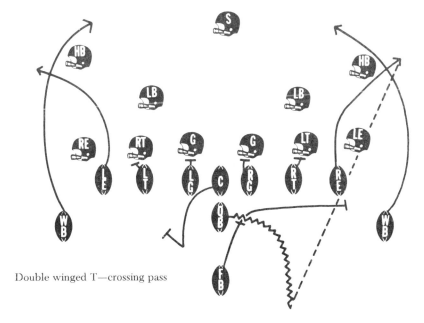

Double winged T—crossing pass

## I FORMATION

Many coaches on both the college and pro levels have had considerable success using the I formation in recent years. The I formation incorporates the running power of the T formation and the opportunity to continue the wide open passing game the pros

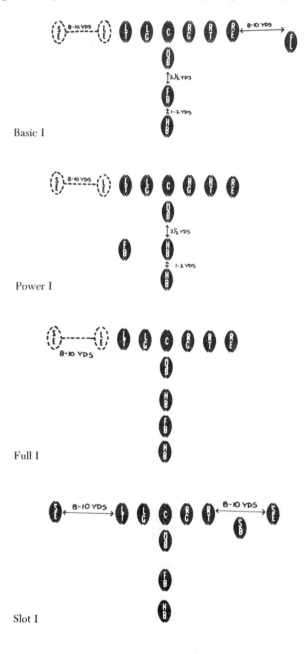

Basic I

Power I

Full I

Slot I

utilize. This is accomplished via the shift and the variations of the I formation. When a team is in a regular or basic I (see diagram) with only two backs behind the quarterback and the wide receivers split, the formation has all the passing advantages of the traditional pro-set. When a team has a third back in the game and lines up in the full I or power I, it is as strong up the middle as in any of the popular running formations.

The shift can be used both ways by teams using the I formation. A team can shift from the I to the pro-set or from a standard pro-set into the I formation. The shift and the unique alignment of the offensive backs adds to the confusion that the I formation can create on the defensive team. It is difficult to key on the second and third back lined up in the backfield, because they are hidden. It is especially difficult on plays up the middle. Needless to say, offensive teams do everything they can to hide the ball and the ball carrier. In the past, the Kansas City Chiefs employed rather short running backs behind a behemoth line with considerable success. The cry from defensive linemen around the league was that before they could find those small backs in the maze of the I, they would be by them.

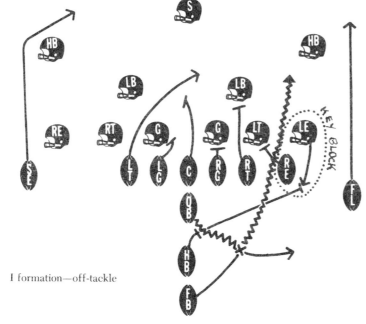

I formation—off-tackle

Like most other offensive formations, there are variations of the I. Hank Stram, when coaching the Kansas City Chiefs, used his tight end in the I behind the quarterback. He did not run many plays from the formation, but forced the defense to adjust when the team would shift and his tight end moved from one side to the other. He had to stop that when 6'10" Morris Stroud replaced Fred Arbanas at tight end. When Stroud was in the I, nobody could see anything. Most pro teams that now use the I formation alternately shift to a standard pro-set, and use some motion in the backfield.

### Strengths

The I formation allows a team to use its best blocker and runner to either side of the line without tipping the play by the set of the backs. It is quick hitting up the middle and can be extremely deceptive with a good ball-handling quarterback. When running play action passes, the quarterback loses a minimum of time, since he does not have to move very far to fake the running play to one of his backs before dropping back to pass.

### Weaknesses

The I formation is slow developing running plays to the outside since the running back coming from the middle has to travel further on the quick pitch than if he were lined up behind the offensive tackle. For the same reason, there is also more time for the corner linebacker to react to the set back going out on a flare pass. When the tight end is in the I, or moves from the I into his normal position, he has less time to study the defense. The vision of the backs in the I may be restricted either by those standing in front of him or by the unusual angles necessary when approaching the line of scrimmage to take a hand off. When running off-tackle, the back must approach at an angle. The slant approach itself is not unusual, but the angle from the I formation is not as wide, and the back has less time to read the defense.

### WISHBONE T OR Y

The wishbone T formation

The wishbone is one of the more popular new offensive formations in football's arsenal. Everyone has acclaimed it but professional coaches. A part of the triple option, which is at the heart of the wishbone, is a running quarterback. Up to now, most pro coaches have thought that the amount of running a Fran Tarkenton or a Bob Griese would have to do to execute the triple option would carry too much of an injury risk. Without the triple option, the wishbone T loses much of its effectiveness.

The wishbone formation is credited to Darryle Royal of Texas University, who won two national championships with it. It helped Alabama and Oklahoma return to national prominence during the early '70's, and countless other teams have adopted it.

The quarterback has three choices when running with the wishbone. He can hand off to the fullback, run the ball himself, cutting inside the third defensive player outside the center, or he can fake the quarterback run and pitch out to the halfback going around the end.

As you can see from the diagram, there is also a triple option pass play that is run from the wishbone T. Good blocking backs are essential if the blocking for the option pass is to be the same as for the run. The offensive guard and tackle will provide the double team blocking which forces the back to pick up the second defensive player. If the wishbone is run from a tight formation, the prospects for an explosive drop-back passing attack are not

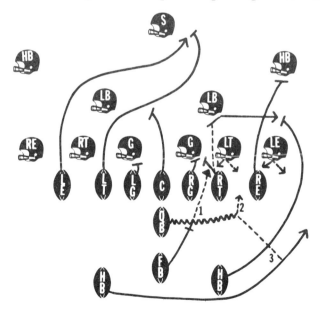

Wishbone T—triple option. First option: quarterback hands off to fullback if tackle moves to outside. Second option: quarterback keeps ball and runs off-tackle if left end moves to the outside. Third option: quarterback pitches to the halfback if the left end crashes down the line to tackle the quarterback.

bright. Most of the passes run from the wishbone will be of the play action variety.

The wishbone often requires the quarterback to run the ball 30 times a game or more, and there are few pro quarterbacks capable of being tackled by the larger defensive ends and linebackers in the N.F.L. and standing up to such a beating. For that reason alone I doubt that it will ever be used by the pros. What is more, it is still a ball control offense when compared to the offensive attacks of the pros and would not be as exciting for the fans. The wishbone in the pros would mean that every quarterback over 30 and many under that age would be relegated to the bench. With them would go the passing game which has made pro football.

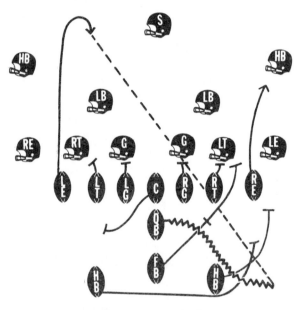

Wishbone T—option hook pass

## Strengths

The wishbone has two basic advantages. Because the fullback lines up so close to the quarterback, he can hit the line with exceptional speed. The speed with which he hits the line makes it particularly difficult for the defense to react correctly. The defense's problem is compounded by the triple option which the quarterback has. The defense is caught in a situation where, if it reacts too quickly, it might be burned by one of the options, and, if it reacts too slowly, it might be by-passed by the fullback. The offensive team never has to concern itself with the defensive alignment when the triple option has been called, since poor blocking angles are not an important consideration. If execution is up to par, the play called in the huddle will always be the correct one.

**Weaknesses**

Proper execution of the wishbone requires an exceptional fullback. The formation was originally designed for the hard charging fullback who would create a perpetual problem for the defensive linemen. The quarterback must be equally talented. He has to be blessed with quick hands and feet as well as the ability to make instantaneous, almost reflex-like decisions. This combination is hard to find. What is more, if one of these two is hurt, the entire offense runs the risk of total collapse.

**THE PRO-SET**

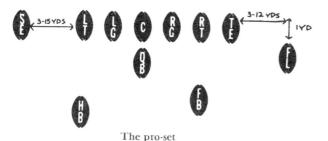

The pro-set

The passing attack is the most exciting aspect of a football game. It is the exceptional passers that pro football has developed which has made the game the number one sport in the country and made the pro-set the number one passing formation. The college coach has only four years to develop an exceptional passer. The pro coach has the advantage of getting an older and more experienced player that he can keep at quarterback for 10 years.

They say it takes four or five years for the average quarterback to develop. There are those like Ken Stabler, Bob Griese, Terry Bradshaw and Bert Jones that do it much faster, but they were still older and more experienced than the college player when they began. The point is that it is difficult for the college coach to find and develop a quarterback in the short time he has to work with him. Despite this, the college and pro games are moving closer together. The colleges are throwing more like the pros, and the pros are using the quarterback to carry the football more often, like the collegians. Colleges are also beginning to adopt the more intricate pro formations. However, it is doubtful that the colleges will ever pass as effectively out of the pro-set as the pros. It is simply too difficult to develop an exceptional passer.

Every pro team without exception uses the pro-set and the pro-set can be incorporated into almost any offensive formation. All that is required to change any formation into a pro-set is to split one end and one back eight to ten yards to opposite sides of the line. It is the importance of the passing game in pro football which makes the pro-set the standard formation. It allows both wide receivers to get downfield quickly and the additional maneuvering room makes it extremely difficult for the defense to cover them with one cornerback.

### Strengths

The use of split men on the flank forces the defense to make adjustments. Since it is extremely difficult for one defensive back to cover the split receivers on a one-for-one basis, most need some help from the inside (see the chapter on the defensive backs). The assistance that most defensive teams strive to provide for the back covering the split man is what weakens the inner portion of the defense and makes the inside running game effective. The linebacker trying to help the cornerback cover the quick sideline pass to the wide receiver makes the defense vulnerable to the off-tackle play.

The blocking effectiveness of the wide or split men will determine, to a large degree, the success of the outside running game. The weak blocker can be hidden out on the flank where he

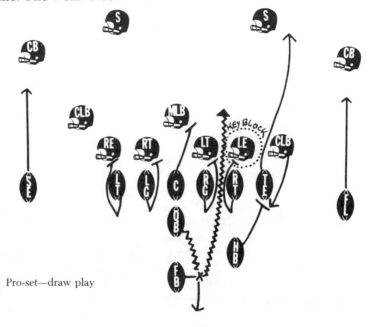

Pro-set—draw play

will not be required to block unless the play is going into his area. Even on the sweep it is not essential for the offensive team to use the split end as a blocker. Since the deep secondary must play the pass before the run, the cornerbacks must cover the wide receiver going up the field on a fly route even though the play actually turns into a sweep to his side of the field. Weak blocking flankers and split ends are often used in this manner rather than as crack back blockers on defenders to their inside. Those teams that run the sweep most effectively, however, do use their wide men as blockers.

The use of the flanker in the pro-set also enables the offense to use variations in the offensive backfield. The vacancy created by moving the flanker outside allows the offense to position the two remaining set backs in any of a number of ways. This makes it more difficult for the defense to type the offense by the position of the backs because they usually vary their alignment on every play. This also enables the offense to use its most effective blocking and running back to best advantage in key situations without tipping the play.

### Weaknesses

The weakness of the pro-set is the loss of a blocking tight end

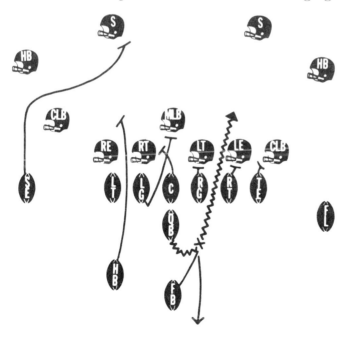

Pro-set—fullback slant

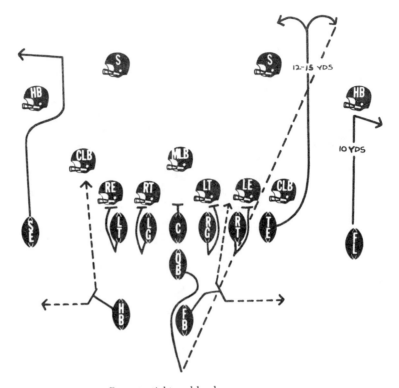

Pro-set—tight end hook pass

along with the faking and blocking of a running back. This can weaken the running game up the middle and off-tackle if the defense does not adjust to the position of the wide receivers. The pro-set requires a good quarterback to keep the threat of a pass to the wide receivers ever present in the minds of the defensive players. Some people also consider the fact that the set backs remaining in the backfield have to learn several positions as a disadvantage. This should not be a problem for a pro back. He must block and run wherever he is and his alignment should not have much to do with his performance.

The pro-set requires good blocking backs to protect the passer. The set back to the side away from the tight end must pick up the corner linebacker blitzing to his side. This assignment would ordinarily fall on the shoulders of the end playing next to the tackle. However, this does not have to turn into a weakness. Good set backs should be drilled and trained to block well from any formation. The fact is, though, that some outstanding running backs, even in the pros, are only fair blockers. In these cases, the blitzing linebacker can be a problem in the pro-set.

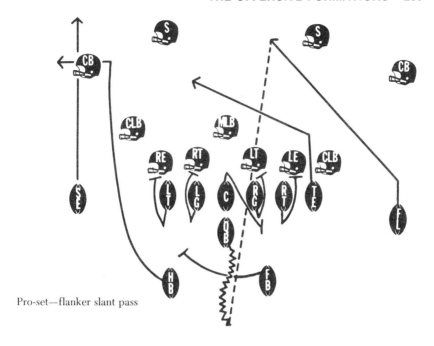

Pro-set—flanker slant pass

## THE MULTIPLE OFFENSE

There is nothing dramatically new in coaches using multiple-type offensive systems. It started back in the days of the single wing. The theory behind the use of the multiple offense is to combine player alignment variations to confuse the defense. Teams using the box and "A" variations of the single wing along with the traditional single wing were using a multiple offense.

Today's team using a multiple offense is likely to use three or more of the offensive formations described in this chapter. Notice that there is little variation in the alignment of the five interior linemen. They will line up the same way and generally have the same blocking assignments regardless of the offensive formation used. This is the advantage of a system such as that used by the Dallas Cowboys. From numerous formations Tony Dorsett can run one basic off-tackle play without changing the blocking of the offensive linemen. The new formation does not affect the linemen's blocking assignments, but might create a better blocking angle by causing the defense to adjust. It might also cause the defense to become confused and fail to adjust, which may help the offense to break the long gainer. In general, use of the multiple offense keeps the defense off balance and forces last minute adjustments as the offense approaches the line of scrimmage.

Most teams using the multiple offense will experiment with

each alignment at the beginning of the game. They will then concentrate on those that seem more effective. For each offensive formation, the defense must adjust its alignment. Failure to do so may cause one offensive formation to be more successful than another.

Offensive personnel changes may influence the effectiveness of a play in various formations. For example, the split end may not be successful when attempting a crackback block on the corner linebacker on the sweep. Using a tight formation and replacing the split end with a bigger tight end capable of blocking the linebacker may make the play a success.

A difference of mere inches in a defensive player's alignment will frequently determine a play's success. The team utilizing the multiple offensive attack can experiment until it finds those inches necessary to create a favorable blocking angle or spreads the defense enough to make a play successful. For example, the defensive team may move its corner linebackers in tight toward the middle when the offensive backfield is in an I formation. The theory behind the move is based on the fact that it will take the offensive back longer to run outside when starting from the I. The position of the linebacker may make it difficult for the offensive end to block him to the outside on the off-tackle play. The linebacker will be induced to move further outside when the offensive backfield lines up in a regular alignment. The few inches the linebacker moves may make it possible for the ends to block him.

All pro teams use a multiple offense. Some confine themselves to the standard pro-set, a tight formation with a full house backfield, and a slot formation in a passing situation. Other teams will use the three formations previously mentioned along with the I formation, winged T, double wing, and double slot. Some have even used the shot gun. The professional player should have little difficulty learning play assignments for the various formations and the different skills each may require. The pressure the multiple offense places on the defense is well worth the additional practice time required to perfect each formation.

The fact that professional teams use a multiple offense does not necessarily mean that they should be used by every high school and college team. A team that executes one basic formation with a reasonable degree of proficiency will be more successful than a team running from five offensive formations with only a modicum of skill. The high school coach must devote much of his time to teaching the fundamentals of blocking and tackling. Devoting an excessive amount of time to implementing numerous formations may hurt a team's performance.

More important than the number of offensive formations is the skill and precision of a team's attack. The player at any level should execute each assignment with poise, confidence and without any hesitation or unnecessary movement. Any fan can recognize the well drilled football team. The coach at the high school level should not try to implement a multiple offense until his team has mastered the essentials of its basic attack.

Regardless of the type or number of formations, the coach's offensive philosophy should be apparent from watching his team perform. You should be able to determine if he is seeking to run a ball control offense, a big play attack or is attempting to balance his offense between the run and pass. The latter will probably be the aim of the coach on 90% of all high school and college teams. However, his personnel will make the final decision for him. The college coach with an outstanding passer and receiver should not be running the ball 90% of the time. The team incapable of running the ball effectively because of its personnel may be forced to pass more than it would like. The quarterback with a weak arm and slow receivers should not throw long. The ideal situation is a balanced attack, but before criticizing the coach that seems to be overemphasizing one aspect of play or using unimaginative formations, you should look at his personnel. It may explain things.

These then are the basic formations which make up the offensive attack. Don't get hung up on memorizing every minute fact at once. Try to see the relationship between the different formations. The following progression (evolution) ought to put you on the road.

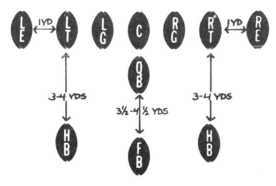

Start with the tight T.

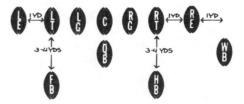

Take an offensive back out of the backfield, move him to the wing, and you have the *winged T*.

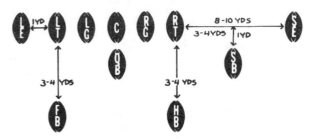

Split one end 8 to 10 yards, move the wing back out another yard or two, and you have the *slot T*.

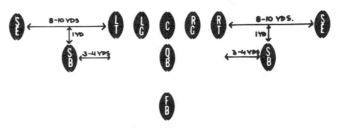

Split the other end and put another offensive back in the slot to form a *double slot*.

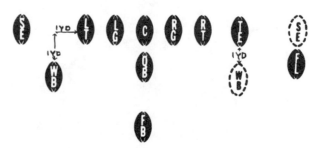

When coaches were ready to go back to the double wing (there was a double wing variation of the single wing), they found it necessary to incorporate line splits, slot backs and split ends.

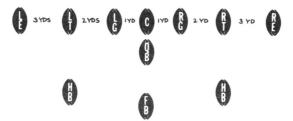

Some coaches were successful using split ends and placing offensive backs on the flank, while others found wide splits in the offensive line effective. They called it the *split T*.

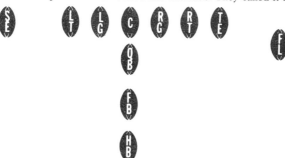

The backs were then aligned directly behind the quarterback in the *I formation*.

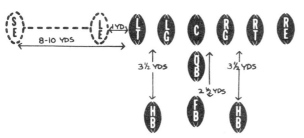

The latest innovation puts the fullback closer to the quarterback than the halfbacks. This is the *wishbone* or *Y*.

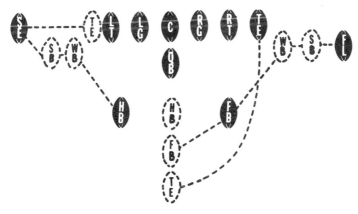

Put them all in the same playbook and you have the multiple offense.

# 2

# THE DEFENSIVE FORMATIONS

The success of any team, at any level of play, requires team-work. To varying degrees, each player on a team is dependent on the play of those next to, behind, or in front of him. The success of the entire offensive unit is dependent on the defense, since the offensive team cannot score unless it has the football. Similarly, the defensive team's statistics will be influenced by the efficiency of the offensive machine. The offensive team that can control the ball for long periods of time makes it easier on the defense than the team that goes in for three quick incomplete passes (each stopping the clock) and punts.

In professional football, despite the dependency of the two units, they each have almost independent identities. On losing teams, where one unit is decidedly stronger than the other, there may be an antagonistic feeling resulting from frustration. You will often hear a member of one unit say that the offense played well, but the defense faltered; or, that "we" played well, but the offense (or defense) fell apart. As would be expected, this phenomenon is not as discernible on teams that are successful, regardless of whether one unit is stronger than another.

The break between the offense and defense begins in the classroom and extends to the practice field and dormitory. Most teams do not bother to have a team meeting each day before dividing into offensive and defensive groups. The members of the offensive team rarely get to talk to the defensive players, except before the meetings begin. On the field, the teams practice separately, except when they find themselves on opposite sides of the line of scrimmage. Players are roomed with others playing the same position for the logical reason that they can discuss their common problems and play assignments. As a result, the offensive player does not get an opportunity to spend much time with his teammates playing defense. The separation off the field extends to where you will usually find players on the same unit killing time together.

The separation between the offensive and defensive teams

often results in "friendly" arguments or discussions which sometimes become heated. They usually center around which unit has contributed more to a team's success and whether the defensive or offensive teams, in general, are more important. The argument frequently carries over to coaches and other interested parties.

I had the opportunity to broadcast a game between the Houston Oilers and the New Orleans Saints during the 1976 season. The producer for NBC Sports, Mike Weissman, was thoughtful enough to save several stories that had gone out on the Associated Press wire service during the week, since they were not carried in the New York newspapers and I normally would not have had an opportunity to see them. He gave them to me at the production meeting the day before the game and I read them that night. I wish that I had never read them.

One story told of an alleged fist fight between offensive center Carl Mauck and the Oilers' fine noseguard, Curley Culp, which started because Culp openly criticized the Oiler offensive unit. The Oilers were in the midst of a disappointing season after being hailed as a threat to the Pittsburgh Steelers in the A.F.C. Central Division prior to the season. The defense was playing well, but the offensive unit was inept. Culp repeated this thought at practice and the altercation with Mauck followed. I assumed that the story had already appeared in the Houston newspapers since it went out on the A. P. wire, and mentioned it in passing during the game which was being seen in the Houston area of the country. To my chagrin, Coach Bum Philips called me first thing on Monday morning and asked: "What the hell are you trying to do, create dissension on this team?" He claimed the story never appeared in the Houston papers and was completely untrue, I apologized and assured him I was not trying to imitate Howard Cosell and be controversial.

It is rare that a head coach will call an announcer. In fact, this was the only time it ever happened to me and points out how sensitive coaches are to any mention of friction between an offensive and defensive unit.

Is the offense or defense more important to a team's success? It is a question as old as football itself.

The proponents of the importance of the offense simply point out the obvious fact that a team cannot win unless it gets points on the scoreboard. An advocate of the importance of the defense would probably counter with the other obvious conclusion that a team cannot lose if the opposition does not score. He is likely to follow with the fact that the offensive team cannot score, regardless of its potency, unless it has possession of the football. Another argument for the defense is that the opposing team that has put a limited number of points on the scoreboard is capable of being defeated up until the very last minute through a turnover or a quick score. The team that has a strong defense is always in the ball game.

A good case can be documented for the defense. There have been several teams in recent years that owe most of their success to the play of their defensive units. In pro football, the Minnesota Vikings of the 1970's, the Dallas Cowboys of the late 1960's, and the New York Giants of the late 1950's all come to mind. However, in each instance the offensive team was not exactly inept. An equally impressive list of teams that achieved success largely through the efforts of their offensive team can be compiled. However, the most convincing case can be made for those teams that have had a balance between their offensive and defensive teams—the Miami Dolphins, the Pittsburgh Steelers and the Oakland Raiders. The conclusion that must eventually be reached is that the offensive and defensive teams are equally important. The relative strength of each will influence the style of play of the other unit.

The three main objectives of the defense are to prevent a score, gain possession of the ball and possibly score while on defense. Preventing a score should be the primary aim of the defense and the foundation on which all defenses should be built. A team should first concentrate on preventing a touchdown by defensing the long pass or run and then concern itself with turning the ball over to the offense or scoring itself. The relative strength of the offense and defense and the game situation will determine the degree of emphasis placed on each defensive objective. These factors, along with a coach's philosophy of defense, will determine whether a team uses a *containing* defense or a *pressure* defense.

## THE CONTAINING DEFENSE

The specific objective of the containing style of defensive play is to prevent a touchdown or long gain by making everything happen in front of and inside the defense. This gives the offense the opportunity to try to control the football. The containing defense does not attempt to throw the ball carrier for a loss. Instead, it aims to allow the offense a maximum of three yards on every play. The offensive team that gains no more than three yards on each of its first three downs will be forced to punt on fourth down. Naturally, it is difficult to keep all pass completions under three yards, especially if the primary aim of the defense is to stop the long gainer. At times, the defensive secondary will be forced to play comparatively loose. However, the prospects for a team making mistakes are increased when the offense puts the ball in the air repeatedly. The containing defense is predicated on the fact that the offense will make mistakes.

The offensive team that is denied the long gainer will be forced to run many plays to move the ball up the field and into scoring range. The defensive team playing a containing style is *challenging* the offense to try to overpower them on every play. With each successive play, the chance of the offense making a costly error increases. Sooner or later, the offensive team will surrender the ball on a fumble, an interception, a blocked kick, or on downs. Occasionally, a missed assignment or a penalty will expedite the process.

Of these errors, the only one that may not be apparent to the fan is the missed assignment. They occur, at all levels of football, with greater frequency than most fans imagine. Every pro player knows his assignments against the various defenses well, and mistakes during practice are rare. It is quite different during a game. The pressure of a game situation and the minor variations in alignment by the defensive team increase the prospects of a missed assignment. The change does not have to be dramatic. A last minute shift or an unexpected "call" from one offensive lineman to another may be enough to cause a player to block the wrong opponent or delay his effort long enough to allow the defensive player to reach the ball carrier untouched. This, in turn, can result not only in a broken play and a probable loss of yardage, but occasionally in a fumble or an interception.

A penalty against the offense is the defensive team's best friend. The longer the offensive team has the ball, the greater the chance a penalty will be called. It may be anything from an off-side or back-in-motion to the more damaging holding or pass interference penalties. It may be caused by a mental lapse on the part of an offensive player preoccupied with the individual battle he is confronted with on the line. It may be the result of a moment's indecision as to whom to block. It may be the result of a last second attempt to compensate for poor position by holding. Since the offensive player's assignment changes with each defense, a penalty can also be the result of misreading the defense. The offensive player may not see a defensive adjustment, or may not hear the quarterback's audible or a teammate's "call" to change the blocking.

Regardless of the reasons, mistakes will be made by the offensive unit. The containing defense relies on them, and would be less effective if they did not occur with regularity.

You can recognize the containing defense by its dullness. The defensive team is likely to remain in one or two basic alignments throughout the game. It can be expected to do the obvious and maintain a constant pattern. The linemen will charge straight into the offensive lineman playing opposite him; the linebackers will refrain from blitzing while tightening up on a running situations and playing loose when the offense is expected to pass; the defensive backfield will always play the pass before it looks for the run. This is standard procedure, regardless of the type of defense.

If you are a great coach like Don Shula, it is possible to play a containing defense which, while remaining predictable, and safe, isn't always dull and uninteresting to the fans. This is exactly what Shula did during the Dolphin Super Bowl years with his "53" and "nickel" defenses. Shula went to these variations primarily because of his personnel. Quite simply, he had a good fourth linebacker in Bob Matheson (who wore #53) and a fine fifth back in Lloyd Mumphord. (Nickel refers to the five defensive backs.) Teams have been substituting a fifth defensive back in long yardage situations and a fourth linebacker in short passing or long running situations for years. Shula simply gave the defenses names and used the same people all the time. He was so predictable in using these variations that everyone in the stands could determine when a substitution was called for and started to cheer themselves when they guessed right. Through it all, Shula remained as conservative as Bud Grant of the Vikings and Chuck Knox of the Bills.

## THE PRESSURE DEFENSE

The specific objective of the *pressure* defense is to force mistakes by the offensive team by penetrating and applying unrelenting pressure. The defensive team strives to throw the offense for a loss of yardage and create a long yardage situation which forces the offense to gamble more and increases the chance of errors. The fan will recognize the pressure defense as the one using stunting defenses, games, a variety of fronts, and the blitz. It is the defense that is more willing to gamble on causing a turnover at the expense of increasing the chances of a touchdown or long gainer.

The team that attempts to penetrate the offense with games and the blitz is restricting its ability to pursue and gang tackle the ball carrier. The blitzing linebacker or lineman stunting away from the direction in which the ball carrier is running has little chance of getting back into a proper path of pursuit. This lack of pursuit increases the chance of the offense breaking a long run. Linebackers involved in stunts or the blitz are also prevented from assisting in pass coverage, which forces the defensive secondary to use man to man coverage. This increases the prospects of the offense hitting the bomb, if the rushing unit fails to reach the quarterback.

Teams utilizing the pressure defense are likely to employ more men on the defensive line and at linebacker than teams using a containing defense. A team blitzing and stunting players must have enough people in position to plug each hole in the offensive line. As was previously stated, the penetrating defensive player will not be able to recover and help stop the ball carrier in other areas of the field. It is a hit or miss situation most of the time. The chances of forcing an offensive mistake or throwing the ball carrier for a loss are greater, but the chances for a long offensive gain are equally great.

## DEVELOPING A DEFENSIVE PHILOSOPHY

If offensive coaches are indeed becoming more daring with the present trend toward the big play offense and more passing on the college and high school levels, then their defensive counterparts are probably becoming more conservative. To a football coach, playing it conservatively on defense implies using the containing defense.

The offensive philosophy of a coach is likely to effect his defensive thinking. The coach that believes in the ball control, three yards and a cloud of dust offense is the coach that may be more inclined to utilize the pressure defense. If he believes that a well coached offensive team can control the ball and move up and down the field without making mistakes, then he is likely to believe that he must used the pressure type of defense which will force the offensive team to make mistakes. He will believe that the only way to stop a ball control offensive team is to refuse to give them an inch, and that it is essential for the defense to move people around and force the issue.

Conversely, the coach that plays an explosive brand of football on offense will probably play the conservative, give them anything but the big play defense. He believes that an offensive team is incapable of consistently moving the ball and putting points on the scoreboard with a ball control style. He will use the defense that allows his team to contain the offense and give ground grudgingly. He remains confident that the offensive team will eventually give up the football on a turnover or fail to make a first down.

Aside from a coach's personal beliefs about offensive football, many other factors must be considered in developing an overall defensive philosophy, and in deciding on specific adjustments for each opponent. The team using a containing defense may modify its approach for certain opponents. To do so, it is necessary only to add some games and blitzes. For a team using a pressure defense, modification means eliminating stunts and playing it straight. In most cases, the defensive personnel keep the same alignment, merely changing their type of charge.

The coach that believes he has superior defensive personnel is more likely to choose to play it conservatively. He does not have to take chances by adding wrinkles and moving his people around. The team with superior personnel will usually attempt to play it straight and overpower the offense. This may change from week to week as new opponents are encountered. The defensive team capable of overpowering one offensive team may be completely ineffective against another.

The opponent's offensive personnel will influence the decision. An opponent with an exceptional passing attack may prompt a coach to use a pressure attack rather than his usual conservative style. He may believe that his linebackers are strong against the run, but weak in defensing the pass. Against a strong running team, he will use a containment defense. But, against the superior passer, he might feel that his linebackers cannot drop back quickly enough to assist the defensive secondary.

Teams preparing to face the Oakland Raider offense often change their defensive philosophy and use a pressure defense. Three reasons are Ken Stabler, Gene Upshaw and Art Shell. Ken Stabler is the best passer (pure or otherwise) in the N.F.L. and Upshaw and Shell are the best tackle-guard combination in the league. Whether the Raiders eventually decide to stress running or passing the football, a defensive coach about to face them can make a strong case for a pressure defense. Given time, Stabler will pick apart any defensive secondary, and it is relatively certain that he will get that time with Upshaw and Shell in front of him. For this reason, many defensive coaches preparing for the Raiders come to the same conclusion and decide to help their defensive secondary. One method is to put in a fifth defensive back. Since Stabler has bad knees, opposing teams would like to force him to scramble. However, because of his strong offensive line, it becomes difficult to pressure him with a standard rush. Many coaches therefore decide to blitz and stunt against the Raiders.

The defensive coach's plight is not eased when he considers how to stop the Raiders running attack. Mark van Eeeghen, Clarence Davis, Carl Garrett and Pete Banaszak can be stopped, but once again how do you stop Upshaw and Shell from opening holes on the left side of the Raider line where they run 70% of the time? The obvious conclusion is that you don't stop them unless you blitz or stunt or overload that side of the line.

A team's offensive strength will naturally influence the play of its defensive unit. The coach that believes his offensive unit can move the ball well against the opposition is more likely to remain in a containing defense. If the offensive team is weak or decimated by injuries, he may be inclined to try to help it by forcing more turnovers.

## CHANGING DEFENSES

There are two ways that a team can alter its defensive style. A team can switch to a pressure defense by stunting, blitzing and using games. It can also increase the pressure on the offense by adding more linemen and linebackers. Every defense consists of two parts: the *forcing* unit and the *containing* unit. The forcing unit is comprised of those players who move across the line at the snap of the ball. They may either be linemen down in a stance or linebackers standing on the line and blitzing across at the snap of the ball. The objective of the forcing unit is to put pressure on the offense. The containing unit is comprised of those linebackers and members of the defensive secondary attempting to force the play inside and keeping the ball in front of them. They will form the major part of the pass defense.

There are teams that put one or two extra defensive linemen in the game when they want to stress the forcing aspect of the defense. However, most teams that want to pressure the offense in the middle of the field will tighten up the defense and blitz one or more linebackers. This gives them the element of surprise and allows them to keep faster people in the game to bolster the entire defensive effort. The obvious danger of placing more people in the forcing unit is that if the ball carrier gets past the line, there are fewer people to contain him in the secondary.

Regardless of a team's overall defensive philosophy, the defensive unit, like the offense, must alter its style of play according to the tactical situation on the field. The score, the time remaining, the down and distance, the weather and the field position of the ball all go into determining whether the emphasis will be placed on the forcing or the containing unit. Of course, when a team is in a first and goal situation on the three yard line, there is no such thing as a containing unit. The defense must prevent any gain and hopefully force an error. In a goal line situation, most teams add people to the forcing unit. This may involve replacing linebackers or defensive backs with defensive linemen, or putting linebackers into the line.

There are a number of ways that the standard defenses can be classified. The two broad categories that are used most often group all defenses as either *odd* or *even*. Those that place a defensive lineman opposite the offensive center are called *odd* defenses or fronts and those that leave the center uncovered by a man in a three point stance are called *even* fronts. The odd fronts employed at the high school and college level usually have five, seven, or nine men down on the defensive line. The even defenses normally employ four, six or eight men. However, there are instances in pro ball where a team places a man head up on the center with four or six men on the line. To add to the confusion, the number of men on the line does not give a true indication of the strength of a defense against the run or pass, unless the number of linebackers, their spacing, and their depth is considered.

A more important method of classifying defenses is to group them according to the number of linemen and linebackers in a particular defense. The *combined* number is called the front. For example, if a defense has five linemen and three linebackers, it has an eight man front. The seven and eight man fronts are seen most often. The seven man fronts include the 4-3, 3-4, 5-2, and 6-1 defenses. The 4-4, 5-3, 6-2, 7-1, and the eight man line comprise the eight man front defenses. The nine man front is broken into the 4-5, 5-4, 6-3, and 7-2.

The eight and nine man fronts are seen most often at the high school level, where the passing game is usually not the dominant factor. Invariably, the pros have come to rely on a seven man front as their basic defense in mid-field. It allows them to use a four deep ("umbrella") coverage in the deep secondary. For our purposes, we shall classify the defenses by the various fronts. The seven man front will be covered in the section on pro defenses.

Defenses can also be classfied by the type of coverage used in the secondary (zone or man) and according to whether or not stunts are employed. These are important considerations and would certainly be included in the scouting report provided to the offensive team.

By dropping back linebackers, and sometimes defensive ends, the zone can be used with any front. Stunting defenses are most effective when run from fronts using two or more linebackers, but they also can be used with any defense.

Each of the defenses diagrammed on the following pages has certain widely recognized strengths and weaknesses. Most coaches attempt to compensate for the inherent weaknesses in a defense by varying the alignment of key personnel. This can be done *before* the snap for all to see, or by having players move into different positions *after* the snap of the ball. The latter is a common practice in the defensive secondary where many coaches attempt to hide the coverage, and makes it more difficult for the quarterback to read the assignments and movement of the individual. Linebackers also frequently attempt to disguise the defense and their particular assignment. For example, a linebacker may be down in a three point stance before the snap of the ball only to drop back into pass coverage once the ball has been snapped. What appeared to be a 5-2 defense was in reality a 4-3.

You may have difficulty in identifying the various defenses despite the diagrams on the following pages. The many different offensive formations and the necessary defensive adjustments sometimes cause one defense to look like another. For example, the 4-4 defense will look entirely different, after adjusting to the double slot offense, than it looks against a tight T formation with a full house backfield. You will see the traditional or "pure" 4-4 as often as you will see the traditional unmodified tight T—hardly ever. It is as important to recognize the adjustments to each offensive formation as it is to recognize the basic defense.

Look for defensive adjustments to the overshifted line, the split of the ends, and the "strength" of the backs (left or right). However, the defensive player making adjustments should not be expected to always line up opposite the opponent he is responsible for. The speed of both players, the relationship of the ball to the hash marks, and movement after the snap must be evaluated. In every instance, the defense should be expected to meet strength with strength. When the offensive team places a set back in the slot between the tight end and the flanker, the defense should compensate by rotating the secondary in that direction or dispatching a linebacker to cover the slot back.

More important than the adjustments to individual movement is who makes the adjustment. The fan who is familiar with both teams' personnel will be better able to evaluate offensive and defensive formations and adjustments. Has a relatively light corner linebacker or a defensive lineman adjusted to an unbalanced line? Anyone can distinguish a lineman from a linebacker by the number on his shirt. Only someone familiar with a team's personnel will be aware of whether the linebacker is almost as big and strong as a defensive lineman.

## EIGHT MAN FRONTS

The number of men used up front by a defensive team will be

influenced by the relative passing effectiveness of the opposition. Basically, we can assume that the more men up front, the better the defense against the run. However, the number of linemen and linebackers must be considered along with their alignment and primary responsibility. Teams using a 4-4 and a gap-8 are both employing an eight man front with three deep backs. The similarity between the two defenses may end there or the two may in fact be almost identical if all the linebackers in the 4-4 charge into gaps in the offensive line at the snap of the ball. The difference then would be determined solely by the size of the linebackers and their effectiveness in plugging the gaps.

The relative strengths of the 4-4 and gap-8 against the pass or run may be entirely different if the four linebackers are playing loosely and dropping back quickly into pass coverage. The same may be said of most of the defenses classified as eight man fronts. Once again, the type of personnel must be considered. Some teams using a 6-2 or 7-1 defense will drop their defensive ends in passing situations after the snap of the ball. Their effectiveness against the pass will depend on their speed, agility and position before the snap. The offensive alignments must also be considered. The defensive end dropping back into pass coverage will be less effective against split ends or a slot back. Consequently, such a maneuver is rarely utilized today, except by teams that change-up by placing a linebacker down on the line in a defensive end's position. It should be used only against a tight offensive formation and in a short yardage situation.

The eight man front (or three deep defense) was considered to be strong against the pass, until the four deep or umbrella defense came into vogue. Because of the increased emphasis on the passing game, more teams at all levels are using a seven man front with four deep backs.

Either zone or man coverage can be used with an eight man front. The number of linebackers and the type of offensive formation determines which is more practical. When in a zone, each deep back is responsible for one-third of the field. It is comparatively easy to teach, since the backs do not have to concern themselves with the broken backfield. It also relieves the deep backs of all responsibility except guarding against the pass. In the umbrella defense, one or two backs are expected to help turn in running plays to the outside. When in three deep coverage, all the defensive backs drop quickly and do not have to concern themselves with the run until the offensive back has crossed the line of scrimmage.

## The 4-4 Defense

Teams that employ stunting defenses with regularity are likely to use the 4-4 as either a basic or change-up defense. Unless stunts and variations are employed, the 4-4 is likely to be weak against the running game, since the offensive team has excellent blocking angles on the linebackers. Their distance from the line of scrimmage also gives the offensive lineman an advantage, unless the linebacker moves forward at the snap of the ball.

The 4-4 defense

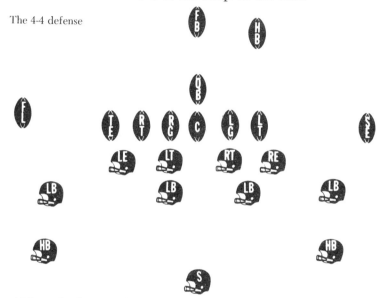

Although the 4-4 defense affords a great deal of flexibility in the use of the linebackers, it is often weak against the pass. Since stunting linebackers are almost always incorporated in this defense, the linebackers will not be able to assist the deep backs on every passing play. If a good rush is not put on the passer, the deep backs may be in trouble. When a linebacker must stunt, he is obliged to move in the direction of the stunt before dropping back to get into pass coverage. This split second delay can make the difference between good pass coverage and an easy touchdown.

The 4-4 alignment has fewer intrinsic weaknesses against a split formation and broken backfield than the other eight man fronts. For this reason, it is often used as a change-up defense in professional football. The success of the defense will often depend on the adaptability of the fourth linebacker.

## The 5-3 Defense

The 5-3 defense is also frequently used with stunts, but can be

The 5-3 defense

played straight just as often. The key to the effectiveness of this defense is the strength of those playing in the middle: the middle guard, the middle linebacker and the safety. If all three are exceptional football players, the 5-3 is likely to be effective against the run and pass. The middle guard is primarily responsible for stopping runs up the middle, while the safety is most important to the defensive secondary using zone coverage against passes. The middle linebacker should help both.

The middle guard has the most difficult assignment in this defense. Both offensive guards as well as the center have the opportunity to reach him quickly, and the distance between him and the defensive tackles on either side of him is great. This makes his job more difficult since the holes between them are harder to close.

## The 6-2 Defense

The 6-2 defense is basically stronger against the run than the pass. The defensive ends sometimes drop back into pass coverage, but more often are assigned to detain the offensive end on the line of scrimmage. Unless the defensive end does this well, the defensive secondary becomes extremely vulnerable. With the advent and increased use of split offensive ends, the 6-2 defense has lost a lot of its effectiveness. One obvious factor is the difficulty the defensive end experiences when he must split with a man in the slot or on the wing and is required to detain him on the line. The

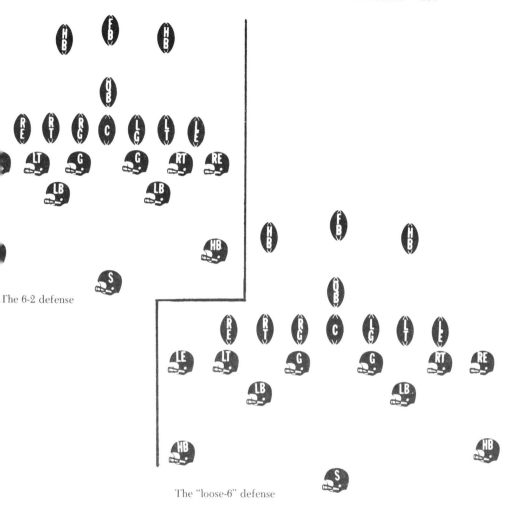

The 6-2 defense

The "loose-6" defense

additional room available to the wide receiver makes this an impractical assignment for any defensive end. It makes more sense for the defense to use a linebacker in the area.

There are several variations of the 6-2 defense. The "loose-6" is employed when the defense is blessed with two outstanding linebackers capable of controlling the offensive tackles, and the defense wishes to concentrate on stopping the outside running game. The "tight-6" is better to counter a strong inside running attack, and requires two extremely fast linebackers that can help stop the outside running game along with the defensive ends. The type of linebackers available and the strength of the offense are considered in determining whether a team uses a "tight-6" or "loose-6" defense.

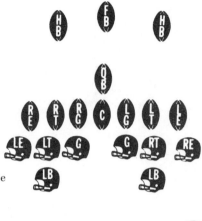

The "tight-6" defense

## Split-6

Align the defense in a gap-8 (see goal line defenses) and then move the two men in gaps on either side of the center into a linebacker's position. You now have a split-6 defense. Like the gap-8, it is strong against the run, but weak against the passing game. This defense was designed to stop the quick hand off on the split T. However, it is weak against the fullback counter up the middle, and wide running plays. The two linebackers must be big enough to stop runs up the middle and still cover a lot of ground in getting to the outside to stop the sweep. This is a hard combination to find.

The "split-6" defense

## The 7-1 Defense

The 7-1 defense is rarely seen today because of its weakness against the passing game. Despite the fact that the defensive ends are assigned to hold up the offensive ends, the defense is particularly weak against the short pass. It is difficult to adapt to offensive variations, and is good only in short yardage situations and against the tight T. For example, when the offensive team sends a man in motion or places a man on the wing, most teams change the alignment of the linebackers. Since there is only one linebacker in the 7-1 defense, there isn't much flexibility.

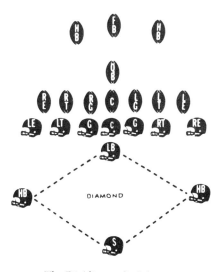

The 7-1 (diamond) defense

## NINE MAN FRONTS

The nine man front was popular in defensing the tight and split T. The additional lineman or linebacker makes the nine man front especially strong against the running game. There is rarely an opportunity to use double team blocking against the nine man front, and in many instances the offensive team is outnumbered at the point of attack or faced with poor blocking angles. However, it is as weak against the pass as it is strong against the run. There are only two deep defensive backs capable of defending against the deep pass.

The extent of the weakness of the nine man front against the pass is dependent on the number of linemen used. A quick glance at the diagrams on the following pages will indicate that the 5-4 defense has a better chance to stop the pass than a 7-2 defense. The 5-4 and 6-3 defenses also give the defensive team more of an opportunity to adjust to split ends, slot backs, wing backs and a broken backfield. Regardless of the specific defense, the nine man front is weak against the pass and the multiple offense seen so often today. This type of defense is used primarily in running situations and as a change-up.

## The 5-4 Defense

The 5-4 (Oklahoma) defense

The 5-4 defense allows a team using a nine man front more flexibility than the 6-3 or 7-2 defenses. Teams using swift and agile outside linebackers that can drop back quickly into pass coverage should not be particularly vulnerable to the pass. However, the smaller they are and the faster the outside linebackers drop back, the more vulnerable the defense becomes to the outside running attack. When the corner linebackers begin to play exceptionally loose, the 5-4 defense begins to look more like a 5-2 front.

The 5-4 defense was originated at Oklahoma University to stop the split T (which Oklahoma itself had great success with). The defense was successful when run properly. Some teams had success with moving the two interior linebackers behind the tackles, but most kept the linebackers opposite the offensive guards. The pressure on the defensive man over the center, always great, became even greater when the linebackers moved to the outside. Some offensive teams had success in trapping the man on the center with either offensive tackle. Other teams had a degree of success by using the option pass or run repeatedly to confuse the corner linebacker and two deep backs. Nevertheless, the 5-4 (also called "the Okie" because of its place of origin) eventually killed the pure split T.

Part of the success the 5-4 had in stopping the split T was due to the additional time the linebackers had to react to the quick hitting attack. Stunts could also be incorporated nicely. Some teams found it beneficial to play their defensive linemen loose to give them more time to react. Regardless of the various reasons coaches offer for the success of the 5-4 in stopping the split T, it could not stop the present-day offensive variations and is rarely used in its original form.

## The 6-3 Defense

The 6-3 is another nine man front designed to neutralize the effectiveness of the split and tight T. Prior to the advent of the T formation, it was rare that a team would utilize more than one or two linebackers at one time in their defensive unit. Offenses relied on overpowering the defense and not on outrunning them. The linebacker confronted with the prospect of being double teamed could not outrun the blockers, but had to take them on at the line of scrimmage. Plays going to the outside did not break quickly which gave the defensive linemen time to react to the sweep. A man with the speed of a linebacker was not necessary. There was no advantage in replacing a bigger and stronger defensive lineman with a faster linebacker when he would be required to handle a double team block in the same manner as the lineman.

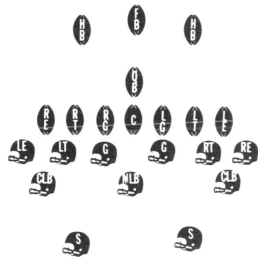

The 6-3 defense

Because of the speed of the T formation, coaches were forced to re-evaluate the role of the linebacker. He was given a new role and increased stature. The faster and more agile linebacker would have a better chance of combatting the swiftness of the split T than the slower defensive lineman. More and faster linebackers were obviously the answer.

Whether the 6-3 defense was the result of taking a linebacker from the 5-4 and putting him down in a three point stance, or evolved by taking a lineman from the 7-2 and placing him at linebacker is unimportant. What is important is that the 6-3, along with the 5-4, helped to neutralize the split T.

Like the 5-4 defense, the 6-3 is weaker against the pass than the run. Fortunately, the split T was a better running than passing formation. The effectiveness of the 6-3 in defensing the pass depends in large measure on the looseness and speed of the outside linebackers.

## The 7-2 Defense

The seven man line was an extremely popular defense during the early days of the T formation. It was a carry-over from the days of the single wing and, with minor variations, could be used against either the single wing of the T formation. This was important during the 1940's and early 1950's, when there were as

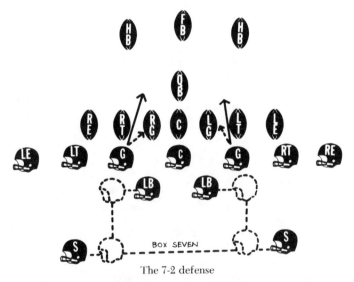

The 7-2 defense

many teams using the single wing as the T formation, and a team would have to prepare for one or the other on a week to week basis.

Like the other nine man fronts, the 7-2 is stronger against the run than the pass. Therefore, a good pass rush is essential and can

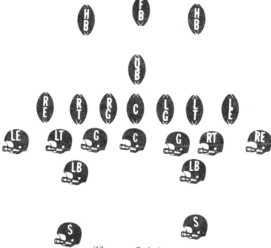

The gap-7 defense

be expected because of the number of linemen rushing the passer. The location of the linebackers will determine the emphasis placed on detaining the ends on the line of scrimmage. When they are aligned to the inside, the ends must be detained. If the linebackers line up deeper and slightly to the outside of the offensive tackles, they will have a better opportunity to cover the ends.

## PRO DEFENSES (SEVEN MAN FRONTS)

### The 4-3 Defense and Its Variations

The basic defense used in pro football since the late 1950's has been the 4-3. It is simply the defense that makes the most sense for pro football. In the chapters on the defense, it was stated that most pro coaches treat the passing and running games as being equally important. A team may run more than it passes, but the potential to do both effectively must always be present. As a result, the pro defense has to be equally strong against both the run and pass. The 4-3 is perfect for the situation. There are four defenders primarily concerned with the run and four men primarily guarding against the pass. The remaining three linebackers can gear their efforts to the immediate situation as determined by the offense and the game variables.

When the linebackers are playing close to the line, the defense may be the equivalent of a five, six, or seven man line depending upon how many linebackers are up tight. When playing deep or dropping back quickly, they can provide more assistance to the

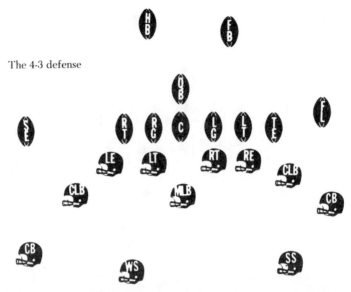

The 4-3 defense

defensive secondary. By varying the primary assignments of the linebackers, the 4-3 defense allows for maximum surprise effect and strategic deployment of personnel. The blitz and the games or stunts involving the linebackers enable the defense to change the number of men in the forcing and containing units without changing personnel or losing the element of surprise.

During the last few years, the odd front in the form of the 3-4 or 30 defense has grown in popularity in pro football. However, many pro teams have used odd fronts over the years. They were variations of the 5-1 or 5-2 and most often were known simply as "fifty" defenses. In most instances, the number of defensive linemen actually in the game at one time does not exceed four. When there are more than four people on the line, one of the defensive tackles simply moves head up on the center and the rest of the line and linebackers make adjustments. The four men in the deep secondary are rarely affected.

You don't need an odd number of men on the defensive line to have an odd defense. The coaches in the N.F.L. have their own terminology for the odd man front. Some merely call it a five right or five left depending on which side of the line the two defensive linemen are stationed. Some teams do not require the defensive tackle to be head up on the center, but move him into one gap, on either side of the center. This would most likely be called an odd front. In effect, all of these are variations of the 4-3 defense, since there are almost always four linemen and three linebackers in the game.

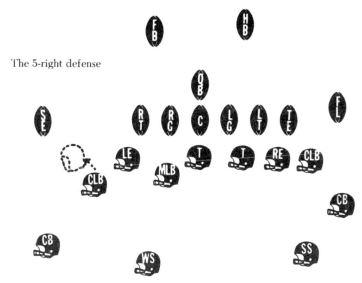

The 5-right defense

The pros also occasionally use a 5-1 defense. In this defense, most teams place the middle linebacker down in a three point stance over the center, with the weak side linebacker directly behind him. The strong side linebacker lines up over the tight end. At times, a fifth defensive lineman will be brought into the game to replace a corner linebacker and line up over the center. The middle linebacker remains in the middle where he is accustomed to playing. The 5-1 is stronger to the side of the tight end, but is used more as a change-up to keep the offense off balance than for its strengths.

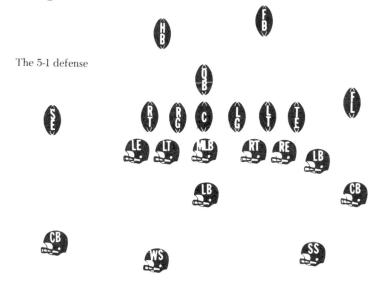

The 5-1 defense

There are some pro teams that use a fourth linebacker as a change-up or in specific situations. It will not look like the 4-4 defense diagrammed above, since the pro-set used on offense will force the defense to spread. If there are linebackers in the middle near the defensive tackles, the pros will call it a 4-4 defense. As in the traditional 4-4, there may be more games and blitzing in this defense than usual.

In short yardage and goal line situations, the pros, like college and high school teams, will use the gap-8 much of the time. If they don't go into a gap-8, they are likely to tighten up the 4-3 and put both corner linebackers down in a three point stance. This defense is generally called a 6-1 and is used most often in short yardage

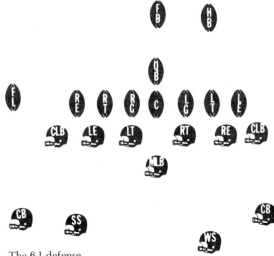

The 6-1 defense

situations at mid-field. At one time it was fashionable to replace regular defensive personnel with exceptionally large offensive linemen or defensive substitutes. If a change is to be made today, you are more likely to see a linebacker replacing a deep back in a short yardage situation.

More and more college teams are going to the seven man front because of its flexibility and lack of glaring weaknesses. You can expect this trend to continue as the college game moves closer to the wide open offensive attacks used by the pros. The three yards and a cloud of dust offense is dead, and so are the defenses that are particularly strong against the running game. The coach striving to implement a balanced offensive attack will necessarily be required to search for balance on defense as well. That balance in defensing the pass and run equally well is provided best by the seven man front.

## The 3-4 Defense

The recent trend to the 3-4 or "30" defense in pro football is a good example of the flexibility and balance of the seven man front. At first glance, it would appear that the use of three interior linemen and four linebackers would make the defensive unit more vulnerable against the running game because of a sacrifice in beef. Perhaps it would have 15 or 20 years ago when most linebackers weighed between 205 and 220 pounds and the emphasis was on strength and size rather than speed on the defensive line. Today, the weight and speed differential between linebacker and defensive lineman is not as great. Linebackers are bigger and defensive

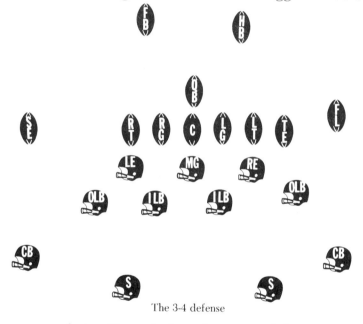

The 3-4 defense

linemen are faster. If you look at the roster of the New England Patriots, you will see that Sam Hunt, one of the two inside linebackers in the 3-4, is bigger than Sugar Bear Hamilton, the Patriot's noseguard. The effectiveness of a seven man front against the run is not determined by whether there is a fourth linebacker or fourth defensive lineman. It is determined by the caliber of that fourth man and how he is utilized.

In 1974, the Patriots were one of the first teams in the N.F.L. to switch to the 3-4 as their basic defense. (There were a number of factors which influenced coach Chuck Fairbanks' decision, not the least of which was the fact that he had more good linebackers than defensive linemen.) When the Patriots switched to the 3-4, they blitzed one of those four linebackers on every play. In effect, they were running the equivalent of a four man line with an added element of surprise because the offensive line never knew which of those four linebackers would be blitzing. The Houston Oilers, who started using the 3-4 about the same time, and the Denver Broncos, who started about a year later, do not blitz a linebacker every time. Again, decisions of that type are determined to a large extent by a team's personnel. Although I haven't questioned all the coaches involved, I think one important consideration in determining whether to blitz a linebacker is the effectiveness of the pass rushers. The Oilers and the Broncos apparently believed that they

Dewey Selmon (61) lined up as a noseguard in the 3-4 formation.

could generate a pass rush with just three men, while the Patriots thought they needed help from one of the linebackers.

When Chuck Fairbanks switched to the 3-4, he said that the primary reason was to get better pursuit to the outside. The Patriots had been weak in defensing the run. Of equal importance was the fact that he had young linebackers inside and when you have two instead of one man in the middle, the pressure on the linebackers is diminished. In 1974, Fairbanks was not only uncertain as to whether inside linebackers Sam Hunt or Steve Nelson could do the job alone, but of the quality of the rest of his defensive personnel as well. The 3-4 allowed Fairbanks to take the pressure off of many of his people by incorporating a great many stunts or games between his linebackers and down linemen. It was designed to keep pressure on opposing offensive linemen, and it worked well for the Pats. They were last in the American Football Conference against the run in 1973 and finished near the top in 1974 after leading the conference in rushing defense most of the season. The problem with the Pats' defense in 1974 was that they put so much emphasis on stopping the run that their pass defense fell apart.

There is no doubt that a seven man front provides great flexibility and allows the defense to put emphasis wherever it wants to. This is true whether a 4-3 or a 3-4 is being used. The Patriots wanted to stop the run and switched to the 3-4. Either by design or inadvertently their linebackers ended up helping the linemen more than the defensive secondary. Eventually, the Patriots achieved balance and the 3-4 worked well for them.

One of the keys to the effectiveness of the 3-4 is the noseguard (or middle guard). If the offensive center can handle the middle guard by himself on the pass and run, the defense is going to have trouble. Remember that the center is at somewhat of a disadvantage because he must snap the ball, and few can handle the noseguard without some help from the offensive guards. Curly Culp, of the Houston Oilers, made a national reputation for himself after being traded from Kansas City for Marv Matuzak and becoming the Oilers' noseguard. Despite all the publicity and the higher salary that went with it, Culp said that he disliked playing the position because he was constantly double-teamed on running plays and sometimes triple-teamed on the pass. Most down linemen feel the same way about the three man defensive line. It is not only the fact that they are more likely to be double-teamed, but that the chance of injury is greater. There are some offensive guards who will wait for the center to straighten up the noseguard on a pass play, and then attempt to cut the noseguard's legs in two while his upper body is tied up with that of the center. The noseguard is a tough position to play and requires a man of great quickness who can not only overpower the first man to block him, but can react to the second block as well. Shorter defensive linemen, such as Culp, Ray Hamilton of New England, and Rubin Carter of Denver, seem to have more success than some of the taller linemen who have played the position. It sounds silly to say that shorter people are quicker than taller people, but it is generally true.

The one thing essential to the success of the 3-4 is excellent overall team speed and quickness. There is no room for huge, lumbering linemen. Because of the many stunts and blitzes incorporated in the defense and the fact that the offense can burn the defense if they call the right play against the blitz or stunt, the defense must have enough speed to pursue effectively and recover. Once again it comes down to people and how they are used.

## GOAL LINE DEFENSES

When the football is inside the defensive team's ten yard line, there is no such thing as a containing defense. The team that allows three yards a down to the offense will allow a touchdown. The closeness of the end line allows the people in the defensive secondary to alter their normal alignment without fear of the quarterback throwing the ball behind them. Unless the ball is inches from the goal line, there is rarely a reason for a defensive back to line up in the end zone. He must play tight and prevent the short bullet-type pass. There is not enough of the playing field available for the receiver to get behind him.

In the middle of the field, the members of the defensive team's forcing unit must be concerned about getting the proper amount of penetration and not being able to pursue the ball carrier. Pursuit becomes less important on the goal line, causing the defensive linemen to alter their style of play. The team that relies on pursuit to stop a play on the goal line will give the offense the two or three yards it requires on each play. The defensive linemen must concern themselves only with penetrating into the offensive back-

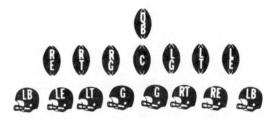

The gap-8 defense

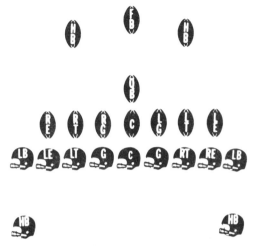

The nine man line

field and stopping the play for no gain or for a loss of yardage. It is in this situation that the submarine charge discussed earlier may be used by the linemen.

One of the problems that some teams and individuals have in a goal line defense is the different charge. The quick and agile defensive lineman, who may be extremely effective at mid-field, quite often lacks the size and strength to be effective in a goal line situation. Quickness is always a valuable asset, but strength is the key to success on the goal line. It is a completely different situation that often requires a lineman to change from a three to a four point stance (two hands on the ground) in order to help him stay low enough to get penetration.

Because of the increased chance of error, most offensive teams attempt to keep the ball out of the air on the goal line. For this reason, the defense will gear its efforts to stopping the run, and change defenses regardless of the success they have experienced with their basic defense. Most teams use a gap-8 defense on the goal line, although some high school and college teams will use a nine man line. In either case, the defensive linemen will strive to penetrate the offensive team's backfield. As you would expect, both the gap-8 and nine man line are exceptionally weak against the pass and not used except on the goal line. When using a nine man line, it is imperative that the defensive man opposite the offensive end detain him on the line of scrimmage.

In most instances, when a team does pass on the goal line, it will use play action passes. However, the pass rush is generally not as effective as one might expect here because of the many people on the forcing unit of the defense. Since their primary objective is to stay low and get penetration of a yard or so, they are not geared to getting the increased penetration necessary to reach the passer. Instead, the defense strives to detain and cover the receivers going downfield.

## STUNTING DEFENSES

Stunting defenses were popular during the late 1950's and early 1960's, but are not used as often today. Rather than involve the entire defense in a stunt, most teams now use small group stunts involving two or sometimes three players. Today, stunts are used

STUNTING DEFENSES

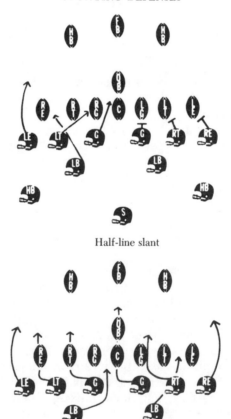

Half-line slant

Looping maneuver (left)

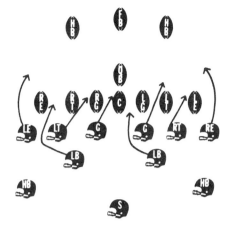

Slanting maneuver (right)

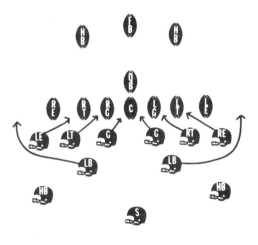

Center slant

as a change-up, or, when necessary, to hide a weakness or counter superior offensive strength. Stunting defenses may be employed in any of the previously diagrammed fronts. They are generally more effective when run from fronts with more than two line-backers, but can be used with only two linebackers, as diagrammed.

The number of teams using half-line stunts and stunts involving the entire defensive front has diminished for several reasons. Like most offensive innovations, the defense eventually caught up and found ways to block stunting linemen and linebackers. When the offense is not expecting a stunt, the defense is likely to experience success the first time they try one. If the offense is well prepared for the stunt, they should be able to handle it from that point on by delaying their charges for a split second and blocking the defender that stunts into their normal area of responsibility.

When stunts were first employed, they created much confusion among the offensive linemen who found themselves trying to block the men lined up directly opposite them regardless of where they moved after the snap of the ball. This led to offensive people running into each other and attempting to block defenders that did not have to be blocked. To counteract this confusion, the offensive linemen adopted area blocking which did the trick.

Defensive coaches found that stunts involving the entire defensive front were unwieldy, and, while the offense was occasionally confused, so was the defense. The key to carrying out a successful stunt is to move quickly into a designated area before the offense can adjust their blocking. Frequently, coaches found that their defensive players became over-anxious and took themselves out of the play. The player moving hard in one direction could not stop his momentum, regain his balance and tackle a ball carrier moving in the direction from whence he came.

Another problem with stunting defenses is the unevenness of team pursuit. Players slanting or looping in the opposite direction from that in which the ball carrier is running will not be able to begin to pursue quickly. They must first reverse their direction, which is not only difficult, but makes them vulnerable to being blocked. Naturally, some players are better equipped to play in a stunting defense than others. Size and strength is less important to the stunting lineman than to the one playing it straight. Speed and quickness are the prerequisites for a stunting defense. For that reason, coaches that believe their teams are out-manned physically will sometimes resort to team stunts. The defensive line that is outweighed by 40 pounds a man may appreciate the opportunity to try to confuse and outrun the offense.

It is rare, at any level of football, for an entire team to be completely overmatched. Coaches continue to try to assist players going up against a physically superior opponent. However, this can be accomplished just as easily with the use of two-man or small group stunts. This type of stunt usually represents less of a gamble. When the entire defense, including the linebackers, are involved in a stunt and the running back gets by the line of scrimmage, there is no one to stop him until he reaches the deep secondary or goal line. When a defensive team employs a tackle-end game, the linebacker will be alerted and may be able to compensate if one of the stunting linemen is cut off and cannot fulfill his assignment.

Like the blitz, consistent stunting involving all or most of the defensive front is considered to be a gamble. Today, it is rarely used as a basic defense. You are likely to see complete team stunts only when a team has fallen behind and begins to panic, or when it is overmatched. Teams with superior personnel will rarely use them under any circumstances.

Games, involving a limited number of defensive players (as opposed to stunts) are used by most teams. They can be effective in accomplishing a number of things. They can prevent the offense from executing a double team block by moving the prospective target. They can make backfield penetration easier and make better pursuit possible. They can help spring a defensive man free to bring down the ball carrier.

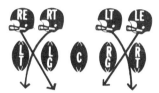

End-tackle game (end moves first)

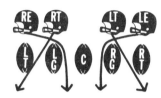

Tackle-end game (tackle moves first)

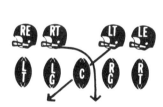

Tackle-tackle game
(either man moves first)

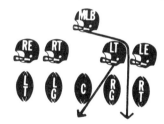

Tackle-middle linebacker game
(tackle moves first)

Occasionally, games put the defense at a disadvantage. They sometimes create wide inviting holes for the offense. They can cause uneven pursuit on the part of those players moving away from the point of attack. When linebackers are involved, they cut down the number of pass defenders.

When you see a defensive team using stunts that require the participation of the entire front, or when a team is using an unusual number of games, look for the reasons. If it is not on the scoreboard and the clock (time remaining), look at the personnel on each team. If the answer is not there, the type of offensive blocking may provide a clue. Teams that use a great deal of double team blocking, cross blocking, trap blocking and use their offensive backs as blockers are more vulnerable to stunting defenses.

The Minnesota Vikings have had one of the best defensive units in the N.F.L. for many years. Until the arrival of Chuck Foreman and the return of Fran Tarkenton, it was their defense that got them into the playoffs and earned them their Super Bowl encounter with the Kansas City Chiefs. The strength in the late '60's and early '70's was the defensive line. When Carl Eller, Alan Page and Jim Marshall arrived in the N.F.L., offensive linemen were not quite as big as they are today. Their relative light playing weights did not create mismatches and the exceptional quickness of all three proved to be a distinct advantage. My hat goes off to Messrs. Eller, Page and Marshall for their ability to maintain that quickness over the years. However, no pro football player is quite as quick at age 37 as he was at age 22 or even at age 27. In order to compensate for the disparity in weight between the Vikings linemen and opposing offensive linemen, the Vikings began to call more "games" during the 1977 season than they ever did before. It must have worked, since the Vikings once again got into the playoffs.

The offensive player has the advantage of knowing where the play is going and on what count. The offensive team has the added advantage of being able to take any alignment that will help it execute the play called in the huddle. The defensive team has the burden of reacting to the movement of the offense. Good defensive alignment involves making adjustments to each change in the offense. This is something that is absolutely necessary and can be easily observed. Just as most offensive formations have their advocates and are run successfully somewhere, you will find that most defensive alignments are also run with success somewhere. The particular defense doesn't matter much unless it is inconsistent with the forcing and containing philosophy previously discussed.

Look for adjustments on the part of the linebackers and defensive backs each time the offense comes out in a different set. When both wide receivers line up on the same side of the line, there should be an adjustment by the secondary. When the set backs line up to the same side, look for the linebackers to move in that direction. Look for things to tighten in short yardage situations and for the linebackers and deep backs to loosen up in a long yardage situation. The examples of suggested adjustments are too numerous to state separately. Look for some adjustment to every offensive change which represents a passing or running threat. These are the basic principles upon which all defenses should be built, regardless of the front used.

# Part Three

# STARTING THE ACTION

## THE HUDDLE

Before the action can begin, the offensive team must be given a play to execute. The play may be sent in by the coach or left to the quarterback to call. In either case, a brief meeting must be held on the field to get the play number and any additional pertinent information to the entire team. The quarterback is the boss in the huddle and is expected to do most of the talking. The quarterback that asserts himself and has the respect of his teammates usually has few problems. Signs of indecision by a quarterback when calling plays can cause a rash of suggestions from wide receivers calling for a pass play; from the running backs calling for a run; and from each lineman calling for the play to be run in his area.

There is other information that can be exchanged between the various players while the huddle is forming. An offensive lineman will frequently tell the running back behind him where he thinks the hole may open. If the opposite defensive lineman is favoring an inside rush, he will advise the back to look to the outside. Information between the backs and linemen is exchanged on pass plays. Chuck Knox wants his offensive linemen to alert the offensive backs when they are about to attempt a change-up block on the opposition. At times, the quarterback may solicit specific information from a teammate. The quarterback can readily see where a player has lined up before the snap of the ball, but does not know where he is going after the snap. It may help him to know.

Sometimes, the amount of talk in the huddle can get out of hand. Alex Hawkins, who has found himself on the hot seat more than once during his career as an analyst for CBS Sports, has always said what was on his mind. Several years ago, CBS fired him for making an observation about a defensive back who was sidelined because both of his hands were broken and in casts. Alex noted: "He gets to know who his friends are when he goes to the john." Eventually, CBS had second thoughts, and brought Alex back a couple of years later. Alex was a sophomore at the University of South Carolina when I was a senior. Even then, he said more than was necessary. Our quarterback was not as authoritative as he should have been and Alex discovered that he could get him to call the plays he wanted. In an important game against arch-rival Clemson it seemed that "The Hawk" was calling all the plays and doing all the talking in the huddle. I was late in returning to the huddle on one play and saw that Hawkins was already bending everyone's ear. Instead of getting into the right tackle slot in the huddle where I belonged, I walked around to the halfback slot and kicked Alex where he sits. Alex got the message and didn't say a word for the rest of the season. I really looked forward to looking at the game films that Monday.

The open huddle was introduced to keep conversation to a minimum. Since the quarterback is facing the entire team, it is more difficult for the players lined up in the rear of the huddle to converse with him. Extensive talking by anyone but the quarterback will be noticed by the coaches on the sidelines. The open huddle also allows the entire team, except for the quarterback, to look at the defense at all times.

The closed huddle is preferred by most coaches. It provides an opportunity for a player with valuable information to talk to a teammate or the quarterback without being detected by the

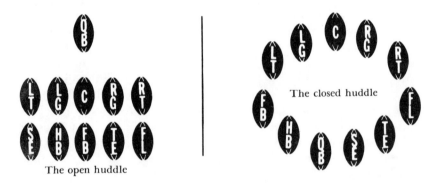

The open huddle

The closed huddle

opposition. The defense does not have to overhear a conversation to gather information. The very fact that two players are talking may tip an upcoming play. There is little chance of any play being tipped in a closed huddle. (When in an open huddle, players may tip the play by looking at the hole or area to which the ball will be carried.) The closed huddle is used by most pro teams, where excessive talking is not a major problem.

The closed huddle, favored by most pro teams.

## PLAY NUMBERING

Much has been said and written about the difficulty that the present-day football player has in learning the vast number of highly technical plays used by such pro coaches as Hank Stram and George Allen. The number of plays that must be learned has been overly exaggerated. Some coaches consider plays run at the same hole in the offensive line as completely different when run from different alignments in the backfield or with different splits by the ends. When counting the number of plays this way, you can get into the hundreds. In reality, though, blocking assignments don't change that often. The same play can be run from 12 different formations, into the same hole, with the blocking assignments remaining the same. There are only so many places to run with the football and so many formations from which plays can be run. The same applies to pass blocking. Learning his plays should not present a problem for any reasonably intelligent player who takes the time to look into his playbook during the first few weeks of practice.

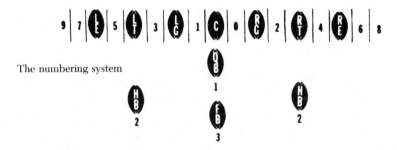

The numbering system

There is a lot of similarity between the play numbering systems used by most teams at all levels of football. The fact that college players can be ready for post season games with a week of preparation indicates that learning plays is not difficult. The similarity in numbering systems makes it easier. There are several systems in use, but most coaches number the holes between offensive linemen. The diagram is self-explanatory. Because of the similarity in numbering systems, coaches vary the even and odd numbers from one side to the other. The number two hole may be on the right side for one team and on the left for another. This is done to prevent teams from picking up audibles or over-hearing plays in the huddle.

The offensive backs also receive numbers in this system. The quarterback may be the "1" back, the halfbacks, the "2" back, and the fullback, the "3" back. The running plays themselves all carry two digits. The first digit indicates the ball carrier and the second where the ball will be carried. For example, the 10 play will be run between the center and right guard with the quarterback carrying the ball. The 22 play will have the halfback run between the right guard and the right tackle. The 33 play will have the fullback carry between the left guard and the left tackle. With some slight variation, this is the basic play numbering system which most teams use.

According to this system, running plays are differentiated from pass plays by assigning specific blocks of numbers to them. Any play from 10 to 59 will be a run. Show passes are assigned numbers from 60 to 99. Play action passes are between 100 and 200. The quick pass requiring fire out protection by the offensive line will take numbers from 200 to 300. Screen passes will form the 400 series.

Words are sometimes included with the numbers when calling plays. The most common backfield maneuvers are diagrammed here. The movement and faking in the offensive backfield varies with each maneuver. The backfield action, if a team does change it from play to play, can be indicated by placing such words as "dive," "slant," or "ride" before the number designating the ball carrier and the hole. A single letter is sometimes used in place of the entire word. The quarterback may simply say "S" for slant or "P" for plunge.

The terms "dive" and "plunge" are usually used to describe the quick hand off to the halfback and fullback respectively. The halfback dives into the line and the fullback plunges. In all the other backfield maneuvers diagrammed, either the halfback or fullback may be designated as the ball carrier, and can carry it into any hole on the line.

On the slant, the ball carrier approaches the line at an angle. On the ride maneuver, the quarterback moves into the line with the

BACKFIELD MANEUVERS

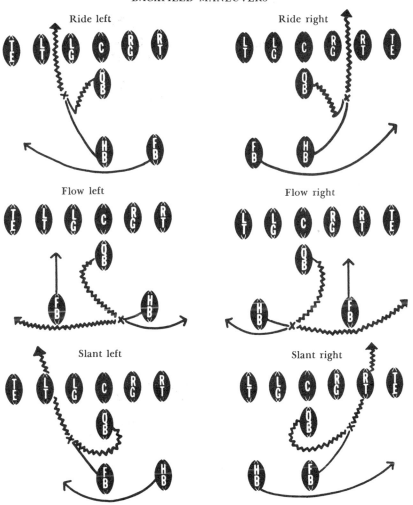

ball carrier for a short distance before handing off the football. He is said to "ride" the ball carrier. Of course, he may fake and then hand off to another back or pass from ride action. Flow action is used on end runs. However, a play can start as a flow maneuver only to have the back break off-tackle. Counter action begins the same way as the flow maneuver, but the ball carrier moves in the opposite direction after taking a step with the flow. The play usually breaks inside the tackles.

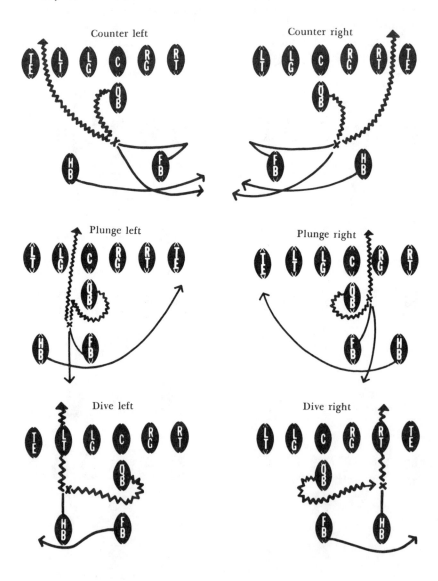

In the pro-set, where only two running backs are used, the type of backfield maneuver may dictate how the backs are to align themselves. For example, the halfback knows that he lines up directly behind the hole on the dive, and the fullback directly behind the quarterback on the plunge, slant and ride. This is not standardized and will vary from team to team. Some teams call the backfield alignment every time. The set of the backs can be altered for each maneuver if the quarterback chooses. The set of the backs is more likely to be altered on pass plays, however, than on the run.

THE BACKFIELD SETS

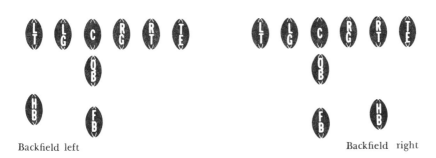

Backfield left                                          Backfield   right

Backfield  split

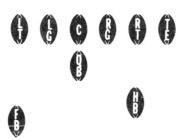

## CALLING SIGNALS

The quarterback calls the play in the huddle and the signals at the line of scrimmage. It helps if he has good diction and a booming voice, but the present-day coach even tries to help his quarterback in this area. He uses one and two syllable words that don't sound alike when devising calls and signals. This makes it easier for all to hear the signals over the roar of the crowd.

The first task of the quarterback in the huddle is to call the formation. If he is running from the pro-set, he might merely say "strong right" or "strong left," which will send the tight end and flanker to one side or the other. If he is running a multiple offense, he might call, "wing right, slot left" or any of the other formations diagrammed in the chapter on the offensive formations.

After setting the formation, he will call the play and the backfield action. "Dive 22" or "D 22" is often all that is necessary. This will tell the team which back will carry the football into which hole, and how the backfield will align itself. On some teams, each backfield maneuver is run from a different backfield set. The word "dive" not only signifies the type of action but to which side the backs will align. On teams where the quarterback must set the backs on every play, he will do this before giving the play. For example, he will say "backs right, counter, thirty-two," or "backs split, counter, thirty-two."

The starting count on which the center will snap the ball is then given and the huddle is usually broken with a hand clap. Most quarterbacks are instructed to call the play on both sides of the huddle and pause before breaking the huddle to allow time for questions. A sample call in the huddle could be: "Slot left, dive 23, on 2." The tight end will line up in the slot to the left side, and the halfback will carry into the three hole on the second count.

Before the widespread use of the face mask, it was common for football players to remove their front teeth and leave them in their lockers during practice. Because it was necessary for the quarterback to be clearly understood, he was often the only player on a team without a gaping space in front of his mouth. Of course, that was the real reason that the quarterback always got the girl.

## THE SHIFT

The offensive team has two choices when it comes out of the huddle. The players can get down into a three point stance immediately, or they can come out with their hands or elbows on their knees and wait to be put into the three point stance by the quarterback. Once a lineman places his hand on the ground, he cannot lift it to change position. The team that comes out and waits to be set by the quarterback has the opportunity of shifting to a more advantageous position if the defense moves or the quarterback checks off. The linemen also have a better opportunity to scan the defense from a semi-upright position. One *disadvantage* of not lining up in a three point stance immediately is that from a semi-upright position it is difficult for the quarterback to move the team into action on his first sound. Pass plays can be run effectively from an upright position, but the lineman is at a distinct disadvantage if he tries to fire out on a running play from such a position. Moving on the first sound can keep the defense off balance. It can also serve to deter shifting defenses and line-backers that have a tendency to move in and out of the line.

If he thinks it desirable, the quarterback of a team which normally shifts has the option of instructing his linemen to assume a three point stance as soon as they reach the line. This will enable the team to move effectively on the first sound. A quarterback will do this when his team has been coming out in a semi-upright position and the defense has been shifting repeatedly after his team sets. Setting immediately restricts the choice of the quarterback checking off, since the offense may not be set in a desirable formation to run a particular play, but the team that is able to move on the first sound and catches the defense while shifting is likely to break a long run.

Like moving on the first sound, the shift also keeps the defense off balance and discourages shifting defenses. The defensive shift is pointless unless the offense is in a set position. If the defense shifts before the offensive team is set in a three point stance, the offense then has an opportunity to make the last move.

The shift allows the offensive line to take wider or narrower splits. At times, the offense may shift a guard or tackle from one side of the center to the other. The shift extends to the backfield and the receivers, where it becomes especially important if the quarterback has changed the play at the line of scrimmage. The shift for the set back in this instance is likely to bring him into a completely different alignment allowing him to run a new play.

## SIGNALS AT THE LINE OF SCRIMMAGE

The quarterback goes through the same procedure each time he takes his position behind the center.

1. He checks the defense quickly and decides if he wants to check off to another play. He will then call a fake or live check off signal (a color or name) and the number of the fake or new play. The signal and number are called on both sides of the line. (The audible will be treated separately later in this chapter.)

2. Some coaches then require the quarterback to identify the defensive alignment for the rest of the team. This is partly because the quarterback is in a better position to see the defense than the rest of the team, and partly to help assure that everyone will be blocking as he should be. The call will be a simple "4-3," or "5-left."

3. The team is then given an opportunity to shift and set itself in a three point stance. The call: "ready-eee" alerts the team to shift, and after a slight pause, the word "down," or "set," will put the team in position to run the play.

4. The starting signals, which may be any series of numbers or words, are then called. "Hut-2, hut-2, hut-2," is commonly used. The entire team will charge on any predetermined "hut" or "2."

The entire call will sound like this "Red—, ride 36—4-3—ready-eee—set—hut-2, hut-2, hut-2."

The quarterback must call a live or fake check off play each time. The exception may be toward the half or the end of the game when time is important. At that time he may simply say: "4-3—ready-eee—set, hut-2, hut-2."

## THE STARTING COUNT

The number or words used to start the team on its play are unimportant. The decision the coach must make is whether to use a rhythmic or a broken cadence. An evenly spaced cadence allows the offensive team to anticipate the call and get a slight jump on the defense. The quarterback will shout: Hut one, hut two, hut three, at regular intervals without any prolonged or uneven pauses. The ball can be snapped on any one of the "huts" or numbers. The problem with a rhythmic cadence is that the defensive team sometimes anticipates the snap. For this reason, the quarterback is instructed to vary the starting count. Still, many fall into a rut and use a favorite number again and again.

The alternative is to pause between calls. This makes it more difficult for both the offense *and* defense to anticipate the count, but many coaches believe that the advantage lies with the offense. Rather then call hut-2, hut-2, the quarterback may call "one and ..." (pause), "two and ..." (no pause), "three and ..." (long pause), and "four and," etc.

The ball can also be snapped on any of the preliminary calls made by the quarterback before starting the count: the first sound, the ready-eee, the "set," the defense, or the fake play call. Toward the end of a game, the defense may be caught napping by using a preliminary call to start the team.

## AUDIBLES (CHECK OFFS)

The audible has long been a subject for discussion by those broadcasting football games on both radio and television. Any prolonged delay with a pronounced shift and the color man is likely to say that there was a check off. Nonsense! The only way to know for certain if a check off is being called is to be aware *of* the signal for the audible and the play calling system. If it were that easy for the color man sitting in the stands to call the audible, the people on the field would pick it up much sooner and react accordingly.

Is the quarterback about to audiblize?

The audible or check off system is a means of changing the play called in the huddle after the team has reached the line of scrimmage. It can be extremely important when the opponent is changing defenses on each play. Some plays are designed to work against specific defenses and do not work well against others. If the team is in the anticipated defense and the quarterback does not see an individual defensive player out of position, there is probably no reason to call an audible. If the defense is well prepared for the play called, though, an audible should be called.

Many teams use a color system to check off, but any group of words will do. It could be names of people, flowers, or even dogs. The quarterback is required to call a live or fake color each times he calls signals at the line. The offense is told before the game which color or name is live. If the live color is called the number following it will be the new play. If a fake color is called, the ensuing number means nothing.

The offensive team is given a list of possible plays that the quarterback may check off to before the game. The formation and blocking assignments have been predetermined and a number is all that is necessary to alert the team. The number on which the ball will be snapped has been provided in advance so that the new play always starts on the same number. If the audible is being used extensively and the quarterback suspects that the defense may be aware of the live color, he can change it at any time. Another alternative is to use a dummy check to confuse the defense. In this instance, the team is forewarned to disregard the live color on a specific play. One thing is certain, you can be sure that the play called on the line will be designed to go in the opposite direction from the one called in the huddle.

Some defensive teams will shift after the color and play number are called. The quarterback can stop this by having the ball snapped on the play number. If the defense is shifting while the offense is putting the ball in play, the offense has a good chance of breaking a play for a long gain. The defensive linemen will not be set and should be blown off the line with ease.

When time is important or the defense is changing alignments on every play, the quarterback may bypass calling a play in the huddle. He may simply call a formation and say "check with me." The play will then be called on the line of scrimmage and every color will be live. A team may have a "double check with me" offense in which the quarterback will call two colors and plays at the line with the second one being live. This would be used when a defensive team continues to shift after the audible.

Many pro teams use a "check with me" offense toward the end of the half, the end of the game, or when the team does not have time to go into a huddle. This is sometimes called the "two-minute-to-go" offense. The team can run a predetermined series of plays or the quarterback can call the play at the line of scrimmage. Either way, time will be saved.

When you're sitting in the stands you can often hear the signals being called. It's a powerful feeling, but it won't help very much unless you have a close friend on the team who is willing to explain the signal system to you and advise you of the live color. Without this information, you will not be able to predict the plays.

In recent years, many quarterbacks have been rigged with microphones during post season all-star games. The announcers are told the signal system and live color, and are then able to advise the viewing audience where the play is going. It can be fun. Most of the time, though, when an announcer tries to predict the plays on his own, he'll be wrong 75% of the time. The fan might think that he's privy to inside information, but, actually, he's been cheated. He's going to look where the announcer expects the play to go and that means that he'll miss a lot of the action.

# Part Four

# HOW TO WATCH
# A FOOTBALL GAME

## Introduction

In the preceding chapters, I have attempted to provide the basic information that a fan will need to enjoy a football game: the terminology, the various positions and their responsibilities, the basic plays, and the basic formations used on offense and defense. The information is by no means complete, but should help you to understand and appreciate what is happening on the field. Through the background provided about each of the 22 players on the field, you should be able to evaluate the individual player and better understand why one formation or defense is successful and another fails.

Despite all the facts that you now have at your disposal, there is no standard or set way to watch a football game. It depends on the individual. To the uninitiated, I would suggest looking at anything that interests you at a given moment. It does not take a knowledgeable viewer to appreciate the explosive offense or gang tackling defense. When in doubt as to where to focus your attention, and if you are a new fan, I would advise you to follow the ball. You will then be certain to see every touchdown, interception, fumble, tackle and most of the outstanding downfield blocks. This is the easy way to watch a football game. If you have gotten to this chapter, I must assume that you are interested in forming intelligent opinions about the players, formations and strategy on display during each game. If you really want to understand the game, you will have to work a little harder.

A pair of active eyes roaming the field *before* the snap will provide a lot of information that will help you evaluate what happens after the snap of the ball. The first thing that you should be aware of is who is in the game, including any replacements sent in at special times. This information can tip a play. Try to find the wide receivers. They are important if a pass play has been called, and are easy to spot. They will be moving out into the flat area by themselves and will not be in the crowd of linemen and backs leaving the huddle. If you do not see at least two wide receivers moving out to the flat area, you have already gathered important information. The team that replaces its wide receivers with another tight end and a good blocking back, and comes out in a full house backfield, should not be expected to throw long. On the other hand, the team that has three, or possibly four, wide receivers in the game at one time should be expected to throw the football. These are extreme situations and are obvious to everyone.

There are more subtle things to look for, though. After identifying the offensive formation, look for adjustments in personnel: the set back who may be lined up slightly to the outside, or unusually wide splits by one or two linemen. When evaluated with other information gathered, such things can often tell a story.

Certain information is more readily available to the fan with a seat high in the stands than to those on the field. Splits in the offensive line are sometimes hard to spot by people in the secondary or on the other side of the field. They are easy to spot from the stands. The team that lines up with wide splits on the same side of the center as both running backs may well be expected to run a dive or power play to that side. The offensive line will split to provide more space for the backs to find running room. The linemen will tighten up on the off-side to make the cutoff block easier, and to get downfield faster.

Look for the offensive backs to tip a play by their alignment. The back with average speed that lines up a little further to the outside may be expected to move in that direction on a quick pitch, after the snap of the ball. Or, there can be other explanations such as trying to get a better blocking angle, or moving into position to get out faster on a flare pass. The information and tips must be pieced together with your knowledge about the strengths of each player, the defense and the offensive formation. Alone it means nothing.

Remember that the information that you pick up often has to be corroborated. The wide split of the offensive back and the possibility of a quick pitch can be *verified* by looking at other things. The offensive tackle in front of the split back may provide a clue. He is warned about the possibility of tipping the play, and coaches will often suggest that he line up closer to the guard when pulling out to lead interference on a quick pitch. At this point the fan's knowledge of the player becomes important. There is no reason to expect the offensive tackle with exceptional speed to cheat to the outside when taking his position next to the offensive guard. However, if the tackle is known to be a slow runner, a wide split may tip the quick pitch.

The game or tactical situation will then confirm the fan's suspicion about the possibility of a quick pitch. The down and distance should be of primary importance. The quick pitch is more of a gamble than the play up the middle. There is a much greater chance of the ball carrier being thrown for a loss. It is not a short yardage play, and should not be expected on third and three. On the other hand, it might be a good call on first and ten. The offensive team's field position will also help determine if the quick pitch is the chosen offensive play. Because of the possibility of the ball carrier losing yardage, it would not be a good call when close to either goal line.

The score could be a factor. A team is more inclined to gamble with a potentially dangerous play in a crucial situation if it is behind on the scoreboard. A team behind by three touchdowns is more likely to use the quick pitch on third and three from midfield than the team sitting on a lead. They will be gambling on picking up a long gain or a quick touchdown.

The condition of the field and weather conditions will provide further clues. When running a quick pitch on a sloppy field, the offense is at a disadvantage. In a long yardage passing situation, when the offense is moving against the wind, the quick pitch may be a good alternative to the pass.

The defensive personnel to the side of the expected quick pitch could provide a clue as to whether this will be the play. On the quick pitch, the offensive team attempts to outrun most of the defensive players on that side of the field. The size, speed and defensive alignment of the players in the area become important. The quick pitch is a good call against a defensive end and linebacker that are playing tight or crashing down the line. It is not a good call against an exceptionally fast defensive end that plays a loose and cautious game. He will be right next to the offensive tackle pulling out to block the cornerback. Since both the corner linebacker and safety will be blocked on the play, their alignment becomes more important than their physical attributes. The linebacker playing tight gives the tight end a better chance to block him. The quarterback is likely to change the play if the linebacker is wide or the safety is close to the line of scrimmage and looks like he is ready to blitz. The flanker must crackback on the safety, and will have difficulty if he is moving across the line of scrimmage.

Finally, you have to evaluate what you have seen during the game so far—as well as tendencies that you have observed during other games. Has the offense run the play successfully in the past?

Has the defense been weak against the quick pitch in the past? The more information evaluated, the better the chance of anticipating an offensive or defensive maneuver.

The viewer familiar with the individual players can go through the entire evaluation process in a matter of seconds. With practice, anyone can learn to take in the entire side of a field with a quick glance. He does not look at the offensive tackle and then the set back, but sees the tackle, back, defensive end, tight end and corner linebacker as a unit. Alignment is relative, and it is impossible to evaluate the position of one player without considering it in relation to the alignment of those around him.

The newly converted football fan has a tendency to devote most of his attention to the offense and overlook the defense. This is a mistake, since an awareness of the defensive alignment and what they are attempting to accomplish can help to better understand the offense. In most instances, you should be looking at one part of the offense in relation to a corresponding part of the defense. However, at the beginning of the game, you should study the *entire* defensive alignment—its strengths, its weaknesses, and how the defense attempts to compensate for them.

The information provided in the chapter on team defense should be applied here. Be aware of the type of "front," and whether the overall objective of the defense is to play a containing or pressure style. The number of linemen and linebackers in the front, the extent of blitzes and games, and the type of coverage in the secondary will indicate the overall objective of the defense. This information can be important in understanding both teams' strategy and tactics.

Be aware of relative distances on defense and adjustments to the offensive alignments. For each change that the offense makes from the pro-set, there should be a corresponding change by the defense. If the set back moves out into the slot, the linebacker on that side should move out toward him if he is assigned to cover him on a pass play. If he does not adjust, the safety must. When one set back moves into a wing back position and the other back lines up on that side of the line, the middle linebacker and corner linebacker on the other side of the line should move toward the wing back. The adjustment is toward the strength of the offensive formation.

Against the standard pro-set, look for indications by the defense which may tip the blitz or the type of coverage being used against the pass. The depth of the linebackers may provide valuable information. If the corner linebacker is up close to the line, you might expect a blitz. A blitz would be especially likely if it is a passing situation and the safety is also up tight in a position to cover the set back or tight end on a quick pass should the corner linebacker blitz. Look for zone coverage if the linebackers are loose or wide. Notice who is covering the wide receiver in the slot. If it is a strong safety who has a reputation for being slow of foot, and the linebacker does not make an adjustment to help, you can expect the quarterback to look for the wide receiver deep.

The depth of the defensive secondary is important. Everyone in the stadium can see the cornerback playing 10 to 12 yards from the wide receiver. If there is no adjustment by the safety or cornerback to cover the flat or short hook area on that side, look for the short pass to the wide receiver. Of course, the variables must be considered once again. If it is third down and 30, the cornerback is not going to be playing tight. The ten yard completion will do little damage, but the bomb may mean the ball game.

If it is a running situation, check the positions of the defensive linemen. Have they adjusted to the splits of the offensive line? Have the linebackers also adjusted to the splits? Have blocking angles developed? If it is a passing situation, notice any unusual alignments by the linemen. If the defensive end is lined up to the inside of the tackle and the defensive tackle is back off the line, you might expect an end-tackle game with the end coming down first into the offensive guard and the defensive tackle going around him to protect and rush from the outside.

At the snap of the ball, look at the offensive guards and keep the quarterback in your field of vision. The guards will tell you whether it is a pass or run. On traps or sweeps, it is the guard who leads the interference. It is true that some teams will send their guards in one direction while the backs and ball go in another. They are hoping that the defense is keying on the guard and will be drawn out of position. But, this does not happen that often. If the guard's movement tells you that it is a running play, check the flow of the backs and look at the offensive line on the side to which the back is moving. Look for a hole large enough for a back to break through. If the hole seems to be opening in another area, determine if the running back can see it and if he makes his cut without slowing down. This is an opportunity to evaluate individuals and determine why a particular play succeeded or failed, at the same time. By the end of the game you will have a good idea of how each player performed and why a team won or lost.

After the ball carrier has been tackled, notice who is standing around on the offensive team (indicating a missed block), and who is still with his block. If you had decided before the start of the play to check the performance of an individual, it may be advisable to devote your attention to him only after you are certain whether it is a pass or a run. If you are intent on looking at the middle linebacker, this won't matter very much. However, it would be foolish to watch the left cornerback if the play is going around the left side. The action is fast but there should be sufficient time to determine the direction of the play and then pick up an individual.

If the offensive guards and the quarterback tell you that the play is a pass, by the way they drop or set up, look downfield to get an overall picture of what is happening. The information gathered before the snap may provide a tip as to who will receive the pass. If one cornerback is tight and the other is playing loose on third down and seven, you should expect the quarterback to throw to the man that is being covered loosely.

After checking the action downfield, glance back at the quarterback to see if he is being rushed and where he is looking. Then, if time permits, look downfield in the direction in which the quarterback was looking to determine if he does have a free man in the area or is just trying to confuse the defense. Most experienced quarterbacks will attempt to deceive the defenders by looking away from the intended receiver until the last possible moment. It's called "looking off" the defender.

Once the ball has been thrown, look for the receiver in the area and the number of defenders near the ball. It should not be difficult to determine if the ball was thrown well and is on target. As was indicated in the chapter on the quarterback, every pass should not be thrown in the same way. Some require more zip than others. Immediately after the play is over, look to see how many defenders were in the area. If the ball is way off target, the position of the other receivers and defenders in the area will indicate whether it was thrown away or if the receiver broke his pattern.

It is rare that a pass pattern has two men running so close to each other that the intended receiver cannot be determined. This occurs occasionally against zone coverage, but almost never happens against man coverage. If you see two receivers close to each other, and the ball seems to be thrown in another direction, you can assume that one of the receivers broke his pattern and zigged when he should have zagged. If a potential receiver is covered by two or three defenders and the ball is obviously overthrown, you can assume that the quarterback threw the ball away. If the receiver is isolated on the defender and the ball is not on target, assume it was poorly thrown.

Once again, the game situation should determine where you will be looking. When it is third and one, don't look at the defensive secondary. When a strong wind is blowing against the passer, look for him to throw to his set backs and tight end. If the wind is behind his back, you might look for the bomb. When time is running out, look for the sideline route which will stop the clock by allowing the receiver to get out of bounds. If it is raining hard and the field is in poor condition, look for the running game up the middle, *not* around the ends.

Naturally, the defense will also be looking for the same things you are, and the offense will come up with the unexpected at times. Most often, though, if you put all the pieces together and look for the obvious, you will guess right.

The above suggested pattern of looking at a football game will assist in helping to determine why a play worked or failed and keep you in the middle of the action. If you are interested in evaluating *individual* performances and abilities, several different patterns may be followed, depending on whom you are interested in evaluating. People on the offensive and defensive lines are easy to evaluate. Watch them for several plays in succession. This will allow you to see how they react in various situations. What does the offensive lineman do when the play is going to the other side? Does he loaf while running downfield, or is he running at full speed and trying to block someone? Is the defensive lineman on the off-side pursuing diligently, or is he going through the motions? These questions can sometimes be answered by looking to see where people are once the play is blown dead. For a real understanding of a position, a player's every action should be watched while the ball is in play.

The fan may want to see what the receiver not expecting the ball does on pass play. In this case, he should look at the quarterback and direct his attention to the receiver to whom the quarterback is not looking. This receiver should be running as hard as he does when he is expecting the ball. It is important to the success of the play. A member of the defensive secondary may be keying the receiver not expecting the ball. If he sees him loafing, he may attempt to help elsewhere and succeed in breaking up the pass. The good receiver always runs exact routes at full speed. When not the intended receiver, he should be setting up future patterns.

The drop of the quarterback may be worth watching from start to finish for a few plays. Does he drop the same way each time, or does he vary according to whom he is looking for? Some quarterbacks will turn and run sideways in anticipation of a pass to their right, and drop straight back when looking for a receiver to their left. This should not happen in the pros.

Think about what you want to see in a player, and pick an opportune moment rather than watching him on every play. You may have to wait a long time before you get the opportunity to see a player perform certain skills. For example, most teams don't use their wide receivers as blockers very often. If this interests you, wait until the guards and the quarterback tell you the play is a sweep or quick pitch and then look at the wide receiver who may be cracking back on someone to the inside. If you are interested in seeing how a cornerback plays against the run, wait for an off-tackle play which should cause him to come up and close the hole.

Tendencies, in particular, should be observed and noted. Does a team always sweep on a particular down? Does the quarterback only throw long on first down? Does he only run the draw on third down? Does the defense blitz only on a specific down? If you can pick up a tendency in the stands, the coaches in the press box should have it also, and adjustments should be made. If the defensive secondary and linebackers are coming up fast on the run, look for the play pass. If they are dropping back quickly in the secondary, look for the run in a passing situation. It may never come and no one may hear your pleas for an adjustment, but it can be fun to second guess the coach and quarterback. The guy sitting next to you may be impressed.

Most important, in watching a football game, though, is not to get frustrated. It takes time to learn the game and put it all together. If you stick with it though, I guarantee you that you'll get there.

Now, let's see how the guys who get paid for it analyze a game. Let's look at the defense through the eyes of the quarterback, the offense through the eyes of the middle linebacker, and the view from the broadcast booth.

# 1

# THE DEFENSE THROUGH THE EYES OF THE QUARTERBACK

When a fan first looks at a defensive alignment, all he sees is people strewn all over the field. There must be some order to this, he thinks to himself, but where to start. To provide a map to this maze, I thought that it might be interesting if we spent a little time looking at the defense through the eyes of the quarterback. The quarterback is the only offensive player on the field who has to look at the defense alignment in its entirety. Of course, he doesn't see everything on every play. But, it is precisely what the quarterback sees when he scans the defense that influences all the action that follows.

The quarterback looks at many different things when scanning the defense. The center of his attention will vary with the type of play called. His first duty is to identify the defense and inform his teammates. The blocking assignments in pro football are more involved than at other levels. Many college teams block an area or a zone: the offensive guard blocks the first man to his side of the center, the tackle the second man (whether on or off the line), and the end the third man from the center. In many instances, the players are not required to know the name of the defense or anything else except how to count to three. Professional coaches usually have a more intricate system and change the offensive line's blocking assignments with each defense it faces. Because there are many different defensive alignments, and only slight variations in the alignment of one or two players may change the defense and the blocking assignments of the entire offense, the quarterback is instructed to identify the defense while calling signals. This helps to avoid missed assignments which might arise.

After recognizing the defense, the quarterback re-evaluates the call he made in the huddle. The audible should only be used when the offense is confronted with an unexpected change. Ten other men must acknowledge the audible in a noisy and pressure filled situation. This can lead to missed assignments, so audibles should be kept to a minimum.

If the quarterback has called a running play in the huddle, he will confine his attention to those people that are primarily assigned to stop the run: the defensive line and the linebackers. The defense may be the one expected and the one a particular play was designed to go against, but one of the linebackers or defensive linemen may be aligned in a position that makes the play more difficult to execute. For example, the defensive tackle may be further off the line of scrimmage than usual and this may indicate a tackle-end game. This would make the draw play or trap called in the huddle more difficult to run. If the quarterback is convinced that the tackle-end game is coming, he will probably check off to another play.

After looking at the defensive line on a running call, the quarterback will check the linebackers to determine any change in position. He looks for tips that indicate a blitz or other movement that might hurt the play. The quarterback knows where his backs and linemen are lined up, where the play is going, and if they can carry out their assignments easily with the linebackers in their present alignment. He must decide if the linebackers are bluffing and trying to confuse his blockers or if they are indeed about to blitz. His decision depends upon what he knows about the linebackers from watching the movies of other games and what they have done to that point in the game.

As an example of how the quarterback thinks, and how the alignment of one man can influence his call, let's look at a situation that existed with the Jets and Patriots while I was playing. Nick Bouniconti was one of the finest middle linebackers in football for many years. He was small for a middle linebacker, but made up for his lack of size with quickness and an uncanny ability to be in the right place at the right time. One of his trade marks was to move from one side of the center to the other in short yardage situations. For several years during the mid-1960's, the Jets tried to take advantage of his movement. The quarterback was told to key Bouniconti and check off to the trap on either the left or right defensive tackle depending on which side of the center Bouniconti was aligned. We ran the trap so often that Bouniconti began to look for it and recognized the audible. It turned into a guessing game between him and the quarterback. Was it a dummy call and was Bouniconti really going to stay on that side of the center or would he move after the audible? The quarterback made the decision, but it was the offensive guard assigned to block Bouniconti that either looked foolish or had a good blocking angle and looked like a hero. I had my share of both.

Ken Stabler surveying the defense before taking the snap.

The quarterback does not spend much time checking the defensive secondary on a running play. Naturally, if he sees a weak safety in a tight position which makes a safety blitz probable, he may check off if a sweep to that side has been called. However, most of the quarterback's attention is directed to the area that the play is set to attack and the alignment of those linemen and linebackers in the path of the ball carrier. What attention he gives to the secondary is geared to finding someone obviously out of position, which would make a particular pass pattern effective. The variables would then determine the advisability of checking off to a pass in a running situation.

Here is an example: the cornerback may be playing extremely tight on the wide receiver because he was burned on several short passes. His position may indicate that a long pass is in order. However, throwing against a strong wind may preclude attempting the bomb until the next quarter.

On a pass play, the quarterback reverses his scanning procedure and starts with the defensive secondary after determining the defense. The focus of his attention depends on the type of pass called and who his primary receiver is. He will first try to determine if the defense is in zone coverage, playing man to man, or using a combination of each. This is extremely difficult since the defense works very hard at making them all look alike before the snap of the ball. Many teams in the N.F.L. switched to the zone during the early '70's and it took some quarterbacks a long time to learn to just recognize zone coverage, much less to handle it effectively. There were several instances of quarterbacks talking about the opposition's man coverage after a game, only to be told that what *looked* like man coverage was really a modified zone. The quarterback must recognize the defense if he is to exploit its weakness. He will not be able to hit his receivers in the dead spots if he does not recognize the defense as a zone.

In analyzing the defense on the pass, the quarterback will check the depths of both the linebackers and the deep secondary. Some linebackers have a tendency to cheat back and to the outside in the zone. They have a lot of area to cover and don't want to be burned. The slower linebacker is especially likely to tip his move.

After checking depths, many quarterbacks will then read the weak safety before the snap, if they plan on throwing to the wide receiver. His alignments may tell the quarterback where he will be going after the snap and the type of coverage in use. The weak safety that is lined up unusually close to the line of scrimmage may be coming in on a safety blitz or attempting to cover for the weak side corner linebacker about to blitz. The safety might also be cheating to cover the split end in the event that he reads the blitz and slants into the area vacated by the corner linebacker. In this case, the weak safety may tip the coverage by the depth of his alignment.

Many weak safeties prefer to line up deep when not assigned to any particular receiver and help where needed. Movement toward the split end may indicate double coverage on him, while movement toward the strong side of the field may tip double coverage on the flanker. In the latter instance, the weak safety would cover the tight end. Depending on the pattern called, the quarterback may switch his attention from the flanker to the tight end who may be able to outmuscle the smaller weak safety for the ball.

It all sounds very complicated, and *is* for the young quarterback. After looking at the same set time after time, though, the experienced quarterback can sometimes pick up even the slightest variation in position. Sometimes he merely has a *feeling* that a particular coverage is coming. With the top quarterbacks, this instinct is right far more often than wrong.

Many quarterbacks turn their attention to the strong safety after the snap of the ball. They want to confirm any tips that they may have picked up from the weak safety. Is the strong safety moving to cover for the weak safety assigned to double cover the split end, or is he moving out to double on the flanker? Much depends on the play called and the options available to the quarterback. If he spots double coverage on both wide receivers and his tight end is blocking, he will be certain to keep his eye on the safety valve in the backfield.

When the quarterback has called a pass that requires him to throw to a back or the tight end, he will probably key the linebackers. If the defense is in a zone, and both a set back and the tight end are going into the same area, there is a good chance that one of the two will be free for a short time. The quarterback will key the linebacker in the area and throw to the receiver that the linebacker is ignoring. Even in man coverage, the quarterback will key the corner linebacker to the side of the flaring back. If the back is flaring to the strong side and the corner linebacker on that side is attempting to hold up the tight end, he is likely to be drawn out of position. The quarterback will then throw to the back. If the corner linebacker does not make contact with the tight end, the quarterback may throw to him. The position of the weak safety before the play started will influence that decision.

At times the quarterback will key the linebacker when throwing to his wide receiver. For example, his primary receiver may be the split end on a slant over the middle. He will not throw the pass if the weak side corner linebacker is in a "walk-away" position about five or six yards outside the offensive tackle.

The quarterback is constantly on the alert for radical changes in the position of anyone on the defensive unit. Has the cornerback tightened up to the point that the split end can beat him deep? Have the two long passes that were completed on him early in the game caused him to loosen up to the point where we can beat him for eight yards any time we want? Have the linebackers started to loosen up since we burned them on those hook passes? Have they tightened because of our running attack and should we throw behind them? Does that cornerback cross his feet on the slant-in and corner? Do they adjust to the slot formation, or is the slower safety trying to cover our wide receiver in the slot? Have they adjusted to the double wing? What do they do when we send a man in motion? Do they overreact in short yardage situations by tightening up too much and over pursuing?

The list of questions the quarterback can ask is long. Each question must be evaluated on the basis of how the defense has adjusted to an offensive move, the personnel involved on both sides of the line, and the variables.

The quarterback takes the information he gathered about various individuals while calling signals at the line of scrimmage, and relates it to a different set of questions he asks before deciding on what play to call in the huddle. The first question he asks himself is whether a particular call will get his team a first down. There may be every indication that a play will gain yardage, but will it provide *enough* yardage? The question is more important on third down than it is on first and ten.

After deciding that a particular play is suitable for a first down against the expected defensive alignment, the quarterback must consider whether the condition of the field is appropriate for a given play. The corner linebacker can be blocked, and the defensive end is playing tight which makes the end sweep look good on the blackboard during team meetings. However, is the sloppy field going to interfere with the running back and the pulling guards, making the call inadvisable? The time remaining and the score must be considered. If time is running out and his team is losing, he may not be able to afford the time it normally takes to run the sweep. Although he believes there is a good chance to pick up a first down with the sweep, he may be forced to attempt a sideline pattern to save time. On the other hand, if his team is winning and the clock is running out, an end run, which takes a comparatively long time to run, may be the ideal call—particularly if there is a good chance of getting a first down.

In the huddle, the quarterback evaluates what he has seen on the previous play against what has happened to that point in the ball game. Say the sweep has been successful on each of the three previous occasions that he called the play. That would make it a good call unless the defense has attempted to adjust to the sweep. (He can check this out before calling the sweep.) The alert quarterback looking to set up his plays will have called a play with the same backfield action as the sweep that he ran on the previous play. When he gets to the line, he can concentrate on seeing if the defense is ripe for the sweep. In the event the defense does change their alignment at the last moment, he may check off to an alternate play. (We'll cover this in the chapter on the game plan.)

None of the above implies that the quarterback will be able to run the best play in each instance. He's going to make his share of mistakes. But, if he's been properly trained, he'll be right far more often than he'll be wrong.

# 2

# THE OFFENSE THROUGH THE EYES
# OF THE MIDDLE LINEBACKER

From the title of this chapter it is obvious that we have assumed that the middle linebacker will be given the assignment of calling defensive signals. Indeed, he is often made the defensive quarterback, but not with the regularity that the offensive quarterback is given the assignment of calling offensive plays. Anyone on the defensive unit may call signals, but it should be a player in a two-point stance (semi-erect) who can easily scan the offense. He should also be in the center of the action where any last minute calls can be heard by everyone. This makes the middle linebacker the natural choice.

Since defensive football has become as sophisticated as the offense, the defensive unit forms a huddle prior to every play. It is in the huddle that the middle linebacker calls the signals and other information is exchanged. It does not take as long as it takes the offensive quarterback to call signals, but coaches have found it necessary. At one time, when a team would remain in one or two defenses all game, a huddle was not used. The defensive signal caller would turn his back to the opposition and give hand signals to his teammates. There have been many jokes and stories about how games were won and lost because the opposing players on the sidelines picked up the signals, and flashed other predetermined hand signals to their quarterback in the huddle. It may have happened and even helped the quarterback to call the right play occasionally. However, if the defenses were so basic and limited that they could be signaled by hand, the difference between them probably did not amount to very much. Today, it would take a middle linebacker with three sets of hands to call the defenses with hand signals.

We should start out by saying that the middle linebacker is not exactly equal to the quarterback as a signal caller. Both call the signals on the field, but the quarterback has more control over his team. He pinpoints the thrust of the offensive effort. Unless the play is sent in from the sidelines, he has complete control while he is in the game. The nature of the defense gives the coach greater control over it. Many adjustments to offensive formations or the alignment of individuals are predetermined. Regardless of the defense called, the defensive unit must adjust to a slot or wing back. The middle linebacker does not have to call such adjustments. They are automatic. The same is true for the minor adjustment made by the linebackers to the alignment of the offensive backs. If the defense had to wait for a cue from the middle linebacker before making such minor adjustments, imagine the confusion that would result when the offense sent a man in motion.

Because of the nature of his responsibilities, the middle linebacker should not be expected to make major adjustments in the middle of a game. The defensive coach is expected to prepare his team for every eventuality. If the defense for a particular offensive set has not been predetermined, it would not be fair to expect the middle linebacker to devise one in the middle of the game.

Then, what is expected of the middle linebacker or whoever is calling defensive signals? Like the quarterback, the middle linebacker must determine his team's objectives on each series of downs. The coaching staff normally dictates the overall objectives that both the offensive and defensive teams will take into a game. The defensive coach might advise his people that the strength of the opposition is off-tackle and around the ends. The overall objective of the defense would then be to stop the outside running game.

The offensive quarterback, after considering many factors, decides on the relationship between the passing and running games. He decides whether he should devote more attention to passing or running on a particular series of downs. The middle linebacker must make the same decision. He decides whether to emphasize a containing or a pressure defense. This will be his overall guideline, and should influence his specific objectives on every play.

Let's say that the middle linebacker goes into the game with the overall objectve of containing the offense based on the premise that his team has superior personnel. In this case, there is no need to take any unnecessary chances. He can safely remain in a containing defense, with only minor variations, as long as his team is winning. He will continue to play it conservatively even when the opposition is backed up to its own goal line on third and ten, when he has an opportunity to apply real pressure.

His overall objective would be quite different in the same situation if his team were behind by two touchdowns and time were running out. In this instance, he would likely try to force an offensive mistake or try to throw the ball carrier for a loss of yardage.

In order to carry out his signal calling tasks, the middle linebacker must have the same qualities as the offensive quarterback. He should be a leader and be intelligent enough to make use of all the tools at his disposal. He has to understand how to use the seven man front, the eight man front, stunts, blitzes, and variations of each defense to best advantage. Like the quarterback, he should know the assignment of every player on every defense at his disposal.

The specific objective of the defense on each play is determined by weighing the immediate facts against the overall objective and the game plan. The middle linebacker is given a game plan and is expected to remain within its confines whenever possible.

To see how the middle linebacker works, let's take a hypothetical situation that is likely to occur on any Saturday or Sunday afternoon in any football game at any level of play. It's the next to last game of the season. The offensive team has a three and six won-lost record and has been mathematically eliminated from winning the division title. The defensive team is 6-3 and tied for first place in the league standings. The defensive team is leading midway in the fourth quarter by a 10-7 score. It's third down and the ball is on the 30 yard line of the defense. Seven yards for a first down. The game has been a defensive battle with both teams relying on their ground games. The offensive team has not thrown a pass in the second half, but they do have the wind at their backs. The fans smell an upset and have been cheering the offensive team as they have driven up and down the field—primarily with a series of running plays inside the tackles.

The overall objective of the middle linebacker has been to play a containing defense, since he believes he has the stronger team and the opposition has demonstrated a willingness to try for a quick score, with the big play, in the past. The quarterback has a weak passing arm, but he does have one fast and capable receiver. As part of its containing philosophy, the defense has been using a seven man front with zone coverage in the secondary. The offense has moved the ball from its own 20 yard line on this drive. What are some of the things that the middle linebacker should be considering?

Because of the time remaining, location of the ball (possibility of a field goal) and the success of the offense on this drive, he should consider a change in his overall objective. Should he change from a containing to a pressure defense? Seven yards is a lot of yardage to pick up on one down, but there is a good possibility of a successful field goal attempt if the offense does not make the first down. Can he allow the opposition to tie the game with less than seven minutes remaining on the clock. Seven minutes is a long time, but his quarterback has not been throwing well or moving his team. A switch to an eight man front would make it more difficult for the opposition to continue to run between the tackles and increase the chance of forcing a turnover or throwing the ball carrier for a loss of yardage. This would make the field goal try more difficult. Conclusion: We'd better switch to an eight man front.

Once the overall objective has been altered the middle linebacker must decide how much of a change to institute. Does he want to become the aggressor and gamble a little or merely put a little more pressure on them by making it more difficult to run with the football. Should he blitz one or perhaps two linebackers, tighten up the alignment of the linebackers, or play it regular? A sudden change in the defensive front coupled with a blitz might confuse the offense and cause someone to break free. On the other hand, it will severely weaken the pass defense and the quarterback might be thinking that the defense isn't expecting a pass since he hasn't thrown all half. The middle linebacker decides that he'll play it safe and not blitz any linebackers. In fact, he decides to get his safety to help the halfback assigned to cover that fast receiver.

Of course the middle linebacker can't forget that if the opposition doesn't go for the bomb, they are likely to run to their right since they are now on the left hashmark and will try to use the wide side of the field to get into better field goal position. He decides to call the "overshift left" variation of this eight man front. That will stop the run to the wide side of the field.

The preceding game situation may sound complicated, but there are many situations that require the defensive signal caller to consider at least as many factors. It is essential that he not overlook anything, since one factor is likely to cancel out or make another one more important. For example, the middle linebacker would not have had to be overly concerned with the bomb if the offense did not have the wind at its back, or if they were not mathematically eliminated from winning the division championship. A team in contention would probably try for the first down and not the touchdown.

The past tendency of the offense to try for the big play in key situations is another important consideration. This is characteristic of weak football teams that have not demonstrated the ability to sustain long drives. The one outstanding receiver, the excitement of the crowd and the fact that a tie means nothing to a team with a 3-6 record justifies the apprehension about the bomb.

Change the yardage necessary for a first down from seven to three yards here, and the middle linebacker's thinking will change completely. A gain of three yards is quite probable for a team that has been running as well as the offensive team in question. The bomb becomes a remote possibility, and the decision to switch from a containing to a pressure defense becomes much easier. The question facing the defensive quarterback is whether to use a goal line defense or merely tighten the eight man front. Most of the factors making the bomb a possibility with seven yards necessary for a first down become unimportant.

Change the yardage necessary for a first down from seven to fifteen and the long pass becomes almost a certainty. In this instance, several other factors bear consideration. Has the offense used the screen or draw play in key long yardage situations in the past? This will determine how quickly the linebackers drop back into pass coverage. The type of formation the offensive team is likely to use becomes important, since the defense will want to try to double cover or help the defender covering that outstanding receiver on the opposing team.

Change the direction of the strong wind and the situation may be altered dramatically. It not only makes the possiblity of the bomb less probable, but changes the thought processes of the middle linebacker regarding the field goal. With the wind blowing against the offensive team, every yard becomes important. A field goal attempt with the ball snapped from the 30 yard line becomes quite a feat for any high school or college player. Kicking against a strong wind makes a successful field goal attempt highly improbable. Even in the pros it would be far from a certainty. Therefore the middle linebacker must be certain that he does not make the field goal attempt tempting to the offense by calling a long yardage defense on third down and 15 and allow them to pick up additional yardage on the ground.

The time remaining on the clock is often important. Change the time remaining in our hypothetical situation from seven minutes to less than two minutes and the middle linebacker has a different set of considerations. The chances of the offensive team getting another opportunity to move the football are not good. With less than two minutes remaining, there will be no next time and a tie game means nothing to a team with a losing record. The line of reasoning that caused the middle linebacker to consider the use of an overshifted defense may not be appropriate. It takes time to sweep the wide side of the field. New factors must be considered. What does history tell us about the offense? Do they have a tendency to run to the wide side of the field? Some teams run more often to the narrow side of the field, since they anticipate a defensive adjustment to the wide side. An overshifted defense may not be necessary.

We could go on and on with this, spelling out each variable and figuring out how the middle linebacker might react to it. The point, though, I think has been made: Even before the ball is snapped, the middle linebacker has a lot to consider.

In order to perform his duties well, the middle linebacker must be well briefed on the opposition, understand the defenses that he has in his arsenal, know his teammates' strengths and weaknesses, and be aware of how the offensive team's tactics and formations in this game compare to what they did in the past.

During the game, the middle linebacker gathers information in the same manner as the offensive quarterback. Just as the offensive quarterback scans the defense, the middle linebacker looks over the offense. What he sees is not likely to influence his actions immediately. As was previously indicated, most defensive adjustments are automatic. However, there are instances when the offense will line up in a completely unexpected alignment for which the defense does not have a predetermined adjustment. In this case, the middle linebacker will often call a change at the line. In most cases his instructions will be directed to the defensive line or linebackers. The defensive backs will rarely be involved because of their distance from the middle linebacker and the difficulty in communicating without tipping the coverage.

Like the quarterback, the middle linebacker looks for specific things to reaffirm his call and gathers information which will help him to make an intelligent call on the next down. The checklist used by the middle linebacker may be as long or longer than the number of things the offensive quarterback looks for on each play. Here are some of the more important things that he will be looking for.

1. The alignment of the offensive backs—This is normally an automatic adjustment on the part of the defensive team. It rarely affects the defensive line, but will affect the alignment of the linebackers or the safety assigned to cover a back coming out of the backfield on a pass route. The alignment of the offensive backs frequently affects the middle linebacker more than anyone else, since he is often responsible for one of the backs on pass coverage.

However, there are other reasons for the middle linebacker to be aware of their alignment. A change in position may explain a number of things, and indicate a defensive adjustment. For example, an offensive attempt to repeatedly isolate an exceptionally fast halfback on one of the linebackers may be prevented by changing the coverage. The weak safety may be assigned to the halfback.

The alignment of the set backs is equally important on running plays. The offensive team may tip a play by constantly running it from the same set of the offensive backs. The alert middle linebacker that spots this can call an automatic adjustment each time the offensive backs line up in a particular set.

2. The split of the receivers and position of the tight end—This is another adjustment that is automatic and affects all members of the defensive secondary as well as the linebackers. The middle linebacker does not have to tell his strong safety to move out with the tight end that lines up in the slot. However, if the offense is having success running a particular play from a certain alignment, an overall adjustment by the defense might be in order.

3. Splits in the offensive line—The middle linebacker must always scan the offensive line to notice any unusual spacing. Large splits may be placing an unjust burden on one of the defensive linemen thereby causing a certain play to work. A defensive change or variation may be necessary to restore balance. This is a situation when the middle linebacker may be able to call an adjustment in the alignment of the defensive line or linebackers at the line of scrimmage. The defensive linemen are taught to make specific adjustments to splits in the offensive line, but cannot see the pattern of the entire offensive line and evaluate the reasons for the splits. It's for the middle linebacker to analyze the situation and make the necessary changes.

4. The ball carrier and point of attack—Hopefully the middle linebacker will be in on the tackle or close enough to it to easily see the ball carrier and where he ran on every play. This will help him determine if the offensive team has found the soft "underbelly" of the defense. Are they picking on a rookie, an injured player, or a weak link in the defense? A variation of the existing defense or a new defensive alignment may compensate for the weakness.

5. The pass receiver or the intended pass receiver and how he reached his destination—As with running plays, the information about what happened in passing situations at various times during a game may help to anticipate an offensive play at a later time. The middle linebacker who anticipates an offensive attack on a particular member of the secondary can help his teammate in a number of different ways. He can try to help him himself, he can

advise another player of the expected offensive call, or he can call a defense with built-in features to guard against the play.

6. Hashmark and yardage tendencies—Teams have definite tendencies from the hashmark and other spots on the field. The middle linebacker must be aware of the formation and play called at all times. This provides an opportunity to evaulate present performance against past tendencies in helping to anticipate future calls from various locations on the field.

7. Type of blocking used by the offense—This is something that a middle linebacker may or may not have an opportunity to notice as the play develops. It is information that is available if he takes the time to question his teammates after the play. A double team, cross block, or trap block may help to explain why a play was successful. More importantly, the information may help the middle linebacker to choose a defense more suitable to stop a successful running or passing attack.

Once again, I have to point out that much of this information will be of no value to the middle linebacker unless he has an understanding of the weapons used on defense and the assignments of all his teammates in each variation. This requires preparation before the game and constant appraisal of the situation throughout the game. Some players cannot do this adequately because they are so wrapped up in their own problems that they have no time to put all the pieces together. They are too busy thinking about how to avoid being knocked off their feet by the offensive center to give much thought to what might be the best defense to call on the ensuing play. You won't find such players calling defensive signals.

Most of the information we have considered as being essential to making the proper defensive call by the middle linebacker has been specific in nature. He must be familiar with the scouting report on the offense. He must understand the specific nature of the defenses in his arsenal. He must be aware of the strengths and weaknesses of his teammates. He must be able to put all this information together and come up with specific defenses for each situation. However, like most leaders, he evaluates the specific information available while trying to adhere to a set of basic general principles. These serve as a guide, and often prevent the decision maker from placing too much emphasis on any one piece of information.

The following are those general principles which most defensive signal callers try to follow:

1. The defense should not gamble when winning.
2. When behind, the extent of the gamble depends on the time

remaining, the field positon and the score.

3. When the ball is between the 25 yard lines, be ready for anything.

4. When you find yourself inside your own 20 yard line, remember what the opposition did to get there.

5. Put yourself in the quarterback's place and ask what he would call against your defensive team.

6. Never forget the offensive axiom of going for the touchdown on first down and concentrating on getting the first down on third down.

7. Make certain that everyone on the defensive unit knows the yardage necessary for a first down.

8. There is more of a reason to gamble if it may force the opposition to kick into the wind.

9. Be cautious about abandoning what has been successful.

10. Anticipate what the offense is expecting and do the opposite.

11. Never forget that football is a game of fundamentals and a team should not rely on deception.

One way to evaluate the signal calling work of the middle linebacker is by trying to determine when major defensive changes have been made. For example, when the defensive team assumes a new formation immediately after following the offense onto the field, you can attribute the change to the coaching staff. When done for the first time during a series of downs with no new player added to the defense, you can safely assume that the middle linebacker instituted the change. The good signal caller does not improvise very often. His success is predicated on his ability to use his existing formations and alignments at the appropriate time. There is less chance of confusion with this type of play caller than with the improvisor.

At times you will notice certain teams shifting alignments at the last possible moment. Unless this happens repeatedly, there is no way to determine if the middle linebacker took it upon himself to make an adjustment. If it happens time after time, you may safely assume that the defensive coaches expected various offensive formations for which defensive adjustments would be required, and prearranged the shift.

I hope that this gives you some indication of the way that the middle linebacker thinks. I would suggest that you try to put yourself in his shoes occasionally when at a game and see if your calls match up to his. Try it. It's a humbling experience and gives you an idea of all the preparation which goes into a football game.

# 3

# THE VIEW FROM THE BOOTH

Most fans see many more games from a seat in their T.V. rooms than they do from a seat in the stands. For that reason, I thought that it would be interesting to take a look at what goes into the packaging of a football game for T.V. The impression that you get at home is sometimes at great odds with the feeling that you get when you are in the stands. Knowing how a broadcast or telecast is put together, and what the television network brass or the radio station manager is interested in will put what you see or hear at home into perspective.

The radio and television executives that hire the announcers are interested in ratings, which help them to keep their jobs. The announcers are interested in pleasing the executives which in turn helps them to keep *their* jobs. You will rarely hear an announcer admit to having worked a dull game. Announcers are expected to try to hold the interest of the listening or viewing audience even when the game is not particularly exciting or important. It is much easier to embellish a radio broadcast than it is to get the television viewer to believe that he is watching a "hard-hitting," "well-executed" game with "tremendous individual effort," when the picture depicts lethargic effort and a comedy of errors.

The above is true for the play-by-play announcer, who is primarily engaged to describe the action as it unfolds, and the analyst who is supposed to explain the *whys* and *hows* of each play as well as the reasons for the success or failure of each team. The analyst especially is expected to make the game more colorful for his audience, which is why he is most often referred to as the "color man."

The radio fan is totally dependent on the words of the announcers. He must rely completely on what they are saying and can form few opinions of his own. Announcers working on radio will claim that the absence of a picture makes their job infinitely harder than television. This is not true. The play-by-play announcer may have to use more words than his counterpart doing a television game, but there is no picture to catch him with the wrong man carrying the ball or making the tackle. It is reported and widely confirmed that Bill Stern, one of the first sportscasters to broadcast football on radio, once found himself with the wrong man carrying the football after describing a very effective 80-yard run. Instead of admitting his error, he merely inserted a ficticious lateral as the runner crossed the goal line.

As a color man, I have found radio much easier than television. The radio announcer can comment on any subject he wants to as long as he finds some thin thread to relate it to the words of the play-by-play man. Who is to say that his observations are unimportant or not related to the action on the field? If he sees something interesting, he can relate it to the audience at any time. The television commentator must relate to the picture even when it does not show anything of interest. Although there is a T.V. set in the broadcast booth, the color man must view the action on the field in order to accurately form opinions on why things are happening. The picture seen on the T.V. screen is often isolated on the quarterback or ball carrier. The color man that looks at the monitor too often will not be able to provide astute analysis. The analyst can never be certain that what caught his eye on the field was seen on the screen. Quite often the play is routine and the real action or color occured somewhere else on the field. He can comment on it, but it loses its importance if the viewer cannot see it. The instant replay also can present a problem for the color man since most often he is not aware of what is being replayed until he sees it along with the viewing audience. We will discuss this further on in the chapter.

Except for playoff and championship games, the television networks usually assign two announcers to each game: a play-by-play man and a color man. (Much of what follows also applies to radio. Differences will be noted.) The notable exception is Monday Night Football. ABC Sports president Roone Arledge was perceptive enough from the very beginning to know that Howard Cosell was not knowledgable enough to fill the role of the color man, and would drive the listening audience to tears if given the play-by-play assignment. The play-by-play man pretty much controls the use of the microphone and the verbose Cosell would rarely give the color man an opportunity to speak. However, Arledge also recognized that Cosell's unique talent would broaden the audience appeal of the show.

When two men are assigned to broadcast a game, each is expected to play a clearly defined role. In addition to describing the action, the play-by-play man sets each play. "It's the Cowboys' ball on Denver's 15 yard line. Second and three." He does not have to talk as much on television as on radio, once the play has begun.

The viewer can see Csonka running off tackle. It is sufficient to say "Csonka behind good blocking going for . . . eight yards . . . and a first down." Or, as has more often been the case since Csonka joined the Giants: "The handoff goes to Csonka who runs into a wall . . . no gain . . . tackle by Jerry Sherk . . . third and three."

It is customary for the analyst to bite his tongue until the play-by-play man stops speaking. The play-by-play man may therefore continue to talk if he feels he has something more to contribute. This can present a problem to the ex-athlete who normally serves as the color man. There are only 30 seconds between each play and if the play-by-play man talks too long, the color man may not have enough time to make his point. An important point loses its impact if made two plays after it has occurred. When two men have worked together long enough, they usually devise a system of hand signals which can be used when one feels he must have the microphone immediately. The play-by-play man is almost always a professional sportscaster who has served his appenticeship and worked his way up to the network level. He has learned the hard way that it is not the quantity of mike time, but the quality of his commentary that is important.

I did the color for the New York Jet games for five years on radio and the Jet pre-season games for five years on television along with television for NBC Sports. Most of that time I worked with Merle Harmon on radio and Charlie Jones on television. However, I have worked with many other announcers over the years. Very few of them try to hog the mike. There have been two exceptions. I did a couple of pre-season games on radio with Bill Mazer some time ago. Bill had done a lot of sports on radio and television, but what he really wanted was Johnny Carson's job. Before coming to New York, he hosted a Carson type talk show in Buffalo and could not forget how good he thought he was. Bill has a rather large ego and is a self-professed expert on every subject, including football. When you worked with Mazer, he did the play-by-play *and* the color. The other guy in the booth was there to confirm Bill's opinions. It went something like this: "Matt Snell off tackle with good blocking at the point of attack by left tackle Winston Hill and left guard Randy Rasmussen who double team-ed defensive tackle Tom Sestak. Snell picked up four yards on the play. Second and six from the Jet 42 yard line. It seemed to me that the Jet right guard was pulling out on the play and was supposed to trap Bills' defensive end Tom Day. However, he tripped over the center's feet and did not get a clean shot at Day. Is that right Sam?" What could Sam say but "Er . . . er . . . ah . . . I guess so Bill, but Hill and Rasmussen really wiped out Sestak didn't they."

Mazer wasn't doing football. He was using the exposure on the

Jet broadcasts to try and land a bigger job. His analysis was sometimes correct, but was more often superficial or completely wrong. As the game went on, I found myself commenting on things that I had not seen or felt were unimportant, in an attempt not to contradict him. Finally, I decided that this had to stop. So, after he analyzed the play and sought my confirmation for yet another time, I countered: "I don't know Bill. I was looking elsewhere." After another question, I simply said: "Well Bill, you know it's impossible to see everything that is happening out there. I wasn't looking downfield at the receivers as you were. I was looking at the pass protection, and a good pass rush caused Namath to throw it away intentionally. I doubt if George Sauer ran the wrong route as you suggested." That got the message across and from then on *he* did play-by-play and *I* did color.

On another ocassion, I was doing a Kansas City-Oakland game for NBC Sports in Kansas City. My play-by-play partner was a fill-in and was trying to impress the network brass back in New York. He had done the Chief games on radio for several years and knew a great deal about the Chiefs. That was part of his problem. He felt that he had to tell the audience everything he knew. The result was incessant chatter totally unrelated to what was being seen on the tube. The game was blacked out in Kansas City and I'm sure the Oakland fans were bored and switched to the 49er game on CBS. In addition to not being given time to make the points I thought were important, we were stepping on each other throughout the game. Both announcers talking at the same time is a definite no-no. He never got another assignment for NBC.

These are two extreme situations. The serious fan who wants to use the information provided does have a problem. He has to decide whether the announcers are making an important point, merely filling air time, or trying to create a balanced broadcast. The networks want *by-play*. Each announcer is expected to contribute reguarly and ideally the two men should occasionally bounce it back and forth in a conversational style. Sometimes it's hard to separate the wheat from the chaff. Here's an example: "Peter Hare has great speed. He grew up on a farm and was so poor that his family could not afford a shotgun. Every day Peter had to run after the rabbits that were eating the crops, and that's how he developed the speed we spoke of." The viewer has to determine if Peter Hare is really that fast or if the announcer merely wanted to work in the poor farm boy story.

This is the type of material that all color men used before ex-athletes broke into the field. They were either newspaper reporters or sportcasters with little technical knowledge of the game. There was a lot of color consisting of background information, anecdotes and human interest stories, but little hard substance. Then came the switch to the jocks. Now there was plenty of information but little human interest and little ability to communicate.

The trend recently has been to find athletes who can communicate and have some broadcasting experience. However, regardless of his ability, the would-be color man probably won't last unless he was a star player or has developed some attention getting trademark: a humorous tone or controversial style. Don Meredith probably has the best sense of humor and timing of anyone on the air. However, he has a lot more going for him. He is bright, articulate and knowledgable. Perhaps one of the reasons that the Monday night broadcast team gets so much attention is the fact that they have the best of humor and controversy. Howard Cosell has the rare ability to sound controversial even when making a routine statement. Frank keeps them informed, Howard makes them angry, and Don makes them laugh. You might not get much football, but all your emotions are taken care of.

Howard was the sports director for WABC radio in New York while I was doing a pre- and post-game show for the New York Met baseball games on the station as well as color on the Jet football games. I had been offered the job after sustaining a knee injury during the 1967 season. Howard lost no time in giving advice. His first words to me were: "You have no special talent. You are not good looking like Frank Gifford. You are not as articulate as Pat Summerall and you are not as well known as Kyle Rote. You must therefore tell it like it is regardless of who gets hurt or you won't last out the year." This was the year the Jets went to the Super Bowl, and Howard tried desperately to get me to criticize Weeb Ewbank. He almost succeeded. Howard recorded his pre-game show during the week, and I became his permanent guest because I was handy and because no one officially connected with the team would talk to him. Cosell's unrelenting attacks on the Jets and particularly on Weeb Ewbank continued through the pre-game show on Super Bowl Sunday. He predicted an easy Baltimore victory, but that did not stop him from jumping on the Jet bandwagon when they won. Howard was waiting at Kennedy Airport with his hat in one hand and a microphone in the other when the team returned home after their surprise victory.

Controversy has worked for Cosell, but others who try it usually fail. The world just isn't ready for another Howard Cosell. Paul McGuire, who does regional games for NBC, has a good sense of humor. I remember him for it when we played together in San Diego during the '60's and it has helped his work in the booth.

Recently, however, McGuire has been making an effort to be controversial. The trail he has left behind indicates that he is in trouble. I followed him into several cities and heard complaints from the front offices of N.F.L. teams about his work. He worked the Jet-Eagle game on the last day of the 1977 season. Prior to that game Walt Michaels announced that he intended to substitute freely and get a look at his young inexperienced players. McGuire believed that this was not fair to the starters who were striving to salvage something from a disappointing season. He is entitled to his opinion and has every right to voice his objection . . . one time. McGuire repeated his view at least four times. It was clear that he was attempting to stir things up. I was at a dinner with assistant coach Dan Henning of the Jets a short time after the game and one of the first things he asked me was what McGuire was trying to pull off.

There is a difference between trying to stir up controversy and merely expressing an opinion which turns out to be controversial. Jim Brown did a Giant game during the 1977 season in which he didn't have many nice things to say, particularly about Larry Csonka, during the game. However, when you consider that Brown's ego is as great as his athletic ability was and that Larry Csonka has seen his best days, it is quite possible that Brown was being honest. Despite his abrasiveness, I agreed with every thing he said that day.

Unless the analyst has sold you on his expertise, be reluctant to accept his more involved statements unless logic or your eyes verify his point of view. He is under a great deal of pressure and it is quite possible that he is mistaken or overly anxious to impress the people back in the studio. Football is not a science. There is almost always room for a conflicting opinion. All announcers are aware of this and a few use it as a license to say just about anything they want. However, the vast majority of announcers do their homework and try to make accurate and appropriate comments.

Let's take a look at the announcer's week. Radio men have it relatively easy since they usually live in the same city as the team they cover on a permanent basis and know its personnel well. They travel with the team and usually develop a good rapport with the coaches who provide much of the information on both teams. Because of this close relationship and the fact that teams can apply pressure on the local station to unload an announcer, you are more likely to hear a biased broadcast on radio. Even if the announcer is intent on being objective, he is likely to concentrate on the team that he knows best and, since he is only heard in his home city, nobody really cares much about the other team. The home town broadcaster generally need put in less preparation time than his network counterpart.

The radio announcer always knows which teams he will be covering. The network T.V. announcer's assignments are less predictable.

Each network ranks it's seven or eight announcing teams and assigns its top teams to the most important games. CBS gives the assignments to their broadcast teams for each of the National Football Conference games they carry two or three weeks in advance. NBC prefers to wait until the Monday or Tuesday before the game in order to determine which games are most important. The most important games to the network are not necessarily the games involving the most successful teams. Heavy population centers such as New York and Los Angeles are more important to the network than San Diego or Cincinnati. NBC has been known to change assignments as late as Thursday because a game has been sold out and will be televised to a major market which would have been blacked out except for the sellout. I was never certain if NBC waited until the last minute because they thought that much of Curt Gowdy or because he had a clause in his contract stating that he would work the number one game and NBC was afraid of a lawsuit.

Each play-by-play and color announcer I know keeps a file on every team in the league. It consists of press releases, newspaper and magazine articles, and notes from previous games that he has broadcast involving the teams he will be covering. Sometime before Thursday or Friday he will review the material in that file before calling the public relations representative of each team. He will ask for lineup changes, injured players and the reasons for a team's success or failure—particularly in last week's game.

The play-by-play announcer will use the information along with that week's press release and the team's press guide to prepare his spotting boards which are used to help him identify important players as each play unfolds. Almost every play-by-play announcer uses the same type of board. The only thing that varies is the size of the information inserts or the board size itself. He will keep these in front of him during the game and the two spotters that sit on either side of him will point to the inserts on the board that represent the people running with or catching the football. The play-by-play announcer does not always need the spotters to tell him who has the football or who made the tackle, though bodies can get entangled and numbers sometimes hard to recognize. A spotter might be anyone familiar with the teams. Writers for small newspapers that travel with the team are often used to spot the visiting team. The public relations man might recommend anyone from an owner's nephew to the president of the team's fan club to spot for the home team. Most experienced announcers use the same people in each city and keep changing until they find someone satisfactory. A statistician also sits in the booth and keeps records on running, passing and kicking yardage.

The spotters and statictician are utilized primarily by the play-by-play man. The analyst does not have to recognize numbers as quickly and will rarely begin to speak about a player unless he recognizes his name and number. The notable exception occurs on the instant replay when the announcer is often unaware of what he will be "analyzing" until it unfolds on the monitor in front of him. It is not only instant replay, but instant analysis as well.

Each announcer leaves for his destination on Friday night or early Saturday morning for a Sunday game. If he can arrive in time for Saturday's practice, most will leave early on Saturday. A lot of preparation and reading is done on the plane.

The practice session that most announcers observe is not as beneficial as one might think. Practice the day before a game is always short and light, with a lot of tine spent on special teams. A sharp eye might catch a slight limp or sore throwing arm that was not reported as an injury. Most often, though, better information is obtained from talking to injured players or other people familiar with the team standing on the sidelines watching practice. If an announcer is lucky, he might see a special play that would have been a surprise if used the next day. However, if the play has not been used before, it is doubtful that the coach will allow his team to practice it in front of the announcer. I once traveled to Cleveland for a season opener on Friday morning in order to be able to watch the longer and more strenuous Friday practice session. Forrest Gregg ran a closed practice and thought I should view films of the previous week'a game instead.

After Saturday's practice, the head coach will usually consent to an interview. The openess and amount of assistance provided varies tremendously with each coach. There are some like Hank Stram who are extremely cooperative and know exactly what type of information will help an announcer. Others, such as Forrest Gregg, are of little assistnace and Bud Grant won't talk at all. Most coaches have been burned by the press or on the air and proceed with the utmost of caution. It is necessary for the announcers to use restraint. I have found it best to ask straightforward questions phrased so that a coach is not in the position of criticizing anyone on the opposing team or his own players. Coaches are also reluctant to heap excessive praise on one of their own players for fear of slighting someone else. Having played for the San Diego Chargers when Chuck Noll was an assistant, I was able to get a private interview with him before the Steelers had "turned the corner" and become a winning football team. Having known him for some time, I decided to ask point blank if he had to find replacements for players A, B, and C before the Steelers could "turn the corner." Chuck thought I was trying to get him to knock his players and very calmly said: "There are no corners on a football field. That's reporter talk. We are always trying to improve our personnel, but replacing the men you named will not necessarily put us in the playoffs." A couple of years later, ex-head coach John Ralston of the Denver Broncos started to talk about "turning the corner." Ralston never said anything once. He repeated the phrase to anyone who would listen and promised that the Broncos would be in the Super Bowl next year. I believe his eternal optimism and the fact that "next year" was in fact three years away cost him his job in Denver. He caused people to expect too much too soon. Perhaps that's why Chuck Noll scoffed at the phrase "turn the corner."

It is prudent to ask questions about strengths rather than about weaknesses. This will allow the coach to be positive and yet properly vague. He will readily say that the opposition has a good outside running attack, but never admit that it is ineffective because they do not have a big back to balance the outside attack. Similarly, he will say that his opponents are "tough inside," when he means that they don't have enough speed to hurt him outside. When asked about the play of an individual, he might say that his pass protection techniques are improving every day or that he is on a weight lifting program to put on body weight. In effect, he is informing you that the first player is weak on pass protection and the second player is not doing an adequate job, perhaps because he is too small. All of this gives the announcer a certain amount of insight. It also provides copy to fill up dead air time. Not infrequently an announcer leaves a coach's office with the feeling that he learned little that will help him on the air, only to find himself quoting or referring to the coach's comments on the air.

After talking to the head coach, a visit to the locker room is customary. Players are a good source of information and will often provide more technical information than the coaches. They are not afraid of being quoted and are often eager to display their knowledge of the game. They will rarely criticize a player they must confront on a head-to-head basis or someone on the opposing team playing the same position they do, but will often comment on the abilities of players they have less direct contact with. They will speak freely about the particular problems they anticipate which may tip off the overall problems which their team faces.

When the last player has left the locker room, the assistant coaches are usually still available. They often echo the comments of the head coach, but provide an opportunity to ask more specific questions about the type of pass coverage used by the opposition and its blitzing or stunting habits. Questions such as: who blitzes most often, who puts on the best pass rush, where the oppostion prefers to run with the ball, or who the quarterback prefers to throw to are all acceptable and readily answered. The assistant coaches' approach to the interview is similar to the players'. They are often completely open about discussing any subject except the particular area they are involved with. Perhaps this is because they don't regard themselves as experts in other areas and believe any information they have could not possibly hurt the team.

After visiting with the assistant coaches, it's a trip up to the public relations office for an update, speed charts, recent press releases and newspaper articles that appeared in the local papers during the week. Some public relations departments send these articles out during the week. The information provided by the public relations representative varies with the rep. Some have extensive technical knowledge, while others limit themselves to the type of anecdotes found in press guides and used by Howard Cosell. They always sound better when Cosell repeats them. The public relations man may say in passing that Lyle Alzado's mother ran a flower shop on Long Island. Cosell will wait until Alzado sacks the quarterback or draws an unnecessary roughness penalty to say: "Dandy, you will never guess where that 270-pound mass of humanity, who can bench press 500 pounds and flip quarterbacks around like so many paperweights, grew up. Yes Dandy, as a boy that hulk of a man worked from 6:00 A.M. to dark every day making floral arrangements in his mother's flower shop. It proves conclusively, as I've always contended, that you don't have to be an insensitive goul to excel on the gridiron." Dandy Don might put it all in perspective, adding: "I do believe that might just make him a 'flower child,' Howard."

The coaches, players and public relations people provide most of the information required by the announcing team. Sometimes, peripheral people provide interesting anecdotes or different slants to a story. Trainers, equipment men or secretaries often know more about a team than anyone else. I used to get many interesting ideas from Dr. James Nicholas, the Jet  orthopedic surgeon. He was very close to the team and had excellent information. The secret though—especially for the analyst—is not always the quantity of information, but how effectively the announcer mixes it together with his own thoughts and opinions and comes up with his own "game plan." By Sunday, he should have a good enough idea of each team's strengths and weaknesses to ascertain which area each offense is likely to attack. He will also have a pretty good idea of what the defense must stop and how they are likely to get it done.

After leaving the stadium, I go back to the hotel and make notes on everyting I can remember. I study the depth charts to memorize numbers and read the articles from the previous week's press. I find that I often relate what happens on Sunday afternoon to previous games. It helps to understand developing trends. For example, if a team failed to pick up two or three yards for a touchdown on several occasions when they ran up the middle, it's easier to explain a pass attempt on third and goal from the three yard line. Newspaper articles are also an excellent source of anecdotes. All this study can get you into trouble, though, if you forget some of the facts.

Willie Lanier was one of the best middle linebackers in the league for many years. During the 1976 season, a rookie named Jimbo Elrod won his starting position. Lanier is a much bigger man at 245 pounds than Elrod, who weighed 210 pounds. The two were playfully wrestling one day during the middle of the season and Elrod hurt his back. I had the facts right, but had insufficient time to develop it on the air and could not clarify it on ensuing plays. Inadvertently, I made it sound like Lanier resented losing his job and used his size to put Elrod out of action in their playful locker room scuffle. I don't remember whether I actually made it sound that way or if Willie's wife merely interpreted it that way. Either way, Willie called NBC, got my number, and was not very concerned about the lack of time and confusion that sometimes exists in the broadcast booth, which I tried to explain to him.

There are two production meetings for a Sunday game. They usually take place in a suite at the hotel about 5:00 P.M. on Saturday afternoon. One involves the producer, director, stage director and technicians. The purpose of this meeting is to discuss the positioning of equipment and people. Immediately after this meeting, the producer and director get together with the announcers. The purpose here is to form the broadcasting game plan. The producer is pretty much in charge of the telecast. He is the man who talks into the ear phones which all announcers wear and coordinates the telecast. The director is responsible for selecting

# BALTIMORE COLTS vs. NEW YORK JETS

SUNDAY, OCTOBER 24, 1976 — SHEA STADIUM, N.Y.

## COLTS OFFENSE

| Pos. | Starter | | |
|---|---|---|---|
| WR | 81 Roger Carr | 88 Ricky Thompson | |
| LT | 64 David Taylor | 67 Bob Van Duyne | |
| LG | 61 Robert Pratt | 67 Bob Van Duyne | |
| C | 57 Ken Mendenhall | 50 Forrest Blue | |
| RG | 66 Elmer Collett | 62 Ken Huff | |
| RT | 75 George Kunz | 67 Bob Van Duyne | |
| TE | 87 Raymond Chester | 85 Jimmie Kennedy | 67 Bob Van Duyne |
| WR | 35 Glenn Doughty | 86 Freddie Scott | |
| QB | 7 Bert Jones | 12 Bill Troup | |
| RB | 26 Lydell Mitchell | 23 Don McCauley | 15 Mike Kirkland |
| RB | 48 Roosevelt Leaks | 23 Don McCauley | 34 Ron Lee |

## COLTS DEFENSE

| Pos. | Starter | | |
|---|---|---|---|
| LE | 72 Fred Cook | 73 Ron Fernandes | |
| LT | 63 Mike Barnes | 74 Ken Novak | |
| RT | 76 Joe Ehrmann | 74 Ken Novak | |
| RE | 78 John Dutton | 73 Ron Fernandes | |
| LLB | 58 Derrel Luce | 56 Dan Dickel | |
| MLB | 59 Jim Cheyunski | 55 Ed Simonini | |
| RLB | 53 Stan White | 54 Sanders Shiver | |
| LCB | 42 Lloyd Mumphord | 25 Ray Oldham | |
| RCB | 31 Nelson Munsey | 25 Ray Oldham | |
| LS | 40 Bruce Laird | 25 Ray Oldham | |
| RS | 20 Jackie Wallace | 33 Randy Hall | 47 Tim Baylor |

## JETS OFFENSE

| Pos. | Starter | | |
|---|---|---|---|
| WR | 89 Lou Piccone | 80 Howard Satterwhite | 83 Jerome Barkum |
| LT | 72 Robert Woods | 75 Winston Hill | |
| LG | 66 Randy Rasmussen | 67 Darrell Austin | 61 John Roman |
| C | 67 Darrell Austin | 65 Joe Fields | |
| RG | 78 Garry Puetz | 67 Darrell Austin | |
| RT | 75 Winston Hill | 78 Garry Puetz | 71 Al Krevis |
| TE | 88 Richard Caster | 86 Richard Osborne | |
| WR | 82 David Knight | 80 Howard Satterwhite | |
| QB | 12 Joe Namath | 14 Richard Todd | |
| RB | 36 Bob Gresham | 43 Jazz Jackson | 45 Louie Giammona |
| RB | 21 Clark Gaines | 49 Ed Marinaro | 35 Steve Davis |

## JETS DEFENSE

| Pos. | Starter | | |
|---|---|---|---|
| LE | 76 Lawrence Pillers | 87 Billy Newsome | |
| LT | 77 Carl Barzilauskas | 74 Larry Faulk | |
| RT | 85 Ed Galigher | 74 Larry Faulk | |
| RE | 81 Richard Neal | 76 Lawrence Pillers | |
| LLB | 51 Greg Buttle | 56 Larry Keller | 55 John Ebersole |
| MLB | 55 John Ebersole | 53 Carl Russ | |
| RLB | 59 Bob Martin | 52 Mike Hennigan | 55 John Ebersole |
| LCB | 23 Shafer Suggs | 46 Rich Sowells | 47 Tommy Marvaso |
| RCB | 38 Ed Taylor | 47 Tommy Marvaso | |
| SS | 27 Phil Wise | 23 Shafer Suggs | 47 Tommy Marvaso |
| FS | 22 Burgess Owens | 38 Ed Taylor | |

## COLTS SPECIALISTS

| | | | |
|---|---|---|---|
| P | 49 David Lee | 15 Mike Kirkland | |
| K | 2 Toni Linhart | | |
| KO | 2 Toni Linhart | | |
| H | 12 Bill Troup | 15 Mike Kirkland | |
| PR | 27 Howard Stevens | 20 Jackie Wallace | |
| KR | 27 Howard Stevens | 40 Bruce Laird | 23 Don McCauley |
| PC | 50 Forrest Blue | 57 Ken Mendenhall | |
| KC | 57 Ken Mendenhall | 50 Forrest Blue | |

## JETS SPECIALISTS

| | | | |
|---|---|---|---|
| P | 3 Duane Carrell | 14 Richard Todd | |
| K | 5 Pat Leahy | | |
| KO | 3 Duane Carrell | | |
| H | 3 Duane Carrell | 14 Richard Todd | |
| PR | 43 Jazz Jackson | 89 Lou Piccone | 45 Louie Giammona |
| KR | 43 Jazz Jackson | 89 Lou Piccone | 45 Louie Giammona |
| PC | 65 Joe Fields | 67 Darrell Austin | |
| KC | 65 Joe Fields | 67 Darrell Austin | |

**TODAY'S OFFICIALS:** Referee—Bob Frederic (71); Umpire—Lou Palazzi (51); Head Linesman—Norm Kragseth (65); Line Judge—Art Holst (33); Back Judge—Don Porter (3); Field Judge—Bob Wortman (84).

An example of a speed chart which all home team public relations departments provide to broadcasters and reporters to help identify the players. The other side of the card contains height, weight, age, pro experience, and college information.

## JETS

| No. | Name | Pos. |
|---|---|---|
| 3 | Carrell, Duane | P |
| 5 | Leahy, Pat | K |
| 12 | Namath, Joe | QB |
| 14 | Todd, Richard | QB |
| 21 | Gaines, Clark | RB |
| 22 | Owens, Burgess | FS-CB |
| 23 | Suggs, Shafer | CB-SS |
| 27 | Wise, Phil | SS |
| 35 | Davis, Steve | RB |
| 36 | Gresham, Bob | CB-S |
| 38 | Taylor, Ed | CB-S |
| 43 | Jackson, Jazz | RB-KR |
| 45 | Giammona, Louie | RB-KR |
| 46 | Sowells, Rich | CB |
| 47 | Marvaso, Tommy | S-CB |
| 49 | Marinaro, Ed | RB |
| 51 | Buttle, Greg | LB |
| 52 | Hennigan, Mike | LB |
| 53 | Russ, Carl | LB |
| 54 | Poole, Steve | LB |
| 55 | Ebersole, John | LB |
| 56 | Keller, Larry | LB |
| 59 | Martin, Bob | T |
| 65 | Roman, John | C |
| 65 | Fields, Joe | C |
| 66 | Rasmussen, Randy | G-G |
| 67 | Austin, Darrell | T |
| 71 | Krevis, Al | T |
| 72 | Woods, Robert | DT |
| 74 | Faulk, Larry | DT |
| 75 | Hill, Winston | DE |
| 76 | Pillers, Lawrence | DE |
| 77 | Barzilauskas, Carl | DT |
| 78 | Puetz, Garry | G-T |
| 80 | Satterwhite, Howard | WR |
| 81 | Neal, Richard | DE |
| 82 | Knight, David | WR |
| 83 | Barkum, Jerome | WR |
| 86 | Osborne, Richard | TE |
| 87 | Newsome, Billy | DE |
| 88 | Caster, Richard | WR-TE |
| 89 | Piccone, Lou | WR-KR |

## COLTS

| No. | Name | Pos. |
|---|---|---|
| 2 | Linhart, Toni | K |
| 7 | Jones, Bert | QB |
| 12 | Troup, Bill | QB |
| 15 | Kirkland, Mike | QB |
| 20 | Wallace, Jackie | S |
| 23 | McCauley, Don | RB |
| 25 | Oldham, Ray | DB |
| 26 | Mitchell, Lydell | RB |
| 27 | Stevens, Howard | KR-RB |
| 31 | Munsey, Nelson | CB |
| 33 | Hall, Randy | S |
| 34 | Lee, Ron | RB |
| 35 | Doughty, Glenn | WR |
| 40 | Laird, Bruce | S |
| 42 | Mumphord, Lloyd | CB |
| 47 | Baylor, Tim | DB |
| 48 | Leaks, Roosevelt | RB |
| 49 | Lee, David | P |
| 50 | Blue, Forrest | C |
| 53 | White, Stan | LB |
| 54 | Shiver, Sanders | LB |
| 55 | Dickel, Dan | LB |
| 56 | Simonini, Ed | LB |
| 57 | Mendenhall, Ken | C |
| 58 | Luce, Derrel | LB |
| 59 | Cheyunski, Jim | LB |
| 61 | Pratt, Robert | G |
| 62 | Huff, Ken | G |
| 63 | Barnes, Mike | DT |
| 64 | Taylor, David | T |
| 66 | Collett, Elmer | G |
| 67 | Van Duyne, Bob | G-T |
| 72 | Cook, Fred | DE |
| 73 | Fernandes, Ron | DE |
| 74 | Novak, Ken | DT |
| 75 | Kunz, George | T |
| 76 | Ehrmann, Joe | DT |
| 78 | Dutton, John | DE |
| 81 | Carr, Roger | WR |
| 85 | Kennedy, Jimmie | TE |
| 86 | Scott, Freddie | WR |
| 87 | Chester, Raymond | TE |
| 88 | Thompson, Ricky | WR |

camera shots and does most of his talking to the five or six men operating the cameras. The producer runs the production meeting. Some treat it like a forum and rely heavily on the announcers for information regarding the game itself—the opening, what to look for, and on whom to isolate. Others, like Dick Auerbach at NBC, feel a need to tell the broadcast team what he wants them to talk about while on camera at the start of the telecast and what he thinks will determine the outcome of the game. After all, he spoke to the public relations man for a good 15 minutes on the telephone during the week and is thoroughly prepared. The public relations representative from the visiting team is usually invited to the production meeting unless the team arrived early and worked out at the stadium, in which case the announcers would have talked to him there. Most visiting teams, however, prefer to have their light Saturday practice at home.

I have been involved in some production meetings that have been major productions themselves and others that have lasted all of 20 minutes. They are more important to the play-by-play man than to the color man. The play-by-play announcer will be given copies of and "lead-ins" to commercials and an outline of the telecast. The outline will contain such items as how the air time at halftime and at the end of the game will be filled. The meeting provides an opportunity to exchange ideas and gets everyone to think alike about the teams involved and the format of the telecast.

Some of the most productive meetings I have attended were conducted over lunch for the Jet pre-season games. Producer Duke Struck and Director John Pecorski got it all together without ever having a formal meeting. Pre-season football games, of course, are not quite like those during the regular season. They are hard to plan because no one knows who is going to be playing much less what is likely to happen during the game. The fact that the outcome of the game is unimportant and the coaches are experimenting changes the announcers' approach drastically.

Sometimes, the broadcast team will stay at the same hotel as the visiting team. This makes it easy to visit with players and coaches in a lobby or coffee shop. Many announcers will make a point of having a drink at the bar after the assistant coaches have completed bed check, which is usually 11:00 P.M. The conversations invariably turn to football and the next day's game. Information gathered at 1:00 A.M. is sometimes spicier than that received earlier.

The announcers usually leave for the stadium on Sunday about three hours before game time. The coaches and players normally arrive at about that time as well, so there is no reason to arrive sooner. Upon arrival, most check out the booth, greet the producer and director in the control room or truck outside the stadium, and then visit each locker room for a quick update from the head coaches or anyone else available. Some locker rooms are closed to everyone and others allow reporters up until an hour before game time. It depends on the coaches. Charlie Jones once told me that it is sometimes advisable to stop in and say hello to the officials, but it never helped me.

Next comes a walk out onto the field. Most assistant coaches visit with their counterparts on the field before the teams come out to warm up. This presents an opportunity to speak to anyone that the announcers may have missed.

Then, it's up to the press room for an early lunch or late breakfast and one last update from the P.R. men from each team. I always take this opportunity to talk to some of the newspaper reporters that cover the teams on a daily basis. Those that take their jobs seriously can often help tie together some loose threads and put other information into perspective. (There is little reason to dwell on a story during the broadcast if the press has covered it extensively during the week and it has become common knowledge.)

It is common for reporters to criticize some announcers in their articles—especially the ex-athletes. This is probably because many of them would like to have the announcer's job. Some writers, like Paul Zimmerman of the *New York Post* would probably do a fine job. Zimmerman has always been deeply involved in football and particularly the Jets. A couple of years ago he tried to pick a successor to Charlie Winner. It's an interesting story and provides some insight into the odd way in which reporters and broadcasters sometimes gather information.

When Chuck Knox was an assistant coach with the Jets, he became friendly with Aaron Lubin, a gentleman that ran a wholesale menswear establishment in New York. All of the Jet players and coaches bought their suits and sports jackets from Aaron, who is a great guy and football fan. After Knox left New York, he stayed in touch with Aaron. One Tuesday evening, in January, 1976, I received a call from Aaron: "Guess who wants to be coach of the Jets?" I then proceeded to name all of the assistant coaches that I knew Aaron had kept in touch with over the years. He finally told me that Chuck was unhappy with the situation in Los Angeles, and that Aaron thought he would be interested in the Jet position. He asked me what I thought he should do to let the Jets know Knox was available. I told him to call general manager Al Ward or Jet president Phil Iselin and tell them. Aaron thought it might be better if some pressure were put on the Jet organization and indicated he would make some additional telephone calls. The next afternoon I was passing a newsstand and happened to see the headline on the back page of the New York Post. It read: "Chuck Knox—Head Coach of the Jets?" Evidently, Paul Zimmerman also thought that Knox should have the Jet job.

About 20 minutes before game time, the producer is ready to rehearse the opening. By this time, he has had an opportunity during the pre-game workout to tape the short segment on the players and coaches that it has become customary to show on the screen as the announcers talk about them. After the rehearsal, there is nothing left to do but settle down and get ready for the game. I take this opportunity to review my notes which by now are substantial. Charlie Jones has always felt that I had too many notes and that I would be better off "winging it" more. His contention has been that there would be more by-play between us if I were not as intent on making all of the points I thought important. He is probably right.

Now, it's game time. The greatest pressure exists during the opening. The producer might have announced that two minutes were allocated for the opening only to shout in your ear, *while you are on the air*, that they are about to kick off. It can be disconcerting and cause even the most professional announcer to pause in the middle of a sentence or lose his train of thought. Time always seems to be the enemy of the color man—during the opening as well as during the game. The play-by-play announcer always gets the mike first and the color man has to work around him. If he takes extra time on the opening, the color man often has to cut short what he has prepared. Without notice, it isn't easy.

During the game the color man has to be extremely succinct. Often, he hasn't time to comment at all. Some think the instant replay is the toughest part of the color man's job. He has two monitors in front of him. One with the picture seen by the viewing audience and the other showing what the isolated camera is following. An isolated camera is one that is used only to record material for replays and normally isolates one aspect of a play. The problem for the color man is that he can't look at both monitors at once and never knows when the producer feels he has something worth showing as an instant replay. The producer will tell the color man when he is about to show a replay and hopefully who he has isolated. Sometimes, he has the numbers right and can tell a trap block from a cross body block. Other times, his attempt to brief the color man with a word or two only makes the job more difficult. The announcers rarely see the replay before they have to comment on it. It is difficult to sound knowledgable when the producer says, "We have Ed White pulling out on a sweep," only to discover that it's Ron Yary on a quick pitch. It becomes even more difficult when the color man begins to talk about something only to be interrupted in the middle of a sentence and told something completely unrelated will be shown as a replay in about two seconds. Through all of this, the color man is expected to make an astute observation about something he may not have seen before, and certainly not merely describe what is being seen. It takes some practice but can be done. This is where the preparation and background information can help. When I don't have a good idea of what is going to unfold on the monitor, I generally talk about the individual until I can determine what is happening and then try to analyze the replay.

Most experienced announcers keep an eye on the replay monitor so that they will know on whom the producer is isolating even if they can't watch him out of the corner of their eye on the play. Knowing who is being isolated will give him some idea of what the replay will show. A good color man knows where every receiver is on a pass play and the blocking assignments on most running plays. Anticipating the replay gives him an added edge. On national games, where two isolated cameras are used to tape replays, the job becomes harder since the moniter can only show where one camera is isolated. The announcer can request certain isolated shots during commercial breaks or on a direct telephone line from the booth to the producer. However, the situation is constantly changing and requires the producer to talk to the announcers during the game. The producer might say in the color man's earphones: "I'll isolate on Dave Casper of the Raiders if you think they might throw to him in this situation." What the color man says *on the air* will tell the producer how he views the idea. If the color man doesn't think it's a good idea, he will not talk about Casper. If he likes the idea, he might say, "This is a situation where they might look for Casper over the middle." If the ball is thrown to Casper, the color man not only knows what's on the replay, but gets credit for calling the right shots.

Al DeRogatis built quite a reputation as a prognosticator while doing the Giant games on radio. This was probably one of the reasons that NBC hired him. Al knew the Giants well and had a lot of inside information. He could also hedge his bet pretty good. In a long yardage situation, he might say, "This is a perfect spot for a long pass to Homer Jones or perhaps a screen pass or draw play." The Giants had only one deep threat and if they didn't throw to him the screen or draw were good choices. When Al was right, his partner, Marty Glickman, would shout it out for the world to hear. Soon, everyone in the stands was listening to the radio to find out what the next play would be. Al didn't have as much success predicting plays on TV because he worked different teams each week. Nevertheless, he was a pro and did a fine job.

At halftime, there are usually eight or nine free minutes. Every announcer uses this time differently. The only thing everyone invariably does is visit the men's room. I will then visit the press room where they usually serve some kind of food. I go for the company and not necessarily the food. There are always scouts, front office people, or injured players present who sometimes come up with a different slant on the game. I recall bumping into Al Davis out in Oakland one year. The Raiders were leading the Jets 28-0 at the half. I asked Davis what he thought and he did three minutes on how lousy his team was playing and how you couldn't count the Jets out of the game with Namath at quarterback. I got back on the air and echoed the last part of his statement about ten seconds before the Raiders' Willie Brown intercepted Namath and made the score 35-0. I wish I hadn't run into Al that day.

Like the fan, the announcer may be looking at almost anything before a given play, but after the snap, he must follow the football since that is what the camera is following. Before the snap, I usually look for many of the same things that the quarterback and middle linebacker look for. At the beginning of the game, I will look for confirmation of the things I expected and, more importantly, things I did not expect—new formations, new players, the type of coverage in the secondary, and people out of alignment. I try to take a quick look at a different player on every play in an attempt to determine who is and who is not doing his job. The winners and losers of individual battles often explain the numbers on the scoreboard. I will look at a player on the snap to see what he will do and then switch to the quarterback or the action downfield. If I have already determined the play to be a pass, I would then look back to the original player to see how he did. On every play, I try to determine why it succeeded or failed. I am looking for the breakdown, error or super effort that provides the explanation. It can best be described as a scanning action designed to take in as much as possible. Most of the time I can put all the pieces together and figure out what happened, but there are other times when I see no more than the viewer at home.

I think it is evident that the involved announcer has an opportunity to obtain much information not readily available to the armchair quarterback. Let him do the legwork for you. If he is well prepared, you can learn much from him since he is a pipeline to the coaches and players. He might repeat many things you have heard before, but is bound to have some new information and perhaps some of his own original thoughts which will help you understand what's happening. This, of course, is the ultimate test for an announcer: how much of what he has said has not been said many times before.

An announcer on the 50 yard line can see many things not readily discernible on a T.V. screen. If he says that a team is using a deep zone, you will understand why the opposing quarterback is throwing so many short passes. If he says that the Minnesota Viking defensive line is undersized and relies on speed and experience, it could explain why the Cleveland Browns continue to pound away up the middle when they are usually more effective outside. He may not have much new information about the men on a team representing your home town, but he can give you a better line on players from other teams.

On the other hand, keep in mind that each fellow in the booth is trying to hold onto his job and can't possibly see everyting that took place on a particular play. He might be bluffing. The network brass is not impressed as much by the accuracy as by style and the ability to hold the viewing audience's interest. If he can accomplish that with humor, controversy, and an occasional homily, it won't matter if he is a bit short on expertise. Listening carefully will tell you whether the announcers are sharp football men intent on passing along information that will help you appreciate the game or if they are trying to be the entertainment themselves.

# Part Five

# THE GAME PLAN

The team game plan consists of three separate parts. The offensive part is comprised of those plays that the coaching staff believes will work against the opposition's defense. The defensive game plan includes defensive fronts and coverages which are expected to stop the opposition's offensive attack. The third phase of the game plan deals with the kicking game and lists details about coverages and returns.

The game plan is often treated with the reverence and secrecy accorded to the recipe for the most popular dish at a good restaurant. It is not only what goes into the recipe that is important, but how the dish is prepared. It is the same with the game plan. The defensive team knows that the opposition will run and pass the football. The question that must be answered is where it will attempt to run and pass, and from what formations. The offensive team knows that the defense will be in certain basic alignments. But, it must anticipate variations and exactly when particular defensive formations will be utilized.

The offensive and defensive game plans are formulated from the answers to two basic questions: What offensive plays will work best against the opposition's defenses? Which defenses will work best against the opposition's offensive attack? In order to answer these questions, the coaching staff must have information about the opposition. Without this information there would be no game plan; just a list of plays which *might* work.

The coaching staff gathers information about the opposition from many sources. All of them are considered forms of scouting. The bulk of this information comes from viewing movies of previous games. Prior to the free exchange of game films by all college and professional teams, which is now a standard practice, scouting was pretty much limited to several scouts or coaches sitting in the stands. Though in-person scouting isn't as important as it once was, most teams continue to dispatch one or two men to scout an opponent in this manner because it provides certain information that cannot readily be determined from viewing films.

Weather conditions are one factor that films usually do not reflect. Wet or windy conditions can explain why certain things happened on the field. Penalties charged to individuals can sometimes explain performances on ensuing plays. The player charged with holding or pass interference sometimes alters his style of play temporarily. The emotional atmosphere created by the home town fans could have had an effect. Answers to these questions and others must come from a man sitting in the stands or press box.

Some coaches still believe that there is no substitute for the first hand information provided from a coach on the scene. Information gathered at the opposition's practice sessions is even more valuable. (This is the reason that some teams conduct closed practices.) Observing a team during practice eliminates the necessity of having to anticipate offensive tactics. The oppostion will know what offensive plays are included in the game plan and the defenses to be employed. This type of scouting is not considered exactly ethical and coaches that attempt to gather information in this manner never admit to it publicly. Even so, it goes on.

During the early years of the American Football League, there was an old deserted house on a hill overlooking Mile High Stadium in Denver. It was possible for someone positioned at a window on the top floor of the house to see the entire field. Most visiting professional teams travel to the city in which they will play a day or two before the game. They are usually allowed to conduct at least one practice session in the stadium to become familiar with any peculiarities of the field. Rumor had it that the Broncos used to put a scout with binoculars in this room when each team came in so that they would be ready. Sid Gillman of San Diego wasn't taking any chances. He took great pains not to tip his game plan during the practice session. Only basic plays were used.

Scouting is rarely so clandestine. In fact, it is sometimes remarkably direct. For example, it is not uncommon for coaches to exchange information about a common opponent. Say team A plays team B on a given Sunday. The coach of team A might call the coach of the team that played team B the preceding week to find out what part of his game plan was successful. This type of exchange of information is common among friends and coaches that have common goals. It is uncommon for teams in the same division to exchange information, but it is common in situations where two teams can benefit by the loss of another team. The coach of a team tied for second place will gladly give information to the coach of the team he is tied with if it will help him to beat the first place team and create a playoff situation. In most cases, it is the unsuccessful coaches that exchange information about the more successful teams in the league.

Any means of gathering information which may provide a clue to the strengths and weaknesses of the opposition or what they are likely to do during a game will be used. Most teams subscribe to the daily newspapers in the cities in which their opponents are located. Information regarding injuries, players with emotional problems, reasons for a win or loss and other bits and pieces can sometimes be tied together with other information to tell a story.

Some coaches occasionally go to extremes to obtain certain inside information. In professional football, players released from one team are sometimes picked up by an opponent merely to "pick his brain." The player will be asked about former teammates and offensive and defensive plays and formations. The latter information is readily available from film, but the strategy behind the use of certain plays from specific formations may not be as evident. It is especially helpful if you can pick up a player just cut by next week's opponent.

Every coach has an offensive and defensive philosophy which he hopes to employ in his game plan. Obviously, adjustments must be made each week for new opponents. Information about individual strengths and weaknesses of the opposition must be evaluated in light of his own personnel. The same must be done for offensive and defensive formations and tendencies.

Before we get to the actual construction of a game plan, let's take a closer look at the information needed and how it is incorporated into the scouting report.

Whether a team gathers its information from a scout in the stands or from looking at films, each play is charted so that patterns can be noted. Specific tendencies are observed about each player along with his team.

## SCOUTING THE OFFENSE

A scout will use various checklists to break down each play and gather information more efficiently. They include many of the same questions that any fan will be asking himself about his favorite team:

1. What is their basic offense?
2. Does the offensive line come out in a three point stance, or are they set by the quarterback?
3. Are plays run more frequently on one count than on another?
4. Does the offensive team run plays quickly?
5. Does the quarterback appear to use many audibles?

6. What type of cadence is used?

7. Is the offensive line as close to the ball as possible?

8. Do the ends split wider on pass plays?

9. Do the wide receivers crackback block on end runs, or do they attempt to take the defensive backs downfield by running deep pass patterns?

10. Does the quarterback tip a pass play by looking at a certain area of the field?

11. Are the splits in the offensive line small or large?

12. Do the offensive backs alter their alignment to carry out specific assignments better?

13. How deep does the quarterback set up to pass?

14. Are there any favorite receivers, and what are their favorite routes?

15. Note the pass protection. Who is the weak link?

16. Note when special plays like the draw and screen are used.

17. Note penalties and against whom they are assessed.

18. Does the team favor the wide side of the field?

19. Do they repeatedly call the same play in key situations?

20. Does the team always pass on a particular down?

21. Does a team call on particular plays, receivers or runners repeatedly in certain situations?

In addition to the general questions asked above, certain questions are asked relating specifically to the running and passing game.

## The Running Game

1. What is their short yardage formation?

2. What is the offensive team's bread and butter play? It will be the play called most often in key situations and may not always be evident from an analysis of the down and distance worksheet.

3. Who is the offensive team's most dangerous runner?

4. What is the strongest part of their offensive line?

5. What is their favorite formation and what plays do they most often run from it?

6. Does a team run to the side of a particular split end if the wide receivers remain on the same side of the field and the tight end moves from one side to another?

7. Is the running attack stronger to the outside or the inside?

8. Does anyone tip the hole into which the run is directed?

9. Are the receivers used as blockers or decoys?

10. Do the basic line splits vary on plays run to the inside or outside?

11. What was used particularly because of weaknesses or strengths in the oppositon and ordinarily would not be emphasized?

## The Passing Game

1. What is their basic passing formation?

2. What is the strength and weakness of the passing attack? Is the passer more effective or are the receivers more effective?

3. How effective are the set backs when picking up the blitz or assisting the offensive linemen?

4. Who is the most dangerous receiver? Is he the quarterback's favorite receiver?

5. How quickly does the passer set up in the pocket?

6. How dangerous is the quarterback when forced to run with the football?

7. Does anyone on the offensive team tip the pass by his alignment?

8. Are screens and draws an integral part of the offensive attack?

9. When are play action passes attempted and are they well executed?

10. Is the quarterback effective when executing roll out passes? When are they called?

11. Does anyone other than the quarterback throw the football?

12. Can we rush the passer? Does the offensive line have a weak spot?

13. Is there a favorite passing formation?

14. Does the quarterback have a tendency to call certain pass patterns from certain areas of the field?

15. How effective are the substitute receivers?

16. Does the offense pass in short yardage situations and what patterns are usually called?

The information gathered by the scouts in the stands and from the game films is put together into an offensive scouting report provided for the defensive team. It provides information on the opposition's personnel and what they are likely to do at various spots on the field. Each coach has his own system of relating the information to his players. Normally, charts will be compiled in addition to descriptive material on the strengths and weaknesses of each player. (See the report on personnel given ahead for examples of the type of descriptions given.)

## SCOUTING THE DEFENSE

The objectives of a team when scouting the opposition's defense are the same as when scouting the offense. Information regarding defensive tendencies, strengths, and weaknesses is gathered and evaluated before the offensive game plan is developed. Checklists and charts similar to those used when scouting the offense are worked out.

### General Points

1. What is their basic defense?
2. What are their short yardage defenses?
3. What are the vulnerable areas of the running defense?
4. What pass patterns are likely to be effective?
5. Does the defense pursue well?
6. Does the opposition play a containing or pressure defense?
7. Does the line play off the ball?
8. How often are games and stunts used?
9. Do the linebackers drop off quickly?
10. Do the deep backs come up quickly on the running game?
11. Do the deep backs rotate to the wide side of the field?
12. When are they vulnerable to the screen or draw play?
13. Are they vulnerable to the play pass or roll out pass?
14. When do they switch to a goal line defense?
15. When is a prevent defense used?
16. Do they react quickly to offensive variations and adjustments?
17. Which offensive formations create the most difficulty for them?
18. Who calls defensive signals?

### The Defensive Line

1. Do they use an odd or even front?
2. Do they shift after the offense sets?
3. Are they stronger in defending the inside or outside?
4. Do they line up off the ball?
5. Who is their best lineman?
6. Who is their weakest lineman?
7. Do they put on a good pass rush?
8. Which side of the line does the most stunting?
9. Are they vulnerable to the screen or draw play?
10. Which linemen can be trapped effectively?
11. Do they split with the offensive line?
12. Do they use any "stack" defenses?

13. Who moves over the offensive center when they shift to an odd front?

14. Do they submarine when in a goal line defense?

15. Are they hand fighters or do they try to overpower the offensive linemen when rushing the passer?

### The Linebackers

1. How qucikly do they get back into pass defense?
2. Are they stronger against the pass or run?
3. Do they vary their alignment according to the situation?
4. Which linebacker is most vulnerable to the pass?
5. Who is strongest against the run?
6. How often do they blitz?
7. Do they tip the blitz?
8. Do they get involved with stunting linemen?
9. Do they come up quickly on play action passes?
10. How do they play the roll out pass?

### The Defensive Secondary

1. Do they use man or zone coverage?
2. What is the depth of the secondary?
3. Which defender can be beaten deep?
4. Which back turns his back to the ball?
5. What is the emotional reaction of a player when a pass is completed against him?
6. Can a defender be "turned" or can we get him to cross his legs?
7. How do they adjust to flankers, slot backs, wing backs and the flood formation?
8. How do they react to play action passes?
9. How important are the linebackers to their pass defense?
10. Will the roll out be effective?
11. How do they react to a man in motion?

## EVALUATING INDIVIDUAL PERSONNEL

Whether scouting the offensive or defensive team, an evaluation of the opposing team's personnel is of major importance. The nature of team defense requires the scout to devote more attention to the individual players on defense. Most teams use just a handful of different defensive alignments. Thus, it is the minor variations or quirks in the play of individuals that become important to the offense. For example, does a lineman line up tight or loose? Does he play soft or tough against the run? Is he a hand fighter when rushing the passer? Does he prefer to take an outside rush on the passer? Can he be blocked to the inside? Is he vulnerable to the trap or draw play?

The answers to the above questions are likely to be as important to the offense as an awareness of the overall defensive alignment expected in a particular situation. Unless a team goes into a goal line or prevent defense, their relative effectiveness against the run or pass will change little. Normally, the only effect a change from a 4-3 to a 5-1 will have on the offense is to require a change in blocking assignments. However, the corner linebacker that tips the blitz by his alignment *does* offer an opportunity for the offense to adjust. A particular defensive alignment may not be noted for its weakness in defending against the sweep, but the defensive end that favors the inside may allow the offense to sweep the end successfully.

Knowing that a specific defense will be used at a particular time will not help the quarterback or anyone else on the offensive team unless other information is provided. The offense must be made aware of how the defensive team adjusts to offensive variations when using the defense, and how individuals play their positions on defense.

The offense has the advantage of knowing where and when the play is executed. Therefore, the defense must be prepared to defend every vulnerable spot on the field. Theoretically, every defense has weak and strong points. If we assume that the 4-3 is equally effective in stopping the run to both sides of the line, the offense should become stronger to one side when a man is placed on the center's nose and the defense remains with four defensive linemen. However, most coaches compensate for inherent weaknesses with adjustments. In this case, the alignment of the linebackers will compensate for the movement of the defensive linemen. Hence, the offense does not usually try to attack what are *supposed* to be the built-in vulnerable areas. They will attack individuals who are overmatched physically or lack experience. Or, they might attempt to capitalize on "dangerous" individual positioning or movement after the snap of the ball. The linebacker that moves head up or inside the tight end is in a dangerous position. His alignment will make it more difficult for him to fulfill his primary responsibility of turning in all running plays directed to the outside.

The scouting report provided for the offense will not only include a chart or summary of where and when to expect defenses, but an outline of what to expect from each player. Every professional player knows what to expect from a 4-3 defense. It is the descriptive paragraphs on the play and adjustments of each man in the defense that are important.

## THE SCOUTING REPORT

The actual scouting report given to the players may be written or dictated to the team. Many coaches still believe that players are more likely to remember information when they must write it down themselves. Either way, they will be given the basic information necessary to execute their assignments well. Here's a scouting report on the Dallas Cowboy defense that might have been given to the Denver Broncos before the 1978 Super Bowl.

*Team:* Dallas Cowboys

*Colors:* Blue and white

*Record:* 14-2

*Playoff Games:* Dallas 37 Chicago 7; Dallas 23 Minnesota 6

*Injuries:* The Cowboys have suffered few injuries during the course of the season and will be completely healthy for the Super Bowl.

*Basic Defenses:* Dallas is exclusively a 4-3 team. They remain in the 4-3 except for goal line situations when they move into a gap-8. They do not change personnel in short yardage situations, but the linebackers will play tight. The defensive tackles remain in a flex position at all times but will alternate from a loose to a tight position

*Coverages:* They are basically a zone team but will change up with man coverage about 30% of the time. At times, they have replaced two linebackers with defensive backs in long yardage situations.

*Blitzing:* Overall, they blitzed 18% of the time during the regular season. They blitzed 7% of the time against the Bears and 22% of the time against the Vikings. Seven out of ten times it will be the weak side linebacker who blitzes. Because of the condition of Craig Morton's hip, we expect Dallas to come 40-50% of the time in passing situations.

*Stunts:* Stunts are used 27% of the time. The flexed position of the tackles makes stunting especially effective. When the tackle is close to the line, we are likely to see a tackle-end game and when the tackle is loose, expect an end-tackle game. We must pick up the stunts or they will eat up our quarterback.

*Shifting:* The linebackers will move, after the offense sets, 20% of the time. D.D. Lewis does it more often than anyone else.

*Pursuit:* The team has excellent pursuit. The linebackers are very active and excellent in pursuit. Defensive tackle Randy White has a linebacker's speed and must be cut off on plays going away from him.

*Team Strengths:* This is the best Dallas team to ever go to the Super Bowl, and the defense has carried them most of the way. The defensive line is the strongest part of the defense. It is the best front four in football. Harvey Martin gets most of the ink, but Randy White is the man we must contain. They have come up with 53 sacks and have yielded just 3.7 yards per rushing play. We believe we can run at Harvey Martin if we can control White. We will use considerable misdirection to slow down White and Martin.

*Team Weaknesses:* The linebacking is the weakest part of the defensive unit, but it certainly is not weak by any standards. Bob Breunig has taken over the middle from the retired Lee Roy Jordon. He is short on experience. Left linebacker Thomas Henderson is just an average linebacker, but can make the big play. D.D. Lewis is a solid performer on the other side. We should be able to run to Henderson's side and right at Breunig. The key will be our ability to handle the defensive line. We will also attempt to throw short over the middle and to Henderson's side. If Craig's hip allows, we will use play action. It will confuse the linebackers. Aaron Kyle is the weak link in the defensive secondary, and the other cornerback, Benny Barnes, can be had. We shall stay away from the safeties.

The above information is helpful, but it is the specific information on individual players which most players look for. In many instances the information provided here will not completely coincide with what was indicated under strengths and weaknesses. A coach may say that his team should be able to run in a certain area, but he will probably refrain from knocking individual players in the scouting report. At least he will not do so in writing. Coaches are traditionally concerned about the possibility of someone seeing the report or of the opposition finding out what is in it and using the information as a psychological tool to inspire their players. Many coaches are also concerned about the possibility of their own players becoming over-confident. Thus, when describing players on the opposition, a coach is more than likely to talk about their weaknesses *in general terms,* allowing his own players to come to the correct conclusion. The "Report on Personnel" on the 1978 Super Bowl Dallas Cowboys is fairly typical for pro football. Red Miller might be emphasizing weaknesses here a bit more than usual in an attempt to build the confidence of his overmatched Broncos.

## REPORT ON PERSONNEL

### Ed Jones #72, Left End, 4th year

At 6'9" and 265 pounds, Jones is the biggest man on the defensive unit. He had his best year ever in 1977 and may eventually live up to his potential. His height can present a problem to the offensive tackle on pass protection. However, he can be handled if we set up on the line of scrimmage and don't give him a running start and an opportunity to use his size. He plays the run and the pass equally well. Like most big men, he does not like to be hit low around the knees. Jones has played a secondary role to Harvey Martin all season. He may be ready to claim equal time of the quarterback. Ate up All Pro Ron Yary of Minnesota in the championship game.

### Jethro Pugh #75, Left Tackle, 13th year

At 6'5" and 250 pounds, Pugh is an average defensive lineman who played in the shadow of Bob Lilly for most of his career. He is not as active as the other members of the front four, but hangs in there and doesn't make mistakes. A tough man to trap and run the draw play against. He will stay low and deliver a hard blow while not taking a side on the guard. However, he is the weakest part of the defensive line and we will run at him.

### Randy White #54, Right Tackle, 3rd year

The smallest defensive lineman at 6'4" and 245 pounds. Played linebacker his first two years with the team but he is already All Pro caliber at tackle. He is fast, quick and tough. He never stops coming and refuses to be blocked. Tough to cut off on plays going away from him. Extremely strong for his size—a weight lifter. He is the man we must control. His extreme aggressiveness makes him vulnerable to the trap and draw plays.

### Harvey Martin #79, Right End, 5th year

At 6'5", 252 pounds, he led the league with 23 quarterback sacks. He is obviously tough to hold out on pass plays but can be blocked on the run. We can trap him and will run the draw play at him and White. It is imperative that the offensive tackle knock his hands away on pass protection. He will take a wide rush and try to outrun the tackle. Will spin and twist a great deal when rushing the passer, but we have confidence in our ability to handle him.

### Bob Breunig #53, Middle Linebacker, 3rd year

6'2", 227 pounds. One of the weak links on the defense. Short on experience. He can be overpowered on plays run at him and we can get to his knees and cut him off on plays to the outside. He will stunt with the flexed tackles. Has good speed but not as quick as Lee Roy Jordan whom he replaced.

### D.D. Lewis #50, Right Linebacker, 9th year

6'1", 215 pounds. He is the most experienced and steadiest performer at linebacker. Better against the pass than the run. Will not let you get a clean shot at him. Tough to run the screen against, and does much of their blitzing.

### Tom Henderson #56, Left Linebacker, 3rd year

6'2", 220 pounds. Henderson can be outstanding, but presently lacks experience. Better against the run than the pass despite three interceptions during the regular season. He can be cut when blitzing, but will go over the block if you throw too soon. We should be able to throw and run in his area.

### Benny Barnes #31, Left Cornerback, 6th year

6'1", 195 pounds. A solid but unspectacular corner. Was a substitute until last season when Mark Washington was injured. Did not intercept a pass all season. Will come up and hit you on the run. We can beat him on hooks and turn-ins.

### Cliff Harris #43, Weakside Safety, 8th year

6'1", 192 pounds. Outstanding football player. Led team with five interceptions. We will have to watch him closely when they are in man coverage and he is free. Reacts well to the flight of the ball. Very effective when he does blitz. He may overreact to play action passes.

### Charlie Waters #41, Strong Safety, 8th year

6'2", 198 pounds. Has good size and will stick you. Waters is just a notch below Harris in ability but may make up for it with intelligence. Calls the coverages in the secondary. Had three interceptions in 1977.

### Aaron Kyle #25, Right Cornerback, 2nd year

At 5'10", he is the smallest and most inexperienced player in the defensive secondary. He is the weak link that we will try to break. He can be beaten long if you catch a few short ones on him. He did not have an interception last season. Relies on Waters for help and guidance during a game. We shall try to isolate him whenever possible.

## THE GAME PLAN

Having accumulated the information mentioned on the preceding pages, the coach now has the basic material needed to put his game plan together. The information must first be weighed against what he knows about his own team. In the case of Denver's Red Miller, can he capitalize on Dallas' weakness at left defensive tackle (Jethro Pugh) or does a weak offensive right guard (Paul Howard) neutralize the advantage? Denver's offensive line is not overwhelming but Howard is a good straight ahead blocker. It therefore makes sense to run at Pugh. Especially, when you consider that Claudie Minor is the Broncos best lineman and that he lines up next to Howard.

I did not give Harvey Martin the respect in Red Miller's theoretical scouting report that Martin normally commands. He received a tremendous amount of publicity for his 23 sacks during the season and if I were the coach of the Broncos, I would have attempted to build the confidence of the very average offensive tackle, Andy Maurer. However, Martin is easily as good against the run as Jones, and Miller would prefer to run to Claudie Minor's side of the line.

Formulating a game plan for the running game must have been a trying experience for Red Miller and the rest of the Bronco offensive coaching staff. There are no weaknesses on the Dallas Defensive line and the linebackers are much better than indicated in the scouting report.

The game plan itself may be no more than a list of plays to be used during a given game. The coach will often tell his players the reasons behind the selection, but they normally will not be written down. The information will be conveyed during a meeting at the beginning of the practice week in which the game plan is presented to the team. At the same time, they usually get diagrams of the opposition's defense.

The first line of the talk to the players will always be the same: "We should win this football game." After that, it changes rather dramatically. In the case of Tom Landry going against Denver the rest of that first sentence would probably be, "if we don't take them lightly." Red Miller's conclusion to the sentence would be, "if we can hold it all together one more week and protect the quarterback." The coach basing his game plan on the information in the scouting report on the Dallas defense provided here would go on to say that "they are a great football team but have several notable weaknesses. We intend to capitalize on their weaknesses whenever we can. Our running attack will be directed at number 75, their left tackle, until he proves that we should be running elsewhere or they take him out of the game. We believe that our right offensive guard can handle him and that Claudie will eat up Jones.

"All passes directed away from their safeties should work. They are their best defensive backs and we will stay away from the middle of the field. Instead, our passing attack will be directed at their right cornerback and their left corner linebacker. For that reason we will be passing from a strong right formation most of the time. Good pass protection is essential to give our pass receivers time to clear out the middle and outrun their defenders on deep patterns. We believe that our set backs can block their linebackers when blitzing, and hope they continue to blitz. Offensive backs should look for the blitz, especially on the weak side.

"Although we will emphasize the passing game and inside running game, we will continue to display a balanced attack. Their best lineman, number 54, White, is vulnerable to the trap and draw plays. For that reason we have added trap 32 and draw 24 to the game plan. We are confident that we can handle him. However, we do want our center to try to help our left guard on drop back passes. We have also added the sucker play to take advantage of White's aggressive play. It will work."

Red Miller is then likely to have announced the rest of the game plan and given the reasons for including each play. Most of the reasons for choosing the plays will revolve around individual strengths and weaknesses or variations in individual alignment or style of play. For example, a sweep to the offensive team's right might be included because Henderson is on that side and they prefer to stay away from Martin and D.D. Lewis. The draw play might be avoided to that side because both Pugh and Jones rush the passer with greater caution than White and Martin.

Pass plays will be selected for the same reasons. With pass plays, it may only be necessary to change the assignment of one player to adjust for individual differences. It may not be necessary to add a new play to capitalize on Aaron Kyle's weakness at right cornerback. All that would be required is for tight end Riley Odoms to change his route to get Waters out of the way on one or two patterns. He may be advised to do so by Miller, when he presents the game plan, or by Morton in the huddle.

Riley Odoms is the best all-around receiver the Broncos have, though Haven Moses made more big plays during the 1977 season. The Broncos would obviously like to isolate Odoms on the strong side linebacker. However, the Cowboys as well as every other team in the league are aware of Odoms' ability and are unlikely to cooperate. Red Miller knows this and has certainly already incorporated everything possible into his standard offense to take advantage of Odoms' exceptional ability. You can be certain that the Broncos design all their pass routes with the hope that the strong safety will be isolated on Odoms.

Of course, while Denver was diligently putting together its

scouting and personnel reports on the Dallas defense as an aid in formulating their game plan, Dallas was working just as hard at analyzing the Denver offense and coming up with a defensive game plan.

Tom Landry would be more positive in stressing the strengths of the Denver offense than Miller was in talking about the Dallas defense. Signaled out for special praise would be Denver right tackle, Claudie Minor, tight end Riley Odoms, fullback Jon Keyworth and quarterback Craig Morton. He would note that Denver has a solid if unspectacular offense—both on the ground and in the air—which cannot be taken lightly.

The Dallas defensive game plan would keep the Cowboys in their usual 4-3 defense for the entire game. It would state overall objectives and perhaps some specific down and yardage situations when a blitz or stunt might be called.

Tom Landry, or more likely Ernie Stautner, the Cowboys' defensive coordinator, might begin his presentation of the game plan by reminding his charges not to be fooled by the unknown names and lack of credentials on the Broncos. "They have been taken lightly for most of the season but just kept beating the toughest teams in the league. If we don't give it our best shot, people will once again begin to say that the Cowboys can't win the big one.

"We must pressure the quarterback. Everyone will expect us to blitz because of Morton's hip, but we feel that our front four can put enough pressure on him without blitzing. We will use more stunts than normally and try to get some pressure up the middle. Since we will not blitz much and their receivers have good speed, we will stay in zone coverage most of the day. We may try a couple of safety blitzes, but I'll send the signal in from the sidelines. We will work hard this week on the tackle-end stunt and make it work.

"I expect them to run to their right side. Minor and Howard are their strongest blockers. Make certain that we don't get hurt in a stunt on a running play. They have had success when running straight at the defense, but watch the break to the outside when Armstrong is in the game."

The coach might then diagram the favorite plays and formations used by the Broncos and where and when to expect them. It might be done on a blackboard or presented in printed form. Any tendencies, such as when Morton likes to throw to his setbacks, would be noted. Special or unusual blocking combinations and other peculiarities would be covered.

After the game plan is presented to the entire team, most teams will then break into groups according to position and continue to discuss the plan of attack with their assistant coaches. Types of blocking might have been changed by the Bronco offensive line coach for Dallas. Miller might have decided that White should have been double teamed, or that cross blocking would work against Pugh and Jones. The offensive backfield coach will make similar adjustments in the alignment of the backs or the type of action that will be used. In most instances, these decisions will first be made in a coaches' meeting with the approval of the head coach.

Most of the information that theoretically is a part of the game plan will be discussed or imparted to the players on the practice field. When practicing running plays against the defenses used by the opposition, previously conceived notions about what the offense can do may have to be abandoned or altered. It is one thing to dissect a defense on a blackboard and another matter to do it on the field of play. Frequently, some of the most ingenious parts of a game plan are developed on the practice field. The game plan given a team during the beginning of the week may be modified several times before game day. This will happen less often when the teams have been long-time rivals and the opposing coaches know each other's style well.

The Dallas defensive personnel proved to be superior to the Denver offense in the 1978 Super Bowl. Unrelenting pressure on the Denver offense caused seven turnovers in the first half—four interceptions and three fumbles. This was the thrust of the Dallas defensive game plan and it worked for them. Denver saw the Dallas stunts up the middle but just couldn't handle them.

## THE KICKING GAME

Like the offense and defense, there must be a scouting report on the opposition's kicking game. The list of details to be noted may not be as extensive, but it *is* equally important. Teams often include wrinkles in their kicking game. The team that is not expecting a reverse on a kick-off or punt return may be burned. Diagrams depicting the blocking on punt and kick returns as well as the coverage on kick-offs and punts are included in the scouting report. The scouting report on the kicking game is given to the team separately a day or two before the game, unless the opposition is known to do something very unorthodox. A simple checklist of things to look for shall suffice here:

### Punting and Place Kicking

1. How long does the punter and place kicker take to get the kick away?

2. Are the blockers on the punt team more anxious to get downfield to cover the kick than to block?

3. Can the kick be blocked? Where?

4. Does the kicker rattle when rushed?

5. Do they do anything else from punt formation except kick the ball?

6. Can we return a kick? Is there a better chance of blocking a kick or returning one?

7. How many steps does the punter take before kicking the ball?

8. Can offensive linemen be "pulled" out of position on the place kick?

9. Is the holder on the place kick a quarterback capable of passing the football?

10. How far can the punter punt and the kicker kick?

## Punt Return

1. Does the opposition concentrate on rushing the punter or returning the punt?

2. How well do they return punts?

3. Who is the most dangerous punt returner?

4. Do they tip the rush or the return?

5. Do they try to detain the offensive linemen?

6. To which side do they usually try to return the punt?

## Kick-off Returns

1. Where do they usually try to return the kick?

2. Who is the most dangerous returner?

3. Do they cross block up front?

4. Is a wedge used and where does it form?

5. When the ball is kicked to one side, is the return to that side automatic?

6. Will changing lanes confuse the blocking up front?

## Kick-offs

1. Will the kicker be intimidated by assigning a blocker to him?

2. Do the men covering stay in their lanes?

3. Where is the team most vulnerable on a return?

4. How do they line up to cover kicks?

5. Who is the safety man?

6. Will cross blocking be effective?

7. What is the usual height and depth of the kick-off?

The game plan is vitally important to the success of any team. In professional football a minimum fine of $500 is imposed on any player who loses his game plan or scouting report, both of which are normally presented to the players on Tuesday morning, after a Sunday game.

To the players, the game plan is merely a list of plays to be practiced and used in the upcoming game. Most players, excluding the quarterback, are more interested in the scouting report. Here is where they will be given information about the opposition that will help them to perform more efficiently. (Most players, in fact, never even see the frequency charts on which the final reports are based.) The offensive lineman is interested only in the ability of the man playing opposite him and where he is likely to align himself in various defenses. The receivers want to know about the defenders that will be covering them. The set backs are interested in how the defenders are likely to react when plays are run at them.

Although the game plan is important, it may be overrated. Some teams make significant adjustments in their offensive and defensive game plan to suit the opposition each week. Other coaches believe in simplicity and attempt to use basic plays that can be effective against all defenses, and basic defenses that do not require major adjustments against any offensive formation. There are examples of success using both philosophies. Football can be made very complicated or extremely basic. It all depends on the inclination of the coach. The only thing that can be said with certainty is that all teams scout and watch movies of the opposition.

Before the advent of movies, teams were often taken by surprise when the opposition assumed a radically different formation. A spread formation would present a problem until the coach was able to make adjustments on the sidelines. It can still present a problem if the defense is not prepared because the offense never showed the formation before. The difference made by the exchanging of films is that a radical departure from the norm can only be used on rare occasions. The team that does come up with a revolutionary change is hampered by the fact that every other coach in the league will have the opportunity to study it and perhaps steal it by the next game. There may be new approaches to football, but nothing stays new for very long.

The extensive use of films has not only done much to neutralize the advantage of wealthy teams that could afford extensive scouting staffs, but has done much to improve the caliber of individual play. Films often reveal mistakes that the naked eye cannot see. The very fact that a player can see his own mistakes makes a tremendous difference. He will learn faster at the lower levels and be better prepared for his opponent at all levels. As he prepares for the upcoming game, he has an opportunity to see what the scouting report describes in detail. Best of all, no team or individual can claim a disadvantage because of fewer scouts.

Of course, new fangled innovations lead to new fangled complaints. Sometimes coaches will complain that opposing coaches have deleted key plays or were late in delivering game films. A team may not be expecting the triple reverse, if the play was taken out of the previous week's film. (This is another reason teams still use live scouts.) When films are delivered late, it gives the opposition less time to prepare the game plan.

The secret to winning football is very often simplicity. The more basic the offensive attack, the less chance of error. The team that makes the fewest errors frequently wins. Once again, the maxim that states that football is a game of execution, and not deception, applies. The most effective game plans are often the simplest, and based on the obvious. Don't allow yourself to be overwhelmed by the esoteric language and the type of coach that deliberately or inadvertently develops a mystique about coaching or the game plan. Take a prolonged look at any two teams you are familiar with, and you are likely to call the areas the offense will attack with the run and pass almost as well as the coaches.

# Part Six

# THE LANGUAGE OF FOOTBALL

**Angle Block**—A blocking maneuver carried out by a player from the offense from the side rather than straight ahead. The angle block is considered to be easier than blocking a player directly in front of the offensive lineman since it usually does not require the blocker to move the defender back off the line of scrimmage. Some teams take wide splits in the offensive line in order to provide good blocking angles for the offensive linemen.

**Area Blocking** (*also called* **Zone Blocking**)—When the members of the offensive line block anyone in a predetermined area of the field. The alternative is man blocking, when each offensive lineman is responsible for a specific man. The area block is used to enable the offensive line to block defensive linemen that are stunting or working games. Because the offensive linemen are responsible for an area rather than an individual, they might find themselves blocking people other than those directly opposite them in the event of "stunting" or "gaming" by the defense.

It is easier for the offensive line to area block when pass protecting, but most teams use the same approach against the run or pass. You might expect the offensive line to be beaten the first time the defense uses a stunt or game, but, after that, they should be on the alert and make the adjustment. Man blocking is much more difficult and not used as often as the area block.

**Audible** (*also called* **Automatic** *or* **Check Off**)—The quarterback changes the play at the line of scrimmage by giving a predetermined verbal signal to alert his team, and then gives numbers that designate a new play. The quarterback may use the audible when the entire defense is in a new alignment that he did not anticipate, or when one defensive player is out of position. There is no reason to use the audible if the defense turns out to be what the quarterback expected. At times, when the defense is changing often, and the quarterback does not know what to expect, he may not call a play in the huddle at all. He'll merely say "check with me" in the huddle, and call the play at the line of scrimmage. There are games when the quarterback may not use any audibles, and others when he will be forced to use them on almost every series of downs.

**Automatic** (*see* **Audible**)

**Back Judge**—An official who lines up on the same side of the field as the line judge and counts the number of defensive players. He also checks when the ball is dead, and sounds his whistle on continuing action fouls. He assists in decisions on catching, recovery, out of bounds and illegal touching of a loose ball. He and the field judge are on the goal line and they are responsible for indicating whether a field goal is high enough and through the uprights. He also has pass interference responsibility.

**Balanced Attack**—A team is said to have a balanced attack if it can move the ball effectively by passing and running. This does not necessarily imply that a team must run and pass an equal number of times during each game or even over the course of a season. A team has a balanced attack when the threat of the run and pass is ever-present, and the defense is forced to remain in a position to defend against either one. When a team is known to be more potent either on the ground or through the air, the defense may align itself so as to overdefend against the opposition's strength.

**Balanced Line**—An equal number of offensive linemen on each side of center. Although the offensive ends are technically considered to be part of the offensive line, they are not considered in determining a balanced or unbalanced line.

Balanced line

Unbalanced line

**Ball Control**—A ball control offense stresses mainly running plays in an effort to keep the clock running while marching up the field. Pass plays attempted when a team is trying to control the ball will normally be short and rarely thrown close to the sideline to prevent the receiver from being thrown out of bounds and stopping the clock.

In pro football, ball control is used when a team is attempting to protect a lead. However, many high school and college teams consider ball control to be a particular philosophy of offense. The theory of the ball control offense is that the opposition cannot score unless they have the ball. If a team can keep the ball most of the time it is more likely to have more points on the scoreboard at the end of the game. A team using a ball control attack will pass the football, but only to keep the defense honest.

**Belly Play** (*also called* **Ride**)—An offensive play where the quarterback fakes a hand off to one back and then moves toward the line of scrimmage with the back receiving the hand off. The belly play is run between the tackles.

**Bird Cage**—The face mask, made of steel tubing, worn by a lineman. It protects the face well, but is seldom worn by backs and receivers since it is more difficult to see out of than the single or double bar mask.

**Blind Slide**—When a player is hit from an angle that does not allow him to see the approaching block. This is a chief contributor to knee injuries since the player being blind sided does not have an opportunity to protect himself or neutralize his opponent's block or tackle. Under normal conditions, when a player is hit with a low tackle or block in the area of his knees, he will try to leave the ground with both feet an instant before contact is made. He does this, when he cannot avoid contact, to prevent a possible knee injury which is more likely to occur when his cleats are planted in the ground. The player that is blind sided does not have an opportunity to take this simple precautionary measure, and a knee or ankle injury often results.

**Blitz** (*also called* **Red Dog** *or* **Dog**)—When one or more of the linebackers or members of the defensive secondary charges across the line of scrimmage at the snap of the ball in an attempt to throw the ball carrier for a loss of yardage. This leaves the defense vulnerable to certain offensive plays, but can result in a turnover or big loss for the offense. It is somewhat of a gamble and is often used by a team that is behind and needs the big play. The blitz is used most often in a passing situation, but there are teams that will use it on any down. The running backs are assigned to pick up the blitzing corner linebackers and deep backs coming from the defensive secondary. The center is responsible for the middle linebacker coming from the standard pro defense (the 4-3).

**Blocked Kick**—A kick is considered blocked when a member of a defensive team obstructs the football after it has been kicked by the kicking team. The ball is free and may be advanced by the recovering team. After a conversion or extra point attempt has been blocked, the ball is dead and may not be advanced.

**Blocking**—Keeping a defensive player from the ball carrier by a member of the offensive team. The offensive player can use any part of his body except his hands. He may not hook his arms around the defender. Tripping is also prohibited.

**Blocking Angle**—The position at which an offensive player puts a block on a defender and which enables him to keep his body between the defender and the ball carrier. It is easier to throw a block from the side, than when the defender is directly opposite the blocker.

**Blocking Back**—Any offensive back that is used primarily as a block. In the old single wing formation the blocking back was the quarterback lined up about one and a half yards behind the line of scrimmage between the guard and tackle. He blocked for tha ball carrier most of the time.

**Bomb**—A long pass usually thrown to a wide receiver in an attempt to score quickly. There is a greater chance of an interception when the ball is thrown deep into the opposition's territory. Throwing the bomb out of desperation will make the chance of an interception even greater. It is usually not wise to throw the bomb when everyone in the stadium is looking for it and the opposition is in a prevent defense.

**Bootleg**—An offensive play that requires the quarterback to fake to an offensive back going around one end and keep the ball in an attempt to run around the opposite end without any lead blockers in front of him. The play is usually called near the goal line when the defensive team can be expected to react quickly to the flow of the offensive backfield. Another reason for saving the bootleg for short yardage situations is that the quarterback is usually not one of the team's better runners and is not expected to outrun the defense for long yardage. The quarterback usually tries to hide the ball against his hip while running with the ball, hence the name *bootleg*.

**Broken Backfield**—When the offensive backs are not aligned in the traditional T formation backfield in which the fullback lines up directly behind the quarterback and the two halfbacks are on either side and slightly in front of the fullback. In a broken backfield, there can be one or two offensive backs in any conceivable alignment.

**Broken Field Running** (*also called* **Open Field Running**)—When a running back has passed the line of scrimmage and has relatively few defenders between himself and the goal line. It provides an opportunity to utilize maneuvers that are not practical when going through the line of scrimmage.

**Broken Pattern** (*also called* **Broken Route**)—When a receiver does not run the pass route called by the quarterback in the huddle. This can be caused by a mental error, or an adjustment forced by the play of the defense.

**Brush Block**—A block deliberately delivered by an offense player at less than full impact. It is used to set up the defensive player of another block by a different offensive player, or to mislead the defense by making it believe that a potential receiver is blocking for the run.

The brush block is used most often by an offensive lineman hitting a defensive lineman before going through to block a linebacker. It is also used by the backs and tight ends to destroy the keys of the defense before going out on a pass route.

**Bullet Pass**—A pass thrown hard and straight. There is usually less chance of an interception when the pass is thrown hard, but on short passes, the ball can be thrown too hard. The quarterback throwing between the linebackers over the middle is more likely to throw the bullet than in other situations.

**Bump and Go** (*also called* **Bump and Run**)—A defensive maneuver where the defensive back lines up as close as possible to a receiver on the line of scrimmage and makes repeated contact with him as he runs downfield. Now, basically illegal.

**Button Hook** (*see* **Hook**)

**Cab Squad** (*also called* **Taxi Squad** *or* **Band Squad**)—Players that practice with a team daily, but are not on the active roster and are ineligible to play. They are usually under contract to the team and may be activated if another player is injured.

The name taxi or cab squad originated when the owner of an N.F.L. team employed these players as cab drivers for one of his enterprises when they were not playing football. The taxi squad has helped many teams insure against injuries and has helped many players gain valuable experience which enabled them to eventually make the team.

**Check Off** (*see* **Audible**)

**Clipping**—Blocking a defensive player from the rear. This is an illegal act unless committed on the line of scrimmage. The penalty is 15 yards from the point of the clip. The clip sometimes becomes a judgment call when the defensive player turns his back to the offensive blocker as he is about to throw the block. The official that sees the defensive player turn his body will probably not call the penalty.

**Clothesline**—When a defensive player swings an extended arm at the head or neck of an offensive player attempting to run by him. Now illegal, it was once a favorite maneuver of defensive ends and linebackers on unsuspecting receivers moving down or across the field. The offensive player often reacted as if he had run into a clothesline at neck height; hence the term.

**Conversion**—The point attempted after a touchdown. In pro or college football, the place kick is used almost exclusively. However, the ball can also be run or thrown over the goal line. When the point after touchdown or conversion is kicked, the ball must travel over the cross bar and between the goal posts. The ball must be kicked from no closer than the two yard line where the ball is placed by the official for the snap by the center.

**Corner Route** (*also called* **Flag Route**)—When the receiver makes his *final* break towards the corner of the end zone where the flag is located. The receiver may make different moves each time he runs this route, but his final move will always be in the direction of the corner. It requires a stronger arm to throw the corner pass than those that break over the middle, since the receiver is moving away from the quarterback.

**Cornerback**—A defensive back aligned to the outside of the safety and corner linebacker. The cornerback is usually assigned to cover the flanker or end, and is generally among the fastest men on the team.

**Count**—The number or word in the signal system on which the ball will be snapped to the quarterback and on which the offensive will move.

The count should be varied to prevent anticipation on the part of the defense. Defensive teams can sometimes be drawn offside if the quarterback has been calling one count repeatedly and then suddenly changes it to a later count without altering the original cadence.

**Counter Play**—A type of offensive backfield action that requires the flow to go in one direction and the ball carrier to move into the line going the opposite way. The ball carrier is often required to take a step in the direction of the flow before moving in the opposite direction to take the hand off. Counter action is normally used on plays run between the offensive tackles.

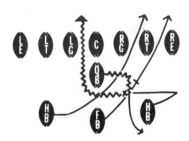

**Coverage**—The type of alignments and methods of defending against the pass in the defensive secondary. A team can use man to man coverage, zone coverage or a combination coverage.

**Crackback Block**—A block thrown by an offensive player moving from an outside alignment toward the center of the field. It will usually be a

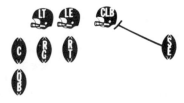

wide receiver blocking in on the corner linebacker, but it can be a man in motion blocking back on someone to his inside. The crackback is the block that often makes the sweep a success.

**Crawling**—An attempt to advance the ball after the official has blown the ball dead. A five yard penalty is supposed to result, but is rarely called in pro football where a ball carrier can get up off the ground and continue running with the football in cases where he has slipped.

**Crossing Pattern**—Two receivers crossing each other's path at a designated point downfield to avoid the defenders. Those crossing can be two wide receivers, the tight end and a wide receiver, or the backs coming out of the backfield. This maneuver sometimes succeeds in confusing the defense allowing one receiver to break free.

**Crowding the Receiver**—When the defensive player covers the receiver tightly, but does not make contact.

**Cup** (*also known as* **Pocket**)—The protective formation of the five interior linemen as they set up to protect the quarterback dropping back to pass. The offensive guards attempt to hold the defensive tackles on the line of scrimmage while the offensive tackles try to ride the defensive ends to the outside. The quarterback is frequently

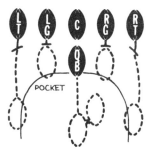

required to "step up into the pocket" if the defensive ends are closing in on him. Stepping up allows the offensive tackles to keep their bodies between the quarterback and the defensive ends.

**Cutback** (*also known as* **Veer** *or* **Going against the Grain**)—When the ball carrier changes his direction to avoid tacklers. This can be a predetermined move on the part of the runner or the result of an active defense closing in on the hole into which the runner was to move. The term "going against the grain" comes from the fact that the defensive people are going in one direction and the back breaks the other way. The *veer* or *cutback* can be to the inside or outside. The terms are used interchangeably but technically the *cutback* occurs when the back cuts to the inside in the direction from which he came, and the *veer* when the back cuts to the outside when the play was designed to go inside. In either case, the ball carrier is going against the grain.

**Cutdown**—A player is cut down or simply cut when he is the victim of a body block either downfield or on the line of scrimmage. A cutdown can be the result of either a cross body block or a shoulder block, but, in either case, it implies a low block below the waist. If a player is knocked down from a high block, he has been "runover," "creamed," or "decked."

**Cut Off Block**—When an offensive player positions himself between the ball carrier and a defender. The block is rarely thrown at the point of attack, which eliminates the necessity of the offensive player moving the defender. The cut off block may be accomplished by a body block, shoulder block or by any other means of preventing the defender from moving laterally. This is a term normally used to describe the assignment of an off-side lineman. He does not have to block his opponent, but merely cut him off.

**Deep Man** (*see* **Long Man**)

**Deep Receiver** (*see* **Long Man**)

**Defensive Holding**—Illegal use of hands by a defensive player *before* the ball is thrown. Pass interference would be called if it occurred after the ball is in the air. The penalty is usually called when a member of the defensive team prevents an offensive player from releasing when attempting to run a pass route. However, it can be called any time a defensive player holds an offensive player's shirt and refuses to release him. The penalty is five yards and an automatic first down.

**Delay** (*see* **Draw Play**)

**Delay Flare** (*see* **Delay Pass**)

**Delay of Game**—When the offensive team fails to begin play within a specified period of time. Usually called when the ball is not snapped within 25 seconds after the referee declares the ball in play.

**Delay Pass** (*also called* **Delay Flare**)—A pass pattern where a potential receiver blocks or fakes a block before running his pass route. It is normally confined to the tight end and set backs, since the defenders assigned to them are likely to move elsewhere if their offensive men do not go out on a pass route eventually freeing them as receivers. The defenders assigned to cover the wide receivers, on the other hand, will stay with them wherever they go.

**Dive**—A running play where the back lines up almost directly behind the hole and runs straight into the line with no faking. The success of the play depends on the quickness of the hand off and the back's ability to

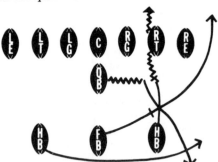

cut if the predetermined hole is closed. The dive is often used in conjunction with option blocking. It is one of the two or three bread and butter plays of the split T, but is used with almost every offensive attack.

**Dog** (*See* **Blitz**)

**Double Coverage** (*also known as* **Double Teaming**)—When two defen-

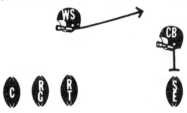

ders are assigned to cover one receiver as he runs his pass route. One defender is usually assigned to guard the receiver short and the other long. The defender assigned to the shallow area will often make contact with the receiver as he leaves the line of scrimmage. He attempts to force him to alter his release and route and tries to destroy the timing between him and the quarterback.

**Double Team Blocking**—When two offensive blockers are assigned to block a defensive player. The frequency of the double team block has diminished of late as offensive formations place increased emphasis on speed. The double team block occurred on almost every play run from the single wing formation.

The double team block used in present-day offensive formations is likely to employ a lineman and a back blocking on one defensive lineman. Also considered a double team block is when one offensive player sets up the block for another with a brush block.

**Double Wing**—An offensive formation in which one offensive player is positioned just outside the weak side tackle. The rest of the pro-set remains the same with two wide receivers and a tight end. The player outside and slightly behind the weak side offensive tackle is usually a

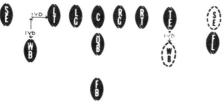

set back, but he can be a receiver sent in to replace one back. The advantage of the double wing is the speed with which the wing back can get downfield. He is also in good position to block to the inside. The weakness is the fact that only one back remains behind the quarterback.

**Down**—A unit of game action. A team has four opportunities to run a play from the line of scrimmage in an attempt to travel ten yards. A down starts with the snap of the ball and ends when the play is completed. When a team has succeeded in moving the football ten yards or more on any given down, it is said to have made a first down. It then has four more chances to make another first down or score a touchdown.

**Down and In**—Any pass route that requires the receiver to run straight downfield and then cut over the middle. The angle of the cut is not clearly defined because of the different terminology used by each team.

**Down and Out**—Any pass route that requires the receiver to run straight downfield and then cut to the outside or sideline. The angle of the cut is not clearly defined.

**Downfield**—To the offensive team, any area on the other side of the line of scrimmage is considered downfield.

**Downfield Block**—Any block thrown beyond the line of scrimmage on one of the defensive players. Downfield blocks are generally more difficult to execute than blocks delivered at the line of scrimmage.

**Draw Play** (*also called* **Delay**)—A running play designed to look like a show pass and draw the defensive players across the line as they would when rushing the passer. The quarterback begins to drop back to pass and then hands off to a running back who carries through the line. The

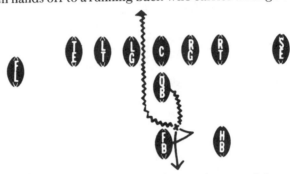

offensive line sets up as it would on the show pass and then tries to take its opponents to one side or the other. The back will run wherever the hole develops. The draw play is particularly effective against a hard charging defensive line and can help to slow down the pass rush if the play is successful.

**Drop Kick**—When the kicker drops the ball and kicks it the instant it makes contact with the ground. This used to be the standard way to kick field goals and points after touchdown.

**Eating the Football**—When the quarterback, trapped behind the line of scrimmage, elects to take a loss rather than throw the ball away and risk an interception. In the event that the quarterback does not see the onrushing defensive player, he is said to be "sacked."

**Eligible Receiver**—Any one of five players on the offensive team eligible to receive a forward pass. Under normal conditions, the two ends and three backfield men (lined up a yard or more behind the line) are eligible. On rare occasions, an interior lineman will become eligible when he is the last man on either side of the line. The quarterback is also an eligible receiver when not passing the ball.

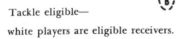

Tackle eligible—

white players are eligible receivers.

**End**—The men that line up on either end of the offensive line. They are eligible to catch a forward pass, and may line up anywhere as long as they remain at the end of the line of scrimmage.

**End Around**—A reverse with either the split end or tight end carrying the ball around the opposite end. The end hesitates at the line of scrimmage for a second and then comes behind the quarterback to take the hand off from him. It is one of those plays that can only be run occasionally since it relies on deception and not execution. The defensive team that reads it early will stop it quickly.

When the flanker runs the play, it is still called the end around despite the fact that the flanker is technically a back.

**End Line**—The last boundary line at each end of the field. The end of the end zone.

**End Zone**—The ten-yard area between the goal line and the end line.

**Even Defense**—Any defensive alignment that does not place a player directly opposite the center on the line of scrimmage. The number of people lined up on the line, at linebacker and in the secondary has no effect in determining whether a defense is even or odd.

**Extra Point**—The conversion or point after touchdown scored by kicking the ball through the uprights, or by running or passing the ball over the goal line. Regardless of how it is scored, it is worth one point.

**Face Guarding**—When a defensive back deliberately obstructs an offensive receiver's vision by placing his hands in front of the receiver's face, or waving his arms frantically. The resulting penalty places the ball at the point of the infraction with a first down.

**Face Masking**—Holding a player by the face mask in an attempt to delay his progress or bring down the ball carrier. It results in a 15-yard penalty if detected by the officials. Face masking is also an extremely dangerous practice.

**Fade Back**—A term used to describe the drop by the quarterback as he moves into position to throw the football on a show pass. It provides the time necessary for him to find his receivers and to release the ball.

**Fair Catch**—When the receiver of a punt feels that he will not be able to advance the ball, he has the option of calling for a fair catch with his team receiving the ball at the point of the catch. He can indicate this choice to the officials by raising one hand over his head. After the receiver signals for a fair catch, the defense cannot make contact with him without being penalized. The receiver, though, must make the catch. If he fumbles, the other team can make the recovery.

**Field Goal**—A kick resulting from a play from scrimmage which travels over the cross bar and between the uprights. The ball must be either place kicked or drop kicked. The offensive team receives three points.

**Field Judge**—The official who covers kicks from scrimmage, passes crossing the defensive goal line, and loose balls. He blows his whistle when the ball is dead or time is out and is responsible for continuing action fouls and decisions involving catching, recovery, out of bounds spot, illegal touching and loose balls across the line of scrimmage. Notifies teams five minutes before the start of the half. Watches for pass interference.

**Fill**—When a set back fills a hole by blocking a defensive lineman not blocked by the offensive lineman opposite him. The back usually fills for a pulling guard preparing a trap block or leading a sweep.

**Fire Protection** (*see* **Quick Pass Protection**)

**First Down**—Advancing the football at least ten yards in no more than four consecutive attempts, giving the offense the opportunity to keep the ball and try for another first down or touchdown.

**Flag** (*see* **Corner Pattern**)—The penalty marker thrown by an official. It is usually a colored handkerchief. Also one of the four flags that mark the four corners of the field.

**Flank** (*also called* **Flat**)—The area that begins several yards outside the tight end and extends to the sideline. It is the area in which the flanker lines up and where the sweep and flare passes are directed.

**Flanker**—An offensive player positioned six to twelve yards outside of his own tight end and one yard behind the line of scrimmage. The flanker is officially a back because only seven men can line up on the line of scrimmage. However, he is used primarily as a receiver because of his ability to get downfield quickly.

**Flare Pass** (*also called* **Swing Pass**)—A pass thrown behind the line of scrimmage to a back moving toward the sideline. The back may have faked into the line or faked a block on a rushing defensive lineman before leaving. The receiver is expected to pick up his yardage *after* receiving the football.

**Flat** (*see* **Flank**)

**Flip Flop**—When offensive or defensive players are moved from one side of the line to the other to compensate for weak personnel. The flip flop is rarely used in pro football, but some high school and college teams have a strong and weak side of the offensive line. One guard, tackle and end always line up next to each other whether it be to the right or left of the offensive center. This is supposed to make it easier for the linemen to learn the plays, and the team's best blockers can be used on the side where the play is to be directed.

The term usually pertains to the safeties in pro football. The safeties *flip flop* so that the strong safety will always line up in front of the tight end.

**Flood**—When two or more receivers are sent into one area of the defensive secondary. The maneuver is generally used to neutralize the effectiveness of the zone defense. When used against man to man coverage, the aim of the offense is to confuse or "pick" the defense by having one receiver run between another receiver and the defender assigned to cover him.

**Flood Formation**—A formation that enables a team to get many re-

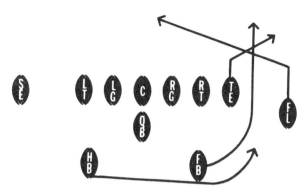

ceivers downfield quickly. It is sometimes known as a "triple" since three receivers line up on one side of the field.

**Flow**—The direction in which the set backs move on a running play or play action pass. It will either be to the right or left. The backs may flow in one direction to draw the defense with them, while the ball carrier may move the other way "against the flow."

**Fly** (*also called* **Go** *or* **Streak**)—A pass route in which a wide receiver runs straight downfield as fast as possible in an attempt to get behind the defender. There is little or no faking. A change of pace may be used by the receiver.

**Fold Block**—When one offensive lineman steps back to allow the man next to him to block the man in front of him, and then moves behind his

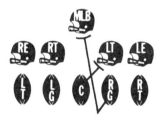

teammate to block a linebacker. It is most often used when the center blocks the defensive tackle lined up over the guard and the guard steps behind him to block the middle linebacker.

**Footsteps** (*also called* **Hearing Footsteps**)—A term used when a receiver drops the football because he was distracted by an approaching defender. It happens at all levels and is usually due to a lack of concentration on the ball.

**Forward Motion** (*also called* **Forward Progress**)—The point where the progress of the ball carrier is stopped and the ball is declared dead. Also, movement toward the opposition's goal line as distinguished from lateral or backward motion.

**Forward Pass**—Any pass thrown by a member of the offensive team which lands closer to the goal line than the point from which it was thrown.

**Forward Wall**—The five offensive linemen: the center, the two guards and the two tackles.

**Foul**—Any violation of a playing rule which leads to a penalty.

**Free Agent**—Used in pro football to designate any player not drafted by a team, but signed to a contract and given an opportunity to make the team.

**Free Kick**—Any kick where the receiving team cannot rush or otherwise interfere with the kicker. Falling into this category are kick-offs, a kick after a safety, and a kick after a fair catch. In the latter case, a field goal attempt may be made. The punt is usually used after a safety. Regardless of what kind of kick is used after a safety or fair catch, the receiving team is free to return the ball as in a regular punt or field goal attempt.

**Free Safety**—The safety not assigned to a specific offensive player. He is usually the deepest man in the defensive backfield. The free safety can be the strong side safety lined up on the side of the tight end, but more often it is the weak side safety who is free. If the strong safety is free on the play, the weak safety will probably be assigned to cover the tight end. Some coaches use the terms weak safety and free safety interchangeably. This is technically wrong since the weak safety is not always free.

**Frequency Chart**—Each alignment, formation and play run by both the offensive and defensive teams is recorded by the opposition. The frequency with which a team reacts a specific way to a given situation is noted and considered in formulating the game plan or in calling plays on the field. For example, the defensive team may have a tendency to blitz on second down and ten. This will show up on the frequency charts and should alert the offense to watch for the blitz on second and ten.

**Front Four**—The two defensive tackles and ends.

**Full House Backfield**—When the offensive team lines up in a traditional T formation with three set backs behind the quarterback and between the offensive tackles. The term is commonly used by those broadcasting pro games since the normal pro alignment employs only two set backs.

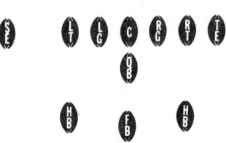

**Fullback**—In a *full house* or standard backfield alignment, the fullback lines up three or four yards directly behind the quarterback. He is usually the biggest man in the backfield and is used primarily to block and carry the ball up the middle or on off-tackle plays. In the pro-set, the fullback can be found anywhere in the backfield.

**Fumble**—When the ball carrier loses possession of the ball before the play is over. The ball is "loose" and can be recovered by any player on the field.

**Game Plan**—The offensive and defensive plans that each team prepares for each opponent. Each team's weaknesses and strengths, tendencies and preferences are considered in formulating the game plan. It is worked out by the coaching staff after viewing movies of the opposition and considering past performances against their team. It is then presented to the offensive and defensive quarterbacks who attempt to adhere to it as closely as possible during the game. Adjustments to new strategy by the opposition are often required.

**Games** (*also called* **Tricks, Stunts** *or* **Deals**)—Defensive tactics that require small groups of linemen and linebackers to exchange assignments after the snap of the ball. This is done to confuse the offensive linemen. It may involve two defensive linemen, a lineman and a

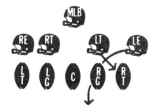

Tackle-end game

linebacker, or a combination of linemen and linebackers. The players involved in a game try not to tip their movement until after the ball is snapped. They align themselves normally and only after the snap do they assume the responsibilities of the player with whom they exchange assignments.

**Gang Tackling**—Two or more defensive players tackling the ball carrier at the same time. This is a sign of good pursuit and aggressive play by the defensive unit. It is essential against an outstanding running back in the open field where he has more room to elude the tackler.

**Gap**—The space between any two offensive or defensive linemen. The splits assumed by the offensive linemen create "gaps" in the line. Defensive linemen are told to line up in the middle of the gap between two players, or to "shoot the gap" if the distance between two players becomes wide enough.

**Gap Defense**—A defensive alignment with all the linemen being placed in the gaps between the offensive linemen. The most common gap defense is the "gap 8" which is usually used in short yardage situations. (See diagram in chapter on team defense.)

**Girdle Pad**—A type of hip pad that allows for more flexibility. It is comprised of several separate pads that fit into a cloth holder worn as shorts. It is worn most often by running backs.

**Go** (*see* **Fly**)

**Goal Line**—The line separating the field of play from the end zone. A player scores a touchdown when the ball penetrates an imaginary vertical plane that rises from the goal line. The touchdown is scored even if he is pushed back after crossing the line.

**Goal Post**—The two poles at each end of the field set 18 feet 6 inches apart and connected by a crossbar 10 feet above the ground and parallel to the end line.

**Going against the Grain** (*see* **Cutback** *and* **Veer**)

**Gridiron**—Term for the playing field rarely used by those involved with the game, except when being facetious. Comes from the visual effect of the lines on the field.

**Grounding**—A rule infraction called when, in the official's judgment, the passer intentionally threw the ball away to avoid being tackled for a loss of yardage behind the line of scrimmage. This is a judgment call and the location of the nearest receiver is the determining factor. In recent years, officials have begun to clamp down on this violation.

**Guard (Offensive)**—The two offensive linemen on either side of the center are the offensive guards. They are important players to watch since their duties frequently carry them to the center of the offensive action when pulling out of the line to trap block or lead interference on the sweep.

**Gun Shy**—Used to describe young players who shy away from contact. Also used to describe the actions of experienced players on particular plays when they attempt to avoid contact. Most often this will occur following a play when a player was injured or hit unusually hard. Players won't admit it, but most of them are gun shy at one time or another.

**Half the Distance**—Any time a penalty would move the ball more than half the distance between the point of the infraction and the goal line, the penalty is reduced to half the distance to the goal line.

**Halfbacks (Defensive)**—The term used on the high school and college levels in place of cornerback.

**Halfbacks (Offensive)**—The two running backs lined up on either side of the fullback in the traditional T alignment. In a broken backfield, the halfback may be aligned anywhere in the offensive backfield. The halfback is normally smaller and faster than the fullback.

**Halftime**—The 20-minute time interval between the first and second halves of a game.

**Hand Fighter**—A defensive lineman who uses his hands to ward off the offensive blocker in order to make the tackle on the runner or get to the passer.

**Hand Off**—An exchange of the football from one offensive player to another.

**Hash Mark**—The set of short lines placed perpendicular to the yard markers 23 yards inside each sideline. If a play ends outside the hash lines, the ball is next put in play from the hash mark. In college and high school football they are 20 yards inside each sideline.

**Hat**—The players' term for the helmet. The phrase "put the hat on him" is another way of saying that a player hit another player hard.

**Head Linesman**—The official who checks offsides, is responsible for the chain crew, and marks forward progress. He also sees if any linemen have crossed the line prior to the pass, marks out of bounds on his side of the field, and watches for illegal receivers.

**High-Low Block (or Tackle)**—When two men are involved in a block or tackle. One makes contact with the upper part of the opponent's body while the other hits the lower part of his body.

**Hitch Routs (see Hook Route)**

**Hook and Go**—A pass route in which the receiver runs the hook route and, after hesitating long enough for the defender to close the gap between them, breaks downfield for a long pass.

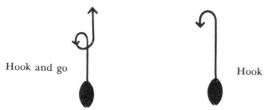

Hook and go                    Hook

**Hook Route (also called Button Hook or Hitch)**—A pass route in which a receiver runs downfield and suddenly stops and turns to face the quarterback. It is usually run eight to twelve yards downfield, and the quarterback attempts to release the ball before the receiver stops and turns to face him. The receiver normally takes a few steps back toward the line as the ball approaches.

**I Formation**—A formation in which two or three backs line up in a straight line directly behind the quarterback. Some teams place the tight end behind the quarterback. In this case it is called the stack I formation.

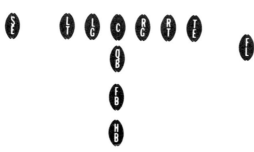

**Illegal Forward Pass**—A pass thrown *after* the quarterback has crossed the line of scrimmage or when he throws to an ineligible receiver.

**Illegal Procedure**—Movement of a member of the offensive line after the team has been set. The movement may be in any direction except across the line of scrimmage, which would result in an offside penalty. Once the offensive lineman places his hand on the ground, he cannot remove it.

**In Motion**—When an eligible receiver runs parallel to or obliquely back from the line of scrimmage before the ball is put in play.

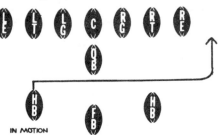

IN MOTION

**Ineligible Receiver** (*also see* **Eligible Receiver**)—An interior offensive lineman (tackle, guard, or center) may not touch a forward pass, or go downfield until after the ball is thrown. They are ineligible receivers. The penalty is 15 yards in either case.

**Influence Block**—Partial contact made by an offensive player designed to cause a defensive player to move a certain way to help set up another block on the defender.

**Inside**—An informal term usually used to refer to the area between the two offensive tackles. A running play designed to break from tackle to tackle is said to go to the "inside." A play breaking outside the offensive tackles breaks to the "outside."

The term is also used to describe a move of the offensive receivers. A receiver that moves toward the center of the field is said to make an *inside* move. A receiver that breaks toward the sideline makes an *outside* move.

**Intentional Grounding** (*see* **Grounding**)

**Interception**—When a defensive player catches a pass intended for an offensive player. Once the ball has been passed it can be caught by an eligible receiver or member of the defensive team. After intercepting the ball, the receiver may return it as far as he can. The intercepting team keeps possession of the football.

**Keeper**—A play in which the quarterback keeps possession of the ball and runs with it himself. It usually occurs in short yardage situations.

**Keys** (*also see* **Reading**)—When a player watches an opponent to try to predict what he is most likely to be doing, he is said to be keying on him. Some of the keys which are used are position, stance, and eye direction. The keys that a player reads on his opponent will affect his actions on that play.

**Kicking Tee**—A rubber object designed to hold the football in an upright position in order to enable the kicker to kick off without anyone holding the ball for him. The tee is not ordinarily used on place kicks.

**Kick-Off**—A free kick used to put the ball in play at the start of the game, at the start of the second half and following touchdowns or field goals.

**Lateral** (*also see* **Pitch**)—A pass thrown to the side or backwards, either overhand or underhand. It may be thrown from any place on the field from one player to another. If fumbled, the defensive team may recover the ball but may not advance it. The lateral may be part of a pre-designed play or be an impromptu action to pick up additional yardage. A lateral becomes a forward pass if the ball ends up closer to the goal line than the point from which it was thrown.

**Line Judge**—The official responsible for timing the game—records all charged time outs—winner of toss—and score. Notes illegal motion behind the line or illegal shift. Times each period and intermission between halves, and, with the field judge, notifies five minutes before the second half. Fires pistol to indicate end of each period. Notifies the referee when two minutes remain in each half. On his side, checks encroachment. Assists the umpire with holding. Assists referee with false starts and forward laterals, and is responsible to know the eligible pass receivers. He marks out of bounds on his side of the field.

**Line of Scrimmage**—An imaginary line extending from sideline to sideline and through the middle of the ball. The offensive and defensive lines take positions on either side of the line of scrimmage to start each play. It is generally referred to as the "line."

**Linebacker**—A defensive player that usually lines up three yards behind the line of scrimmage, between the defensive linemen and the defensive secondary. His primary responsibility will vary according to the game situation. In short yardage situations, he is responsible for stopping the run. In long yardage situations, he becomes primarily responsible for the pass.

**Linesman** (*also called* **Head Linesman**)—The official primarily responsible for actions pertaining to infractions on the line of scrimmage prior to the snap of the ball, such as offsides. The linesmen also follows the play action on his side of the field, and is in charge of the chain crew.

**Live Color**—The color pre-designated as the one to signal an audible at the line of scrimmage (see **Audible**). There may be more than one live color and it may be changed during the course of the game.

**Loft**—A long, high pass that the receiver has an opportunity to run under, as opposed to a bullet pass. The quarterback usually lofts the ball on a "go" route.

**Log Block**—When a trapping offensive lineman blocks his man to the inside rather than attempts to drive him out beyond the hole. It is used against hard charging defensive linemen who close the hole quickly.

**Long Man** (*also called* **Deep Man** *or* **Deep Receiver**)—The receiver that is farthest downfield on a given pass pattern.

**Look-In**—A quick pass over the center. It is usually thrown immediately after the quarterback takes the snap from the center, but can be used to

describe any route where the receiver runs straight downfield and then breaks over the middle.

**Looping** (*also see* **Stunting Defense**)—A maneuver on a stunting defense that requires one of the defensive players involved in the stunt to move slightly backward and around a teammate in a looping manner.

**Loose Ball**—A ball in play but not in the possession of any player. It may be recovered by anyone on either team.

**Man-Head-On** (*also called* **Man-On-Nose**)—When a defensive player is lined up on the line of scrimmage in a three or four point stance directly opposite an offensive lineman.

**Man in Motion**—The action of back running behind the line in his own backfield before the snap of the ball. A back may run parallel to or obliquely back from the line of scrimmage. Only one man may be in motion at a given time and he may not be running toward the line of scrimmage. The man in motion is used to cause the defense to make last-minute adjustments.

**Man to Man Coverage**—A type of coverage in the defensive secondary in which each defender is assigned to a specific receiver. Against the standard pro-set, the cornerbacks are assigned to the wide receivers, the strong safety to the tight end, the weak side safety to a set back (or remains free), and the linebackers to the set backs.

**Middle Linebacker**—In the traditional pro 4-3 defense, the linebacker in the middle of the offensive line facing the offensive center. He will be aligned one to four yards from the ball, depending on the situation.

**Mike**—A term used by many teams to identify the middle linebacker.

**Multiple Foul**—Two or more fouls by the same team on the same down.

**Multiple Offense**—An offensive attack utilizing many different offensive formations. The purpose of the multiple offense is to utilize the best formation for each play, to keep the defense guessing, and to make it more difficult for the defense to pick up tip-offs. When a team aligns itself in the same formation on every play, there is a tendency for the offensive players to cheat, at times, in order to get into better position to accomplish particular assignments. This is not necessary when a team runs a multiple offense, since, theoretically, each formation is the best for the play called.

**Near Back**—The offensive back positioned on the side of the line to which the play is designed to go. The back on the opposite side is the far back.

**Neutral Zone**—The area between the offensive and defensive lines defined by the length of the ball.

**Odd Defense** (*also called* **Odd Front**)—A defensive line spacing with a defensive lineman placed directly opposite the offensive center. The man opposite the center is usually the defensive tackle, but may be the defensive end.

**Offset Defense**—A defense in which one of the defensive tackles (usually the weak side tackle) lines up in the gap between the offensive guard and the center. It is a variation of the 4-3 defense used to beef up the defense against the strong side of the offensive line.

**Off-Side**—The side of the line opposite that to which the play is being run. The players on the off-side are sometimes designated the off-side guard, the off-side tackle, the off-side back, etc.

**Offside Penalty**—Movement by any player, either offensive or defensive, *across* the line of scrimmage before the snap. The penalty is five yards.

**One-on-One**—A situation where one offensive player and one defensive player are pitted against each other in any area of the playing field without either receiving any help from a teammate.

**On-Side**—The side of the line to which the play is directed. The players on the on-side are sometimes designated the on-side guard, the on-side tackle, the on-side back, etc.

**Onside Kick**—A short kick-off tried with the hope that the kicking team will recover the ball. The kick-off is a free ball. As long as the kick-off travels more than ten yards, it can be recovered by either team. The onside kick is normally used when a team is behind by several touchdowns or when little time remains in a close game. It is strictly a gamble since, when it fails, it gives the opposition the ball at mid-field.

**Open Field**—An area beyond the line of scrimmage free of defenders.

**Option Blocking**—A type of blocking for running plays that allows the offensive lineman to fire into the middle of the defensive player and drive him in any direction that the defender chooses to move. The running back keys the block and moves away from the defensive player. The option block is easier to deliver than the shoulder block that requires a man to be moved in a given direction. In many cases, in the option block, the offensive blocker does not have to drive his opponent off the line, but merely has to keep contact long enough for the back to run by the man being blocked.

**Option Pass** (*also called* **Run Pass**)—A play which starts out as a sweep with the running back then having the option of continuing to run or throwing a pass. His decision will be influenced by the play of the deep backs covering the receiver on the side to which he is running. If a deep back comes up to cover the run, the running back will pass the football.

If he stays with the receiver, the back will continue to run.

**Option Running** (*see* **Pick-a-Hole**)

**Outside**—The area between the tight end and the sideline on one side and the weak side tackle and the sideline on the other.

**Over the Top**—When a running back attempts to dive over the offensive and defensive lines in an attempt to get the first down or go over the goal line. It is a move by the back to counter the effect of submarining defensive linemen. It is only used when the distance to be made is short and the defense can be expected to tighten.

**Overshift**—An alignment by the defensive team where the linemen are set strong to one side of the line, lining up more men on one side than on the other to counter offensive formation strength.

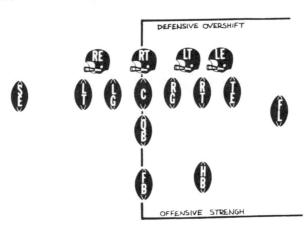

**Pass Interference**—The illegal action of a player keeping an eligible man from getting to or catching a forward pass. It can be called on either the offense or the defense. Both men have an equal right to the ball and may collide without penalty as long as they are going for the ball. The penalty for defensive interference is a first down at the spot of the foul; for offensive interference it is 15 yards from the line of scrimmage.

**Pass Pattern**—A combination of pass routes by two or more receivers. The term is used interchangeably with pass route, which is the individual path and faking movements used by a receiver to elude the defender and get into a position to catch the ball. In this book, a distinction is made between route and pattern.

**Pass Protection**—The act of keeping defensive players away from the passer until he throws the football. The type of protection will vary with the type of pass being thrown. See *show pass* and *quick pass protection*.

**Penalty Marker** (*also called* **Flag**)—A piece of cloth carried by an official and thrown to the ground after calling a rule violation.

**Personal Foul**—A major penalty resulting in a loss of 15 yards called against the team of an offensive or defensive player guilty of commit-ting an illegal act of aggression against another player. Personal fouls are called for such things as unncessary roughness, clipping, hurdling, piling on, striking with fists, kicking, and running into the passer or kicker.

**Pick**—When one receiver attempts to get into a position to prevent a defender from covering a teammate. Downfield blocking is not per-mitted on a pass play, but the receivers are permitted to run anywhere they please. Therefore, one receiver may "accidently" run a route which will impede the movement of a pass defender. This sometimes occurs accidently, but is more frequently planned.

**Pick-a-Hole** (*also known as* **Option Running**)—When the running back is given the option of running any place a hole develops. This is a style of running that goes along with option blocking by the offensive line. The runner must look at the blocking up front as he approaches the line and picks the open hole. He will usually key one of the offensive or defensive linemen.

**Piling On**—A 15-yard penalty resulting when a player deliberately jumps or falls on the ball carrier or anyone else, after the whistle has blown. It is often a judgment call since a player frequently has difficulty in stopping.

**Pitch** (*also known as a* **Toss, Lateral,** *or* **Pitchout**)—An underhand or overhand throw either to the side or backwards. The terms "pitch" and "toss" are usually confined to laterals made by the quarterback when moving along the line of scrimmage. The term "lateral" is more frequently used when a player passes to the side or backwards in the open field.

**Place Kick**—A general term which includes the field goal attempt, point after touchdown, and kick-off. The ball is kicked in each case from a fixed position on the ground. It may be held there by another player in all situations, but a kicking tee may be used for the kick-off.

**Play Action Pass**—A pass play on which a running play is first faked by the offensive team. The offensive line fires out as they would on the run; the running back fakes into the line as he would on the run; and the quarterback fakes the hand off to him before looking downfield for his receiver. The object is to make the defensive team think it is executing a running play and hopefully cause the defensive secondary to come up to stop the run.

**Play Book**—The notebook used to hold all offensive and defensive plays, and other notes regarding team play and individual assign-ments. The plays may be printed, mimeographed or hand written.

**Play Progression**—A series of offensive plays, each having the same or similar action. For example, the flow of the backs and the initial movement of the offensive line is the same on the trap play as on the sweep. The object is to momentarily confuse or mislead the defense. The defensive back or linebacker keying the pulling guard has no way to know whether the guard is pulling to trap block or to lead interference on an end run. Pass plays may also be called in progression.

**Plunge**—A backfield maneuver with the fullback carrying the ball into the middle of the offensive line. The quarterback continues to move backward after the hand off to the fullback, and fakes a hand off to the halfback.

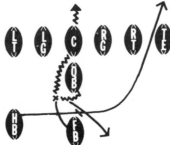

**Pocket** (*see* **Cup**)

**Pop**—A hard hit by an offensive or defensive player.

**Post Route**—A pass route in which the receiver runs downfield and breaks diagonally for the goal post on his final cut.

**Power I**—A variation of the I formation where one offensive back lines up in the traditional position of the T formation halfback behind the offensive tackle, and the remaining two backs align themselves behind

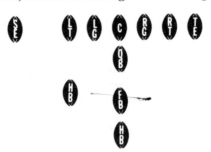

the quarterback in the I formation. It is called the power I because the offensive team has more power to the side of the back not in the I.

**Power Play**—Any play where a set back runs into a given hole before the running back carrying the football comes through.

**Power Sweep** (*also called* **Sweep**)—A term popularized during the

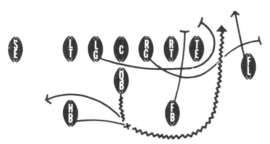

Lombardi era at Green Bay. An end run with two linemen leading interference. The other set back usually fakes into the line or blocks one of the defensive linemen. The sweep develops more slowly than the quick pitch, since the running back must "belly" back to give the off-side guard time to get out in front of him. There is no real difference between the power sweep and the sweep.

**Prevent Defense** (*also called* **Victory Defense**)—A defense used to prevent the long pass. It may involve a change in personnel or merely a change in the deployment of the people in the game. The defensive backs will line up deeper and give the receiver the opportunity to catch the short pass, but not the bomb. Some teams use only three defensive linemen when in a prevent defense. Other teams will sometimes drop a fast defensive end into pass defense. When in a prevent defense a team is in deep zone coverage.

**Primary Receiver**—The first man the quarterback will look for on a given pass play.

**Pro-Set**—The standard offensive formation used in professional football where there is a split end, tight end, flanker back, and only two set backs. The positioning of the set backs may vary from play to play,

along with the splits of the tight end and wide receivers. The advantage of the pro-set is the speed with which a maximum number of receivers can get downfield into position to catch a pass. The pro-set provides equal potential for running and passing the football.

**Pull** (*also called* **Pull Out**)—The action taken by an offensive lineman in which he quickly steps back and moves in a lateral direction to trap block or lead interference on a sweep.

**Pump**—A simulated throw by the quarterback used to get the defender to move in a particular direction. It is also used to get the free defensive backs to look and move away from the direction the quarterback will eventually throw the football.

**Punt**—The act of kicking the ball over to the defending team, usually in a fourth down situation when a team does not have a good chance at a first down and is too far away to try for a field goal. If the punted ball is untouched, it is dead where it stops and belongs to the defending team. If the ball goes out of bounds, it is put in play at that point by the defending team. If the defending team touches the ball and does not control it, it is then a "free" ball. The punting team, however, may "down" the ball by merely touching it. The receiving team takes control where the ball has been touched.

**Pursuit**—The action of the defensive team when running down the ball carrier. Good pursuit is essential for effective gang tackling and overall good defense.

**Quarterback Draw**—An offensive play designed to look like a show pass and draw the defensive linemen across the line as they would rush the

passer. The quarterback begins to drop back as he would on a show pass, and then runs the ball up the middle.

**Quarterback Sneak**—An offensive play where the quarterback takes the snap from the center and moves ahead directly behind him. The play is used in short yardage situations or when an unusually wide gap exists between the defensive linemen. The offensive line uses wedge blocking on the play. The quarterback sneak is considered a safe call in the goal line or short yardage situation since there is no hand off involved.

**Quick Kick**—When the offensive team punts unexpectedly by shifting into a short punt formation. The purpose of the quick kick is to surprise the defense and kick the ball before they can deploy a safety in a position to catch and return the kick. Because of the advantage of surprise, the quick kick usually occurs on third down.

**Quick Opener** (*also see* **Dive**)—An offensive play where the quarterback hands off to the set back going straight into the line.

**Quick Pass Protection** (*also called* **Fire Protection**)—Pass protection in which the offensive linemen fire out into the men head on them in an attempt to get their arms and hands down. The offensive player fires into the knees or lower part of the defender's body. The linemen are not expected to keep the opposition out as long as on a show pass. Quick pass protection is only used when the quarterback is expected to release the ball soon after the snap.

**Quick Release**—The ability of the quarterback to get rid of the ball quickly once he spots an open receiver.

**Reading**—When an offensive or defensive player looks at one or more keys, he is "reading" the defense or the defender. Reading takes place before and after the snap of the ball, and is more important at certain positions. Being able to read the defense to determine the type of pass coverage is extremely important to the success of a quarterback. On defense, reading the offensive backfield and the receivers is most important to the free safety.

**Red Dog** (*see* **Blitz**)

**Referee**—The official primarily responsible for control of the game. His duties include marking the ball for play; declaring the ball dead or in play; signaling rule infractions; and pacing off penalties. He is positioned behind the offensive backfield at the start of each play.

**Release**—The act of moving off the line of scrimmage and downfield. There may or may not be any contact with an opponent. The term is usually reserved for the release of a receiver who the opposition is attempting to detain on the line. There are several moves a receiver may employ in releasing.

Also refers to the release of the ball by a passer

**Remaining Back**—The offensive back not carrying the ball on a given play, or the back not leaving the backfield to run a pass route.

**Reverse**—Any play which starts in one direction, and ends up in the opposite direction. The reverse is usually run to the outside, but it can

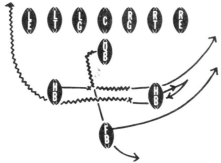

also be run off-tackle. The ball carrier may be a running back or an offensive end (end around).

**Reverse Field**—When a runner changes direction and begins to run in the opposite direction.

**Ride Action**—A type of faking in the offensive backfield that requires the quarterback to move a short distance with the running back who is faking into the line. The quarterback is said to "ride" the back into the line.

**Roll Out**—The action of a quarterback running toward one side or another before passing. There may be a preliminary fake into the line by a running back.

**Rotation**—Movement in the defensive secondary to adjust to the strength of the offensive formation or to help cover the wide side of the field. The rotation may take place before the snap of the ball, or the defensive team may attempt to hide the defensive formation by

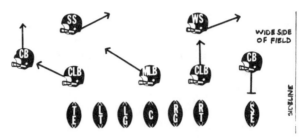

rotating *after* the snap of the ball. Rotation is normally associated with a type of zone coverage, and involves linebackers.

**Roughing the Kicker**—The rule book says that the kicker may not be touched after kicking the ball. Contact of any kind will result in a roughing the kicker penalty unless the ball is touched in the process or the defensive player is knocked into the kicker by a member of the kicker's team.

**Run Pass** (*see* **Option Pass**)

**Runback**—Return of a punt, kick-off, missed field goal or intercepted pass.

**Running Back**—Any of the offensive backs used primarily to run with the football—the fullback or either halfback in the traditional T formation.

**Rushing**—Yardage gained by the offensive team running from the line of scrimmage with the ball. Yardage gained by the kick return teams is not included in a team's total rushing yardage.

**Rushing the Passer** —Pursuit by the defense to try to throw the quarterback for a loss or force him to rush his pass.

**Sack**—When the quarterback is thrown for a loss while attempting to pass.

**Safety**—When a ball carrier on the offensive team is tackled with the ball in his own end zone. Two points are awarded to the defensive team. A safety is also scored when a punt is blocked out of the end zone, or when a bad snap or fumble rolls out of the offensive team's end zone.

When a defender intercepts a pass or catches a kick and his momentum carries him into the end zone, it is ruled a touchback and the ball is carried out to the 20-yard line.

Also refers to the deepest defenders in the secondary. See "strong safety" and "weak safety."

**Safety Blitz**—When one of the safeties in the defensive secondary leaves his normal postion after the snap of the ball and charges into the offensive backfield in an attempt to throw the ball carrier for a loss of yardage. The safety blitz is usually carried out by the weak side safety, but the strong safety will sometimes blitz. He does it less often because he is normally assigned to cover the tight end and is often slower moving than the weak safety.

**Safety Valve** (*also see* **Flare Pass**)—A short pass to one of the set backs leaving the backfield when the other receivers are covered. The set back provides a safety valve against the quarterback being thrown for a loss of yardage.

**Scat Back**—An informal term used to describe a fast, but usually small, running back. This type of back is normally used to carry the football on plays to the outside.

**Scramble**—When the quarterback is forced to leave the huddle and take evasive action after his pass protection has broken down. Scrambling can be distinguished from a roll out or play pass by the action of the offensive linemen. If they are not pulling out or firing out into the defense, it is usually an impromptu action on the part of the quarterback.

**Screen Pass**—When the offensive line allows the defense to get by them after a short delay, and forms a wall in front of a set back who receives a pass behind the line of scrimmage and runs with the football. The

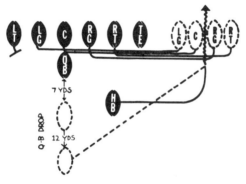

quarterback keeps backing up to make the defensive linemen believe they have beaten the offensive linemen they are playing opposite. The key to running the screen pass well is timing and the acting ability of all members of the offensive team. The screen is often used against a team that is rushing the passer well. The screen pass may be run behind a wall of linemen that has formed on either side of the line or right up the middle.

**Scrimmage**—The action that takes place from the snap of the ball until the down ends or the offensive team loses possession of the ball. Also refers to practice under game conditions.

**Secondary**—The *players* in the defensive backfield, or the *area* beyond the line of scrimmage that they are assigned to cover. The secondary is made up of the two cornerbacks, the strong side safety and the weak side safety.

**Secondary Receiver**—The receiver that the quarterback will look for if his primary receiver cannot get free.

**Set Back**—A general term for the offensive backs that line up behind the quarterback. The term refers more to the *positioning* of people than the position that they play. Thus, if the tight end lined up in the backfield on one play, he would be a set back on that play.

**Shift**—When the offensive or defensive team moves in unison from one formation to another prior to the snap of the ball. The shift may involve one player or many players. It may be done to keep the opposition guessing or as a last minute adjustment to an unexpected change by the opposition.

**Shoestring Tackle**—A tackle made around the ball carrier's ankles.

**Shooting the Gap**—When a defensive lineman or linebacker attempts to charge through a gap between two offensive linemen without making contact with either one of them. He may attempt to shoot the gap as part of a "game" or take it upon himself when the split between the two offensive players in front of him becomes too wide.

**Shotgun Formation**—A formation in which the quarterback stands alone, about seven yards behind the line of scrimmage, and takes a

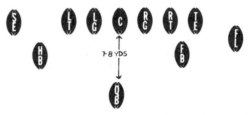

direct snap from center. It is a passing formation, and allows the quarterback more time to scan the defense and find a free receiver. Used especially toward the end of the half or the end of the game.

**Sideline**—The stripe running the length of the field and marking the outside edge of the field and the end zones. The sideline itself is out of bounds. Also refers to a pass pattern run toward the sideline.

**Sideline and Go**—The receiver runs a *sideline* route and then breaks deep on a *go* route. The quarterback should pump as the break for the sideline is made. It is most effective after several sideline routes have been successful. In general, it works well against a defender that is playing tight.

Sideline and go                                    Sideline

**Sideline Route**—A pass route where the receiver runs anywhere from five to twelve yards downfield and then makes a 90 degree break toward the sideline. Timing is more important than faking on the part of the receiver. The quarterback should anticipate the receiver's final cut and release the ball before he breaks for the sideline. The ball should be thrown low and to the outside.

**Single Wing**—An offensive formation that was once widely used, but is now rarely seen. It relies on power plays and double team blocking. It

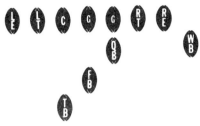

is not an effective passing formation and all of its plays are slow in developing. See chapter on team offense.

**Slam**—When an offensive player makes a shoulder block into a defender and then releases downfield to make another block.

**Slant Play**—An offensive running play where the back approaches the line of scrimmage at an angle, rather than straight ahead. Its advantage is that the back can break without difficulty into any one of a number of holes in the line.

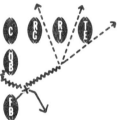

**Slant Route**—A pass route in which the receiver runs downfield a few yards and then breaks at an angle over the middle. The quarterback must throw the ball hard and low between the linebackers.

**Slot**—The gap between the weak side tackle and the split end or between the tight end and the flanker. Offensive teams place receivers in the "slot" to allow them to get downfield faster, and to make it difficult for the defense to double cover one of the wide receivers.

**Slot Back**—Any back lined up in the slot on either side of the offensive line. The slot formation is normally a passing formation used to get another receiver downfield quickly or to force single coverage on the wide receiver.

**Snap**—The initiation of the play by the center when he passes the ball between his legs.

**Spearing**—When a defensive player deliberately dives head first into an offensive player that has been knocked to the ground. A penalty will be called if a deliberate attempt to injure the offensive player with the helmet has been made.

**Special Teams** (*also called* **Suicide Squads**)—All of the kicking teams including: the kick-off team, kick-off return team, punt team, punt return team, and place kick team. They are called suicide squads because of the great incidence of injuries to those assigned to the special teams. In pro football, these assignments normally go to second stringers and rookies.

**Split**—The spacing between offensive linemen. The offensive line splits to force open the gaps in the defensive line thus allowing the backs sufficient running room. Splitting is sometimes done to create favorable blocking angles for the linemen, or to put a lineman into a more favorable position to carry out his assignment.

**Split End** (*also called* **Open End** *or* **Spread End**)— A wide receiver normally on the opposite side of the line from the tight end. The functions of the split end are usually interchangeable with those of the flanker. Both positions are known collectively as wide receivers.

**Split T Formation**—An offensive formation popular and successful during the 1950's. It is characterized by large splits in the offensive line, and a quick hitting attack. Much of the success teams had with the split

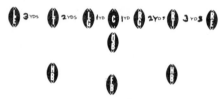

T was due to the inability of the opposition to adjust to the splits. The defensive linemen would split with the offense creating huge holes for the backs to run through. Defensive teams were also unaccustomed to coping with such a fast hitting formation.

**Spotter**—An assistant to the radio or television broadcast team that identifies players for the play by play man. He usually sits next to him and points to a chart listing all of the players' numbers when he "spots" the number of the ball carrier and tackler.

**Spread Formation** (*see* **Shotgun**)

**Square Out** (*see* **Sideline**)

**Stack**—A defensive alignment where a linebacker lines up directly behind a defensive lineman. Their relative positions make it easy to employ stunts and shoot the gaps on either side of the offensive linemen they are opposite. The lineman will charge to one side of the offensive lineman with the linebacker moving into the other gap.

**Stack Defense**—Usually used to describe a 4-4 defense with the linebackers aligned directly behind the front four defensive linemen. It is also used to describe any defense where at least two linebackers are stacked directly behind two defensive linemen.

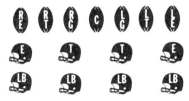

**Statue of Liberty**—An end sweep where the quarterback takes the ball from the center and drops back as if he were going to pass the football. An offensive back or receiver runs behind him and, as he passes, the quarterback raises his arm as if he were about to throw the ball. The player passing behind the quarterback takes the ball and runs around end. The Statue of Liberty was once a popular play but is rarely seen today at any level of football.

**Straight Arm**—A technique used by a runner to ward off an opposing tackler by extending one arm into his head as he approaches to make the tackle. The elbow is locked as the ball carrier strikes with the heel of his hand. The straight arm is normally used in the open field when there is only one tackler to elude and there are no other alternatives for the runner. When a running back takes a hand off into the line of scrimmage, he will not use the straight arm.

**Streak** (*see* **Fly**)

**Strong Safety**—The safety that lines up on the strong side of the line opposite the tight end, seven to ten yards downfield. He is usually assigned to cover the tight end when his team is in man coverage.

**Strong Side**—The side of the line where the tight end aligns himself in the pro-set. There will be an extra man on that side, hence the designation strong side.

**Stunting** (*see* **Games**)

**Stunting Defense**—A type of defensive play where the defensive line and linebackers are involved in stunts most of the time. Stunting defenses usually involve all of the people on the defensive line. For example, the defensive linemen may all move to cover the assignments of the players to their immediate right, while the linebackers move to the left.

**Stutter Step**—A short, choppy stepping action by a running back when attempting to avoid a would-be tackler.

**Submarine**—A maneuver by a defensive lineman intent on not being driven off the line of scrimmage. He accomplishes this by charging extremely low *under* or sometimes *between* the lineman opposite him. The submarine is normally used in a short yardage or goal line situation when the offense is expected to run up the middle. The disadvantage is the difficulty the submarining lineman has in pursuing the ball carrier if the play does not come directly at him.

**Sudden Death**—A scheme used to break ties in play-off or championship games. The teams flip a coin at the start of the overtime, to see who kicks off and who receives. The first team to score by any means is the winner.

**Suicide Squad**—The special teams used in kicking situations. They are called the suicide squads because of the high incidence of injury associated with the kicking teams and the open field blocking required by those playing on them. In pro ball, the suicide squads are normally manned by younger players rather than the 22 starters.

**Sweep** (*see* **Power Sweep**)

**Swing Pass** (*see* **Flare Pass**)

**T Formation**—An offensive formation in which the quarterback lines up directly behind the center and takes the snap from him. The fullback is

a few yards behind the quarterback and the two halfbacks set to the outside of the fullback to form a T. The fullback is usually deeper than the two halfbacks.

**Tackle**—An offensive lineman positioned between the guard and end. Usually the biggest man on the offensive line.

A defensive lineman playing opposite the offensive guards. Usually the biggest man on the defensive team.

**Tackle Eligible** (*see* **Eligible Receiver**)—A rarely-seen formation in which a tackle is placed on the end of the offensive line and becomes eligible to catch a pass. The offensive team hopes that the defense will not cover the tackle when he moves downfield.

**Tailback**—The deepest back in a single wing formation positioned almost directly behind the offensive center. His depth varies, but it is usually five yards.

**Taxi Squad** (*see* **Cab Squad**)

**Tee**—A piece of rubber used to hold the football in an upright position for the place kicker when kicking off.

**Three Point Stance**—The position most players assume as the play is about to begin. The legs are spread about shoulder width and in a parallel position. The player crouches low enough to comfortably place one hand on the ground 18 inches in front of him. The three point stance is the best position for moving out quickly to either side or straight ahead. It is also the most advantageous position from which a block may be made on an opposing player. The term "three point" refers to the two legs and one hand which maintain contact with the ground.

**Tight End**—A receiver positioned one to four yards outside the offensive tackle and on the line of scrimmage. His basic assignments are to block and catch the short pass. In pro football, the tight end lines up on the same side as the flanker—what is known as the *strong side*. In pro football, the end on the other end of the line is split three to twelve yards and known as the *split* end.

**Timing Patterns**—A series of routes on a play in which receivers make their final breaks at different times and at different distances downfield. This allows the quarterback to find his secondary and tertiary receivers more easily. For example, the flanker may be assigned to make his final move to the sideline at eight yards, the tight end over the middle at 12 yards, and the split end to run a corner route. Knowing all of this helps the quarterback scan the field systematically.

**Tip Off** (*also called* **Telegraph**)—When a team or a player tips off his future intentions through certain mannerisms before the play. It is these tips which the opposition keys on or reads.

**Toss of the Coin**—Before the game the referee flips a coin in the presence of both team captains. The captain of the visiting team makes the call (heads or tails) and the winner of the toss has the choice of receiving the opening kick-off or choosing the goal which his team will defend. At the start of the second half the team that lost the toss has the option of receiving the kick-off or defending a specific goal.

**Touchback**—A situation that results when a kick-off is downed in the end zone, a pass is intercepted in the end zone, a punt goes into or out of the end zone, or a field goal is missed and goes into or out of the end zone. The defensive or receiving team takes possession on its own 20-yard line. A touchback only occurs when the opposing team causes the ball to go into the end zone in one of the above mentioned ways. A blocked punt recovered in the end zone results in a touchdown and an offensive player who carries the ball into his end zone on his own momentum is charged with a safety.

**Touchdown**—When a player carries the ball into the opposition's end zone. Six points are awarded.

**Trap** (*also called* **Mousetrap**)—When an offensive lineman leaves (pulls out of) his regular position in the line and moves behind the line to block a man that has intentionally been allowed to cross the line of scrimmage without being blocked. The purpose of the trap block is to surprise the defensive linemen and give the trapping offensive lineman a good blocking angle as he approaches from the side.

**Tricks** (*see* **Games**)

**Triple** (*also see* **Flood**)—When three potential pass receivers line up on one side of the field in order that all three can get downfield

**Turn In**—A pass pattern in which one of the receivers runs downfield and loops in over the middle. The extent of the loop varies from team to team.

**Turn Out**—A pass pattern in which one of the receivers runs downfield and loops to the outside to catch the football.

**Turning the Corner**—When a player on the offensive team, running laterally to the outside, turns upfield. The expression is generally reserved for the running back carrying the football, but a pulling guard can also turn the corner when leading interference.

**Two Minute Offense**—When the offensive team runs a predetermined series of plays or is told what play to run at the line of scrimmage instead of conferring in the huddle before each play. This is done in order to conserve time when a quick score is needed toward the end of the half or game. When in a two minute offense, a team will usually stress pass plays which can be run off without much time elapsing.

**Two Minute Warning**—A time out is called by the official when there are two minutes remaining in the first half and in the game.

**Two-on-One**—When two players are assigned to block one member of the defensive team. This is sometimes called a high-low block, since one player hits the opponent high and the other low at the same time.

The term also refers to two defensive players assigned to cover one pass receiver.

**Two Point Stance**—When a player is standing or crouching, but does not have a hand on the ground. It is used by the linebackers, defensive backs and wide receivers.

**Type**—When an offensive or defensive team allows the opposition to determine an upcoming play or defense because it has been using a stereotyped alignment. For example, the offensive team will type itself if it always lines up with two set backs in the same alignments when running off-tackle. This team might try to avoid being typed by lining up the same formation when running into other areas of the line.

A defensive team may type itself by using zone coverage in the secondary when in an odd front and man coverage in the secondary when in an even front. Coaches and players are more likely to recognize "tips" of this sort when watching movies of the opposition prior to the game, than during the game itself.

**Umpire**—The official that has primary jurisdiction over faulty equipment, conduct, and action of the players on the scrimmage line. He also assists the referee on decisions involving possession of the ball in close proximity to the line of scrimmage. He is in charge of keeping records of all time-outs.

**Up** (*alternate term for* **Fly**)

**Veer**—When a running back moves at an angle to either side. His path is usually determined by the flow of the defensive pursuit. However, some teams have plays with a predetermined veer by the running back.

**Victory Defense**—The term is used to describe the defense designed to stop the long gain because it is generally used when a team has a lead.

**Weak Safety**—The safety on the opposite side of the field from the tight end. He may or may not be free.

**Weak Side**—The side of the offensive formation away from the tight end and flanker. Most teams will alternate the side of the tight end, so that the weak side may vary from play to play.

**Wedge**—A formation used on kick-off returns in which players line up shoulder to shoulder in front of the ball carrier.

**Wedge Blocking**—When members of the offensive line block the area to their inside whether a defender is in the area or not. The line attempts to move forward, shoulder to shoulder, in front of the ball carrier.

**Wedge Breaker**—The member of the kick-off team assigned to knock down or separate the wedge formed by the kick-off return team. He will usually dive into the legs of the players forming the wedge.

**Wide Receiver**—The flanker, split end, or any other receiver set more than six yards from his tight end or offensive tackle.

**Wide Side**—When the ball is placed on one of the hash marks, the area between the ball and the sideline furthest from it is called the wide side of the field.

**Wing**—An offensive halfback positioned outside his own end or offensive tackle. His depth may vary, but he will not be split more than a few yards. If the split is more than a few yards, the halfback is in a slot formation.

**Wishbone T** (*also known as the* **Y** *Formation*)—A recent offensive innovation that has proven to be effective on the high school and college levels. It is not used in professional football because of the danger to the quarterback and the fact that it is not an especially

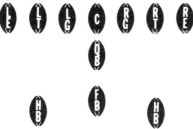

effective passing formation. The advantage of the wishbone T is the proximity of the fullback to the line of scrimmage and the various "options" that can be run from the formation. (See chapter on team offense.)

**X**—A crossing pattern by two wide receivers. Also a term applied to one of the wide receivers by some coaches.

**Y**—A symbol designating the tight end on some football teams. Also an alternate name for the wishbone formation.

**Yardage Chain**—A metal chain 10 yards long attached to two rods or yardsticks used to measure first downs.

**Zig In**—A pass route where the receiver runs downfield, cuts to the inside, cuts back to the outside and finally breaks to the inside to catch the football.

**Zig Out**—A pass route where the receiver cuts to the outside, cuts back to the inside, and then makes his final break to the outside.

**Zone Blocking** (*see* **Area Blocking**)

**Zone Defense**—A type of coverage in the defensive secondary where the defenders are assigned to areas of the field rather than to individual receivers. The zone is gaining increased favor in professional football. It has always been popular at the high school and college levels.